A Practical English Grammar

Fourth edition

A Practical English Grammar

A. J. Thomson
A. V. Martinet

Oxford University Press

Oxford University Press
Great Clarendon Street, Oxford OX2 6DP

Oxford   New York
Auckland   Bangkok   Buenos Aires   Cape Town   Chennai
Dar es Salaam   Delhi   Hong Kong   Istanbul   Karachi   Kolkata
Kuala Lumpur   Madrid   Melbourne   Mexico City   Mumbai
Nairobi   São Paulo   Shanghai   Taipei   Tokyo   Toronto

Oxford and *Oxford English* are trade marks of
Oxford University Press

ISBN 0 19 431342 5 (paperback)
ISBN 019 431347 6 (hardback)

First published 1960 (reprinted seven times)
Second edition 1969 (reprinted ten times)
Third edition 1980 (reprinted eight times)
Fourth edition 1986
Twenty fourth impression 2003

Printed in China

Preface to the fourth edition

A Practical English Grammar is intended for intermediate and
post-intermediate students. We hope that more advanced learners
and teachers will also find it useful.

The book is a comprehensive survey of structures and forms,
written in clear modern English and illustrated with numerous
examples. Areas of particular difficulty have been given special
attention. Differences between conversational usage and strict
grammatical forms are shown but the emphasis is on
conversational forms.

In the fourth edition the main changes are as follows:

1 Explanations and examples have been brought up to date.

2 There is now more information on countable and uncountable
  nouns, attributive and predicative adjectives, adverbs of place,
  sentence adverbs, cleft sentences, prepositions, conjunctions,
  modal verbs, perfect tenses, infinitive constructions, the
  passive, purpose clauses and noun clauses.

3 Some material has been rearranged to make comparisons
  easier. For example, parts of chapters on *can, may, must* etc.
  are now grouped by function; verbs of liking and preference
  have a chapter to themselves; suggestions and invitations have
  joined the chapter on commands, requests and advice.

4 The contents list now summarizes every section heading, and
  there is a new index containing many more entries and
  references.

In this edition the sign ' ~ ' is frequently used to denote a change
of speaker in examples of dialogue. Note also that although the
sign ' = ' sometimes connects two words or expressions with the
same meaning, it is often used more freely, e.g. to indicate a
transformation from active to passive or direct to indirect speech.

We wish to thank all at Oxford University Press who have
assisted in the preparation of the fourth edition. We would also
like to thank Professor Egawa of Nihon University, Japan,
Professor René Dirven of Duisburg University, West Germany
and other colleagues for their friendly and helpful suggestions.

London, November 1985   A.J.T., A.V.M.

Contents

Contents

Contents

Contents

Contents

1 Articles and **one, a little/a few, this, that**

1 **a/an** (the indefinite article)

The form **a** is used before a word beginning with a consonant, or a vowel with a consonant sound:

a man   *a hat*   *a university*   *a European*
a one-way street

The form **an** is used before words beginning with a vowel (**a, e, i, o, u**) or words beginning with a mute **h**:

an apple   *an island*   *an uncle*
an egg   *an onion*   *an hour*

or individual letters spoken with a vowel sound:

an L-plate   *an MP*   *an SOS*   *an 'x'*

a/an is the same for all genders:

a man   *a woman*   *an actor*   *an actress*   *a table*

2 Use of **a/an**

a/an is used:

A   Before a singular noun which is countable (i.e. of which there is more than one) when it is mentioned for the first time and represents no particular person or thing:

I need a visa.   *They live in a flat.*   *He bought an ice-cream.*

B   Before a singular countable noun which is used as an example of a class of things:

A car must be insured =
All cars/Any car must be insured.
A child needs love =
All children need/Any child needs love.

C   With a noun complement. This includes names of professions:

It was an earthquake.   *She'll be a dancer.*   *He is an actor.*

D   In certain expressions of quantity:

a lot of   *a couple*
a great many   *a dozen* (but *one dozen* is also possible)
a great deal of

E   With certain numbers:
> *a hundred*   *a thousand*   (See 349.)

Before **half** when **half** follows a whole number:
> 1½ *kilos* = *one and a half kilos* or *a kilo and a half*

But ½ *kg* = *half a kilo* (no **a** before *half*), though *a* + *half* + noun is sometimes possible:
> *a half-holiday*   *a half-portion*   *a half-share*

With ⅓, ¼, ⅕ etc. **a** is usual: *a third*, *a quarter* etc., but **one** is also possible. (See 350.)

F   In expressions of price, speed, ratio etc.:
> *5p a kilo*   *£1 a metre*   *sixty kilometres an hour*
> *10p a dozen*   *four times a day*

(Here a/an = **per**.)

G   In exclamations before singular, countable nouns:
> *Such a long queue!*   *What a pretty girl!*   But
> *Such long queues!*   *What pretty girls!*

(Plural nouns, so no article. See 3.)

H   **a** can be placed before Mr/Mrs/Miss + surname:
> *a Mr Smith*   *a Mrs Smith*   *a Miss Smith*

a Mr Smith means 'a man called Smith' and implies that he is a stranger to the speaker. *Mr Smith*, without *a*, implies that the speaker knows Mr Smith or knows of his existence.

(For the difference between **a/an** and **one**, see 4. For **a few** and **a little**, see 5.)

3   Omission of a/an

a/an is omitted:

A   Before plural nouns.
a/an has no plural form. So the plural of *a dog* is *dogs*, and of *an egg* is *eggs*.

B   Before uncountable nouns (see 13).

C   Before names of meals, except when these are preceded by an adjective:
> *We have breakfast at eight.*
> *He gave us a good breakfast.*

The article is also used when it is a special meal given to celebrate something or in someone's honour:
> *I was invited to dinner* (at their house, in the ordinary way) but
> *I was invited to a dinner given to welcome the new ambassador.*

4 a/an and one

A **a/an** and **one** (adjective)

1 When counting or measuring time, distance, weight etc. we can use
either **a/an** or **one** for the singular:

> £1 = *a/one pound*   £1,000,000 = *a/one million pounds*

(See chapter 36.)

But note that in *The rent is £100 a week* the **a** before *week* is not
replaceable by **one** (see 2 F).

In other types of statement **a/an** and **one** are not normally
interchangeable, because **one** + noun normally means 'one only/not
more than one' and **a/an** does not mean this:

> *A shotgun is no good.* (It is the wrong sort of thing.)
> *One shotgun is no good.* (I need two or three.)

2 Special uses of **one**

(a) **one** (adjective/pronoun) used with **another/others**:

> *One (boy) wanted to read, another/others wanted to watch TV.*
> (See 53.)
> *One day he wanted his lunch early, another day he wanted it late.*

(b) **one** can be used before *day/week/month/year/summer/winter* etc. or
before the name of the day or month to denote a particular time when
something happened:

> *One night there was a terrible storm.*
> *One winter the snow fell early.*
> *One day a telegram arrived.*

(c) **one day** can also be used to mean 'at some future date':

> *One day you'll be sorry you treated him so badly.*
> (*Some day* would also be possible.)

(For **one** and **you**, see 68.)

B **a/an** and **one** (pronoun)

one is the pronoun equivalent of **a/an**:

> *Did you get a ticket? ~ Yes, I managed to get one.*

The plural of **one** used in this way is **some**:

> *Did you get tickets? ~ Yes, I managed to get some.*

5 a little/a few and little/few

A **a little/little** (adjectives) are used before uncountable nouns:

> *a little salt/little salt*

a few/few (adjectives) are used before plural nouns:

> *a few people/few people*

All four forms can also be used as pronouns, either alone or with **of**:

> *Sugar? ~ A little, please.*
> *Only a few of these are any good.*

B **a little, a few** (adjectives and pronouns)

a little is a small amount, or what the speaker considers a small amount. **a few** is a small number, or what the speaker considers a small number.

only placed before **a little/a few** emphasizes that the number or amount really is small in the speaker's opinion:

Only a few of our customers have accounts.

But **quite** placed before **a few** increases the number considerably:

I have quite a few books on art. (quite a lot of books)

C **little** and **few** (adjectives and pronouns)

little and **few** denote scarcity or lack and have almost the force of a negative:

There was little time for consultation.
Little is known about the side-effects of this drug.
Few towns have such splendid trees.

This use of **little** and **few** is mainly confined to written English (probably because in conversation **little** and **few** might easily be mistaken for **a little/a few**). In conversation, therefore, **little** and **few** are normally replaced by **hardly any**. A negative verb + **much/many** is also possible:

We saw little = We saw hardly anything/We didn't see much.
Tourists come here but few stay overnight =
Tourists come here but hardly any stay overnight.

But **little** and **few** can be used more freely when they are qualified by *so, very, too, extremely, comparatively, relatively* etc.

fewer (comparative) can also be used more freely.

I'm unwilling to try a drug I know so little about.
They have too many technicians, we have too few.
There are fewer butterflies every year.

D **a little/little** (adverbs)

1 **a little** can be used:

(a) with verbs: *It rained a little during the night.*
They grumbled a little about having to wait.

(b) with 'unfavourable' adjectives and adverbs:
a little anxious   a little unwillingly
a little annoyed   a little impatiently

(c) with comparative adjectives or adverbs:
The paper should be a little thicker.
Can't you walk a little faster?

rather could replace **a little** in (b) and can also be used before comparatives (see 42), though **a little** is more usual.

In colloquial English **a bit** could be used instead of **a little** in all the above examples.

2 **little** is used chiefly with **better** or **more** in fairly formal style:

His second suggestion was little (= not much) better than his first.
He was little (= not much) more than a child when his father died.

It can also, in formal English, be placed before certain verbs, for example *expect, know, suspect, think*:

He little expected to find himself in prison.
He little thought that one day . . .
Note also the adjectives *little-known* and *little-used*:
a little-known painter   a little-used footpath

6 the (the definite article)

A Form
the is the same for singular and plural and for all genders:

the boy	*the girl*	*the day*
the boys	*the girls*	*the days*

B Use
The definite article is used:

1 When the object or group of objects is unique or considered to be unique:
    the earth   the sea   the sky   the equator   the stars

2 Before a noun which has become definite as a result of being mentioned a second time:
    His car struck a tree; you can still see the mark on the tree.

3 Before a noun made definite by the addition of a phrase or clause:
    the girl in blue   the man with the banner
    the boy that I met   the place where I met him

4 Before a noun which by reason of locality can represent only one particular thing:
    Ann is in the garden. (the garden of this house)
    Please pass the wine. (the wine on the table)
Similarly: *the postman* (the one who comes to us), *the car* (our car), *the newspaper* (the one we read).

5 Before superlatives and *first, second* etc. used as adjectives or pronouns, and *only*:
    the first (week)   the best day   the only way

C the + singular noun can represent a class of animals or things:
    The whale is in danger of becoming extinct.
    The deep-freeze has made life easier for housewives.
But *man,* used to represent the human race, has no article:
    If oil supplies run out, man may have to fall back on the horse.
the can be used before a member of a certain group of people:
    The small shopkeeper is finding life increasingly difficult.
the + singular noun as used above takes a singular verb. The pronoun is he, she or it:
    The first-class traveller pays more so he expects some comfort.

D the + adjective represents a class of persons:
    the old = old people in general (see 23)

E   **the** is used before certain proper names of seas, rivers, groups of islands, chains of mountains, plural names of countries, deserts, regions:

> *the Atlantic*   *the Netherlands*
> *the Thames*   *the Sahara*
> *the Azores*   *the Crimea*
> *the Alps*   *the Riviera*

and before certain other names:

> *the City*   *the Mall*   *the Sudan*
> *the Hague*   *the Strand*   *the Yemen*

the is also used before names consisting of noun + **of** + noun:

> *the Bay of Biscay*   *the Gulf of Mexico*
> *the Cape of Good Hope*   *the United States of America*

the is used before names consisting of adjective + noun (provided the adjective is not *east, west* etc.):

> *the Arabian Sea*   *the New Forest*   *the High Street*

the is used before the adjectives *east/west* etc. + noun in certain names:

> *the East/West End*   *the East/West Indies*
> *the North/South Pole*

but is normally omitted:

> *South Africa*   *North America*   *West Germany*

the, however, is used before *east/west* etc. when these are nouns:

> *the north of Spain*   *the West* (geographical)
> *the Middle East*   *the West* (political)

Compare *Go north* (adverb: in a northerly direction) with *He lives in the north* (noun: an area in the north).

F   **the** is used before other proper names consisting of adjective + noun or noun + **of** + noun:

> *the National Gallery*   *the Tower of London*

It is also used before names of choirs, orchestras, pop groups etc.:

> *the Bach Choir*   *the Philadelphia Orchestra*   *the Beatles*

and before names of newspapers (*The Times*) and ships (*the Great Britain*).

G   **the** with names of people has a very limited use. **the** + plural surname can be used to mean 'the . . . family':

> *the Smiths = Mr and Mrs Smith (and children)*

the + singular name + clause/phrase can be used to distinguish one person from another of the same name:

> *We have two Mr Smiths. Which do you want? ~ I want the Mr Smith who signed this letter.*

the is used before titles containing *of* (*the Duke of York*) but it is not used before other titles or ranks (*Lord Olivier, Captain Cook*), though if someone is referred to by title/rank alone **the** is used:

> *The earl expected . . .*   *The captain ordered . . .*

Letters written to two or more unmarried sisters jointly may be addressed *The Misses* + surname: *The Misses Smith*.

7 Omission of **the**

A The definite article is not used:

1 Before names of places except as shown above, or before names of people.

2 Before abstract nouns except when they are used in a particular sense:
Men fear death but
The death of the Prime Minister left his party without a leader.

3 After a noun in the possessive case, or a possessive adjective:
the boy's uncle = the uncle of the boy
It is my (blue) book = The (blue) book is mine.

4 Before names of meals (but see 3 C):
The Scots have porridge for breakfast but
The wedding breakfast was held in her father's house.

5 Before names of games: *He plays golf.*

6 Before parts of the body and articles of clothing, as these normally prefer a possessive adjective:
Raise your right hand.   He took off his coat.
But notice that sentences of the type:
She seized the child's collar.
I patted his shoulder.
The brick hit John's face.
could be expressed:
She seized the child by the collar.
I patted him on the shoulder.
The brick hit John in the face.
Similarly in the passive:
He was hit on the head.   He was cut in the hand.

B Note that in some European languages the definite article is used before indefinite plural nouns but that in English **the** is never used in this way:
Women are expected to like babies. (i.e. women in general)
Big hotels all over the world are very much the same.
If we put **the** before *women* in the first example, it would mean that we were referring to a particular group of women.

C *nature*, where it means the spirit creating and motivating the world of plants and animals etc., is used without **the**:
If you interfere with nature you will suffer for it.

8 Omission of **the** before **home**, before **church, hospital, prison, school** etc. and before **work, sea** and **town**

A **home**
When *home* is used alone, i.e. is not preceded or followed by a descriptive word or phrase, **the** is omitted:
He is at home.

home used alone can be placed directly after a verb of motion or verb of motion + object, i.e. it can be treated as an adverb:

> *He went home.   I arrived home after dark.   I sent him home.*

But when *home* is preceded or followed by a descriptive word or phrase it is treated like any other noun:

> *They went to their new home.*
> *We arrived at the bride's home.*
> *For some years this was the home of your queen.*
> *A mud hut was the only home he had ever known.*

B   **bed, church, court, hospital, prison, school/college/university**

the is not used before the nouns listed above when these places are visited or used for their primary purpose. We go:

to bed to sleep or as invalids	*to hospital* as patients
to church to pray	*to prison* as prisoners
to court as litigants etc.	*to school/college/university* to study

Similarly we can be:

in bed, sleeping or resting	*in hospital* as patients
at church as worshippers	*at school* etc. as students
in court as witnesses etc.	

We can be/get back (or be/get home) *from school/college/university.*
We can *leave school, leave hospital,* be released *from prison.*

When these places are visited or used for other reasons **the** is necessary:

> *I went to the church to see the stained glass.*
> *He goes to the prison sometimes to give lectures.*

C   **sea**

We go *to sea* as sailors. To be *at sea* = to be on a voyage (as passengers or crew). But to go *to* or be *at the sea* = to go *to* or be *at the seaside.* We can also live *by/near the sea.*

D   **work** and **office**

work (= place of work) is used without **the**:

> *He's on his way to work.   He is at work.*
> *He isn't back from work yet.*

Note that *at work* can also mean 'working'; *hard at work* = working hard:

> *He's hard at work on a new picture.*

office (= place of work) needs **the**: *He is at/in the office.*
To be *in office* (without **the**) means to hold an official (usually political) position. To be *out of office* = to be no longer in power.

E   **town**

the can be omitted when speaking of the subject's or speaker's own town:

> *We go to town sometimes to buy clothes.*
> *We were in town last Monday.*

9 this/these, that/those (demonstrative adjectives and pronouns)

A Used as adjectives, they agree with their nouns in number. They are the only adjectives to do this.

> *This beach was quite empty last year.*
> *This exhibition will be open until the end of May.*
> *These people come from that hotel over there.*
> *What does that notice say?*
> *That exhibition closed a month ago.*
> *He was dismissed on the 13th. That night the factory went on fire.*
> *Do you see those birds at the top of the tree?*

this/these/that/those + noun + *of* + *yours/hers* etc. or *Ann's* etc. is sometimes, for emphasis, used instead of *your/her* etc. + noun:

> *This diet of mine/My diet isn't having much effect.*
> *That car of Ann's/Ann's car is always breaking down.*

Remarks made with these phrases are usually, though not necessarily always, unfavourable.

B **this/these, that/those** used as pronouns:

> *This is my umbrella. That's yours.*
> *These are the old classrooms. Those are the new ones.*
> *Who's that (man over there)? ~ That's Tom Jones.*

After a radio programme:

> *That was the concerto in C minor by Vivaldi.*

this is is possible in introductions:

> ANN (to TOM): *This is my brother Hugh.*
> ANN (to HUGH): *Hugh, this is Tom Jones.*
> TELEPHONE CALLER: *Good morning. This is/I am Tom Jones . . .*

I am is slightly more formal than *This is* and is more likely to be used when the caller is a stranger to the other person. The caller's name + *here* (*Tom here*) is more informal than *This is*.

those can be followed by a defining relative clause:

> *Those who couldn't walk were carried on stretchers.*

this/that can represent a previously mentioned noun, phrase or clause:

> *They're digging up my road. They do this every summer.*
> *He said I wasn't a good wife. Wasn't that a horrible thing to say?*

C **this/these, that/those** used with **one/ones**
When there is some idea of comparison or selection, the pronoun **one/ones** is often placed after these demonstratives, but it is not essential except when **this** etc. is followed by an adjective:

> *This chair is too low. I'll sit in that (one).*
> *I like this (one) best.*
> *I like this blue one/these blue ones.*

2 Nouns

10 Kinds and function

A   There are four kinds of noun in English:
Common nouns: *dog, man, table*
Proper nouns: *France, Madrid, Mrs Smith, Tom*
Abstract nouns: *beauty, charity, courage, fear, joy*
Collective nouns: *crowd, flock, group, swarm, team*

B   A noun can function as:
The subject of a verb: *Tom arrived.*
The complement of the verbs **be, become, seem**: *Tom is an actor.*
The object of a verb: *I saw Tom.*
The object of a preposition: *I spoke to Tom.*
A noun can also be in the possessive case: *Tom's books.*

11 Gender

A   Masculine: men, boys and male animals (pronoun **he/they**).

Feminine: women, girls and female animals (pronoun **she/they**).

Neuter: inanimate things, animals whose sex we don't know and
sometimes babies whose sex we don't know (pronoun **it/they**).
Exceptions: ships and sometimes cars and other vehicles when
regarded with affection or respect are considered feminine. Countries
when referred to by name are also normally considered feminine.
>   *The ship struck an iceberg, which tore a huge hole in her side.*
>   *Scotland lost many of her bravest men in two great rebellions.*

B   Masculine/feminine nouns denoting people

1   Different forms:

(a)		
boy, girl	*gentleman, lady*	*son, daughter*
bachelor, spinster	*husband, wife*	*uncle, aunt*
bridegroom, bride	*man, woman*	*widower, widow*
father, mother	*nephew, niece*

Main exceptions:

| | |
--- | --- | ---
baby | *infant* | *relative*
child | *parent* | *spouse*
cousin | *relation* | *teenager*

(b)		
duke, duchess	*king, queen*	*prince, princess*
earl, countess	*lord, lady*

2 The majority of nouns indicating occupation have the same form:

    artist   *cook*   *driver*   *guide*
    assistant   *dancer*   *doctor*   etc.

Main exceptions:

    actor, actress   *host, hostess*
    conductor, conductress   *manager, manageress*
    heir, heiress   *steward, stewardess*
    hero, heroine   *waiter, waitress*

Also *salesman, saleswoman* etc., but sometimes *-person* is used instead of *-man, -woman: salesperson, spokesperson.*

C Domestic animals and many of the larger wild animals have different forms:

    bull, cow   *duck, drake*   *ram, ewe*   *stallion, mare*
    cock, hen   *gander, goose*   *stag, doe*   *tiger, tigress*
    dog, bitch   *lion, lioness*

Others have the same form.

12   Plurals

A The plural of a noun is usually made by adding **s** to the singular:

    day, days   *dog, dogs*   *house, houses*

s is pronounced /s/ after a **p, k** or **f** sound. Otherwise it is pronounced /z/.

When **s** is placed after **ce, ge, se** or **ze** an extra syllable (/ɪz/) is added to the spoken word.

Other plural forms

B Nouns ending in **o** or **ch, sh, ss** or **x** form their plural by adding **es**:

    tomato, tomatoes   *brush, brushes*   *box, boxes*
    church, churches   *kiss, kisses*

But words of foreign origin or abbreviated words ending in **o** add **s** only:

    dynamo, dynamos   *kimono, kimonos*   *piano, pianos*
    kilo, kilos   *photo, photos*   *soprano, sopranos*

When **es** is placed after **ch, sh, ss** or **x** an extra syllable (/ɪz/) is added to the spoken word.

C Nouns ending in **y** following a consonant form their plural by dropping the **y** and adding **ies**:

    baby, babies   *country, countries*   *fly, flies*   *lady, ladies*

Nouns ending in **y** following a vowel form their plural by adding **s**:

    boy, boys   *day, days*   *donkey, donkeys*   *guy, guys*

D Twelve nouns ending in **f** or **fe** drop the **f** or **fe** and add **ves**. These nouns are *calf, half, knife, leaf, life, loaf, self, sheaf, shelf, thief, wife, wolf*:

    loaf, loaves   *wife, wives*   *wolf, wolves*   etc.

The nouns *hoof, scarf* and *wharf* take either **s** or **ves** in the plural:
    hoofs or *hooves*   *scarfs* or *scarves*   *wharfs* or *wharves*
Other words ending in **f** or **fe** add **s** in the ordinary way:
    cliff, cliffs   *handkerchief, handkerchiefs*   *safe, safes*

E   A few nouns form their plural by a vowel change:
    foot, feet   *louse, lice*   *mouse, mice*   *woman, women*
    goose, geese   *man, men*   *tooth, teeth*
The plurals of *child* and *ox* are *children, oxen*.

F   Names of certain creatures do not change in the plural.
fish is normally unchanged. *fishes* exists but is uncommon.
Some types of fish do not normally change in the plural:
    carp   *pike*   *salmon*   *trout*
    cod   *plaice*   *squid*   *turbot*
    mackerel
but if used in a plural sense they would take a plural verb.
Others add **s**:
    crabs   *herrings*   *sardines*
    eels   *lobsters*   *sharks*
deer and *sheep* do not change: *one sheep, two sheep*.
Sportsmen who shoot *duck, partridge, pheasant* etc. use the same form
for singular and plural. But other people normally add **s** for the
plural: *ducks, partridges, pheasants*.
The word *game*, used by sportsmen to mean an animal/animals hunted,
is always in the singular, and takes a singular verb.

G   A few other words don't change:
    aircraft, craft (boat/boats)   *quid* (slang for £1)
    counsel (barristers working in court)
Some measurements and numbers do not change (see chapter 36).
For uncountable nouns, see 13.

H   Collective nouns, *crew, family, team* etc., can take a singular or plural
verb; singular if we consider the word to mean a single group or unit:
    Our team is the best
or plural if we take it to mean a number of individuals:
    Our team are wearing their new jerseys.
When a possessive adjective is necessary, a plural verb with **their** is
more usual than a singular verb with **its**, though sometimes both are
possible:
    The jury is considering its verdict.
    The jury are considering their verdict.

I   Certain words are always plural and take a plural verb:
    clothes   *police*
garments consisting of two parts:
    breeches   *pants*   *pyjamas*   *trousers*   etc.
and tools and instruments consisting of two parts:
    binoculars   *pliers*   *scissors*   *spectacles*
    glasses   *scales*   *shears*   etc.

Also certain other words including:

arms (weapons)	*particulars*
damages (compensation)	*premises/quarters*
earnings	*riches*
goods/wares	*savings*
greens (vegetables)	*spirits* (alcohol)
grounds	*stairs*
outskirts	*surroundings*
pains (trouble/effort)	*valuables*

J   A number of words ending in **ics**, *acoustics, athletics, ethics, hysterics, mathematics, physics, politics* etc., which are plural in form, normally take a plural verb:

His mathematics are weak.

But names of sciences can sometimes be considered singular:

Mathematics is an exact science.

K   Words plural in form but singular in meaning include *news*:

The news is good

certain diseases:

mumps   rickets   shingles

and certain games:

billiards   darts   draughts
bowls   dominoes

L   Some words which retain their original Greek or Latin forms make their plurals according to the rules of Greek and Latin:

crisis, crises /'kraɪsɪs/, /'kraɪsiːz/   *phenomenon, phenomena*
erratum, errata   *radius, radii*
memorandum, memoranda   *terminus, termini*
oasis, oases /əʊ'eɪsɪs/, /əʊ'eɪsiːz/

But some follow the English rules:

dogma, dogmas   gymnasium, gymnasiums
formula, formulas (though *formulae* is used by scientists)

Sometimes there are two plural forms with different meanings:

appendix, appendixes or *appendices* (medical terms)
appendix, appendices (addition/s to a book)
index, indexes (in books), *indices* (in mathematics)

Musicians usually prefer Italian plural forms for Italian musical terms:

libretto, libretti   tempo, tempi

But **s** is also possible: *librettos, tempos.*

M   Compound nouns

1   Normally the last word is made plural:

boy-friends   break-ins   travel agents

But where *man* and *woman* is prefixed both parts are made plural:

men drivers   women drivers

2 The first word is made plural with compounds formed of verb + **er** nouns + adverbs:

    hangers-on   lookers-on   runners-up

and with compounds composed of noun + preposition + noun:

    ladies-in-waiting   sisters-in-law   wards of court

3 Initials can be made plural:

    MPs (Members of Parliament)
    VIPs (very important persons)
    OAPs (old age pensioners)
    UFOs (unidentified flying objects)

13 Uncountable nouns (also known as non-count nouns or mass nouns)

A 1 Names of substances considered generally:

bread	*cream*	*gold*	*paper*	*tea*
beer	*dust*	*ice*	*sand*	*water*
cloth	*gin*	*jam*	*soap*	*wine*
coffee	*glass*	*oil*	*stone*	*wood*

2 Abstract nouns:

advice	*experience*	*horror*	*pity*
beauty	*fear*	*information*	*relief*
courage	*help*	*knowledge*	*suspicion*
death	*hope*	*mercy*	*work*

3 Also considered uncountable in English:

baggage	*damage*	*luggage*	*shopping*
camping	*furniture*	*parking*	*weather*

These, with *hair, information, knowledge, news, rubbish*, are sometimes countable in other languages.

B Uncountable nouns are always singular and are not used with **a/an**:

    I don't want (any) advice or help. I want (some) information.
    He has had no experience in this sort of work.

These nouns are often preceded by **some, any, no, a little** etc. or by nouns such as *bit, piece, slice* etc. + **of**:

a bit of news	*a grain of sand*	*a pot of jam*
a cake of soap	*a pane of glass*	*a sheet of paper*
a drop of oil	*a piece of advice*	

C Many of the nouns in the above groups can be used in a particular sense and are then countable. They can take **a/an** in the singular and can be used in the plural. Some examples are given below.

hair (all the hair on one's head) is considered uncountable, but if we consider each hair separately we say *one hair, two hairs* etc.:

    Her hair is black. Whenever she finds a grey hair she pulls it out.

We drink *beer, coffee, gin,* but we can ask for *a (cup of) coffee, a gin, two gins* etc. We drink *wine,* but enjoy *a good wine.* We drink it from *a glass* or from *glasses.* We can walk in *a wood/woods.*

experience meaning 'something which happened to someone' is countable:
> *He had an exciting experience/some exciting experiences*
> (= adventure/s) *last week.*

work meaning 'occupation/employment/a job/jobs' is uncountable:
> *He is looking for work/for a job.*

works (plural only) can mean 'factory' or 'moving parts of a machine'.
works (usually plural) can be used of literary or musical compositions:
> *Shakespeare's complete works*

D Some abstract nouns can be used in a particular sense with **a/an**:
a help:
> *My children are a great help to me.*   *A good map would be a help.*

a relief:
> *It was a relief to sit down.*

a knowledge + of:
> *He had a good knowledge of mathematics.*

a dislike/dread/hatred/horror/love + of is also possible:
> *a love of music*   *a hatred of violence*

a mercy/pity/shame/wonder can be used with **that**-clauses
introduced by **it**:
> *It's a pity you weren't here.*   *It's a shame he wasn't paid.*

it + be + a pity/shame + infinitive is also possible:
> *It would be a pity to cut down these trees.*

E **a fear/fears, a hope/hopes, a suspicion/suspicions**
These can be used with **that**-clauses introduced by **there**:
> *There is a fear/There are fears that he has been murdered.*

We can also *have a suspicion that . . .*
Something can arouse *a fear/fears, a hope/hopes, a suspicion/suspicions.*

14   The form of the possessive/genitive case

A **'s** is used with singular nouns and plural nouns not ending in **s**:

a man's job	*the people's choice*
men's work	*the crew's quarters*
a woman's intuition	*the horse's mouth*
the butcher's (shop)	*the bull's horns*
a child's voice	*women's clothes*
the children's room	*Russia's exports*

B A simple apostrophe (') is used with plural nouns ending in **s**:

a girls' school	*the students' hostel*
the eagles' nest	*the Smiths' car*

C Classical names ending in **s** usually add only the apostrophe:
> *Pythagoras' Theorem*   *Archimedes' Law*   *Sophocles' plays*

D Other names ending in **s** can take **'s** or the apostrophe alone:
> *Mr Jones's (or Mr Jones' house)*   *Yeats's (or Yeats') poems*

E   With compounds, the last word takes the **'s**:
   my brother-in-law's guitar
Names consisting of several words are treated similarly:
   Henry the Eighth's wives   the Prince of Wales's helicopter
's can also be used after initials:
   the PM's secretary   the MP's briefcase   the VIP's escort
Note that when the possessive case is used, the article before the person or thing 'possessed' disappears:
   the daughter of the politician = the politician's daughter
   the intervention of America = America's intervention
   the plays of Shakespeare = Shakespeare's plays

15   Use of the possessive/genitive case and **of** + noun

A   The possessive case is chiefly used of people, countries or animals as shown above. It can also be used:

1   Of ships and boats: *the ship's bell, the yacht's mast*

2   Of planes, trains, cars and other vehicles, though here the **of** construction is safer:
   a glider's wings or *the wings of a glider*
   the train's heating system or *the heating system of the train*

3   In time expressions:
   a week's holiday   today's paper   tomorrow's weather
   in two years' time   ten minutes' break   two hours' delay
   a ten-minute break, a two-hour delay are also possible:
   We have ten minutes' break/a ten-minute break.

4   In expressions of money + **worth**:
   £1's worth of stamps   ten dollars' worth of ice-cream

5   With **for** + noun + **sake**: *for heaven's sake, for goodness' sake*

6   In a few expressions such as:
   a stone's throw   journey's end   the water's edge

7   We can say either *a winter's day* or *a winter day* and *a summer's day* or *a summer day*, but we cannot make spring or autumn possessive, except when they are personified: *Autumn's return*.

8   Sometimes certain nouns can be used in the possessive case without the second noun. *a/the baker's/butcher's/chemist's/florist's* etc. can mean 'a/the baker's/butcher's etc. shop'.
Similarly, *a/the house agent's/travel agent's* etc. (office) and *the dentist's/doctor's/vet's* (surgery):
   You can buy it at the chemist's.   He's going to the dentist's.
Names of the owners of some businesses can be used similarly:
   Sotheby's, Claridge's
Some very well-known shops etc. call themselves by the possessive form and some drop the apostrophe: *Foyles, Harrods*.

Names of people can sometimes be used similarly to mean
' . . .'s house':
We had lunch at Bill's.   *We met at Ann's.*

B   **of** + noun is used for possession:

1   When the possessor noun is followed by a phrase or clause:
The boys ran about, obeying the directions of a man with a whistle.
I took the advice of a couple I met on the train and hired a car.

2   With inanimate 'possessors', except those listed in A above:
the walls of the town   *the roof of the church*   *the keys of the car*
However, it is often possible to replace noun X + **of** + noun Y by
noun Y + noun X in that order:
the town walls   *the church roof*   *the car keys*
The first noun becomes a sort of adjective and is not made plural:
the roofs of the churches = *the church roofs* (see 16)
Unfortunately noun + **of** + noun combinations cannot always be
replaced in this way and the student is advised to use **of** when in doubt.

16   Compound nouns

A   Examples of these:

1   Noun + noun:
ˈLondon ˈTransport   ˈFleet Street   ˈTower ˈBridge
ˈhall ˈdoor   ˈtraffic warden   ˈpetrol tank
ˈhitch-hiker   ˈsky-jacker   ˈriver bank
ˈkitchen ˈtable   ˈwinter ˈclothes

2   Noun + gerund:
ˈfruit picking   ˈlorry driving   ˈcoal-mining
ˈweight-lifting   ˈbird-watching   ˈsurf-riding

3   Gerund + noun:
ˈwaiting list   ˈdiving-board   ˈdriving licence
ˈlanding card   ˈdining-room   ˈswimming pool

B   Some ways in which these combinations can be used:

1   When the second noun belongs to or is part of the first:
ˈshop ˈwindow   ˈpicture frame   ˈcollege ˈlibrary
ˈchurch bell   ˈgarden ˈgate   ˈgear lever
But words denoting quantity: *lump, part, piece, slice* etc. cannot be used
in this way:
a piece of cake   *a slice of bread*

2   The first noun can indicate the place of the second:
ˈcity ˈstreet   ˈcorner ˈshop   ˈcountry ˈlane   ˈstreet market

3   The first noun can indicate the time of the second:
ˈsummer ˈholiday   ˈSunday ˈpaper   ˈNovember ˈfogs
ˈspring ˈflowers   ˈdawn ˈchorus

4   The first noun can state the material of which the second is made:

ǀsteel ǀdoor   ǀrope ǁladder   ǀgold ǀmedal
ǀstone ǀwall   ǀsilk ǀshirt

wool and *wood* are not used here as they have adjective forms: *woollen* and *wooden*. *gold* has an adjective form *golden*, but this is used only figuratively:

a golden handshake   a golden opportunity   golden hair

The first noun can also state the power/fuel used to operate the second:

ǀgas ǀfire   ǀpetrol engine   ǀoil ǀstove

5   The first word can indicate the purpose of the second:

ǀcoffee cup   ǀescape hatch   ǀchess board
ǀreading lamp   ǀskating rink   ǀtin opener
ǀgolf club   ǀnotice board   ǀfootball ground

6   Work areas, such as *factory, farm, mine* etc., can be preceded by the name of the article produced:

ǀfish-farm   ǀgold-mine   ǀoil-rig

or the type of work done:

ǀinspection pit   ǀassembly plant   ǀdecompression chamber

7   These combinations are often used of occupations, sports, hobbies and the people who practise them:

ǀsheep farming   ǀsheep farmer   ǀpop singer
ǀwind surfing   ǀwater skier   ǀdisc jockey

and for competitions:

ǀfootball match   ǀtennis tournament   ǀbeauty contest   ǀcar rally

8   The first noun can show what the second is about or concerned with. A work of fiction may be a ǀdetective/murder/mystery/ghost/horror/spy story. We buy ǀbus/train/plane tickets. We pay ǀfuel/laundry/milk/telephone bills, ǀentry fees, ǀincome tax, ǀcar insurance, ǀwater rates, ǀparking fines.

Similarly with committees, departments, talks, conferences etc.:

ǀhousing committee, ǀeducation department, ǀpeace talks

9   These categories all overlap to some extent. They are not meant to be mutually exclusive, but aim to give the student some general idea of the uses of these combinations and help with the stress.

C   As will be seen from the stress-marks above:

1   The first word is stressed in noun + gerund and gerund + noun combinations, when there is an idea of purpose as in B5 above, and in combinations of type B7 and B8 above.

2   Both words are usually stressed in combinations of types A1, B1-3 above, but inevitably there are exceptions.

3   In place-name combinations both words usually have equal stress:

ǀKing's ǀRoad   ǀWaterloo ǀBridge   ǀLeicester ǀSquare

But there is one important exception. In combinations where the last word is *Street*, the word *Street* is unstressed:

ǀBond Street   ǀOxford Street

3 Adjectives

17 Kinds of adjectives

A   The main kinds are:
   (a) Demonstrative: *this, that, these, those* (see 9)
   (b) Distributive: *each, every* (46); *either, neither* (49)
   (c) Quantitative: *some, any, no* (50); *little/few* (5); *many, much* (25); *one, twenty* (349)
   (d) Interrogative: *which, what, whose* (54)
   (e) Possessive: *my, your, his, her, its, our, your, their* (62)
   (f) Of quality: *clever, dry, fat, golden, good, heavy, square* (19)

B   Participles used as adjectives
   Both present participles (**ing**) and past participles (**ed**) can be used as adjectives. Care must be taken not to confuse them. Present participle adjectives, *amusing, boring, tiring* etc., are active and mean 'having this effect'. Past participle adjectives, *amused, horrified, tired* etc., are passive and mean 'affected in this way'.
   The play was boring. (The audience was bored.)
   The work was tiring. (The workers were soon tired.)
   The scene was horrifying. (The spectators were horrified.)
   an infuriating woman (She made us furious.)
   an infuriated woman (Something had made her furious.)

C   Agreement
   Adjectives in English have the same form for singular and plural, masculine and feminine nouns:
   a good boy, good boys   a good girl, good girls
   The only exceptions are the demonstrative adjectives **this** and **that**, which change to **these** and **those** before plural nouns:
   this cat, these cats   that man, those men

D   Many adjectives/participles can be followed by prepositions: *good at, tired of* (see 96).

18 Position of adjectives: attributive and predicative use

A   Adjectives in groups (a) - (e) above come before their nouns:
   this book   which boy   my dog
   Adjectives in this position are called attributive adjectives.

B   Adjectives of quality, however, can come either before their nouns:
   a rich man   a happy girl

or after a verb such as (a) *be, become, seem*:

    Tom became rich.   *Ann seems happy.*

or (b) *appear, feel, get/grow* (= become), *keep, look* (= appear), *make, smell, sound, taste, turn*:

    Tom felt cold.   *He got/grew impatient.*

    He made her happy.   *The idea sounds interesting.*

Adjectives in this position are called predicative adjectives. Verbs used in this way are called link verbs or copulas.

C   Note on link verbs (see also 169)

A problem with verbs in B(b) above is that when they are not used as link verbs they can be modified by adverbs in the usual way. This confuses the student, who often tries to use adverbs instead of adjectives after link verbs. Some examples with adjectives and adverbs may help to show the different uses:

    He looked calm (adjective) = *He had a calm expression.*

    He looked calmly (adverb) *at the angry crowd.* (*looked* here is a deliberate action.)

    She turned pale (adjective) = *She became pale.*

    He turned angrily (adverb) *to the man behind him.* (*turned* here is a deliberate action.)

    The soup tasted horrible (adjective). (It had a horrible taste.)

    He tasted the soup suspiciously (adverb). (*tasted* here is a deliberate action.) .

D   Some adjectives can be used only attributively or only predicatively, and some change their meaning when moved from one position to the other.

bad/good, big/small, heavy/light and **old**, used in such expressions as *bad sailor, good swimmer, big eater, small farmer, heavy drinker, light sleeper, old boy/friend/soldier* etc.; cannot be used predicatively without changing the meaning: *a small farmer* is a man who has a small farm, but *The farmer is small* means that he is a small man physically. Used otherwise, the above adjectives can be in either position. (For **little, old, young**, see also 19 B.)

chief, main, principal, sheer, utter come before their nouns.

frightened may be in either position, but **afraid** and **upset** must follow the verb and so must **adrift, afloat, alike** (see 21 G), **alive, alone, ashamed, asleep**.

The meaning of **early** and **late** may depend on their position:

an early/a late train means a train scheduled to run early or late in the day. *The train is early/late* means that it is before/after its proper time.

poor meaning 'without enough money' can precede the noun or follow the verb.

poor meaning 'unfortunate' must precede the noun.

poor meaning 'weak/inadequate' precedes nouns such as *student, worker* etc. but when used with inanimate nouns can be in either position:

    He has poor sight.   *His sight is poor.*

E Use of **and**

With attributive adjectives **and** is used chiefly when there are two or more adjectives of colour. It is then placed before the last of these:

a green and brown carpet   *a red, white and blue flag*

With predicative adjectives **and** is placed between the last two:

The day was cold, wet and windy.

19 Order of adjectives of quality

A Several variations are possible but a fairly usual order is: adjectives of
(a) size (except **little**; but see C below)
(b) general description (excluding adjectives of personality, emotion etc.)
(c) age, and the adjective **little** (see B)
(d) shape
(e) colour
(f) material
(g) origin
(h) purpose (these are really gerunds used to form compound nouns: |*walking stick, riding boots*).

a long sharp knife   *a small round bath*
new hexagonal coins   *blue velvet curtains*
an old plastic bucket   *an elegant French clock*

Adjectives of personality/emotion come after adjectives of physical description, including **dark, fair, pale**, but before colours:

a small suspicious official   *a long patient queue*
a pale anxious girl   *a kindly black doctor*
an inquisitive brown dog

B **little**, **old** and **young** are often used, not to give information, but as part of an adjective-noun combination. They are then placed next to their nouns:

Your nephew is a nice little boy.   *That young man drives too fast.*

little + **old** + noun is possible: *a little old lady*. But **little** + **young** is not.

When used to give information, **old** and **young** occupy position (c) above:

a young coloured man   *an old Welsh harp*

Adjectives of personality/emotion can precede or follow **young/old**:

a young ambitious man   *an ambitious young man*

young in the first example carries a stronger stress than **young** in the second, so the first order is better if we wish to emphasize the age.

little can be used similarly in position (c):

a handy little calculator   *an expensive little hotel*
a little sandy beach   *a little grey foal*

But **small** is usually better than **little** if we want to emphasize the size.

(For **little** meaning 'a small amount', see 5.)

C **fine, lovely, nice**, and sometimes **beautiful**, + adjectives of size
(except **little**), shape and temperature usually express approval of the
size etc. If we say *a beautiful big room, a lovely warm house, nice/fine
thick steaks* we imply that we like big rooms, warm houses and
thick steaks.
fine, lovely and **nice** can be used similarly with a number of other
adjectives:
   fine strong coffee   a lovely quiet beach   a nice dry day
When used predicatively, such pairs are separated by **and**:
   The coffee was fine and strong.
   The day was nice and dry.
beautiful is not much used in this sense as a predicative adjective.

D **pretty** followed by another adjective with no comma between them is
an adverb of degree meaning **very/quite**: *She's a pretty tall girl* means
She is quite/very tall. But *a pretty, tall girl* or, more usually, *a tall, pretty
girl* means a girl who is both tall and pretty.

20 Comparison

A There are three degrees of comparison:

Positive	Comparative	Superlative
dark	*darker*	*darkest*
tall	*taller*	*tallest*
useful	*more useful*	*most useful*

B One-syllable adjectives form their comparative and superlative by
adding **er** and **est** to the positive form:
   bright   brighter   brightest
Adjectives ending in **e** add **r** and **st**:
   brave   braver   bravest

C Adjectives of three or more syllables form their comparative and
superlative by putting **more** and **most** before the positive:
   interested   more interested   most interested
   frightening   more frightening   most frightening

D Adjectives of two syllables follow one or other of the above rules.
Those ending in **ful** or **re** usually take **more** and **most**:
   doubtful   more doubtful   most doubtful
   obscure   more obscure   most obscure
Those ending in **er, y** or a consonant + **le** usually add **er, est** or **r, st**:
   clever   cleverer   cleverest
   pretty   prettier   prettiest (note that the **y** becomes **i**)
   gentle   gentler   gentlest

E   Irregular comparisons:

bad	*worse*	*worst*
far	*farther*	*farthest* (of distance only)
	further	*furthest* (used more widely; see F, G)
good	*better*	*best*
little	*less*	*least*
many/much	*more*	*most*
old	*elder*	*eldest* (of people only)
	older	*oldest* (of people and things)

F   **farther/farthest** and **further/furthest**
Both forms can be used of distances:
> *York is farther/further than Lincoln or Selby.*
> *York is the farthest/furthest town* or
> *York is the farthest/furthest of the three.*

(In the last sentence **farthest/furthest** are pronouns. See 24 B.)
further can also be used, mainly with abstract nouns, to mean
'additional/extra':
> *Further supplies will soon be available.*
> *Further discussion/debate would be pointless.*

Similarly: *further enquiries/delays/demands/information/instructions* etc.
furthest can be used similarly, with abstract nouns:
> *This was the furthest point they reached in their discussion.*
> *This was the furthest concession he would make.*

(For adverb use, see 32.)

G   **far** (used for distance) and **near**
In the comparative and superlative both can be used quite freely:
> *the farthest/furthest mountain   the nearest river*

But in the positive form they have a limited use.
far and **near** are used chiefly with *bank, end, side, wall* etc.:
> *the far bank* (the bank on the other side)
> *the near bank* (the bank on this side of the river)

near can also be used with *east*, and **far** with *north, south, east*
and *west*.

With other nouns **far** is usually replaced by *distant/remote* and **near** by
nearby/neighbouring: *a remote island, the neighbouring village.*
For **far** (adverb), see 32; for **near** (adverb or preposition), see 30 C.

H   **elder, eldest; older, oldest**
elder, eldest imply seniority rather than age. They are chiefly used for
comparisons within a family: *my elder brother, her eldest boy/girl*;
but **elder** is not used with **than**, so **older** is necessary here:
> *He is older than I am.* (**elder** would not be possible.)

In colloquial English **eldest, oldest** and **youngest** are often used of
only two boys/girls/children etc.:
> *His eldest boy's at school; the other is still at home.*

This is particularly common when **eldest, oldest** are used as
pronouns:
> *Tom is the eldest.* (of the two)   (See 24 B.)

21 Constructions with comparisons (see also 341)

A   With the positive form of the adjective, we use **as . . . as** in the
affirmative and **not as/not so . . . as** in the negative:
A boy of sixteen is often as tall as his father.
He was as white as a sheet.
Manslaughter is not as/so bad as murder.
Your coffee is not as/so good as the coffee my mother makes.

B   With the comparative we use **than**:
The new tower blocks are much higher than the old buildings.
He makes fewer mistakes than you (do).
He is stronger than I expected =
I didn't expect him to be so strong.
It was more expensive than I thought =
I didn't think it would be so expensive.
When **than . . .** is omitted, it is very common in colloquial English to
use a superlative instead of a comparative: *This is the best way* could be
said when there are only two ways.
(See comparatives, superlatives used as pronouns, 24 B.)

C   Comparison of three or more people/things is expressed by the
superlative with **the . . . in/of**:
This is the oldest theatre in London.
The youngest of the family was the most successful.
A relative clause is useful especially with a perfect tense:
It/This is the best beer (that) I have ever drunk.
It/This was the worst film (that) he had ever seen.
He is the kindest man (that) I have ever met.
It was the most worrying day (that) he had ever spent.
Note that **ever** is used here, not **never**. We can, however, express
the same idea with **never** and a comparative:
I have never drunk better beer.   I have never met a kinder man.
He had never spent a more worrying day.
Note that **most** + adjective, without **the**, means **very**:
You are most kind means *You are very kind.*
most meaning **very** is used mainly with adjectives of two or more
syllables: *annoying, apologetic, disobedient, encouraging, exciting,
helpful, important, misleading* etc.

D   Parallel increase is expressed by the **the** + comparative . . . **the** +
comparative:
HOUSE AGENT: *Do you want a big house?*
ANN: *Yes, the bigger the better.*
TOM: *But the smaller it is, the less it will cost us to heat.*

E   Gradual increase or decrease is expressed by two comparatives joined
by **and**:
The weather is getting colder and colder.
He became less and less interested.

F   Comparison of actions with gerunds or infinitives:
>   *Riding a horse is not as easy as riding a motor cycle.*
>   *It is nicer/more fun to go with someone than to go alone.*
(See 341.)

G   Comparisons with **like** (preposition) and **alike**:
>   *Tom is very like Bill.   Bill and Tom are very alike.*
>   *He keeps the central heating full on. It's like living in the tropics.*

H   Comparisons with **like** and **as** (both adverb and adjective expressions
are shown here)
In theory **like** (preposition) is used only with noun, pronoun or gerund:
>   *He swims like a fish.   You look like a ghost.*
>   *Be like Peter/him: go jogging.*
>   *The windows were all barred. It was like being in prison.*
and **as** (conjunction) is used when there is a finite verb:
>   *Do as Peter does: go jogging.*
>   *Why don't you cycle to work as we do?*
But in colloquial English **like** is often used here instead of **as**:
>   *Cycle to work like we do.*

I   **like** + noun and **as** + noun:
>   *He worked like a slave.* (very hard indeed)
>   *He worked as a slave.* (He was a slave.)
>   *She used her umbrella as a weapon.* (She struck him with it.)

22   than/as + pronoun + auxiliary

A   When the same verb is required before and after **than/as** we can use an
auxiliary for the second verb. This auxiliary is not contracted.
>   *I earn less than he does.* (less than he earns)
The same tense need not be used in both clauses:
>   *He knows more than I did at his age.*

B   When the second clause consists only of **than/as** + **I/we/you** + verb,
and there is no change of tense, it is usually possible to omit the verb:
>   *I'm not as old as you (are).   He has more time than I/we (have).*
In formal English we keep **I/we**, as the pronoun is still considered to be
the subject of the verb even though the verb has been omitted. In
informal English, however, **me/us** is more usual:
>   *He has more time than me.   They are richer than us.*

C   When **than/as** is followed by **he/she/it** + verb, we normally keep the
verb: *You are stronger than he is.*
But we can drop the verb and use **he/she/they** in very formal English
or **him/her/them** in very colloquial English.
These rules apply also to comparisons made with adverbs:
>   *I swim better than he does/better than him.*
>   *They work harder than we do/harder than us.*
>   *You can't type as fast as I can/as fast as me.*

23 **the** + adjective with a plural meaning

A **blind, deaf, disabled, healthy/sick, living/dead, rich/poor, unemployed** and certain other adjectives describing the human character or condition can be preceded by **the** and used to represent a class of persons. These expressions have a plural meaning; they take a plural verb and the pronoun is **they**:

The poor get poorer; the rich get richer.

the can be used in the same way with national adjectives ending in **ch** or **sh**:

the Dutch   .the Spanish   the Welsh

and can be used similarly with national adjectives ending in **se** or **ss**:

the Burmese   the Chinese   the Japanese   the Swiss

though it is just possible for these to have a singular meaning.

B Note that **the** + adjective here refers to a group of people considered in a general sense only. If we wish to refer to a particular group, we must add a noun:

These seats are for the disabled.
The disabled members of our party were let in free.
The French like to eat well.
The French tourists complained about the food.

Some colours can be used in the plural to represent people but these take **s** like nouns: *the blacks, the whites.*

C **the** + adjective can occasionally have a singular meaning:

the accused (person)   the unexpected (thing)

24 Adjectives + **one/ones** and adjectives used as pronouns

A Most adjectives can be used with the pronouns **one/ones**, when **one/ones** represents a previously mentioned noun:

Don't buy the expensive apples; get the cheaper ones.
Hard beds are healthier than soft ones.
I lost my old camera; this is a new one.

Similarly with a number + adjective:

If you haven't got a big plate, two small ones will do.

B Adjectives used as pronouns

first/second etc. can be used with or without **one/ones**; i.e. they can be used as adjectives or pronouns:

Which train did you catch? ~ I caught the first (one).

the + superlative can be used similarly:

Tom is the best (runner).   The eldest was only ten.

and sometimes **the** + comparative:

Which (of these two) is the stronger?

But this use of the comparative is considered rather literary, and in informal English a superlative is often used here instead:

Which (of these two) is the strongest?

Adjectives of colour can sometimes be used as pronouns:
> *I like the blue (one) best.*

Colours of horses, especially **bay, chestnut, grey** are often used as pronouns and take **s** in the plural:
> *Everyone expected the chestnut to win.*
> *The coach was drawn by four greys.*

25 many and much (adjectives and pronouns)

A   **many** and **much**

many (adjective) is used before countable nouns.
much (adjective) is used before uncountable nouns:
> *He didn't make many mistakes.   We haven't much coffee.*

They have the same comparative and superlative forms **more** and **most**:
> *more mistakes/coffee   most men/damage*

many, much, more, most can be used as pronouns:
> *He gets a lot of letters but she doesn't get many.*
> *You have a lot of free time but I haven't much.*

more and **most** can be used quite freely, and so can **many** and **much**, with negative verbs (see above examples). But **many** and **much** with affirmative or interrogative verbs have a restricted use.

B   **many** and **much** with affirmative verbs

many is possible when preceded (i.e. modified) by **a good/a great**.
Both are possible when modified by **so/as/too**.
> *I made a good many friends there.*
> *He has had so many jobs that . . .*
> *She read as much as she could.*
> *They drink too much (gin).*

When not modified, **many**, as object or part of the object, is usually replaced by **a lot/lots of** (+ noun) or by **a lot** or **lots** (pronouns).
much, as object or part of the object, is usually replaced by **a great/good deal of** (+ noun) or **a great/good deal** (pronouns):
> *I saw a lot/lots of seabirds. I expect you saw a lot too.*
> *He spends a lot/lots of/a great deal of money on his house.*

As subject or part of the subject, either **many** or **a lot (of)** etc. can be used, but **much** here is normally replaced by one of the other forms.
much, however, is possible in formal English:
> *Much will depend on what the minister says.*

Compare negative and affirmative sentences:
> *He hasn't won many races.*
> *You've won a lot/lots of races* or *You've won a lot* or
> *You've won a great many (races).*

> *He didn't eat much fruit.*
> *She ate a lot/lots of fruit/a great deal of fruit* or
> *She ate a lot/a great deal.*

C   **many** and **much** with interrogative verbs
Both can be used with **how**: *How many times? How much?*
In questions where **how** is not used, **many** is possible, but **a lot (of)**
etc. is better when an affirmative answer is expected:
Did you take a lot of photos? I expect you did.
much without **how** is possible but the other forms are a little more
usual:
Did you have a lot of snow/much snow last year?
(For **much** as an adverb, see 33.)

26   Adjectives + infinitives

A   Some of the most useful of these adjectives are given below, grouped
roughly according to meaning or type. Some adjectives with several
meanings may appear in more than one group. (For adjectives +
prepositions, see 96.)
Starred adjectives can also be used with **that**-clauses. Sometimes
that . . . should is more usual. (See 236.)
In sections B-E, with the exception of B2, the constructions are
introduced by **it**. (For introductory **it**, see 67.) If **it + be . . .** is
preceded by **find/think/believe** etc. **that** it is sometimes possible to
omit **that** and the verb **be**:
He found that it was impossible to study at home =
He found it impossible to study at home.

B 1 **it + be + adjective (+ of + object) + infinitive** is used chiefly with
adjectives concerning:
(a) character: **brave, careless, cowardly, cruel, generous, good/
nice (= kind), mean, rude, selfish, wicked, wrong** (morally)
etc., and **fair*/just*/right*** with negative or interrogative verbs, or
(b) sense: **clever, foolish, idiotic*, intelligent, sensible, silly,
stupid.**
absurd*, ludicrous*, ridiculous* and **unreasonable*** are
sometimes also possible.
It was kind of you to help him. (You helped him. This was kind.)
It was stupid (of them) to leave their bicycles outside.
of + object can be omitted after group (b) adjectives, and sometimes
after group (a) adjectives, except **good** and **nice**. (Omission of **of** +
object would change the meaning of **good** and **nice**. See E.)

2   Pronoun + **be** + adjective + noun + infinitive is also possible with the
above adjectives and with a number of others, including:
astonishing*, curious*, extraordinary*, funny* (= **strange***),
odd*, queer*, surprising* etc. and **pointless, useful, useless**
It was a sensible precaution to take.
That was a wicked thing to say.
Comments of this type can sometimes be expressed as exclamations:
What a funny way to park a car!   What an odd time to choose!

The adjective is sometimes omitted in expressions of disapproval:
What a (silly) way to bring up a child!
What a time to choose!
Example with a **that**-clause:
It is strange/odd/surprising that he hasn't answered.

C   **it + be** + adjective + infinitive is possible with **advisable***,
inadvisable*, better*, best, desirable*, essential*, good (=
advisable), **important*, necessary*, unnecessary*, vital*** and
with **only + fair*/just*/right***:
Wouldn't it be better to wait? ~ No, it's essential to book in advance.
for + object can be added except after **good** (where it would change
the meaning; see E below) and after **just**:
It won't be necessary for him to report to the police.
It is only fair for him to have a chance.
inessential and **unimportant** are not normally used, but
not essential is possible.

D   **it + be** + adjective (+ **for** + object) + infinitive is possible with
**convenient*, dangerous, difficult, easy, hard*, possible*,
impossible, safe, unsafe.** (For **possible that**, see 27 E.)
Would it be convenient (for you) to see Mr X now?
It was dangerous (for women) to go out alone after dark.
We found it almost impossible to buy petrol. (See A above.)
The above adjectives, with the exception of **possible**, can also be used
in the noun + **be** + adjective + infinitive construction:
This cake is easy to make.
The instructions were hard to follow.
This car isn't safe to drive.

E   **it + be** + adjective/participle + infinitive is also possible with adjectives
and participles which show the feelings or reactions of the person
concerned:

agreeable	*dreadful**	*lovely**	*terrible**
awful*	*good*/nice**	*marvellous**	*wonderful**
delightful*	*(= pleasant)*	*splendid**	etc.
disagreeable	*horrible**	*strange**	

and with the present participles of:

alarm*	*bewilder*	*discourage**	*excite**	*surprise**
amaze*	*bore*	*disgust**	*frighten*	*terrify*
amuse*	*depress**	*embarrass*	*horrify**	*upset*
annoy*	*disappoint**	*encourage**	*interest**	etc.
astonish*				

fun (= an exciting experience) and **a relief** can be used similarly.
It's awful to be alone in such a place.
It's boring to do the same thing every day.
It was depressing to find the house empty.
It would be fun/exciting/interesting to canoe down the river.
It was a relief to take off our wet boots.

for + object is quite common after **lovely, interesting, marvellous, nice, wonderful** and possible after the other adjectives:

It's interesting (for children) to see a house being built.
It was marvellous (for the boys) to have a garden to play in.

Note that **for** + object placed after **good** restricts the meaning of **good** to **healthy/beneficial**: *It's good for you to take regular exercise.* (**good** + infinitive can have this meaning but can also mean **pleasant/kind/advisable**. See B, C above.)

it + **be** + adjective + noun + infinitive is also possible with the above adjectives/participles:

It was an exciting ceremony to watch.
It was a horrible place to live (in).

F Somewhat similar meanings can be expressed by subject + adjective + infinitive with **angry*, delighted*, dismayed*, glad*, happy*, pleased*, relieved*, sad*, sorry*** and the past participles of the verbs in E above: *I'm delighted to see you.*

The most useful infinitives here are *to find/learn/hear/see*, but **glad/happy/sad/sorry** are also often followed by *to say/tell/inform* and sometimes by other infinitives:

He was glad to leave school.
She was dismayed to find the door locked.

G Subject + **be** + adjective/participle + infinitive with: **able/unable; apt, inclined, liable, prone; prepared, not prepared** (= **ready/willing/unwilling), reluctant; prompt, quick, slow**:

We are all apt to make mistakes when we try to hurry.
I am inclined to believe him.   I am prepared/ready to help him.
He was most reluctant to lend us the money.
He was slow to realize that times had changed =
He realized only slowly that times had changed.

27 Adjectives + infinitive/**that**-clause/preposition constructions

A **due, due to, owing to, certain, sure, bound, confident**

due, used of time, can take an infinitive:

The race is due to start in ten minutes.

But it can also be used alone:

The plane was due (in) at six. It is an hour overdue.

due to (preposition) means 'a result of':

The accident was due to carelessness.

owing to means 'because of':

Owing to his carelessness we had an accident.

due to should be preceded by subject + verb, but English people are careless about this and often begin a sentence with **due to** instead of with **owing to**.

certain and **sure** take infinitives to express the speaker's opinion. **bound** is also possible here:

Tom is certain/sure/bound to win. (The speaker is confident
of this.)

But subject + **certain/sure** + **that**-clause expresses the subject's
opinion:

Tom is sure that he will win. (Tom is confident of victory.)

confident that could replace **certain/sure that** above, but
confident cannot be followed by an infinitive.

sure, certain, confident can be followed by **of** + noun/pronoun or
gerund:

Unless you're early you can't be sure of getting a seat.

bound can take an infinitive, as shown above, but not a **that**-clause.

bound + infinitive can also mean 'under an obligation':

According to the contract we are bound to supply the materials.

B   **afraid (of), ashamed (of), sorry (for or about)**

afraid of, ashamed of, sorry for/about + noun/pronoun or gerund:

She is afraid of heights/of falling.

*He was ashamed of himself (for behaving so badly)/ashamed of
behaving so badly.*

I'm sorry for breaking your window. (apology)

I'm sorry about your window. (apology/regret)

I'm sorry for Peter. (pity)

afraid, ashamed, sorry can be followed by an infinitive:

She was afraid to speak. (She didn't speak.)

I'd be ashamed to take his money. (I don't/won't take it.)

I'm sorry to say that we have no news.

or by a **that**-clause:

I'm ashamed that I've nothing better to offer you.

She's afraid (that) he won't believe her. (fear)

I'm afraid (that) we have no news. (regret)

I'm sorry (that) you can't come.

(For the difference in meaning between these three constructions, see
271. For **I'm afraid not/so**, see 347.)

C   **anxious (about), anxious** + infinitive, **anxious that**

anxious (+ **about** + noun/pronoun) means **worried**:

I'm anxious (about Tom). His plane is overdue.

be anxious (+ **for** + noun/pronoun) + infinitive = 'to desire/to wish':

I'm very anxious (for him) to see the Carnival.

anxious + **that** . . . + **should** is possible in very formal English:

The committee is anxious that this matter should be kept secret.

D   **fortunate** and **lucky** can take either a **that**-clause or an infinitive, but
there is usually a difference of meaning.

It is fortunate/lucky that usually means 'It's a good thing that':

It's lucky that Tom has a car.

It's lucky that he passed his test. (Now he can drive himself to the
station/take the children to the seaside etc.)

It's lucky for us that he has a car. (He can give us a lift etc.)

Subject + **be** + **fortunate/lucky** + infinitive, however, emphasizes the subject's good fortune:

> *He's lucky to have a car.* (Many people haven't got one.)
> *He was lucky to pass his test.* (He wasn't really up to the standard.)

is/are + **fortunate/lucky** + present infinitive is used mainly with static verbs. With **was/were** or the continuous or perfect infinitive there is a wider choice:

> *You were fortunate to escape unharmed.*
> *You are lucky to be going by air.*
> *He is lucky to have sold his house before they decided to build the new airport.*

It is lucky/unlucky can, however, be followed by the infinitive of any verb:

> *It is unlucky to break a mirror.* (It brings misfortune.)

fortunate and **unfortunate** are not used here but can be used in the other constructions. They are chiefly found in more formal English.

These adjectives can also be used alone or with a noun:

> *I wasn't lucky.*   *He's fortunate.*
> *Thirteen's my lucky number.*   *He's a fortunate man.*

E   **possible, probable** and **likely** can take a **that**-clause introduced by **it**. **likely** can also be used with subject + infinitive

>   (a) *It's possible that he'll come today* =
>   (b) *Perhaps he'll come/He may come today.*
>   (a) *It's probable that he'll come today* =
>   (b) *He'll probably come today.*

In each case the (b) form is more usual than the (a) but the **that**-clause is convenient when we want to modify the adjectives:

> *It's just/quite possible that . . .*
> *It's not very probable that . . .*

With **likely** both forms are equally useful:

> *It's quite likely that he'll come today* =
> *He's quite likely to come today.*

is/are + subject + **likely** + infinitive is very useful as it supplies an interrogative form for **may** (= **be possible**):

> *Is he likely to ring today?*

possible, probable, likely can be used without a **that**-clause when it is quite clear what this would be:

> *Do you think he'll sell his house?* ~ *It's quite possible/probable/likely (that he'll sell it).*

F   **aware** and **conscious** take a **that**-clause or **of** + noun/pronoun or gerund:

> *It'll be dangerous.* ~ *I'm aware that it'll be dangerous/I'm aware of that.*
> *I was conscious of being watched* =
> *I felt that someone was watching me.*

conscious used by itself has a physical meaning:

> *I had only a local anaesthetic. I was conscious the whole time.*

4 Adverbs

28 Kinds of adverbs

Manner: *bravely, fast, happily, hard, quickly, well* (see 35)
Place and direction: *down, far, here, near, there, up, west* (36)
Time: *now, soon, still, then, today, yet* (37)
Frequency: *always, never, occasionally, often, twice* (38)
Sentence: *certainly, definitely, luckily, surely* (40)
Degree: *fairly, hardly, rather, quite, too, very* (41)
Interrogative: *when? where? why?* (60)
Relative: *when, where, why* (75 E)

Form and use

29 The formation of adverbs with ly

A Many adverbs of manner and some adverbs of degree are formed by
adding **ly** to the corresponding adjectives:
    final, finally   immediate, immediately   slow, slowly
Spelling notes
(a) A final **y** changes to **i**: *happy, happily.*
(b) A final **e** is retained before **ly**: *extreme, extremely.*
    Exceptions: *true, due, whole* become *truly, duly, wholly.*
(c) Adjectives ending in a consonant + **le** drop the **e** and add **y**:
    gentle, gently   simple, simply
Note that the adverb of **good** is **well**.

B Adjectives ending in **ly**
daily, weekly, monthly etc., **kindly** and sometimes **leisurely** can be
adjectives or adverbs, but most other adjectives ending in **ly**, e.g.
friendly, likely, lonely etc., cannot be used as adverbs and have no
adverb form. To supply this deficiency we use a similar adverb or
adverb phrase (= adverbial):
    likely (adjective)   *probably* (adverb)
    friendly (adjective)   *in a friendly way* (adverbial)

C Some adverbs have a narrower meaning than their corresponding
adjectives or differ from them.
coldly, coolly, hotly, warmly are used mainly of feelings:
    We received them coldly. (in an unfriendly way)
    They denied the accusation hotly. (indignantly)
    She welcomed us warmly. (in a friendly way)

But **warmly dressed** = wearing warm clothes.

coolly = **calmly/courageously** or **calmly/impudently**:

He behaved very coolly in this dangerous situation.

presently = **soon**: *He'll be here presently.*

(See also 30 B. For **barely, scarcely,** see 44. For **surely,** see 40 A.)

30 Adverbs and adjectives with the same form

A

back	*hard**	*little*	*right**
*deep**	*high**	*long*	*short**
*direct**	*ill*	*low*	*still*
early	*just*.*	*much/more/most**	*straight*
enough	*kindly*	*near**	*well*
far	*late**	*north/east* etc.	*wrong**
fast	*left*	*pretty**	

*See B below.

Used as adverbs:
Come back soon.
You can dial Rome direct.
The train went fast.
They worked hard. (energetically)
an ill-made road
Turn right here.
She went straight home.
He led us wrong.

Used as adjectives:
the back door
the most direct route
a fast train
The work is hard
You look ill/well
the right answer
a straight line
This is the wrong way.

B Starred words above also have **ly** forms. Note the meanings.

deeply is used chiefly of feelings:

He was deeply offended.

directly can be used of time or connection:

He'll be here directly. (very soon)

The new regulations will affect us directly/indirectly.

(For **hardly,** see 44.)

highly is used only in an abstract sense:

He was a highly paid official.   *They spoke very highly of him.*

justly corresponds to the adjective **just** (fair, right, lawful), but **just** can also be an adverb of degree. (See 41.)

lately = **recently**: *Have you seen him lately?*

mostly = **chiefly**

nearly = **almost**: *I'm nearly ready.*

prettily corresponds to the adjective **pretty** (attractive):

Her little girls are always prettily dressed.

But **pretty** can also be an adverb of degree meaning **very**:

The exam was pretty difficult.

rightly can be used with a past participle to mean **justly** or **correctly**:

He was rightly/justly punished.

I was rightly/correctly informed.

But in each case the second adverb would be more usual.
shortly = **soon, briefly** or **curtly**.
wrongly can be used with a past participle:
> *You were wrongly (incorrectly) informed.*

But *He acted wrongly* could mean that his action was either incorrect or morally wrong.

C   **long** and **near** (adverbs) have a restricted use.

1   **long**
longer, longest can be used without restriction:
> *It took longer than I expected.*

But **long** is used mainly in the negative or interrogative:
> *How long will it take to get there?* ~ *It won't take long.*

In the affirmative **too/so** + **long** or **long** + **enough** is possible.
Alternatively **a long time** can be used:
> *It would take too long.*
> *It would take a long time.*

In conversation **(for) a long time** is often replaced by **(for) ages**:
> *I waited for ages.*
> *It took us ages to get there.*

2   **near**
nearer, nearest can be used without restriction:
> *Don't come any nearer.*

But **near** in the positive form is usually qualified by **very/quite/so/too** or **enough**:
> *They live quite near.*   *Don't come too near.*
> *You're near enough.*

The preposition **near** with noun, pronoun or adverb is more generally useful:
> *Don't go near the edge.*
> *The ship sank near here.*

D   **far** and **much** also have a restricted use. See 32 and 33.

31   Comparative and superlative adverb forms

A   With adverbs of two or more syllables we form the comparative and superlative by putting **more** and **most** before the positive form:

Positive	Comparative	Superlative
quickly	*more quickly*	*most quickly*
fortunately	*more fortunately*	*most fortunately*

Single-syllable adverbs, however, and **early**, add **er, est**:

hard	*harder*	*hardest*
early	*earlier*	*earliest* (note the **y** becomes **i**)

B   Irregular comparisons:

well	*better*	*best*
badly	*worse*	*worst*
little	*less*	*least*
much	*more*	*most*
far	*farther*	*farthest* (of distance only)
	further	*furthest* (used more widely; see 32 A)

32   far, farther/farthest and further/furthest

A   **further, furthest**
These, like **farther/farthest**, can be used as adverbs of place/distance:
> *It isn't safe to go any further/farther in this fog.*

But they can also be used in an abstract sense:
> *Mr A said that these toy pistols should not be on sale.*
> *Mr B went further and said that no toy pistols should be sold.*
> *Mr C went furthest of all and said that no guns of any kind should be sold.*

B   **far**: restrictions on use
far in the comparative and superlative can be used quite freely:
> *He travelled further than we expected.*

far in the positive form is used chiefly in the negative and interrogative:
> *How far can you see? ~ I can't see far.*

In the affirmative **a long way** is more usual than **far**, and **a long way away** is more usual than **far away**:
> *They sailed a long way.   He lives a long way away.*

But **very far away** is possible, and so is **so/quite/too + far** and **far + enough**:
> *They walked so far that . . .   They walked too far.*
> *We've gone far enough.*

far can be used with an abstract meaning:
> *The new law doesn't go far enough.*
> *You've gone too far!* (You've been too insulting/overbearing/ insolent etc.)

far, adverb of degree, is used with comparatives or with **too + positive** forms:
> *She swims far better than I do.   He drinks far too much.*

33   much, more, most

A   **more** and **most** can be used fairly freely:
> *You should ride more.   I use this room most.*

But **much**, in the positive form, has a restricted use.

B   **much** meaning **a lot** can modify negative verbs:
> *He doesn't ride much nowadays.*

In the interrogative **much** is chiefly used with **how**. In questions
without **how**, **much** is possible but **a lot** is more usual:
>   *How much has he ridden?*   *Has he ridden a lot/much?*
In the affirmative **as/so/too** + **much** is possible. Otherwise **a lot/
a good deal/a great deal** is preferable:
>   *He shouts so much that . . .*   *I talk too much.*
But *He rides a lot/a great deal.*

C   **very much** meaning **greatly** can be used more widely in the
affirmative. We can use it with *blame, praise, thank* and with a number
of verbs concerned with feelings: *admire, amuse, approve, dislike,
distress, enjoy, impress, like, object, shock, surprise* etc.:
>   *Thank you very much.*   *They admired him very much.*
>   *She objects very much to the noise they make.*
much (= **greatly**), with or without **very**, can be used with the
participles *admired, amused, disliked, distressed, impressed, liked,
shocked, struck, upset*:
>   *He was (very) much admired.*
>   *She was (very) much impressed by their good manners.*

D   **much** meaning **a lot** can modify comparative or superlative adjectives
and adverbs:
>   *much better*   *much the best*   *much more quickly*
much too can be used with positive forms:
>   *He spoke much too fast.*

E   **most** placed before an adjective or adverb can mean **very**. It is mainly
used here with adjectives/adverbs of two or more syllables:
>   *He was most apologetic.*   *She behaved most generously.*
(See 21 C.)

34   Constructions with comparisons (see also 341)

When the same verb is required in both clauses we normally use an
auxiliary for the second verb (see 22).

A   With the positive form we use **as . . . as** with an affirmative verb, and
as/so . . . as with a negative verb:
>   *He worked as slowly as he dared.*
>   *He doesn't snore as/so loudly as you do.*
>   *It didn't take as/so long as I expected.*

B   With the comparative form we use **than**:
>   *He eats more quickly than I do/than me.*
>   *He played better than he had ever played.*
>   *They arrived earlier than I expected.*
the + comparative . . . **the** + comparative is also possible:
>   *The earlier you start the sooner you'll be back.*

C With the superlative it is possible to use **of** + noun:
   He went (the) furthest of the explorers.
   But this construction is not very common and such a sentence would
   normally be expressed by a comparative, as shown above.
   A superlative (without **the**) + **of all** is quite common, but **all** here
   often refers to other actions by the same subject:
   He likes swimming best of all. (better than he likes anything else)
   of all can then be omitted.

D For comparisons with **like** and **as**, see 21 H, I.

Position

35 Adverbs of manner

A Adverbs of manner usually come after the verb:
   She danced beautifully
   or after the object when there is one:
   He gave her the money reluctantly.   *They speak English well.*
   Do not put an adverb between verb and object.

B When we have verb + preposition + object, the adverb can be either
   before the preposition or after the object:
   He looked at me suspiciously or *He looked suspiciously at me.*
   But if the object contains a number of words we put the adverb before
   the preposition:
   He looked suspiciously at everyone who got off the plane.

C Similarly with verb + object sentences the length of the object affects
   the position of the adverb. If the object is short, we have verb + object
   + adverb, as shown in B above. But if the object is long we usually put
   the adverb before the verb:
   She carefully picked up all the bits of broken glass.
   He angrily denied that he had stolen the documents.
   They secretly decided to leave the town.

D Note that if an adverb is placed after a clause or a phrase, it is normally
   considered to modify the verb in that clause/phrase. If, therefore, we
   move *secretly* to the end of the last example above, we change the
   meaning:
   They secretly decided . . . (The decision was secret.)
   They decided to leave the town secretly. (The departure was
   to be secret.)

E Adverbs concerned with character and intelligence, **foolishly,
   generously, kindly, stupidly** etc., when placed before a verb,
   indicate that the action was foolish/kind/generous etc.:
   I foolishly forgot my passport.   *He generously paid for us all.*
   He kindly waited for me.   *Would you kindly wait?*

Note that we could also express such ideas by:
> *It was foolish of me to forget.*
> *It was kind of him to wait.*
> *Would you be kind enough to wait?* (See 252.)

The adverb can come after the verb or after verb + object, but the meaning then changes:
> *He spoke kindly = His voice and words were kind*

is not the same as *It was kind of him to speak to us.*
> *He paid us generously = He paid more than the usual rate*

is not the same as *It was generous of him to pay us.*

Note the difference between:
> *He answered the questions foolishly* (His answers were foolish) and
> *He foolishly answered the questions.* (Answering was foolish./It was foolish of him to answer at all.)

F **badly** and **well** can be used as adverbs of manner or degree. As adverbs of manner they come after an active verb, after the object or before the past participle in a passive verb:

> *He behaved badly.*   *He read well.*
> *He paid her badly.*   *She speaks French well.*
> *She was badly paid.*   *The trip was well organized.*

badly as an adverb of degree usually comes after the object or before the verb or past participle:

> *The door needs a coat of paint badly/The door badly needs a coat of paint.*
> *He was badly injured in the last match.*

well (degree) and **well** (manner) have the same position rules:

> *I'd like the steak well done.*
> *He knows the town well.*
> *Shake the bottle well.*
> *The children were well wrapped up.*

The meaning of **well** may depend on its position. Note the difference between:

> *You know well that I can't drive* (There can be no doubt in your mind about this) and
> *You know that I can't drive well.* (I'm not a good driver.)

well can be placed after **may/might** and **could** to emphasize the probability of an action:

> *He may well refuse = It is quite likely that he will refuse.*

(For **may/might as well**, see 288.)

G **somehow, anyhow**

somehow (= in some way or other) can be placed in the front position or after a verb without object or after the object:

> *Somehow they managed.*   *They managed somehow.*
> *They raised the money somehow.*

anyhow as an adverb of manner is not common. But it is often used to mean 'in any case/anyway'. (See 327.)

36 Adverbs of place and direction

abroad, away, everywhere, far, here, there etc.

A   If there is no object, these adverbs are usually placed after the verb:
She went away.   He lives abroad.   Bill is upstairs.
But they come after verb + object or verb + preposition + object:
She sent him away.   I looked for it everywhere.
(But see chapter 38 for verb + adverb combinations such as *pick up, put down* etc.)
Adverb phrases, formed of preposition + noun/pronoun/adverb, follow the above position rules:
The parrot sat on a perch.   He stood in the doorway.
He lives near me.
But see also E below.

B   **somewhere, anywhere** follow the same basic rules as **some** and **any**:
I've seen that man somewhere.
Can you see my key anywhere? ~ No, I can't see it anywhere.
Are you going anywhere? (ordinary question) but
Are you going somewhere? (I assume that you are.)
nowhere, however, is not normally used in this position except in the expression **to get nowhere** (= to achieve nothing/to make no progress):
Threatening people will get you nowhere. (You'll gain no advantage by threatening people.)
But it can be used in short answers:
Where are you going? ~ Nowhere. (I'm not going anywhere.)
It can also, in formal English, be placed at the beginning of a sentence and is then followed by an inverted verb:
Nowhere will you find better roses than these. (See 45.)

C   **here, there** can be followed by **be/come/go** + noun subject:
Here's Tom.   There's Ann.   Here comes the train.
There goes our bus.
here and **there** used as above carry more stress than **here/there** placed after the verb. There is also usually a difference in meaning.
Tom is here means he is in this room/building/town etc. But *Here's Tom* implies that he has just appeared or that we have just found him. *Tom comes here* means that it is his habit to come to this place, but *Here comes Tom* implies that he is just arriving/has just arrived.
If the subject is a personal pronoun, it precedes the verb in the usual way:
There he is.   Here I am.   Here it comes.
But **someone** and **something** follow the verb:
'There's someone who can help you.
Note that the same sentence, spoken without stress on *There*, would mean that a potential helper exists. (See 117.)

D   Someone phoning a friend may introduce himself/herself by
     name + **here**:
>   ANN (on phone): *Is that you, Tom? Ann here* or *This is Ann.*
     She must not say *Ann is here* or *Here is Ann.*

E   The adverbs **away** (= off), **down, in, off, out, over, round, up** etc.
     can be followed by a verb of motion + a noun subject:
>   *Away went the runners.*
>   *Down fell a dozen apples.*
>   *Out sprang the cuckoo.*
>   *Round and round flew the plane.*
     But if the subject is a pronoun it is placed before the verb:
>   *Away they went.*   *Round and round it flew.*
     There is more drama in this order than in subject + verb + adverb but
     no difference in meaning.

F   In written English adverbials introduced by prepositions (*down,
     from, in, on, over, out of, round, up* etc.) can be followed by verbs
     indicating position (*crouch, hang, lie, sit, stand* etc.), by verbs of
     motion, by *be born, die, live* and sometimes other verbs:
>   *From the rafters hung strings of onions.*
>   *In the doorway stood a man with a gun.*
>   *On a perch beside him sat a blue parrot.*
>   *Over the wall came a shower of stones.*
     The first three of these examples could also be expressed by a
     participle and the verb *be*:
>   *Hanging from the rafters were strings of onions.*
>   *Standing in the doorway was a man with a gun.*
>   *Sitting on a perch beside him was a blue parrot.*
     But a participle could not be used with the last example unless the
     shower of stones lasted for some time.

37   Adverbs of time

A   **afterwards, eventually, lately, now, recently, soon, then,
     today, tomorrow** etc. and adverb phrases of time: **at once, since
     then, till** (6.00 etc.)
     These are usually placed at the very beginning or at the very end of the
     clause, i.e. in front position or end position. End position is usual with
     imperatives and phrases with **till**:
>   *Eventually he came/He came eventually.*
>   *Then we went home/We went home then.*
>   *Write today.*   *I'll wait till tomorrow.*
     (For **lately, recently**, see also 185.)
     With compound tenses, **eventually, lately, now, recently, since**
     and **soon** can come after the auxiliary:
>   *We'll soon be there.*

B **before, early, immediately** and **late** come at the end of the clause:
> *He came late.   I'll go immediately.*

But **before** and **immediately**, used as conjunctions, are placed at the beginning of the clause:
> *Immediately the rain stops we'll set out.*

C **since** and **ever since** are used with perfect tenses (see 187 D).
since can come after the auxiliary or in end position after a negative or interrogative verb; **ever since** (adverb) in end position.
Phrases and clauses with **since** and **ever since** are usually in end position, though front position is possible:
> *He's been in bed since his accident/since he broke his leg.*

D **yet** and **still** (adverbs of time)
yet is normally placed after verb or after verb + object:
> *He hasn't finished (his breakfast) yet.*

But if the object consists of a large number of words, **yet** can be placed before or after the verb:
> *He hasn't yet applied/applied yet for the job we told him about.*

still is placed after the verb **be** but before other verbs:
> *She is still in bed.*

yet means 'up to the time of speaking'. It is chiefly used with the negative or interrogative.
still emphasizes that the action continues. It is chiefly used with the affirmative or interrogative, but can be used with the negative to emphasize the continuance of a negative action:
> *He still doesn't understand.* (The negative action of 'not understanding' continues.)
> *He doesn't understand yet.* (The positive action of 'understanding' hasn't yet started.)

When stressed, **still** and **yet** express surprise, irritation or impatience. Both words can also be conjunctions (see 327).

E **just**, as an adverb of time, is used with compound tenses:
> *I'm just coming.   (See also 183.)*

(For **just** as an adverb of degree, see 41.)

38 Adverbs of frequency

(a) **always, continually, frequently, occasionally, often, once, twice, periodically, repeatedly, sometimes, usually** etc.
(b) **ever, hardly ever, never, rarely, scarcely ever, seldom**

A Adverbs in both the above groups are normally placed:

1 After the simple tenses of **to be**:
> *He is always in time for meals.*

2 Before the simple tenses of all other verbs:
> *They sometimes stay up all night.*

3   With compound tenses, they are placed after the first auxiliary, or, with interrogative verbs, after auxiliary + subject:

He can never understand.

You have often been told not to do that.

Have you ever ridden a camel?

Exceptions

(a) **used to** and **have to** prefer the adverb in front of them:

You hardly ever have to remind him; he always remembers.

(b) Frequency adverbs are often placed before auxiliaries when these are used alone, in additions to remarks or in answers to questions:

Can you park your car near the shops? ~ Yes, I usually can.

I know I should take exercise, but I never do.

and when, in a compound verb, the auxiliary is stressed:

I never 'can remember.   She hardly ever 'has met him.

Similarly when **do** is added for emphasis:

I always 'do arrive in time!

But emphasis can also be given by stressing the frequency adverb and leaving it in its usual position after the auxiliary:

You should 'always check your oil before starting.

B   Adverbs in group (a) above can also be put at the beginning or end of a sentence or clause.

Exceptions

always is rarely found at the beginning of a sentence/clause except with imperatives.

often, if put at the end, normally requires **very** or **quite**:

Often he walked.   He walked quite often.

C   Adverbs in group (b) above, **hardly ever, never, rarely** etc. (but not **ever** alone), can also be put at the beginning of a sentence, but inversion of the following main verb then becomes necessary:

Hardly/Scarcely ever did they manage to meet unobserved.

(For **hardly, barely, scarcely**, see 44.)

hardly/scarcely ever, never, rarely and **seldom** are not used with negative verbs.

D   **never, ever**

never is chiefly used with an affirmative verb, never with a negative. It normally means 'at no time':

He never saw her again.   I've never eaten snails.

They never eat meat. (habit)

I've never had a better flight.

(For **never** + comparative, see 21 C.)

never + affirmative can sometimes replace an ordinary negative:

I waited but he never turned up. (He didn't turn up.)

never + interrogative can be used to express the speaker's surprise at the non-performance of an action:

Has he never been to Japan? I'm surprised, because his wife is Japanese.

ever means 'at any time' and is chiefly used in the interrogative:
   Has he ever marched in a demonstration? ~ No, he never has.
ever can be used with a negative verb and, especially with compound tenses, can often replace **never** + affirmative:
   I haven't ever eaten snails.
This use of **ever** is less common with simple tenses.
ever + affirmative is possible in comparisons (see 21 C) and with suppositions and expressions of doubt:
   I don't suppose he ever writes to his mother.
(For **hardly/scarcely** + **ever**, see A – C above. For **ever** after **how** etc., see 61, 85.)

39 Order of adverbs and adverb phrases of manner, place and time when they occur in the same sentence

Expressions of manner usually precede expressions of place:
   He climbed awkwardly out of the window.
   He'd study happily anywhere.
But **away, back, down, forward, home, in, off, on, out, round** and **up** usually precede adverbs of manner:
   He walked away sadly.   *She looked back anxiously.*
   They went home quietly.   *They rode on confidently.*
(See also 36 E.)
here and **there** do the same except with the adverbs **hard, well, badly**: *He stood there silently* but *They work harder here.*
Time expressions can follow expressions of manner and place:
   They worked hard in the garden today.
   He lived there happily for a year.
But they can also be in front position:
   Every day he queued patiently at the bus stop.

40 Sentence adverbs

These modify the whole sentence/clause and normally express the speaker's/narrator's opinion.

A   Adverbs expressing degrees of certainty
   (a) **actually** (= in fact/really), **apparently, certainly, clearly, evidently, obviously, presumably, probably, undoubtedly**
   (b) **definitely**
   (c) **perhaps, possibly, surely**
Adverbs in group (a) above can be placed after **be**:
   He is obviously intelligent.
before simple tenses of other verbs:
   They certainly work hard.   *He actually lives next door.*
after the first auxiliary in a compound verb:
   They have presumably sold their house.

at the beginning or at the end of a sentence or clause:
> *Apparently he knew the town well.*
> *He knew the town well apparently.*

definitely can be used in the above positions but is less usual at the beginning of a sentence.

perhaps and **possibly** are chiefly used in front position, though the end position is possible.

surely is normally placed at the beginning or end, though it can also be next to the verb. It is used chiefly in questions:
> *Surely you could pay £1?   You could pay £1, surely?*

Note that though the adjectives **sure** and **certain** mean more or less the same, the adverbs differ in meaning.

certainly = **definitely**:
> *He was certainly there; there is no doubt about it.*

But **surely** indicates that the speaker is not quite sure that the statement which follows is true. He thinks it is, but wants reassurance.
> *Surely he was there?* (I feel almost sure that he was.)

B   Other sentence adverbs
admittedly, (un)fortunately, frankly, honestly*, (un)luckily, naturally*, officially* etc. are usually in the front position though the end position is possible. They are normally separated from the rest of the sentence by a comma. Starred adverbs can also be adverbs of manner.
> *Honestly, Tom didn't get the money.* (Sentence adverb. *honestly* here means 'truthfully'. The speaker is assuring us that Tom didn't get the money.)
> *Tom didn't get the money honestly* (adverb of manner) = *Tom got the money dishonestly.*

41   Adverbs of degree

absolutely, almost, barely, completely, enough, entirely, even, extremely, fairly, far, hardly, just, much, nearly, only, pretty, quite, rather, really, scarcely, so, too, very etc.
(For **(a) little**, see 5 D; for **fairly** and **rather**, see 42; for **hardly, scarcely, barely**, see 44; for **quite**, see 43.)

A   An adverb of degree modifies an adjective or another adverb. It is placed before the adjective or adverb:
> *You are absolutely right.   I'm almost ready.*

But **enough** follows its adjective or adverb:
> *The box isn't big enough.*
> *He didn't work quickly enough.*   (See also 252 B.)

B   **far** requires a comparative, or **too** + positive:
> *It is far better to say nothing.   He drives far too fast.*

much could replace **far** here. It can also be used with a superlative:
> *This solution is much the best.*

C   The following adverbs of degree can also modify verbs:
almost, barely, enough, hardly, just, (a) little, much, nearly, quite, rather, really and **scarcely**. All except **much, a little** and **enough** are then placed before the main verb:

> *He almost/nearly fell.*   *I am just going.*
> *Tom didn't like it much but I really enjoyed it.*

(For **much**, see 33. For **(a) little**, see 5 D.)

D   **only** can also modify verbs. In theory it is placed next to the word to which it applies, preceding verbs, adjectives and adverbs and preceding or following nouns and pronouns:

> (a) *He had only six apples.* (not more than six)
> (b) *He only lent the car.* (He didn't give it.)
> (c) *He lent the car to me only.* (not to anyone else)
> (d) *I believe only half of what he said.*

But in spoken English people usually put it before the verb, obtaining the required meaning by stressing the word to which the **only** applies:

> *He only had ǀsix apples* is the same as (a) above.
> *He only lent the car to ǀme* is the same as (c) above.
> *I only believe ǀhalf* etc. is the same as (d) above.

E   **just**, like **only**, should precede the word it modifies:

> *I'll buy just one.*   *I had just enough money.*

It can also be placed immediately before the verb:

> *I'll just buy one.*   *I just had enough money.*

But sometimes this change of order would change the meaning:

> *Just sign here* means *This is all you have to do.*
> *Sign just here* means *Sign in this particular spot.*

fairly, rather, quite, hardly etc.

42   **fairly** and **rather**

A   Both can mean 'moderately', but **fairly** is chiefly used with 'favourable' adjectives and adverbs (*bravely, good, nice, well* etc.), while **rather** is chiefly used in this sense before 'unfavourable' adjectives and adverbs (*bad, stupidly, ugly* etc.):

> *Tom is fairly clever, but Peter is rather stupid.*
> *I walk fairly fast but Ann walks rather slowly.*

Both can be used similarly with participles:

> *He was fairly relaxed; she was rather tense.*
> *a fairly interesting film*   *a rather boring book*

The indefinite article, if required, precedes **fairly** but can come before or after **rather**:

> *a fairly light box*   *a rather heavy box/rather a heavy box*

With adjectives/adverbs such as *fast, slow, thin, thick, hot, cold* etc., which are not in themselves either 'favourable' or 'unfavourable', the speaker can express approval by using **fairly** and disapproval by using

rather: *This soup is fairly hot* implies that the speaker likes hot soup, while *This soup is rather hot* implies that it is a little too hot for him.

B **rather** can be used before *alike, like, similar, different* etc. and before comparatives. It then means 'a little' or 'slightly':

Siamese cats are rather like dogs in some ways.

The weather was rather worse than I had expected.

rather a is possible with certain nouns: *disappointment, disadvantage, nuisance, pity, shame* and sometimes *joke*:

It's rather a nuisance (= a little inconvenient) *that we can't park here.*

It's rather a shame (= a little unfair) *that he has to work on Sundays.*

fairly cannot be used in these ways.

C **rather** can be used before certain 'favourable' adjectives/adverbs such as *amusing, clever, good, pretty, well* but its meaning then changes; it becomes nearly equivalent to **very**, and the idea of disapproval vanishes: *She is rather clever* is nearly the same as *She is very clever.* **rather** used in this way is obviously much more complimentary than **fairly**. For example the expression *It is a fairly good play* would, if anything, discourage others from going to see it. But *It is rather a good play* is definitely a recommendation. Occasionally **rather** used in this way conveys the idea of surprise:

I suppose the house was filthy. ~ No, as a matter of fact it was rather clean.

D **rather** can also be used before *enjoy, like* and sometimes before *dislike, object* and some similar verbs:

I rather like the smell of petrol.   He rather enjoys queueing.

rather can be used in short answers to questions with the above verbs:

Do you like him? ~ Yes I do, rather.

rather + *like/enjoy* is often used to express a liking which is a surprise to others or to the speaker himself. But it can also be used to strengthen the verb: *I rather like Tom* implies more interest than *I like Tom.*

(For **would rather**, see 297, 298.)

43 quite

This is a confusing word because it has two meanings.

A It means 'completely' when it is used with a word or phrase which can express the idea of completeness (*all right, certain, determined, empty, finished, full, ready, right, sure, wrong* etc.) and when it is used with a very strong adjective/adverb such as *amazing, extraordinary, horrible, perfect*:

The bottle was quite empty.   You're quite wrong.

It's quite extraordinary; I can't understand it at all.

B When used with other adjectives/adverbs, **quite** has a slightly
weakening effect, so that **quite good** is normally less complimentary
than **good. quite** used in this way has approximately the same meaning
as **fairly** but its strength can vary very much according to the way it is
stressed:

> *quite* '*good* (weak *quite*, strong *good*) is very little less than 'good'.
> '*quite* '*good* (equal stress) means 'moderately good'.
> '*quite good* (strong *quite*, weak *good*) is much less than 'good'.

The less **quite** is stressed the stronger the following adjective/adverb
becomes. The more **quite** is stressed the weaker its adjective/
adverb becomes.

Note the position of **a/an**: *quite a long walk, quite an old castle.*

quite can also modify *enjoy, like, agree* and *understand (the reason)*:

> *It was a difficult journey but we quite enjoyed it.*
> *I can't tell you without Tom's consent. ~ I quite understand.*

44 hardly, scarcely, barely

hardly, scarcely and **barely** are almost negative in meaning.

hardly is chiefly used with **any, ever, at all** or the verb **can**:

> *He has hardly any money.* (very little money)
> *I hardly ever go out.* (I very seldom go out.)
> *It hardly rained at all last summer.*
> *Her case is so heavy that she can hardly lift it.*

But it can also be used with other verbs:

> *I hardly know him.* (I know him only very slightly.)

Be careful not to confuse the adverbs **hard** and **hardly**:

> *He looked hard at it.* (He stared at it.)
> *He hardly looked at it.* (He gave it only a brief glance.)

scarcely can mean 'almost not' and could replace **hardly** as used
above: *scarcely any/scarcely ever* etc.

But **scarcely** is chiefly used to mean 'not quite':

> *There were scarcely twenty people there.* (probably fewer)

(For **hardly/scarcely** with inversion, see 45 and 342 E.)

barely means 'not more than/only just':

> *There were barely twenty people there.* (only just twenty)
> *I can barely see it.* (I can only just see it.)

Inversion of the verb

45 Inversion of the verb after certain adverbs

Certain adverbs and adverb phrases, mostly with a restrictive or
negative sense, can for emphasis be placed first in a sentence or clause
and are then followed by the inverted (i.e. interrogative) form of the

verb. The most important of these are shown below. The numbers indicate paragraphs where an example will be found.

hardly ever (see 38 A, C)	*on no account*
hardly . . . when (342 E)	*only by*
in no circumstances	*only in this way*
neither/nor (112 D)	*only then/when*
never	*rarely*
no sooner . . . than (342 E)	*scarcely ever*
not only	*scarcely . . . when*
not till	*seldom*
nowhere (36 B)	*so* (112 A)

I haven't got a ticket. ~ Neither/Nor have I.
I had never before been asked to accept a bribe.
Never before had I been asked to accept a bribe.
They not only rob you, they smash everything too.
Not only do they rob you, they smash everything too.
He didn't realize that he had lost it till he got home.
Not till he got home did he realize that he had lost it.
This switch must not be touched on any account.
On no account must this switch be touched.
He was able to make himself heard only by shouting.
Only by shouting was he able to make himself heard.
This remedy rarely failed.
Rarely did this remedy fail.
He became so suspicious that . . .
So suspicious did he become that . . .

Note also that a second negative verb in a sentence can sometimes be expressed by **nor** with inversion:

He had no money and didn't know anyone he could borrow from.
He had no money, nor did he know anyone he could borrow from.
(**neither** would be less usual here.)

(For adverbs and adverb phrases followed by inversion of verb and noun subject, e.g. *Up went the rocket; By the door stood an armed guard*, see 36 C, E, F.)

5 all, each, every, both, neither, either, some, any, no, none

46   all, each, every, everyone, everybody, everything
(for **all** and **each**, see also 48)

A   **all** compared to **every**
Technically, **all** means a number of people or things considered as a group while **every** means a number of people or things considered individually. But in practice **every** and its compounds are often used when we are thinking of a group.

B   **each** (adjective and pronoun) and **every** (adjective)
each means a number of persons or things considered individually.
every can have this meaning but with **every** there is less emphasis on the individual.
Every man had a weapon means 'All the men had weapons', and implies that the speaker counted the men and the weapons and found that he had the same number of each. *Each man had a weapon* implies that the speaker went to each man in turn and checked that he had a weapon.
each is a pronoun and adjective: *Each (man) knows what to do.*
every is an adjective only: *Every man knows . . .*
each can be used of two or more persons or things, and is normally used of small numbers. **every** is not normally used of very small numbers.
Both take a singular verb. The possessive adjective is **his/her/its**.
(For the reciprocal pronoun **each other**, see 53 C, 70 B.)

C   **everyone/everybody** and **everything** (pronouns)
everyone/everybody + singular verb is normally preferred to **all (the) people** + plural verb, i.e. we say *Everyone is ready* instead of *All the people are ready*. There is no difference between **everyone** and **everybody**.
everything is similarly preferred to **all (the) things**, i.e. we say *Everything has been wasted* instead of *All the things have been wasted*.
The expressions **all (the) people, all (the) things** are possible when followed by a phrase or clause:
> *All the people in the room clapped.*
> *I got all the things you asked for.*
Otherwise they are rarely used.
(For pronouns and possessive adjectives with **everyone/everybody**, see 51 C, 69.)

47 both

both means 'one and the other'. It takes a plural verb.
both can be used alone or followed by a noun:
Both (doors) were open
or by (**of**) + **the/these/those** or possessives:
both (of) the wheels   both (of) your wheels
or by **of** + **us/you/them**:
Both of us knew him.
A personal pronoun + **both** is also possible:
We both knew him. (See 48.)
both . . . and . . . can be used to emphasize a combination of two
adjectives, nouns, verbs etc.:
It was both cold and wet.
He is both an actor and a director.
He both acts and directs.

48 all/both/each + of and alternative constructions

A **all** (pronoun) can be followed by **of** + **the/this/these/that/those/**
possessives and proper nouns.
both (pronoun) + **of** can be used similarly but with plural forms only.
The **of** here is often omitted especially with **all** + a singular
noun/pronoun.

> *all the town*   *all (of) Tom's boys*
> *all his life*   *both (of) the towns*
> *all (of) these*   *both (of) his parents*

B With **all/both** + **of** + personal pronoun the **of** cannot be omitted:
all of it   both of them
But there is an alternative construction, personal pronoun + **all/both**:
all of it is replaceable by *it all*.
all of us = *we all* (subject), *us all* (object).
all of you is replaceable by *you all*.
all of them = *they all* (subject), *them all* (object).
Similarly:
both of us = *we both* or *us both*
both of you = *you both*
both of them = *they both* or *them both*
All of them were broken = *They were all broken.*
All/Both of us went = *We all/both went.*
We ate all/both the cakes.
We ate all/both of them.
We ate them all/both.

C When one of these pronoun + **all/both** combinations is the subject of a
compound tense the auxiliary verb usually precedes **all/both**:
We are all waiting.   You must both help me.

be is also placed before **all/both** except when it is used in short answers etc.:

We are all/both ready but

Who is ready? ~ We all are/We both are.

Other auxiliaries used alone and simple tenses of ordinary verbs follow **all/both**:

You all have maps.   They both knew where to go.

D **each**, like **both**, can be followed by **of** + **these/those** etc. (plural forms only). The **of** here cannot be omitted:

each of the boys   each of these

each of us/you/them can, however, be replaced by pronoun + **each**:

each of you = you each

each of us = we each (subject), *us each* (indirect object)

each of them = they each (subject), *them each* (indirect object)

We each sent in a report.

They gave us each a form to fill in.

Note that **each of us/you/them** is singular:

Each of us has a map.

But **we/you/they each** is plural:

We each have a map.

Verbs used with **we/you/they each** follow the patterns given in C above for **all** and **both**:

They have each been questioned.

49   neither, either

A 1 **neither** means 'not one and not the other'. It takes an affirmative singular verb. It can be used by itself or followed by a noun or by **of** + **the/these/those**/possessives or personal pronouns:

(a) *I tried both keys but neither (of them) worked.*

(b) *Neither of them knew the way/Neither boy knew . . .*

(c) *I've read neither of these (books).*

2 **either** means 'any one of two'. It takes a singular verb and, like **neither**, can be used by itself or followed by a noun/pronoun or by **of** + **the/these/those** etc.

3 **either** + negative verb can replace **neither** + affirmative except when **neither** is the subject of a verb. So **either** could not be used in (a) or (b) above but could in (c):

I haven't read either of these (books).

Though **either** cannot be the subject of a negative verb, it can be subject or object of an affirmative or interrogative verb:

Either (of these) would do.

Would you like either of these?

4 Pronouns and possessive adjectives with **neither/either** used of people should technically be **he/him, she/her** and **his/her**, but in

colloquial English the plural forms are generally used:
> *Neither of them knows the way, do they?*
> *Neither of them had brought their passports.*

B **neither . . . nor, either . . . or**
neither . . . nor + affirmative verb is an emphatic way of combining two negatives:

(a) *Neither threats nor arguments had any effect on him.*
(b) *They said the room was large and bright but it was neither large nor bright.*
(c) *He neither wrote nor phoned.*

either . . . or + negative verb can replace **neither . . . nor** except when **neither . . . nor** is the subject of a verb, as in (a) above. So:

(b) *. . . but it wasn't either large or bright* and
(c) *He didn't either write or phone.*

either . . . or cannot be the subject of a negative verb but can be the subject or object of affirmative or interrogative verbs and is used in this way to express alternatives emphatically:

> *You can have either soup or fruit juice.* (not both)
> *You must either go at once or wait till tomorrow.*
> *It's urgent, so could you either phone or telex?*

(For **either** used in additions to remarks, see 112. For **neither/nor** followed by inversion, see 45, 112.)

50 some, any, no and none (adjectives and pronouns)

A 1 **some** and **any** mean 'a certain number or amount'. They are used with or instead of plural or uncountable nouns. (For **some/any** with singular nouns, see C below.)

some is a possible plural form of **a/an** and **one**:

> *Have a biscuit/some biscuits.   I ate a date/some dates.*

some, any and **none** can be used with **of** + **the/this/these/those/** possessives/personal pronouns:

> *Some of the staff can speak Japanese.*
> *Did any of your photos come out well?*

2 **some** is used:
With affirmative verbs:

> *They bought some honey.*

In questions where the answer 'yes' is expected:

> *Did some of you sleep on the floor?* (I expect so.)

In offers and requests:

> *Would you like some wine?*
> *Could you do some typing for me?*

(See also C.)

3 **any** is used:
With negative verbs:

> *I haven't any matches.*

5 all, each, every etc.

With **hardly, barely, scarcely** (which are almost negatives):
I have hardly any spare time.
With **without** when **without any . . . = with no . . .** :
He crossed the frontier without any difficulty/with no difficulty.
With questions except the types noted above:
Have you got any money?
Did he catch any fish?
After **if/whether** and in expressions of doubt:
If you need any more money, please let me know.
I don't think there is any petrol in the tank.
(See also C.)

B **no** (adjective) and **none** (pronoun)
no and **none** can be used with affirmative verbs to express a negative:
I have no apples. I had some last year but I have none this year.
no + noun can be the subject of a sentence:
No work was done.
No letter(s) arrived.
none as the subject is possible but not very usual:
We expected letters, but none came.
none + of, however, is quite usual as subject:
None of the tourists wanted to climb the mountain.

C **some** or **any** used with singular, countable nouns
some here usually means 'an unspecified or unknown':
Some idiot parked his car outside my garage.
or other can be added to emphasize that the speaker isn't very interested:
He doesn't believe in conventional medicine; he has some remedy or other of his own.
any can mean 'practically every', 'no particular (one)':
Any book about riding will tell you how to saddle a horse.
Any dictionary will give you the meaning of these words.

51 someone, somebody, something, anyone, anybody, anything, no one, nobody, nothing

A Compounds with **some, any** and **no** follow the above rules:
Someone wants to speak to you on the phone.
Someone/Somebody gave me a ticket for the pop concert. ~
No one/Nobody has ever given me a free ticket for anything.
Do you want anything from the chemist?
Would anyone/anybody like a drink?
Note also:
I drink anything = I don't mind what I drink.
Anyone will tell you where the house is.
(See 50 C.)

B   **someone, somebody, anyone, anybody, no one, nobody** can be
possessive:

> *Someone's passport has been stolen.*
> *Is this somebody's/anybody's seat?*
> *I don't want to waste anyone's time.*

C   Pronouns and possessive adjectives with **someone, somebody,
anyone, anybody, no one, nobody, everyone, everybody**

These expressions have a singular meaning and take a singular verb so
personal pronouns and possessive adjectives should logically be
he/she, him/her, his/her. However in colloquial English plural forms
are more common:

> *Has anyone left their luggage on the train?*
> *No one saw Tom go out, did they?*

But with **something, anything, nothing** we still use **it:**

> *Something went wrong, didn't it?*

52   **else** placed after **someone/anybody/nothing** etc.

A   **someone/somebody/something, anyone/anybody/anything,
no one/nobody/nothing, everyone/everybody/everything** and
the adverbs **somewhere, anywhere, nowhere, everywhere** can
be followed by **else:**

> *someone else/somebody else* = some other person
> *anyone else/anybody else* = any other person
> *no one else/nobody else* = no other person
> *everyone else/everybody else* = every other person
> *something else* = some other thing

> *I'm afraid I can't help you. You'll have to ask someone else.* ~
> *There isn't anyone else/There's no one else to ask.*

else used with adverbs:

> *somewhere else* = in/at/to some other place
> *anywhere else* = in/at/to any other place
> *nowhere else* = in/at/to no other place

> *Are you going anywhere else?*

B   **someone/somebody, anyone/anybody, no one/nobody + else** can
be possessive:

> *I took someone else's coat.*
> *Was anyone else's luggage opened?*
> *No one else's luggage was opened.*

53 another, other, others with one and some

A another, other, others

	Adjective	Pronoun
Singular	*another*	*another*
Plural	*other*	*others*

Have you met Bill's sisters? ~ I've met one. I didn't know he had another (sister). ~ Oh, he has two others/two other sisters.

B one . . . another/other(s), some . . . other(s)

One student suggested a play, another (student)/other students/others wanted a concert.

Some tourists/Some of the tourists went on the beach; others explored the town.

C one another and each other

Tom and Ann looked at each other =
Tom looked at Ann and Ann looked at Tom.

Both **one another** and **each other** can be used of two or more, but **each other** is frequently preferred when there are more than two.

6 Interrogatives: wh-? words and how?

54 Interrogative adjectives and pronouns

For persons: subject   *who* (pronoun)
                 object   *whom, who* (pronoun)
                 possessive   *whose* (pronoun and adjective)
For things: subject/object   *what* (pronoun and adjective)
For persons or things when the choice is restricted:
                 subject/object   *which* (pronoun and adjective)
The same form is used for singular and plural.
what can also be used for persons (see 58 D).

55 Affirmative verb after **who, whose** etc. used as subjects

who, whose, which, what when used as subjects are normally followed by an affirmative, not an interrogative, verb:
> *Who pays the bills?* (affirmative verb)
> *Whose/Which horse won?* (affirmative verb)
> *What happened?/What went wrong?* (affirmative verb; possible answers: *We missed the train/had an accident.*)

But with **who, whose** etc. + **be** + noun or personal/distributive pronoun, an interrogative verb is used:
> *Who are you?*   *Whose is this?*   *What is that noise?*

With **who, whose** etc. used as objects of a verb or preposition an interrogative verb is, of course, necessary.

56 Examples of the use of **who, whom, whose, which** and **what**

A **who, whom, whose**
who as subject:
> *Who keeps the keys?* (affirmative verb)
> *Who took my gun?* (affirmative verb)
> *Who are these boys?* (interrogative verb)

who, whom as objects of a verb:
Normal English: *Who did you see?*
Very formal English: *Whom did the committee appoint?*

whose as subject:
> *Whose car broke down?* (affirmative verb)
> *Whose (books) are these?* (interrogative verb)

whose as object of a verb:
> *Whose umbrella did you borrow?*

71

B **which**
which as subject:
> *Which pigeon arrived first?* (affirmative verb)
> *Which of them is the eldest?* (affirmative verb)

which as object of a verb:
> *Which hand do you use?*   *Which of these dates would you prefer?*

C **what**
what as subject:
> *What caused the explosion?* (affirmative verb)
> *What kind of tree is that?* (interrogative verb)

what as object of a verb:
> *What paper do you read?*   *What did they eat?*

57 who, whom, which and what as objects of prepositions

A **who, whom**
In formal English we use preposition + **whom**:
> *With whom did you go?*   *To whom were you speaking?*

But in ordinary English we usually move the preposition to the end of the sentence. The **whom** then normally changes to **who**:
> *Who did you go with?*   *Who were you speaking to?*

B **which, what**
In formal English we use preposition + **which/what**:
> *To which address did you send it?*
> *On what do you base your theory?*

In informal English we move the preposition to the end of the sentence:
> *Which address did you send it to?*
> *What do you base your theory on?*

58 Uses of what

A **what** is a general interrogative used for things:
> *What bird is that?*   *What makes that noise?*
> *What country do you come from?*   *What did he say?*

B **what** + action + **for?** means 'why?' and often expresses disapproval:
> *What did you do that for?* can mean
> *Why did you do such an odd thing/such a stupid thing?*

C **what** + **be ... like?** is a request for a description or comment:
> *What was the exam like?* ~ *It was very difficult.*
> *What was the weather like?* ~ *It was very windy.*
> *What's the food like in your hostel?* ~ *It's quite good.*

Used of people it may concern either appearance or character:
> *What's he like?* ~ *He's short and fat and wears glasses* or
> *He's a very talkative, friendly man.*

what does he/she/it look like? concerns appearance only, and can also mean 'What does he/she/it resemble?':

What does she look like? ~ She is tall and glamorous. She looks like
a film star.
What does it look like? ~ It's black and shiny. It looks like coal.

D **what is he?** means 'What is his profession?':
What is his father? ~ He is a tailor.
what (adjective) used for persons is not common: *What students are*
you talking about? is possible, but *Which students . . . ?* would be much
more usual.

E **what** and **how** in questions about measurements
We can use **what** + **age/depth/height/length/width** but in
conversation it would be more usual to say **how old/deep/high/tall/**
long/wide?
what size/weight? is usual when an exact answer is required,
though **how big/heavy?** is also possible.
What age are you?/What is your age?/How old are you?
What height is he?/What is his height?/How tall is he?
What is the weight of the parcel?/How heavy is it?
What size do you take in shoes?

59 **which** compared with **who** and **what**

A Examples of **which** and **what** used for things:
What will you have to drink?
There's gin, whisky and sherry: which will you have?
What does it cost to get to Scotland? ~ It depends on how you
go. ~ Which (way) is the cheapest or *Which is the cheapest (way)?*
I've seen the play and the film. ~ What did you think of them?
Which (of them) did you like best?

B Examples of **which** and **who** used for people:
Who do you want to speak to? ~ I want to speak to Mr Smith. ~
We have two Smiths here. Which (of them) do you want?
which (pronoun) of people is not used alone as subject of a verb:
Which of you knows the formula? ('of you' is essential.)
Who knows the formula? would also be possible.

C **which** (adjective) can be used of people when there is only a very
slight idea of restriction:
Which poet (of all the poets) *do you like best?*
what would be possible here and would be more logical, but **what**
(adjective) for people is normally avoided.

60 Interrogative adverbs: **why, when, where, how**

A **why?** means 'for what reason?':
Why was he late? ~ He missed the bus.

B **when?** means 'at what time?':
 When do you get up? ~ 7 a.m.

C **where?** means 'in what place?':
 Where do you live? ~ In London.

D **how?** means 'in what way?':
 How did you come? ~ I came by plane.
 How do you start the engine? ~ You press this button.

how can also be used:

1 With adjectives (see 25 C):
 How strong are you? How important is this letter?
 (For **how** + **old/high** etc., see 58 E.)

2 With **much** and **many**:
 How much (money) do you want?
 How many (pictures) did you buy?

3 With adverbs:
 How fast does he drive? How often do you go abroad?
 How badly was he hurt? How soon can you come?
 Note that *How is she?* is an enquiry about her health, but *What is she like?* is a request for a description. (See 58 C.)
 Do not confuse *How are you?* with *How do you do?* When two people are introduced each says *How do you do?* This is a greeting rather than a question. (See 126.)

61 ever placed after who, what, where, why, when, how

 Where ever have you been? I've been looking for you everywhere!
 Who ever told you I'd lend you the money? I've no money at all!
ever here is not necessary in the sentence but is added to emphasize the speaker's surprise/astonishment/anger/irritation/dismay. It has the same meaning as *on earth/in the world*.
Such sentences are always spoken emphatically and the intonation will convey the speaker's emotion:
 Why ever did you wash it in boiling water? (dismay)
 Who ever are you? (The other person is presumably an intruder.)
 Who ever left the door open? (What stupid person left it open?)
 Where ever have you put my briefcase? (I can't find it anywhere.)
 What ever are you doing in my car? (astonishment/annoyance)
 When ever did you leave home? (You must have left very early.)
 How ever did he escape unhurt? (The car was a complete wreck.)
Note also **why ever not?** and **what ever for?**:
 You mustn't wear anything green. ~ Why ever not? (I can't understand the reason for this prohibition.)
 Bring a knife to class tomorrow. ~ What ever for? (I can't understand what I need a knife for.)
(For **whoever, whatever** etc. written as one word, see 85.)

7 Possessives, personal and reflexive pronouns: **my, mine, I, myself** etc.

62 Possessive adjectives and pronouns

Possessive adjectives	Possessive pronouns
my	*mine*
your	*yours*
his/her/its	*his/hers*
our	*ours*
your	*yours*
their	*theirs*

Note that no apostrophes are used here. Students should guard against the common mistake of writing the possessive **its** with an apostrophe. *it's* (with an apostrophe) means *it is*.
The old form of the second person singular can be found in some bibles and pre-twentieth century poetry:
> *thy   thine*

one's is the possessive adjective of the pronoun **one**.

63 Agreement and use of possessive adjectives

A   Possessive adjectives in English refer to the possessor and not to the thing possessed. Everything that a man or boy possesses is **his** thing; everything that a woman or girl possesses is **her** thing:
> *Tom's father is his father* but
> *Mary's father is her father.*

Everything that an animal or thing possesses is **its** thing:
> *A tree drops its leaves in autumn.*
> *A happy dog wags its tail.*

But if the sex of the animal is known, **his/her** would often be used.
If there is more than one possessor, **their** is used:
> *The girls are with their brother.*
> *Trees drop their leaves in autumn.*

Note that the possessive adjective remains the same whether the thing possessed is singular or plural:
> *my glove, my gloves   his foot, his feet*

75

B   Possessive adjectives are used with clothes and parts of the body:
    She changed her shoes.   He injured his back.
    (But see also 7 A6.)

C   To add emphasis, **own** can be placed after **my, your, his** etc. and
    after **one's**:
    my own room   her own idea
    own can be an adjective, as above, or a pronoun:
    a room of one's own
    Note the expression:
    I'm on my own = I'm alone.

64   Possessive pronouns replacing possessive adjectives + nouns

A   *This is our room or This (room) is ours.*
    This is their car. That car is theirs too.
    You've got my pen.
    You're using mine. Where's yours?

B   The expression **of mine** etc. means 'one of my' etc.:
    a friend of mine = one of my friends
    a sister of hers = one of her sisters

65   Personal pronouns

A   Form

		Subject	Object
Singular:	first person	*I*	*me*
	second person	*you*	*you*
	third person	*he/she/it*	*him/her/it*
Plural:	first person	*we*	*us*
	second person	*you*	*you*
	third person	*they*	*them*

The old form of the second person singular is:
    thou (subject)   *thee* (object)

B   Use of subject and object forms

1   **you** and **it** present no difficulty as they have the same form for subject
    and object:
    Did you see the snake? ~ Yes, I saw it and it saw me. ~ Did it
    frighten you?

2   First and third person forms (other than **it**)
    (a) **I, he, she, we, they** can be subjects of a verb:
    I see it.   He knows you.   They live here.
    or complements of the verb **to be**: *It is I.*

Normally, however, we use the object forms here:
> *Who is it? ~ It's me.*
> *Where's Tom? ~ That's him over there.*

But if the pronoun is followed by a clause, we use the subject forms:
> *Blame Bill! It was he who chose this colour.*

(b) **me, him, her, us, them** can be direct objects of a verb:
> *I saw her.   Tom likes them.*

or indirect objects:
> *Bill found me a job.   Ann gave him a book.   (See 66.)*

or objects of a preposition:
> *with him   for her   without them   to us*

66   The position of pronoun objects

A   An indirect object comes before a direct object:
> *I made Ann/her a cake.   I sent Bill the photos.*

However, if the direct object is a personal pronoun it is more usual to place it directly after the verb and use **to** or **for**:
> *I made it for her.   I sent them to him.   (See 88.)*

The position rule does not apply to **one, some, any, none** etc.:
> *He bought one for Ann* or *He bought Ann one.*
> *He gave something to Jack* or *He gave Jack something.*

B   Pronoun objects of phrasal verbs
With many phrasal verbs a noun object can be either in the middle or at the end:
> *Hand your papers in/Hand in your papers.*
> *Hang your coat up/Hang up your coat.*
> *Take your shoes off/Take off your shoes.*

A pronoun object, however, must be placed in the middle:
> *hand them in   hang it up   take them off*

(See chapter 38.)

67   Uses of **it**

A   **it** is normally used of a thing or an animal whose sex we don't know, and sometimes of a baby or small child:
> *Where's my map? I left it on the table.*
> *Look at that bird. It always comes to my window.*
> *Her new baby is tiny. It only weighs 2 kilos.*

B   **it** can be used of people in sentences such as:
> ANN (on phone): *Who is that/Who is it?*
> BILL: *It's me.*
> *Is that Tom over there? ~ No, it's Peter.*

C   **it** is used in expressions of time, distance, weather, temperature, tide:
> *What time is it? ~ It is six.*
> *What's the date? ~ It's the third of March.*

How far is it to York? ~ It is 400 kilometres.
How long does it take to get there? ~ It depends on how you go.
It is raining/snowing/freezing.   It's frosty.   It's a fine night.
It's full moon tonight.   In winter it's/it is dark at six o'clock.
It is hot/cold/quiet/noisy in this room.
It's high tide/low tide.

Note also:

It's/It is three years since I saw him =
I haven't seen him for three years. (See 188.)

(For **it is time** + subject + past tense, see also 293.)

D   Introductory **it**

1   **it** can introduce sentences of the following type ('cleft sentences'):
It was ¹Peter who lent us the money. (not Paul)
It's ¹today that he's going. (not tomorrow)
it is used even with a plural noun:
It's ¹pilots that we need, not ground staff.
(See also 76.)

2   When an infinitive is subject of a sentence, we usually begin the
sentence with **it** and put the infinitive later; i.e. we say:
It is easy to criticize instead of
To criticize is easy.
It is better to be early instead of
To be early is better.
It seems a pity to give up now instead of
To give up now seems a pity.
If **it + be** is preceded by **find/think (that),** the **be** and the **that**
can often be omitted:
He thought (that) it (would be) better to say nothing.
We found it impossible to get visas.

3   **it** can be used similarly when the subject of a sentence is a clause. It
would be possible to say:
That he hasn't phoned is odd.
That prices will go up is certain.
But it would be much more usual to say:
It's odd that he hasn't phoned.
It's certain that prices will go up.
Other examples:
It never occurred to me that perhaps he was lying.
It struck me that everyone was unusually silent.

E   **it/this** can represent a previously mentioned phrase, clause or verb:
He smokes in bed, though I don't like it. (*it* = his smoking in bed)
He suggested flying, but I thought it would cost too much.
(*it* = flying)

F   **it** also acts as a subject for impersonal verbs:
it seems   it appears   it looks   it happens

68 you, one and they as indefinite pronouns

A **you** and **one**

As subjects, either can be used:
> *Can you/one camp in the forest?*

As objects, **you** is the normal pronoun:
> *They fine you for parking offences.*

you is more common in ordinary conversation. It is a more 'friendly' pronoun and implies that the speaker can imagine himself in such a position.

one is more impersonal and less often used, though the possessive **one's** is quite common:
> *It's easy to lose one's/your way in Venice.*

The correct possessive form must be used:
> *One has to show one's pass at the door.*
> *You have to show your pass at the door.*

If instead of **one** or **you** we use a singular noun, the possessive adjective will obviously be **his** or **her**:
> *One must do one's best.*
> *A traveller has to guard his possessions.*

B **they**

they is used as subject only. **they** can mean 'people':
> *they say = people say, it is said*
> *They say it is going to be a cold winter.*

they can also mean 'the authority concerned', i.e. the government/ the local council/one's employers/the police etc.:
> *They want to make this a one-way street.*

69 Use of they/them/their with neither/either, someone/everyone/no one etc.

These expressions are singular and take a singular verb. Their personal pronouns therefore should be **he/she** and the possessive adjectives should be **his/her** (**he/his** for males and mixed sexes; **she/her** for females). But many native speakers find this troublesome and often use **they/their**, even when only one sex is involved:
> *Neither of them remembered their instructions.*
> *Would someone lend me their binoculars?*
> *Everyone has read the notice, haven't they?*
> *No one objected, did they?*   (See also 51 C.)

70 Reflexive pronouns

A These are: **myself, yourself, himself, herself, itself, ourselves, yourselves, themselves.** Note the difference between the second person singular **yourself**, and the second person plural **yourselves**. The indefinite reflexive/emphasizing pronoun is **oneself**.

B   **myself, yourself** etc. are used as objects of a verb when the action of
    the verb returns to the doer, i.e. when subject and object are the same
    person:
    I cut myself.   He can't shave himself.
    It is not always easy to amuse oneself on holiday.
    Tom and Ann blamed themselves for the accident.
    This refrigerator defrosts itself.
    Note the change of meaning if we replace the reflexive pronoun by the
    reciprocal pronoun **each other**:
    Tom and Ann blamed each other. (Tom blamed Ann and Ann
    blamed Tom. See 53 C.)

C   **myself, yourself** etc. are used similarly after a verb + preposition:
    He spoke to himself.   Did she pay for herself?
    Look after yourself.   Take care of yourselves.
    I'm annoyed with myself.   He sat by himself. (alone)
    She addressed the envelope to herself.
    But if the preposition indicates locality, we use the ordinary, not the
    reflexive, pronouns:
    Did you take your dog with you?
    They put the child between them.
    Had he/Did he have any money on him?

71   myself, himself, herself etc. used as emphasizing pronouns

    myself etc. can also be used to emphasize a noun or pronoun:
    The King himself gave her the medal.
    self is then stressed in speech.
    When used in this way the pronoun is never essential and can be
    omitted without changing the sense. It usually emphasizes the subject
    of the sentence and is placed after it:
    Ann herself opened the door.   Tom himself went.
    Alternatively it can be placed after the object if there is one:
    Ann opened the door herself
    or after an intransitive verb:
    Tom went himself.
    If the intransitive verb is followed by a preposition + noun, the
    emphasizing pronoun can be placed after this noun:
    Tom went to London himself or *Tom himself went to London.*
    When it emphasizes another noun it is placed immediately after it:
    I saw Tom himself.   I spoke to the President himself.
    She liked the diamond itself but not the setting.
    Note the difference between:
    I did it myself (It was done by me and not by someone else) and
    I did it by myself (I did it without help).

8 Relative pronouns and clauses

There are three kinds of relative clauses: defining (see 72-7), non-defining (78-81) and connective (82).

72 Defining relative clauses

These describe the preceding noun in such a way as to distinguish it from other nouns of the same class. A clause of this kind is essential to the clear understanding of the noun. In the sentence:

The man who told me this refused to give me his name

'who told me this' is the relative clause. If we omit this, it is not clear what man we are talking about. Notice that there is no comma between a noun and a defining relative clause.

Defining relative clauses usually follow **the** + noun, but they can also be used with **a/an** + noun, plural nouns without **the** and the pronouns **all, none, anybody, somebody** etc. and **those**.

Clauses following **a/an** + noun, plural nouns without **the** and **somebody/someone/something** sometimes define their noun/pronoun only indirectly. The noun/pronoun in these cases is usually the object of a verb or preposition:

I met someone who said he knew you.

The book is about a girl who falls in love with . . .

Sometimes these clauses are separated from their noun/pronoun by a word or phrase:

There's a man here who wants . . .

I saw something in the paper which would interest you.

But normally relative clauses should be placed directly after their noun or pronoun:

The noise that he made woke everybody up.

She was annoyed by something that I had said.

73 Relative pronouns used in defining relative clauses

The forms are as follows:

	Subject	Object	Possessive
For persons	who	whom/who	whose
	that	that	
For things	which	which	whose/of which
	that	that	

74 Defining relative clauses: persons

A   Subject: **who** or **that**
who is normally used:
> *The man who robbed you has been arrested.*
> *The girls who serve in the shop are the owner's daughters.*
> *Only those who had booked in advance were allowed in.*
> *Would anyone who saw the accident please get in touch with
> the police?*

But **that** is a possible alternative after **all, everyone, everybody, no
one, nobody** and **those**:
> *Everyone who/that knew him liked him.*
> *Nobody who/that watched the match will ever forget it.*

B   Object of a verb: **whom** or **who** or **that**
The object form is **whom**, but this is considered very formal. In spoken
English we normally use **who** or **that** (**that** being more usual than
who), and it is still more common to omit the object pronoun
altogether:
> *The man whom I saw told me to come back today* or
> *The man who I saw . . .* or *The man that I saw . . .* or
> *The man I saw . . .* (relative pronoun omitted)
> *The girls whom he employs are always complaining about their pay* or
> *The girls who he employs . . .* or *The girls that he employs . . .* or
> *The girls he employs . . .*

C   With a preposition: **whom** or **that**
In formal English the preposition is placed before the relative pronoun,
which must then be put into the form **whom**:
> *the man to whom I spoke*
In informal speech, however, it is more usual to move the preposition
to the end of the clause. **whom** then is often replaced by **that**, but it is
still more common to omit the relative altogether:
> *the man who/whom I spoke to* or
> *the man that I spoke to* or *the man I spoke to*
Similarly:
> *The man from whom I bought it told me to oil it* or
> *The man who/that I bought it from . . .* or
> *The man I bought it from . . .*
> *The friend with whom I was travelling spoke French* or
> *The friend who/that I was travelling with . . .* or
> *The friend I was travelling with . . .*

D   Possessive
whose is the only possible form:
> *People whose rents have been raised can appeal.*
> *The film is about a spy whose wife betrays him.*

75 Defining relative clauses: things

A Subject
Either **which** or **that**. **which** is the more formal:
This is the picture which/that caused such a sensation.
The stairs which/that lead to the cellar are rather slippery.
(See also B below.)

B Object of a verb
which or **that**, or no relative at all:
The car which/that I hired broke down or *The car I hired . . .*
which is hardly ever used after **all, everything, little, much, none, no** and compounds of **no**, or after superlatives. Instead we use **that**, or omit the relative altogether, if it is the object of a verb:
All the apples that fall are eaten by the pigs.
This is the best hotel (that) I know.

C Object of a preposition
The formal construction is preposition + **which**, but it is more usual to move the preposition to the end of the clause, using **which** or **that** or omitting the relative altogether:
The ladder on which I was standing began to slip or
The ladder which/that I was standing on began to slip or
The ladder I was standing on began to slip.

D Possessive
whose + a clause is possible but **with** + a phrase is more usual:
a house whose walls were made of glass   a house with glass walls

E Relative adverbs: **when, where, why**
Note that **when** can replace **in/on which** (used of time):
the year when (= in which) *he was born*
the day when (= on which) *they arrived*
where can replace **in/at which** (used of place):
the hotel where (= in/at which) *they were staying*
why can replace **for which**: *The reason why he refused is . . .*
when, where and **why** used in this way are called relative adverbs.

76 Cleft sentences: **it** + **be** + noun/pronoun + defining relative clause

It was ¹Tom who helped us. (not Bill or Jack)
It was ¹Ann that I saw. (not Mary)
When the object is a proper noun, as above, **that** is more usual than **who**. With all other objects, **that** is the correct form:
It's the manager that we want to see.
It was wine that we ordered. (not beer)
that is usual for non-personal subjects:
It's speed that causes accidents, not bad roads.

77 A relative clause replaced by an infinitive or a participle

A   Infinitives can be used:

1   After **the first/second** etc. and after **the last/only** and sometimes after superlatives:

the last man to leave the ship =
the last man who left/leaves the ship
the only one to understand =
the only one who understood/understands

Notice that the infinitive here replaces a subject pronoun + verb. It could not be used to replace an object pronoun + verb. For example the clause in *the first man that we saw* could not be replaced by an infinitive, for *the first man to see* would have a completely different meaning. If, however, **that** is the subject of a passive verb, e.g. *the first man that was seen*, we can replace the clause by a passive infinitive: *the first man to be seen.*

2   When there is an idea of purpose or permission:

He has a lot of books to read. (books that he can/must read)
She had something to do. (something that she could do/had to do)
They need a garden to play in. (a garden they can play in)

Note that here the infinitive replaces a verb + relative pronoun as object.

It might be thought that these two uses of the infinitive would lead to confusion but in practice this is very rare as the meaning of the infinitive is made clear by the rest of the sentence.

By itself the phrase *the first man to see* could mean either *the first man that we must see* (*man* is the object) or *the first man who saw* (*man* is the subject), but when it is part of a sentence we can see at once which meaning is intended:

The first man to see is Tom =
The first man that we must see is Tom, while
The first man to see me was Tom =
The first man who saw me was Tom.

B   Present participles can be used:

1   When the verb in the clause is in the continuous tense:

People who are/were waiting for the bus often shelter/sheltered in my doorway =
People waiting for the bus often shelter/sheltered . . .

2   When the verb in the clause expresses a habitual or continuous action:

Passengers who travel/travelled on this bus buy/bought their tickets in books = Passengers travelling . . .
Boys who attend/attended this school have/had to wear uniform = Boys attending . . .
a law which forbids/forbade the import = a law forbidding the import
a notice which warns/warned people = a notice warning people
an advertisement which urges/urged = an advertisement urging

Similarly:

> *a petition asking*   *a letter ordering/demanding/telling*
> *a placard protesting*   *placards protesting*

3   When a verb in the clause expresses a wish, i.e. when the verb in the
     clause is *wish, desire, want, hope* (but not *like*):

> *people who wish/wished to go on the tour* =
> *people wishing to go on the tour*
> *fans who hope/hoped for a glimpse of the star* =
> *fans hoping for a glimpse of the star*

4   A non-defining clause (see 78 below) containing one of the above verbs,
     or any verb of knowing or thinking, e.g. *know, think, believe, expect*, can
     be similarly replaced by a present participle:

> *Peter, who thought the journey would take two days, said . . .* =
> *Peter, thinking the journey would take two days, said . . .*
> *Tom, who expected to be paid the following week, offered . . .* =
> *Tom, expecting to be paid the following week, offered . . .*
> *Bill, who wanted to make an impression on Ann, took her to . . .* =
> *Bill, wanting to make an impression on Ann, took her to . . .*

78   Non-defining relative clauses

A   Non-defining relative clauses are placed after nouns which are definite
     already. They do not therefore define the noun, but merely add
     something to it by giving some more information about it. Unlike
     defining relative clauses, they are not essential in the sentence and can
     be omitted without causing confusion. Also unlike defining relatives,
     they are separated from their noun by commas. The pronoun can never
     be omitted in a non-defining relative clause. The construction is fairly
     formal and more common in written than in spoken English.

B   Relative pronouns used in non-defining relative clauses:

	Subject	Object	Possessive
For persons	*who*	*whom/who*	*whose*
For things	*which*	*which*	*whose/of which*

79   Non-defining relative clauses: persons

A   Subject: **who**
     No other pronoun is possible. Note the commas:

> *My neighbour, who is very pessimistic, says there will be no apples
> this year.*
> *Peter, who had been driving all day, suggested stopping at
> the next town.*

Clauses such as these, which come immediately after the subject of the main verb, are found mainly in written English. In spoken English we would be more likely to say:

My neighbour is very pessimistic and says . . .

Peter had been driving all day, so/and he suggested . . .

But clauses placed later in the sentence, i.e. clauses coming after the object of the main verb, are quite common in conversation:

I've invited Ann, who lives in the next flat.

Clauses following a preposition + noun are also common:

I passed the letter to Peter, who was sitting beside me.

B Object: **whom, who**

The pronoun cannot be omitted. **whom** is the correct form, though **who** is sometimes used in conversation:

Peter, whom everyone suspected, turned out to be innocent.

As noted above, a non-defining clause in this position is unusual in spoken English. We would be more likely to say:

Everyone suspected Peter, but he turned out to be innocent.

But non-defining clauses coming later in the sentence, i.e. after the object of the main verb or after a preposition + noun, are common in conversation:

She wanted Tom, whom she liked, as a partner; but she got Jack, whom she didn't like.

She introduced me to her husband, whom I hadn't met before.

C Object of a preposition: **whom**

The pronoun cannot be omitted. The preposition is normally placed before **whom**:

Mr Jones, for whom I was working, was very generous about overtime payments.

It is however possible to move the preposition to the end of the clause. This is commonly done in conversation, and **who** then usually takes the place of **whom**:

Mr Jones, who I was working for, . . .

If the clause contains an expression of time or place, this will remain at the end:

Peter, with whom I played tennis on Sundays, was fitter than me

could become

Peter, who/whom I played tennis with on Sundays, was fitter than me.

D Possessive: **whose**

Ann, whose children are at school all day, is trying to get a job.

This is George, whose class you will be taking.

In conversation we would probably say:

Ann's children are at school all day, so she . . .

This is George. You will be taking his class.

80 all, both, few, most, several, some etc. + of + whom/which

This form can be used for both people and things. See examples below. For each a more informal equivalent is given in brackets:

> *Her sons, both of whom work abroad, ring her up every week.*
> *(Both her sons work abroad, but they ring her up every week.)*
> *He went with a group of people, few of whom were correctly equipped for such a climb.*
> *(He went with a group of people; few of them . . .)*
> *The buses, most of which were already full, were surrounded by an angry crowd.*
> *(Most of the buses were full, and/but they were surrounded by an angry crowd.)*
> *I met the fruit-pickers, several of whom were university students.*
> *(I met the fruit-pickers; several of them were . . .)*
> *I picked up the apples, some of which were badly bruised.*
> *(I picked up the apples; some of them . . .)*
> *The house was full of boys, ten of whom were his own grandchildren.*
> *(The house was full of boys; ten of them . . .)*

81 Non-defining relative clauses: things

A Subject: **which**
that is not used here:
> *That block, which cost £5 million to build, has been empty for years.*
> *The 8.15 train, which is usually very punctual, was late today.*

In speech we would be more likely to say:
> *That block cost £5 million to build and has been empty for years.*
> *The 8.15 train is usually punctual; but it was late today.*

B Object: **which**
that is not used here, and the **which** can never be omitted:
> *She gave me this jumper, which she had knitted herself* or
> *She gave me this jumper; she had knitted it herself.*
> *These books, which you can get at any bookshop, will give you all the information you need* or
> *These books will give you all the information you need. You can get them at any bookshop.*

C Object of a preposition
The preposition comes before **which**, or (more informally) at the end of the clause:
> *Ashdown Forest, through which we'll be driving, isn't a forest any longer* or
> *Ashdown Forest, which we'll be driving through, isn't a forest any longer.*
> *His house, for which he paid £10,000, is now worth £50,000* or
> *His house, which he paid £10,000 for, is now . . .*

D **which** with phrasal verbs
Combinations such as *look after, look forward to, put up with* (see chapter 38) should be treated as a unit, i.e. the preposition/adverb should not be separated from the verb:

This machine, which I have looked after for twenty years, is still working perfectly.
Your inefficiency, which we have put up with far too long, is beginning to annoy our customers.

E Possessive: **whose** or **of which**
whose is generally used both for animals and things. **of which** is possible for things, but is unusual except in very formal English.

His house, whose windows were all broken, was a depressing sight.
The car, whose handbrake wasn't very reliable, began to slide backwards.

82 Connective relative clauses

The pronouns are **who, whom, whose, which**. Commas are used as with non-defining clauses. Connective clauses do not describe their nouns but continue the story. They are usually placed after the object of the main verb:

I told Peter, who said it wasn't his business
or after the preposition + noun:
I threw the ball to Tom, who threw it to Ann.
They can be replaced by **and/but** + **he/she** etc.:
I threw the ball to Tom and he threw it . . .
I told Peter, but he said . . .
Sometimes it may be difficult to say whether a clause in this position is non-defining or connective, but there is no need for students to make this distinction, as the two forms are the same.
More examples of connective clauses:

He drank beer, which made him fat =
He drank beer and it made him fat.
We went with Peter, whose car broke down before we were halfway there =
We went with Peter but his car broke down before we were halfway there.

We can use **one/two** etc., **few/several/some** etc. + **of** + **whom/which** as shown in 80:

I bought a dozen eggs, six of which broke when I dropped the box.
He introduced me to his boys, one of whom offered to go with me.
The lorry crashed into a queue of people, several of whom had to have hospital treatment.

which can also stand for a whole clause:

The clock struck thirteen, which made everyone laugh.
He refused to do his share of the chores, which annoyed the others.
(His refusal annoyed them.)

The rain rattled on the roof all night, which kept us awake.
She was much kinder to her youngest child than she was to the
others, which made the others jealous.

83 what (relative pronoun) and which (connective relative)

what = the thing that/the things that:
What we saw astonished us =
The things that we saw astonished us.
When she sees what you have done she will be furious =
When she sees the damage that you have done she will be furious.
Be careful not to confuse the relative **what** with the connective relative
which. Remember that **which** must refer to a word or group of words
in the preceding sentence, while **what** does not refer back to anything.
The relative **what** is also usually the object of a verb, while the
connective **which** is usually the subject:
He said he had no money, which was not true.
Some of the roads were flooded, which made our journey more
difficult.
(See also 82.)

84 The importance of commas in relative clauses

Remember that a defining relative clause is written without commas.
Note how the meaning changes when commas are inserted:
  (a) *The travellers who knew about the floods took another road.*
  (b) *The travellers, who knew about the floods, took another road.*
In (a) we have a defining relative clause, which defines or limits the
noun *travellers*. This sentence therefore tells us that only the travellers
who knew about the floods took the other road, and implies that there
were other travellers who did not know and who took the flooded road.
In (b) we have a non-defining clause, which does not define or limit the
noun it follows. This sentence therefore implies that all the travellers
knew about the floods and took the other road.
  (c) *The boys who wanted to play football were disappointed when*
      it rained.
  (d) *The boys, who wanted to play football, were disappointed . . .*
Sentence (c) implies that only some of the boys wanted to play football.
There were presumably others who didn't mind whether it rained or
not. Sentence (d) implies that all the boys wanted to play and all were
disappointed.
  (e) *The wine which was in the cellar was ruined.*
  (f) *The wine, which was in the cellar, was ruined.*
Sentence (e) implies that only some of the wine was ruined.
Presumably some was kept elsewhere and escaped damage.
Sentence (f) states that all the wine was in the cellar and ruined.

85 whoever, whichever, whatever, whenever, wherever, however

These have a variety of meanings and can introduce relative and other clauses. The other clauses do not technically belong to this chapter but it seems best to group these **-ever** forms together.

A **whoever** (pronoun) and **whichever** (pronoun and adjective) can mean 'the one who', 'he who', 'she who':

> *Whoever gains the most points wins the competition.*
> *Whichever of them gains the most points wins.*
> *Whichever team gains the most points wins.*
> *Whoever gets home first starts cooking the supper.*
> *Whichever of us gets home first starts cooking.*
> *Whoever cleans your windows doesn't make a good job of it.*

B **whatever** (pronoun and adjective), **whenever, wherever**:

> *You can eat what/whatever you like.* (anything you like)
> *When you are older you can watch whatever programme you like.*
> *My roof leaks when/whenever it rains.* (every time it rains)
> *You will see this product advertised everywhere/wherever you go.*
> *Go anywhere/wherever you like.*

C **whoever, whichever, whatever, whenever, wherever, however** can mean 'no matter who' etc.:

> *If I say 'heads, I win; tails you lose', I will win whatever happens* or *whichever way the coin falls.*
> *Whatever happens don't forget to write.*
> *I'll find him, wherever he has gone.* (no matter where he has gone)

whatever you do is often placed before or after a request/command to emphasize its importance:

> *Whatever you do, don't mention my name.*

however is an adverb of degree and is used with an adjective or another adverb:

> *I'd rather have a room of my own, however small (it is), than share a room.*
> *However hard I worked, she was never satisfied.*

D **whatever, wherever** can indicate the speaker's ignorance or indifference:

> *He lives in Wick, wherever that is.* (I don't know where it is, and I'm not very interested.)
> *He says he's a phrenologist, whatever that is.* (I don't know what it is and I'm not very interested.)

who ever? when ever? what ever? etc. may be written as separate words, but the meaning then changes (see 61):

> *I lost seven kilos in a month.* ~ *How ever did you lose so much in such a short time?*
> BILL (suspiciously): *I know all about you.*
> TOM (indignantly): *What ever do you mean?*
> *Where ever did you buy your wonderful carpets?*

9 Prepositions

86 Introduction

Prepositions are words normally placed before nouns or pronouns (but see 87 about possible alternative positions). Prepositions can also be followed by verbs but, except after **but** and **except**, the verb must be in the gerund form:

> *He is talking of emigrating.*
> *They succeeded in escaping.*

The student has two main problems with prepositions. He has to know (a) whether in any construction a preposition is required or not, and (b) which preposition to use when one is required.

The first problem can be especially troublesome to a European student, who may find that a certain construction in his own language requires a preposition, whereas a similar one in English does not, and vice versa: e.g. in most European languages purpose is expressed by a preposition + infinitive; in English it is expressed by the infinitive only:

> *I came here to study.*

The student should note also that many words used mainly as prepositions can also be used as conjunctions and adverbs. Where this is the case it will be pointed out in the following paragraphs.

87 Alternative position of prepositions

A Prepositions normally precede nouns or pronouns. In two constructions, however, it is possible in informal English to move the preposition to the end of the sentence:

1 In questions beginning with a preposition + **whom/which/what/ whose/where**:

> *To whom were you talking?* (formal)
> *Who were you talking to?* (informal)
> *In which drawer does he keep it?* (formal)
> *Which drawer does he keep it in?* (informal)

It used to be thought ungrammatical to end a sentence with a preposition, but it is now accepted as a colloquial form.

2 Similarly in relative clauses, a preposition placed before **whom/which** can be moved to the end of the clause. The relative pronoun is then often omitted:

> *the people with whom I was travelling* (formal)
> *the people I was travelling with* (informal)
> *the company from which I hire my TV set* (formal)
> *the company I hire my TV set from* (informal)

B   But in phrasal verbs the preposition/adverb remains after its verb, so the formal type of construction is not possible. *the children I was looking after* could not be rewritten with **after** + **whom** and *Which bridge did they blow up?* could not be rewritten with **up** + **which**.

88   Omission of **to** and **for** before indirect objects

A 1   A sentence such as *I gave the book to Tom* could also be expressed *I gave Tom the book*, i.e. the indirect object can be placed first and the preposition **to** omitted.
We can use this construction with the following verbs: *bring, give, hand, leave* (in a will), *lend, offer, pass* (= hand), *pay, play* (an instrument/piece of music), *promise, sell, send, show, sing, take, tell* (= narrate, inform):
>   *I showed the map to Bill = I showed Bill the map.*
>   *They sent £5 to Mr Smith = They sent Mr Smith £5.*

2   Similarly *I'll find a job for Ann* could be expressed *I'll find Ann a job* (putting the indirect object first and omitting **for**). This construction is possible after *book, build, buy, cook,* (*bake, boil, fry* etc.), *fetch, find, get, keep, knit, leave, make, order, reserve*:
>   *I'll get a drink for you = I'll get you a drink.*
>   *I bought a book for James = I bought James a book.*

B   Normally either construction can be used. But:

1   The construction without preposition is preferred when the direct object is a phrase or a clause:
>   *Tell her the whole story.*
>   *Show me what you've got in your hand.*

2   The construction with preposition is preferred:
(a) When the indirect object is a phrase or a clause:
>   *We kept seats for everyone on our list/for everyone who had paid.*
>   *I had to show my pass to the man at the door.*

(b) When the direct object is **it** or **them**. Sentences such as *They kept it for Mary, She made them for Bill, We sent it to George* cannot be expressed by a verb + noun + pronoun construction.
If the indirect object is also a pronoun (*I sent it to him*) it is sometimes possible to reverse the pronouns and omit **to** (*I sent him it*), but this cannot be done with **for** constructions and is better avoided.
This restriction does not apply to other pronoun objects:
>   *He gave Bill some.   He didn't give me any.*
>   *He bought Mary one.   I'll show you something.*

C   *promise, show, tell* can be used with indirect objects only, without **to**:
>   *promise us   show him   tell him*

read, write can be used similarly, but require **to**:
>   *read to me   write to them*

play, sing can be used with **to** or **for**:
    play to us   *play for us*   *sing to us*   *sing for us*

89   Use and omission of **to** with verbs of communication

A   Verbs of command, request, invitation and advice, e.g. *advise, ask, beg, command, encourage, implore, invite, order, recommend, remind, request, tell, urge, warn*, can be followed directly by the person addressed (without **to**) + infinitive:
    They advised him to wait.
    I urged her to try again.   (See 244.)
The person addressed (without **to**) can be used after *advise, remind, tell, warn* with other constructions also:
    He reminded them that there were no trains after midnight.
    They warned him that the ice was thin/warned him about the ice.
But note that *recommend* (= advise) when used with other constructions needs **to** before the person addressed:
    He recommended me to buy it but *He recommended it to me.*
He recommended me (for the post) would mean 'He said I was suitable'.
When *ask* is used with other constructions the person addressed is often optional. The preposition **to** is never used here:
    He asked (me) a question.
    He asked (me) if I wanted to apply.
    She asked (her employer) for a day off.

B   *call* (= shout), *complain, describe, explain, grumble, murmur, mutter, say, shout, speak, suggest, talk, whisper* need **to** before the person addressed, though it is not essential to mention this person:
    Peter complained (to her) about the food.
    She said nothing (to her parents).
    He spoke English (to them).
shout at can be used when the subject is angry with the other person:
    He shouted at me to get out of his way.
Compare with *He shouted to me* which means he raised his voice because I was at a distance.

90   Time and date: **at, on, by, before, in**

A   **at, on**

at a time:
    at dawn   *at six*   *at midnight*   *at 4.30*

at an age:
    at sixteen/at the age of sixteen
    She got married at seventeen.

on a day/date:
    on Monday   *on 4 June*   *on Christmas Day*

Exceptions
> *at night*
> *at Christmas, at Easter* (the period, not the day only)

on the morning/afternoon/evening/night of a certain date:
> *We arrived on the morning of the sixth.*

It is also, of course, possible to say:
> *this/next Monday* etc., *any Monday, one Monday*

B **by, before**

by a time/date/period = at that time or before/not later than that date. It often implies 'before that time/date':
> *The train starts at 6.10, so you had better be at the station by 6.00.*

by + a time expression is often used with a perfect tense, particularly the future perfect (see 216):
> *By the end of July I'll have read all those books.*

before can be preposition, conjunction or adverb:
> *Before signing this . . .* (preposition)
> *Before you sign this . . .* (conjunction)
> *I've seen him somewhere before.* (adverb)

(See 195 B, 342.)

C **on time, in time, in good time**

on time = at the time arranged, not before, not after:
> *The 8.15 train started on time.* (It started at 8.15.)

in time/in time for + noun = not late; **in good time (for)** = with a comfortable margin:
> *Passengers should be in time for their train.*
> *I arrived at the concert hall in good time (for the concert).* (Perhaps the concert began at 7.30 and I arrived at 7.15.)

D **on arrival, on arriving, on reaching, on getting to**

on arrival/on arriving, he . . . = when he arrives/arrived, he . . .
on can also be used similarly with the gerund of certain other verbs (chiefly verbs of information):
> *On checking, she found that some of the party didn't know the way.*
> *On hearing/Hearing that the plane had been diverted, they left the airport.*

The **on** in the last sentence could be omitted. (See 277.)

E **at the beginning/end, in the beginning/end, at first/at last**

at the beginning (of)/at the end (of) = literally at the beginning/end:
> *At the beginning of a book there is often a table of contents.*
> *At the end there may be an index.*

in the beginning/at first = in the early stages. It implies that later on there was a change:
> *In the beginning/At first we used hand tools. Later we had machines.*

in the end/at last = eventually/after some time:
> *At first he opposed the marriage, but in the end he gave his consent.*

91 Time: **from, since, for, during**

A **from, since** and **for**

1 **from** is normally used with **to** or **till/until**:
  Most people work from nine to five.
from can also be used of place:
  Where do you come from?

2 **since** is used for time, never for place, and means 'from that time to the time referred to'. It is often used with a present perfect or past perfect tense (see 185-8, 194).
  He has been here since Monday. (from Monday till now)
  He wondered where Ann was. He had not seen her since their quarrel.
since can also be an adverb (see 37, 185-8):
  He left school in 1983. I haven't seen him since.
since can also be a conjunction of time:
  He has worked for us ever since he left school.
  It is two years since I last saw Tom =
  I last saw Tom two years ago/I haven't seen Tom for two years.
(For **since** with other types of clause, see 338.)

3 **for** is used of a period of time: **for six years, for two months, for ever**:
  Bake it for two hours.
  He travelled in the desert for six months.
for + a period of time can be used with a present perfect tense or past perfect tense for an action which extends up to the time of speaking:
  He has worked here for a year. (He began working here a year ago and still works here.)
for used in this way is replaceable by **since** with the point in time when the action began:
  He has worked here since this time last year.

B **during** and **for**
during is used with known periods of time, i.e. periods known by name, such as Christmas, Easter or periods which have been already defined:
  during the Middle Ages   during 1941
  during the summer (of that year)
  during his childhood
  during my holidays
The action can either last the whole period or occur at some time within the period:
  It rained all Monday but stopped raining during the night. (at some point of time)
  He was ill for a week, and during that week he ate nothing.
for (indicating purpose) may be used before known periods:
  I went there/I hired a car/I rented a house for my holidays/for the summer.

for has various other uses:
> *He asked for £5.   I paid £1 for it.*
> *I bought one for Tom.* (See 88.)

for can also be a conjunction and introduce a clause (see 330).

92 Time: **to, till/until, after, afterwards** (adverb)

A **to** and **till/until**

to can be used of time and place; **till/until** of time only.
We can use **from . . . to** or **from . . . till/until**:
> *They worked from five to ten/from five till ten.* (*at five to ten* would mean 'at 9.55'.)

But if we have no **from** we use **till/until**, not **to**:
> *Let's start now and work till dark.* (**to** would not be possible here.)

till/until is often used with a negative verb to emphasize lateness:
> *We didn't get home till 2 a.m.*
> *He usually pays me on Friday but last week he didn't pay me till the following Monday.*

till/until is very often used as a conjunction of time:
> *We'll stay here till it stops raining.*
> *Go on till you come to the level crossing.*

But note that if 'you come to' is omitted, the **till** must be replaced by **to**:
> *Go on to the level crossing.*

B **after** and **afterwards** (adverb)

after (preposition) must be followed by a noun, pronoun or gerund:
> *Don't bathe immediately after a meal/after eating.*
> *Don't have a meal and bathe immediately after it.*

If we do not wish to use a noun/pronoun or gerund, we cannot use **after**, but must use **afterwards** (= **after that**) or **then**:
> *Don't have a meal and bathe immediately afterwards.*
> *They bathed and afterwards played games/played games afterwards* or *They bathed and then played games.*

afterwards can be used at either end of the clause and can be modified by **soon, immediately, not long** etc.:
> *Soon afterwards we got a letter.*
> *We got a letter not long afterwards.*

after can also be used as a conjunction:
> *After he had tuned the piano it sounded quite different.*

93 Travel and movement: **from, to, at, in, by, on, into, onto, off, out, out of**

A We travel **from** our starting place **to** our destination:
> *They flew/drove/cycled/walked from Paris to Rome.*
> *When are you coming back to England?*

We also send/post letters etc. **to** people and places. (But see note on
home below.)

B   **arrive at/in, get to, reach** (without preposition)
We **arrive in** a town or country, **at** or **in** a village, **at** any other
destination:
They arrived in Spain/in Madrid.
I arrived at the hotel/at the airport/at the bridge/at the crossroads.
get to can be used with any destination, and so can **reach**:
He got to the station just in time for his train.
I want to get to Berlin before dark.
They reached the top of the mountain before sunrise.
get in (**in** = adverb) can mean 'arrive at a destination'. It is chiefly
used of trains:
What time does the train get in? (reach the terminus/our station)
Note also **get there/back** (**there, back** are adverbs).

C   **home**
We can use a verb of motion etc. + **home** without a preposition:
It took us an hour to get home.
They went home by bus.
But if **home** is immediately preceded by a word or phrase a preposition
is necessary:
She returned to her parents' home.
We can **be/live/stay/work** etc. **at home**, **at** + . . . + **home** or
in + . . . + **home**. But **in** cannot be followed directly by **home**:
You can do this sort of work at home or at/in your own home.

D   Transport: **by, on, get in/into/on/onto/off/out of**
We can travel **by** car (but **in** the/my/Tom's car), **by** bus/train/
plane/helicopter/hovercraft etc. and **by** sea/air. We can also travel **by** a
certain route, or **by** a certain place (though **via** is more usual):
We went by the M4.   We went via Reading.
We can walk or go **on** foot. We can cycle or go **on** a bicycle or **by**
bicycle. We can ride or go **on** horseback.
We get **into** a public or private vehicle, or get **in** (adverb).
We get **on/onto** a public vehicle, or get **on** (adverb).
But we go **on board** a boat (= embark).
We get **on/onto** a horse/camel/bicycle.
We get **out of** a public or private vehicle, or get **out** (adverb).
We get **off** a public vehicle, a horse, bicycle, etc., or get **off** (adverb).

E   **get in/into/out/out of** can also be used of buildings, institutions and
countries instead of **go/come/return** etc. when there is some difficulty
in entering or leaving. **in** and **out** here are used as adverbs.
*I've lost my keys! How are we going to get into the flat/
to get in?* (adverb)
The house is on fire! We had better get out! (adverb)
It's difficult to get into a university nowadays.

F   Giving directions: **at, into, to** etc. (prepositions), **along, on**
(prepositions and adverbs) and **till** (conjunction):

> *Go along the Strand till you see the Savoy on your right.*
> *The bus stop is just round the corner.*
> *Turn right/left at the Post Office/at the second traffic lights.*
> *Go on* (adverb) *past the post office.*
> *Turn right/left into Fleet Street.*
> *Take the first/second etc. turning on/to the right* or *on/to your right.*
> *Go on* (adverb) *to the end of the road.* (**till** could not be used here.)
> *You will find the bank on your left halfway down the street.*
> *When you come out of the station you will find the bank opposite*
> *you/in front of you.*
> *Get out (of the bus) at the tube station and walk on* (adverb) *till you*
> *come to a pub.*
> *Get off (the bus) and walk back* (adverb) *till you come to some*
> *traffic lights.*

Be careful not to confuse **to** and **till** (see 92 A).

94   at, in; in, into; on, onto

A   **at** and **in**
(For **arrive at/in**, see 93 B.)

at

We can be **at** home, **at** work, **at** the office, **at** school, **at** university,
at an address, **at** a certain point e.g. **at** the bridge, **at** the crossroads,
at the bus-stop.

in

We can be **in** a country, a town, a village, a square, a street, a room,
a forest, a wood, a field, a desert or any place which has boundaries or
is enclosed.

But a small area such as a square, a street, a room, a field might be
used with **at** when we mean 'at this point' rather than 'inside'.

We can be **in** or **at** a building. **in** means inside only; **at** could mean
inside or in the grounds or just outside. If someone is 'at the station' he
could be in the street outside, or in the ticket office/waiting room/
restaurant or on the platform.

We can be **in** or **at** the sea, a river, lake, swimming pool etc.
in here means actually in the water:

> *The children are swimming in the river.*

at the sea/river/lake etc. means 'near/beside the sea'. But **at sea**
means 'on a ship'.

B   **in** and **into**
in as shown above normally indicates position.
into indicates movement, entrance:

> *They climbed into the lorry.*   *I poured the beer into a tankard.*
> *Thieves broke into my house/My house was broken into.*

With the verb **put**, however, either **in** or **into** can be used:
> *He put his hands in/into his pockets.*

in can also be an adverb:
> *Come in = Enter.*   *Get in* (into the car).

C   **on** and **onto**

on can be used for both position and movement:
> *He was sitting on his case.*   *Snow fell on the hills.*
> *His name is on the door.*   *He went on board ship.*

onto can be used (chiefly of people and animals) when there is movement involving a change of level:
> *People climbed onto their roofs.*   *We lifted him onto the table.*
> *The cat jumped onto the mantelpiece.*

on can also be an adverb:
> *Go on.*   *Come on.*

95   above, over, under, below, beneath etc.

A   **above** and **over**

above (preposition and adverb) and **over** (preposition) can both mean 'higher than' and sometimes either can be used:
> *The helicopter hovered above/over us.*
> *Flags waved above/over our heads.*

But **over** can also mean 'covering', 'on the other side of', 'across' and 'from one side to the other':
> *We put a rug over him.*
> *He lives over the mountains.*
> *There is a bridge over the river.*

all over + noun/pronoun can mean 'in every part of':
> *He has friends all over the world.*

above can have none of these meanings.

over can mean 'more than' or 'higher than'.
above can mean 'higher than' only.
Both can mean 'higher in rank'. But *He is over me* would normally mean 'He is my immediate superior', 'He supervises my work'. **above** would not necessarily have this meaning.
If we have a bridge over a river, *above the bridge* means 'upstream'.
over can be used with meals/food/drink:
> *They had a chat over a cup of tea.* (while drinking tea)

In the combination **take** + a time expression + **over** + noun/pronoun, **over** can mean 'to do/finish' etc.:
> *He doesn't take long over lunch/to eat his lunch.*
> *He took ages over the job.* (He took ages to finish it.)

above can also be an adjective or adverb meaning 'earlier' (in a book, article etc.):
> *the above address* (the previously mentioned address)
> *see B above* (the previously mentioned section B)

B **below** and **under**
below (preposition and adverb) and **under** (preposition) can both mean 'lower than' and sometimes either can be used. But **under** can indicate contact:

> *She put the letter under her pillow.*
> *The ice crackled under his feet.*

With **below** there is usually a space between the two surfaces:

> *They live below us.* (We live on the fourth floor and they live on the third.)

Similarly: *We live above them.* (See A above.)
below and **under** can mean 'junior in rank'. But *He is under me* implies that I am his immediate superior. **below** does not necessarily have this meaning.
(Both **over** and **under** can be used as adverbs, but with a change of meaning.)

C **beneath** can sometimes be used instead of **under**, but it is safer to keep it for abstract meanings:

> *He would think it beneath him to tell a lie.* (unworthy of him)
> *She married beneath her.* (into a lower social class)

D **beside, between, behind, in front of, opposite**
Imagine a theatre with rows of seats: A, B, C etc., Row A being nearest the stage.

		Stage		
Row A	Tom	Ann		Bill
Row B	Mary	Bob		Jane

This means that:

> *Tom is beside Ann; Mary is beside Bob etc.*
> *Ann is between Tom and Bill; Bob is between Mary and Jane.*
> *Mary is behind Tom; Tom is in front of Mary.*

But if Tom and Mary are having a meal and Tom is sitting at one side of the table and Mary at the other, we do not use **in front of**, but say:

> *Tom is sitting opposite Mary* or *Tom is facing Mary.*

But *He stood in front of me* could mean either 'He stood with his back to me' or 'He faced me'.
People living on one side of a street will talk of the houses on the other side as *the houses opposite (us)* rather than *the houses in front of us*.
With other things, however, these restrictions do not apply:

> *She put the plate on the table in front of him.*
> *She sat with a book in front of her.*
> *Where's the bank? ~ There it is, just in front of you!*
> *There's a car-park in front of/at the back of the hotel.*

E Don't confuse **beside** with **besides**.
beside = at the side of:

> *We camped beside a lake.*

besides (preposition) = in addition to/as well as:
> *I do all the cooking and besides that I help Tom.*
> *Besides doing the cooking I help Tom.*

besides (adverb) means (a) 'in addition to that/as well as that':
> *I do the cooking and help Tom besides*

and (b) 'in any case/anyway':
> *We can't afford oysters. Besides, Tom doesn't like them.*

(See 327.)

F **between** and **among**

between normally relates a person/thing to two other people/things, but it can be used of more when we have a definite number in mind:
> *Luxembourg lies between Belgium, Germany and France.*

among relates a person/thing to more than two others; normally we have no definite number in mind:
> *He was happy to be among friends again.*
> *a village among the hills*

G **with** could also be used instead of **among** in the last sentence above. Also, of course, with a singular object:
> *He was with a friend.*

Examples of other uses:
> *He cut it with a knife.*
> *Don't touch it with bare hands.*
> *The mountains were covered with snow.*
> *I have no money with me/on me.*
> *He fought/quarrelled with everyone.*

In descriptions:
> *the girl with red hair*
> *the boy with his hands in his pockets*
> *the man with his back to the camera/with his feet on his desk*

H **but** and **except** (prepositions)

These have the same meaning and are interchangeable.

but is more usual when the preposition + object is placed immediately after *nobody/none/nothing/nowhere* etc:
> *Nobody but Tom knew the way.*
> *Nothing but the best is sold in our shops.*

except is more usual when the preposition phrase comes later in the sentence:
> *Nobody knew the way except Tom*

and after *all/everybody/everyone/everything/everywhere* etc.

but is more emphatic than **except** after *anybody/anything/anywhere* etc.:
> *You can park anywhere but/except here.* (You can't park here.)

but and **except** take the bare infinitive (see 98).

(For **but for** in conditional sentences, see 226. For **but** as a conjunction, see 326.)

96 Prepositions used with adjectives and participles

Certain adjectives and past participles used as adjectives can be
followed by a preposition + noun/gerund. (For verbs + prepositions,
see 97.)

Usually particular adjectives and participles require particular
prepositions. Some of these are given below; others can be found by
consulting a good dictionary, which after any adjective will give the
prepositons that can be used with it.

about, at, for, in, of, on, to, with used with certain adjectives and
participles:

absorbed in	*involved in*
according to	*keen on*
accustomed to (see 163)	*liable for/to*
afraid of (27 B, 271)	*nervous of*
anxious for/about (27 C)	*owing to* (27 A)
ashamed of	*pleased with*
aware of (27 F)	*prepared for*
bad at/for	*proud of*
capable of	*ready for*
confident of	*responsible for/to*
due to/for (27 A)	*scared of*
exposed to	*sorry for/about* (27 B)
fit for	*successful in*
fond of	*suspicious of*
frightened of/at	*terrified of*
good at/for	*tired of*
interested in	*used to* (163)

He was absorbed in his book.
She is afraid/frightened/scared of the dark.
According to Tom it's 2.30. (Tom says it's 2.30.)
He is bad/good at chess. (a bad/good player)
Running is bad/good for you. (unhealthy/healthy)
They are very keen on golf.
Drivers exceeding the speed limit are liable to a fine.
*The management is not responsible for articles left in
customers' cars.*
I'm sorry for your husband. (I pity him.)
I'm sorry for forgetting the tickets. (apology)
I'm sorry about the tickets. (apology or regret)

(For *good/kind* etc. + **of**, *It was kind of you to wait*, see 26 B.)

97 Verbs and prepositions

A large number of verb + preposition combinations are dealt with in
chapter 38. But there are a great many other verbs which can be
followed by prepositions and some of these are listed below. More can
be found in any good dictionary.

accuse sb of	*insist on*
apologize (to sb) for	*live on* (food/money)
apply to sb/for sth	*long for*
ask for/about	*object to*
attend to	*occur to*
beg for	*persist in*
believe in	*prefer sb/sth to sb/sth*
beware of	*prepare for*
blame sb for	*punish sb for*
charge sb with (an offence)	*quarrel with sb about*
compare sth with	*refer to*
comply with	*rely on*
conform to	*remind sb of*
consist of	*resort to*
deal in	*succeed in*
depend on	*suspect sb of*
dream of	*think of/about*
fight with sb for	*wait for*
fine sb for	*warn sb of/about*
hope for	*wish for*

Do you believe in ghosts?
They were charged with receiving stolen goods.
You haven't complied with the regulations.
For a week she lived on bananas and milk.
It never occurred to me to insure the house.
They persisted in defying the law.
When arguments failed he resorted to threats.

Notice also **feel like** + noun/pronoun = feel inclined to have
something:
Do you feel like a drink/a meal/a rest?
feel like + gerund = feel inclined to do something:
I don't feel like walking there.
(For **like** used in comparisons, see 21 G-I.)
Passive verbs can of course be followed by **by** + agent; but they can
also be followed by other prepositions:
The referee was booed by the crowd.
The referee was booed for his decision/for awarding a penalty.

98   Gerunds after prepositions

A   It has already been stated in 86 that verbs placed immediately after prepositions must be in the gerund form:

He left without paying his bill.

I apologize for not writing before.

She insisted on paying for herself.

Before signing the contract, read the small print.

(See also 259.)

A few noun + preposition + gerund combinations may also be noted:

There's no point in taking your car if you can't park.

What's the point of taking your car if you can't park?

Is there any chance/likelihood of his changing his mind?

Have you any objection to changing your working hours?

I am in favour of giving everyone a day off.

B   The only exceptions to the gerund rule are **except** and **but** (preposition), which take the bare infinitive:

I could do nothing except agree.

He did nothing but complain.

However, if **but** is used as a conjunction, it can be followed directly by either full infinitive or gerund:

Being idle sometimes is agreeable, but being idle all the time might become monotonous.

To be idle sometimes is agreeable, but to be idle all the time etc.

99   Prepositions/adverbs

Many words can be used as either prepositions or adverbs:

He got off the bus at the corner. (preposition)

He got off at the corner. (adverb)

The most important of these are **above, about, across, along, before, behind, below, besides, by, down, in, near, off, on, over, past, round, since, through, under, up**:

They were here before six. (preposition)

He has done this sort of work before. (adverb)

Peter is behind us. (preposition)

He's a long way behind. (adverb)

She climbed over the wall. (preposition)

You'll have to climb over too. (adverb)

When the meeting was over the delegates went home. (adverb; here *over* = finished)

The shop is just round the corner. (preposition)

Come round (to my house) any evening. (adverb)

He ran up the stairs. (preposition)

He went up in the lift. (adverb)

Many of these words are used to form phrasal verbs (see chapter 38):

The plane took off. (left the ground)

He came round. (recovered consciousness)

10 Introduction to verbs

100 Classes of verbs

A There are two classes of verbs in English:

1 The auxiliary verbs (auxiliaries): *to be, to have, to do; can, could, may, might, must, ought, shall, should, will, would; to need, to dare* and *used.*

2 All other verbs, which we may call ordinary verbs:
    to work   *to sing*   *to pray*

B *be, have, do, need* and *dare* have infinitives and participles like ordinary verbs, but *can, could, may, might, must, ought, shall, should, will* and *would* have neither infinitives nor participles and therefore have only a restricted number of forms. (For *used*, see 162 A.)

Before studying auxiliaries it may be helpful to consider ordinary verbs, most of whose tenses are formed with auxiliaries.

Ordinary verbs

101 Principal parts of the active verb

	Affirmative	Negative
Present infinitive	*to work*	*not to work*
Present continuous infinitive	*to be working*	*not to be working*
Perfect infinitive	*to have worked*	*not to have worked*
Perfect continuous infinitive	*to have been working*	*not to have been working*
Present participle and gerund	*working*	*not working*
Perfect participle and gerund	*having worked*	*not having worked*
Past participle	*worked*	

In regular verbs the simple past and the past participle are both formed by adding **d** or **ed** to the infinitive. Sometimes the final consonant of the infinitive has to be doubled, e.g. *slip, slipped* (see spelling rules, 355). For irregular verbs, see 364.

The present participle and gerund are always regular and are formed by adding **ing** to the infinitive. The rule concerning the doubling of the final consonant of the infinitive before adding **ing** applies here also (see spelling rules, 355).

102 Active tenses

A Form

Present	simple	*he works* (see 172)
	continuous	*he is working* (164)
	perfect	*he has worked* (182)
	perfect continuous	*he has been working* (190)
Past	simple	*he worked* (175)
	continuous	*he was working* (178)
	perfect	*he had worked* (194)
	perfect continuous	*he had been working* (197)
Future	simple	*he will work* (207)
	continuous	*he will be working* (211)
	perfect	*he will have worked* (216)
	perfect continuous	*he will have been working* (216)
Present	conditional	*he would work* (219)
	conditional continuous	*he would be working* (219)
Perfect	conditional	*he would have worked* (220)
	conditional continuous	*he would have been working*

B Affirmative contractions
The auxiliaries **be, have, will, would** are contracted as follows:

am	*'m*	*have*	*'ve*	*will*	*'ll*
is	*'s*	*has*	*'s*	*would*	*'d*
are	*'re*	*had*	*'d*		

Note that **'s** can be **is** or **has** and **'d** can be **had** or **would**:
He's going = He is going.
He's gone = He has gone.
He'd paid = He had paid.
He'd like a drink = He would like a drink.

These contractions are used after pronouns, **here, there**, some question words (see 104), and short nouns:
Here's your pen.   The twins've arrived.
The car'd broken down.

Affirmative contractions are not used at the end of sentences:
You aren't in a hurry but I am.
(**I'm** would not be possible here.)

shall/should, **was** and **were** are not written in a contracted form but are often contracted in speech to /ʃl, ʃəd, wəz/ and /wə(r)/.

C Stress
Auxiliaries used to form tenses are normally unstressed. The stress falls on the main verb.

103 Negatives of tenses

A   The simple present tense: third person singular *does not/doesn't* +
infinitive; other persons *do not/don't* + infinitive.
The simple past tense negative for all persons is *did not/didn't* +
infinitive.
Contractions are usual in speech:

> *He does not/doesn't answer letters.*
> *They do not/don't live here.*
> *I did not/didn't phone her.*
> *She did not/didn't wait for me.*

The negative of all other tenses is formed by putting **not** after the
auxiliary.
Contractions are usual in speech:

> *He has not/hasn't finished.*
> *He would not/wouldn't come.*

B   Negative contractions
The auxiliaries **be, have, will, would, shall, should, do** are
contracted as follows:

> *am not*   *'m not*
> *is not*   *isn't* or *'s not*
> *are not*   *aren't* or *'re not*
> *I'm not going and Tom isn't going/Tom's not going.*
> *We aren't going/We're not going.*

have not and **has not** contract to **haven't** and **hasn't**, but in perfect
tenses **'ve not** and **'s not** are also possible:

> *We haven't seen him/We've not seen him.*
> *He hasn't/He's not come yet.*

will not contracts to **won't**, though **'ll not** is also possible. **shall not**
contracts to **shan't**:

> *I won't go/I'll not go till I hear and I shan't hear till tomorrow.*

Other verb forms are contracted in the usual way by adding **n't**.
Negative contractions can come at the end of a sentence:

> *I saw it but he didn't.*

C   In English a negative sentence can have only one negative expression in
it. Two negative expressions give the sentence an affirmative meaning:
Nobody did nothing means that everyone did something.
So *never, no* (adjective), *none, nobody, no one, nothing, hardly, hardly
ever* etc. are used with an affirmative verb. We can say:

> *He didn't eat anything* or
> *He ate nothing.*
> *He doesn't ever complain* or
> *He never complains.*
> *We haven't seen anyone* or
> *We have seen no one.*
> *They didn't speak much* or
> *They hardly spoke at all/They hardly ever spoke.*

104 Interrogative for questions and requests

A Simple present tense interrogative: *does he/she/it* + infinitive;
do I/you/we/they + infinitive.
Simple past tense interrogative: *did* + subject + infinitive.
> *Does Peter enjoy parties?*   *Did he enjoy Ann's party?*

In all other tenses the interrogative is formed by putting the subject after the auxiliary:
> *Have you finished?*   *Are you coming?*

B Contractions of auxiliaries used in the interrogative

1 **am, is, are, have, had, will** and **would**
After *how, what, who, where, why,* these can be contracted as shown in 102 B:
> *How will/How'll he get there?*   *What has/What's happened?*

is and **will** can also be contracted after *when*:
> *When is/When's he coming?*

will can also be contracted after *which*:
> *Which will/Which'll you have?*

When the verb comes first as in A above, it is not contracted in writing except in negative interrogative forms. But in speech it is usually contracted.

2 **shall, should, do** and **did** are not written in contracted form, although **do you** is sometimes written **d'you**. In speech **shall, should** and **do you** are often contracted to /ʃl, ʃəd, djuː/.

C The interrogative form is used for questions, but it is not used:

1 When the question is about the identity of the subject:
> *Who told you?*   *What happened?*

2 In indirect speech:
> *He said, 'Where does she live?'* = *He asked where she lived.*

3 If we place before the question a prefix such as *Do you know, Can you tell me, I want to know, I'd like to know, I wonder/was wondering, Have you any idea, Do you think*:
> *What time does it start?* but *Have you any idea what time it starts?*
> *Where does Peter live?* but *I wonder where Peter lives.*
> *Will I have to pay duty on this?* but
> *Do you think I'll have/Do you know if I'll have to pay duty?*

D Requests are usually expressed by the interrogative:
> *Can/Could you help me?*   *Will/Would you pay at the desk?*
> *Would you like to come this way?*
> *Would you mind moving your car?*

But here again, if before the request we put a phrase such as *I wonder/was wondering* or *Do you think*, the verb in the request changes from interrogative to affirmative:
> *Could you give me a hand with this?* but
> *I wonder/was wondering/wondered if you could give me a hand* or
> *Do you think you could give me a hand?*

In indirect speech the problem does not arise, as indirect requests are

expressed by a verb such as **ask** with object + infinitive:
He asked me to give him a hand.

E   The interrogative is used in question tags after a negative verb:
You didn't see him, did you?   (See 110.)

F   When, for emphasis, words/phrases such as *never, rarely, seldom, only when, only by, not only, not till* are placed first in a sentence the following main verb is put into the inverted (= interrogative) form:
Only when we landed did we see how badly the plane had been damaged.   (See 45.)

105   Negative interrogative

A   This is formed by putting **not** after the ordinary interrogative:
Did you not see her?   Is he not coming?
But this form is almost always contracted:
Didn't you see her?   Isn't he coming?
Note that **not** is now before the subject.
am I not? has an irregular contraction: *aren't I?*

B   The negative interrogative is used when the speaker expects or hopes for an affirmative answer:
Haven't you finished yet? · Don't you like my new dress?
CHILD: *Can't I stay up till the end of the programme?*
I could wait ten minutes. ~ Couldn't you wait a little longer?

C   The negative interrogative is also used in question tags after an affirmative sentence:
You paid him, didn't you?
She would like to come, wouldn't she?   (See 110.)

Auxiliary verbs

106   Auxiliaries and modal auxiliaries

Principal auxiliaries	Modal auxiliaries		Semi-modals
to be	*can*	*could*	*to need*
to have	*may*	*might*	*to dare*
to do	*must*	*had to*	*used*
	ought		
	shall	*should*	
	will	*would*	

Auxiliaries help to form a tense or an expression, hence the name.
They combine with present or past participles or with infinitives to form the tenses of ordinary verbs:
I am coming.   He has finished.   I didn't see them.

They combine with infinitives to indicate permission, possibility, obligation, deduction etc. as will be shown in the following chapters:
He can speak French.   You may go.   We must hurry.

107 Auxiliaries: forms and patterns

A **be, have** and **do** (the principal auxiliaries)

Infinitive	Present tense	Past tense	Past participle
to be	*am, is, are*	*was*	*been*
to have	*have, has*	*had*	*had*
to do	*do, does*	*did*	*done*

1 In the negative and interrogative, **be** and **do** follow the auxiliary pattern:
Negative, verb + **not**:
He isn't coming.   It did not matter.
Interrogative, subject + verb:
Was he waiting?   Does she see us?

2 **have** normally follows the auxiliary pattern:
Has he (got) to go?
but sometimes uses **do/did** forms:
Does he have to go?

3 **be** takes the full infinitive:
They are to wait for us at the station.
have takes the full infinitive except in two constructions
(see 119 A, 120).
do takes the bare infinitive: *Did he write?*

4 **be, have** and **do**, when used as auxiliaries, require a participle or infinitive, though in answers, comments etc. this is often understood but not mentioned:
Have you seen it? ~ Yes, I have (seen it).

5 **be** (see 115), **have** and **do** can also be used as ordinary verbs with independent meanings; i.e. **have** can mean 'possess' (see 122), **do** can mean 'perform/occupy oneself' etc. (see 126).
be or **have** or **do** can then be the only verb in a sentence:
He is lazy.   He has no job.   He does nothing.
do is then conjugated with **do/did**:
What do you do in the evenings?
and **have** can be conjugated in either way:
Have you (got) time?/Do you have time?

B **can, could, may, might, must, ought, will, would, shall** and **should** (the modal auxiliaries)

Modal verbs have no final **s** in the third person singular:
I must, he must   I can, he can

They always form their negative and interrogative according to the auxiliary pattern:

will not   ought not . . .
will he . . . ?   ought he . . . ?

They have no proper past tenses; four past forms exist, **could, might, should, would**, but they have only a restricted use.

Modal verbs have no infinitives or participles and therefore cannot be used in the continuous tenses.

All modal verbs except **ought** are followed by the bare infinitive:

You should pay but *You ought to pay.*

A modal verb always requires an infinitive, though sometimes this is understood but not mentioned:

Can you understand? ~ Yes, I can (understand).

C   **need, dare** and **used** (the semi-modals)

1   When used as auxiliaries, **need** and **dare** can conform to the modal pattern. They then take the bare infinitive:

He need not wait.

But they can also use the **do/did** forms, and then take the full infinitive with **to**:

He doesn't dare to interrupt.
They didn't need to wait. (See 149.)

need and **dare** can also be used as ordinary verbs, and are then inflected and have the usual participles:

He needs help.   They dared me to jump.

2   **used**, sometimes referred to as **used to**, is used only in the past. For its negative and interrogative it usually follows the auxiliary pattern:

I used not/usedn't to go.

But though technically **used** has no infinitive, the forms **didn't use to** and **did** he/she etc. **use to?** are quite often heard.

Use of auxiliaries in short answers, agreements etc.

Auxiliaries are extremely important in conversation because in short answers, agreements, disagreements with remarks, additions to remarks etc. we use auxiliaries instead of repeating the original verb.

108   Auxiliaries in short answers

Questions requiring the answer **yes** or **no**, i.e. questions such as *Do you smoke?* or *Can you ride a bicycle?*, should be answered by **yes** or **no** and the auxiliary only. The original subject, if a noun, is replaced by a pronoun. Pronoun subjects may change as shown:

Do you smoke? ~ *Yes, I do (not Yes, I smoke).*
Is that Ann? ~ *Yes, it is/No, it isn't.*
Did the twins go? ~ *Yes, they did/No, they didn't.*
Will there be an exam? ~ *Yes, there will/No, there won't.*

If there is more than one auxiliary in the question, the first should be used in the answer:

Should he have gone? ~ *Yes, he should.*

Questions with **must** I/he etc. or **need** I/he etc. are answered *Yes, you/he etc. must* or *No, you/he etc. needn't*:

Must I/Need I take all these pills? ~ *Yes, you must/No, you needn't.* (See 147.)

An answer with **yes** or **no** without the auxiliary would be less polite.

109 Agreements and disagreements with remarks

A Agreements with affirmative remarks are made with **yes/so/of course** +
+ affirmative auxiliary. If there is an auxiliary in the first verb this is
repeated. If there is no auxiliary **do, does** or **did** is used:

He works too hard. ~ *Yes, he does.*
There may be a strike. ~ *Yes, there may.*
Living in London will be expensive. ~ *(Yes,) of course it will.*
That's Ann! ~ *Oh, so it is.*

B Disagreements with negative remarks are made with **yes/oh yes** +
affirmative auxiliary. The auxiliary is stressed here.

I won't have to pay. ~ *Oh yes, you ˈwill!*
My alarm didn't ring! ~ *Oh yes, it ˈdid!*
There isn't any salt in this. ~ *Yes, there ˈis.*
Bread won't make me fat. ~ *Oh yes, it ˈwill.*

C Agreements with negative remarks are made with **no** + negative
auxiliary:

It wouldn't take long to get there. ~ *No, it wouldn't.*
I haven't paid you yet. ~ *No, you haven't.*
The boys mustn't be late. ~ *No, they mustn't.*
The door can't have been locked. ~ *No, it can't.*

D Disagreements with affirmative remarks are expressed by
no/oh no + negative auxiliary:

Ann'll lend it to you. ~ *Oh no, she won't.*
Peter gets up too late. ~ *No, he doesn't.*
There is plenty of time. ~ *No, there isn't.*
Prices are coming down. ~ *Oh no, they aren't.*

but can be used when disagreeing with an assumption. The assumption
may be expressed by a question:

Why did you travel first class? ~ *But I didn't!*

110 Question tags

These are short additions to sentences, asking for agreement or confirmation.

A   After negative statements we use the ordinary interrogative:
You didn't see him, did you?
Ann can't swim, can she?
That isn't Tom, is it?
After affirmative statements we use the negative interrogative:
Peter helped you, didn't he?
Mary was there, wasn't she?
Negative verbs in the tags are usually contracted.
Irregular: *I'm late, aren't I?*
Note that **let's** has the tag **shall**: *Let's go, shall we?*
The subject of the tag is always a pronoun.

B   Examples of question tags after negative statements:
Peter doesn't smoke, does he?
Ann isn't studying music, is she?
Bill didn't want to go, did he?
James wasn't driving the car, was he?
You haven't ridden a horse for a long time, have you?
The twins hadn't seen a hovercraft before, had they?
They couldn't understand him, could they?
There wasn't enough time, was there?
People shouldn't drop litter on pavements, should they?
Ann hasn't got colour TV, has she?
Note that statements containing words such as *neither, no* (adjective), *none, no one, nobody, nothing, scarcely, barely, hardly, hardly ever, seldom* are treated as negative statements and followed by an ordinary interrogative tag:
No salt is allowed, is it?
Nothing was said, was it?
Peter hardly ever goes to parties, does he?
When the subject of the sentence is *anyone, anybody, no one, nobody, none, neither* we use the pronoun **they** as subject of the tag:
I don't suppose anyone will volunteer, will they?
No one would object, would they?
Neither of them complained, did they?

C   Question tags after affirmative statements
With the simple present tense we use **don't/doesn't?** in the tag. With the simple past tense we use **didn't?**
Edward lives here, doesn't he?
You found your passport, didn't you?
After all other tenses we just put the auxiliary verb into the negative interrogative:
Mary's coming tomorrow, isn't she?
Peter's heard the news, hasn't he?

Remember that **'s** = **is** or **has**, and **'d** = **had** or **would**:
Peter'd written before you phoned, hadn't he?
Mary'd come if you asked her, wouldn't she?
You'd better change your wet shoes, hadn't you?
The boys'd rather go by air, wouldn't they?

With *everybody, everyone, somebody, someone* we use the pronoun **they**:
Everyone warned you, didn't they?
Someone had recognized him, hadn't they?

Negative interrogative tags without contractions are possible but the word order is different:
You saw him, did you not?
This is a much less usual form.

D   Intonation
When question tags are used the speaker doesn't normally need information but merely expects agreement. These tags are therefore usually said with a falling intonation, as in statements.
Sometimes, however, the speaker does want information. He is not quite sure that the statement is true, and wants to be reassured. In this case the question tag is said with a rising intonation and the important word in the first sentence is stressed, usually with a rise of pitch. (See *Structure Drills 1*, 11-13.)

111   Comment tags

A   These are formed with auxiliary verbs, just like question tags, but after an affirmative statement we use an ordinary interrogative tag; after a negative statement we use a negative interrogative tag.
A comment tag can be added to an affirmative statement. It then indicates that the speaker notes the fact.
You saw him, did you? = Oh, so you saw him.
You've found a job, have you? = Oh, so you've found a job.
Comment tags can also be spoken in answer to an affirmative or negative statement:
I'm living in London now. ~ Are you?
I didn't pay Paul. ~ Didn't you?
When used in this way the tag is roughly equivalent to *Really!* or *Indeed!*

B   The chief use of these tags is to express the speaker's reaction to a statement. By the tone of his voice he can indicate that he is interested, not interested, surprised, pleased, delighted, angry, suspicious, disbelieving etc.
The speaker's feelings can be expressed more forcibly by adding an auxiliary:
I borrowed your car. ~ Oh, you did, did you?
I didn't think you'd need it. ~ Oh, you didn't, didn't you?
i.e. before an ordinary interrogative we use an affirmative auxiliary verb, before a negative interrogative we use a negative verb.

Again, the meaning depends on the tone of voice used. The speaker may be very angry, even truculent; but the form could also express admiration or amusement.

112   Additions to remarks

A   Affirmative additions to affirmative remarks can be made by subject + auxiliary + **too/also** or by **so** + auxiliary + subject, in that order. If there is an auxiliary in the first remark, it is repeated in the addition:
   Bill would enjoy a game and Tom would too/so would Tom.
If there is no auxiliary, **do/does/did** is used in the addition; i.e. instead of saying *Bill likes golf and Tom likes golf (too)* we can say *Bill likes golf and Tom does too/so does Tom.*
The additions can, of course, be spoken by another person:
   The boys cheated! ~ The girls did too!/So did the girls!
   I'm having a tooth out tomorrow. ~ So'm I!
When both remarks are made by the same person, both subjects are usually stressed. When they are made by different people the second subject is stressed more strongly than the first.

B   Affirmative additions to negative remarks are made with **but** + subject + auxiliary:
   Bill hasn't got a licence. ~ But Donald has.
   She doesn't eat meat but her husband does.
   The horse wasn't hurt but the rider was.

C   Negative additions to affirmative remarks are made with **but** + subject + negative auxiliary:
   He likes pop music but I don't.
   You can go but I can't.
   Peter passed the test but Bill didn't.

D   Negative additions to negative remarks are made with **neither/nor** + auxiliary + subject:
   Tom never goes to concerts, neither does his wife.
   Ann hasn't any spare time. ~ Neither/Nor have I.
   I didn't get much sleep last night. ~ Neither/Nor did I.
These additions can also be made with subject + negative auxiliary + **either**:
   He didn't like the book; I didn't either.
   They don't mind the noise; we don't either.
Alternatively, we can use the whole verb + object, if there is one, + **either**:
   I didn't like it either.   We don't mind it either.

11 be, have, do

be as an auxiliary verb

113 Form and use in the formation of tenses

A Form

Principal parts: *be, was, been*
Gerund/present participle: *being*

Present tense:

Affirmative	Negative	Interrogative
I am/I'm	*I am not/I'm not*	*am I?*
you are/you're	*you are not/you're not*	*are you?*
he is/he's	*he is not/he's not*	*is he?*
she is/she's	*she is not/she's not*	*is she?*
it is/it's	*it is not/it's not*	*is it?*
we are/we're	*we are not/we're not*	*are we?*
you are/you're	*you are not/you're not*	*are you?*
they are/they're	*they are not/they're not*	*are they?*

Alternative negative contractions: *you aren't, he isn't* etc.
Negative interrogative: *am I not/aren't I? are you not/aren't you?*
is he not/isn't he? etc.

Past tense:

Affirmative	Negative	Interrogative
I was	*I was not/wasn't*	*was I?*
you were	*you were not/weren't*	*were you?*
he/she/it was	*he/she/it was not/wasn't*	*was he/she/it?*
we were	*we were not/weren't*	*were we?*
you were	*you were not/weren't*	*were you?*
they were	*they were not/weren't*	*were they?*

Negative interrogative: *was I not/wasn't I? were you not/weren't you?*
was he not/wasn't he? etc.

The forms are the same when **be** is used as an ordinary verb.
Other tenses follow the rules for ordinary verbs. But **be** is not
normally used in the continuous form except in the passive and as
shown in 115 B.

B Use to form tenses

be is used in continuous active forms: *He is working/will be working* etc., and in all passive forms: *He was followed/is being followed.*

Note that **be** can be used in the continuous forms in the passive:
Active: *They are carrying him.*
Passive: *He is being carried.*

(For **be** used in the continuous with adjectives, see 115 B.)

114 be + infinitive

A The **be** + infinitive construction, e.g. *I am to go*, is extremely important and can be used in the following ways:

1 To convey orders or instructions:
No one is to leave this building without the permission of the police.
(no one must leave)
He is to stay here till we return. (he must stay)
This is a rather impersonal way of giving instructions and is chiefly used with the third person. When used with **you** it often implies that the speaker is passing on instructions issued by someone else. The difference between (a) *Stay here, Tom* and (b) *You are to stay here, Tom* is that in (a) the speaker himself is ordering Tom to stay, while in (b) he may be merely conveying to Tom the wishes of another person.

This distinction disappears of course in indirect speech, and the **be** + infinitive construction is an extremely useful way of expressing indirect commands, particularly when the introductory verb is in the present tense:
He says, 'Wait till I come.' =
He says that we are to wait till he comes.
or when there is a clause in front of the imperative:
He said, 'If I fall asleep at the wheel wake me up.' =
He said that if he fell asleep at the wheel she was to wake him up.

It is also used in reporting requests for instructions:
'Where shall I put it, sir?' he asked =
He asked where he was to put it.   (See also 318 B.)

2 To convey a plan:
She is to be married next month.
The expedition is to start in a week's time.
This construction is very much used in newspapers:
The Prime Minister is to make a statement tomorrow.
In headlines the verb **be** is often omitted to save space:
Prime Minister to make statement tomorrow.
Past forms:
He was to go. (present infinitive)
He was to have gone. (perfect infinitive)

The first of these doesn't tell us whether the plan was carried out or not. The second is used for an unfulfilled plan, i.e. one which was not carried out:

> *The Lord Mayor was to have laid the foundation stone but he was taken ill last night so the Lady Mayoress is doing it instead.*

B   **was/were** + infinitive can express an idea of destiny:

> *He received a blow on the head. It didn't worry him at the time but it was to be very troublesome later.* (turned out to be/proved troublesome)
> *They said goodbye, little knowing that they were never to meet again.* (were destined never to meet)

C   **be about** + infinitive expresses the immediate future:

> *They are about to start.* (They are just going to start/They are on the point of starting.)

just can be added to make the future even more immediate:

> *They are just about to leave.*

Similarly in the past:

> *He was just about to dive when he saw the shark.*

be on the point of + gerund has the same meaning as **be about** + infinitive, but is a shade more immediate.

be as an ordinary verb

Form: as for **be** used as an auxiliary (see 113 A).

115   be to denote existence, be + adjective

A   **be** is the verb normally used to denote the existence of, or to give information about, a person or thing:

> *Tom is a carpenter.*   *The dog is in the garden.*
> *Malta is an island.*   *The roads were rough and narrow.*
> *Gold is a metal.*   *Peter was tall and fair.*

B   **be** is used to express physical or mental condition:

> *I am hot/cold.*   *He was excited/calm.*
> *They will be happy/unhappy.*

With certain adjectives, e.g. *quiet/noisy, good/bad, wise/foolish*, it is possible to use the continuous form of **be**, e.g. *Tom is being foolish*, to imply that the subject is showing this quality at this time. Compare *Tom is being foolish*, which means Tom is talking or acting foolishly now, with *Tom is foolish*, which means that Tom always acts or talks foolishly. Similarly, *The children are being quiet* means they are playing quietly now, but *The children are quiet* might mean that they usually play quietly.

Other adjectives include:

annoying	*generous/mean*
cautious/rash	*helpful/unhelpful*
clever/stupid	*irritating*
difficult	*mysterious*
economical/extravagant	*optimistic/pessimistic*
formal	*polite*
funny	*selfish/unselfish*

With some of these, e.g. *stupid, difficult, funny, polite*, the continuous form may imply that the subject is deliberately acting in this way:

You are being stupid may mean *You are not trying to understand.*
He is being difficult usually means *He is raising unnecessary objections.*
He is being funny usually means *He is only joking. Don't believe him.*
She is just being polite probably means *She is only pretending to admire your car/clothes/house* etc.

C   **be** is used for age:

How old are you? ~ I'm ten/I am ten years old. (not *I'm ten years*)
How old is the tower? ~ It is 400 years old. (*years old* must be used when giving the age of things.)

D   Size and weight are expressed by **be**:

How tall are you?/What is your height? ~ I am 1·65 metres.
How high are we now? ~ We're about 20,000 feet.
What is your weight? or *What do you weigh/How much do you weigh? ~ I am 65 kilos* or *I weigh 65 kilos.*

E   **be** is used for prices:

How much is this melon? or *What does this melon cost? ~ It's £1.*
The best seats are (= cost) *£25.*

116   there is/are, there was/were etc.

A   When a noun representing an indefinite person or thing is the subject of the verb **be** we normally use a **there** + **be** + noun construction. We can say *A policeman is at the door* but *There is a policeman at the door* would be more usual.

Note that, though **there** appears to be the subject, the real subject is the noun that follows the verb, and if this noun is plural the verb must be plural too:

There are two policemen at the door.

In the above sentences both constructions (noun + **be** and **there** + **be** + noun) are possible. But when **be** is used to mean *exist/happen/ take place* the **there** construction is necessary:

There is a mistake/There are mistakes in this translation.

These sentences could not be rewritten *A mistake is/Mistakes are* etc.

In the following examples (R) is placed after the example when the **there** construction is replaceable by noun/pronoun + verb:

> *There have been several break-ins this year.*
> *There will be plenty of room for everyone.*
> *There were hundreds of people on the beach.* (R)

B   **there** can be used similarly with *someone/anyone/no one/something* etc.:

> *There's someone on the phone for you.* (R)

C   **there + be + something/nothing/anything** + adjective is also possible:

> *Is there anything wrong (with your car)?* (R) ~
> *No, there's nothing wrong with it.* (R)
> *There's something odd/strange about this letter.*

D   A noun or *someone/something* etc. could be followed by a relative clause:

> *There's a film I want to see.*   *There's something I must say.*

or by an infinitive:

> *There's nothing to do.* (nothing that we can do/must do; see 250)

E   The **there** construction can be used with another auxiliary + **be**:

> *There must be no doubt about this.*   *There may be a letter for me.*

or with **seem + be, appear + be**:

> *There seems to be something wrong here.*

F   **there** used as above is always unstressed.
Be careful not to confuse **there** used in this way with **there**, stressed, used as an adverb:

> 'There's a man I want to see.* (He is standing by the door.)

Compare with:

> *There's a man I want to see.* (This man exists.)

117   it is and there is compared

For uses of **it is**, see 67.
Some examples may help to prevent confusion between the two forms:

1   **it is** + adjective; **there is** + noun:

> *It is foggy* or *There is a fog.*
> *It was very wet* or *There was a lot of rain.*
> *It won't be very sunny* or *There won't be much sun.*

2   **it is, there is** of distance and time:

> *It is a long way to York.*
> *There is a long way still to go.* (We have many miles still to go.)
> *It is time to go home.* (We always start home at six and it is six now.)
> *There is time for us to go home and come back here again before the film starts.* (That amount of time exists.)

3   **it is**, used for identity, and **there is** + noun/pronoun:

> *There is someone at the door. I think it's the man to read the meters.*
> *There's a key here. Is it the key of the safe?*

4   **it is**, used in cleft sentences (see 67 D), and **there is**:
    It is the grandmother who makes the decisions. (the grandmother,
    not any other member of the family)
    . . . and there's the grandmother, who lives in the granny-flat.
    (the grandmother exists)

have as an auxiliary verb

118   Form and use in the formation of tenses

A   Form

    Principal parts: *have, had, had*
    Gerund/present participle: *having*

    Present tense:

Affirmative	Negative	Interrogative
I have/I've	*I have not/haven't*	*have I?*
you have/you've	*you have not/haven't*	*have you?*
he has/he's	*he has not/hasn't*	*has he?*
she has/she's	*she has not/hasn't*	*has she?*
it has/it's	*it has not/hasn't*	*has it?*
we have/we've	*we have not/haven't*	*have we?*
you have/you've	*you have not/haven't*	*have you?*
they have/they've	*they have not/haven't*	*have they?*

    Alternative negative contractions (chiefly used in perfect tenses): *I've not,*
    you've not, he's not etc.
    Negative interrogative: *have I not/haven't I? have you not/haven't you?*
    has he not/hasn't he? etc.

    Past tense:
    Affirmative: *had/'d* for all persons
    Negative: *had not/hadn't* for all persons
    Interrogative: *had I?* etc.
    Negative interrogative: *had I not/hadn't I?* etc.

    Other tenses follow the rules for ordinary verbs.

B   Use to form tenses
    have is used with the past participle to form the following tenses:
    Present perfect: *I have worked.*
    Past perfect: *I had worked.*
    Future perfect: *I will/shall have worked.*
    Perfect conditional: *I would/should have worked.*

119 have + object + past participle

A   This construction can be used to express more neatly sentences of the type 'I employed someone to do something for me'; i.e. instead of saying *I employed someone to clean my car* we can say *I had my car cleaned*, and instead of *I got a man to sweep my chimneys* ('got' here = paid/persuaded etc.), we can say *I had my chimneys swept*.

Note that this order of words, i.e. **have** + object + past participle, must be observed as otherwise the meaning will be changed: *He had his hair cut* means he employed someone to do it, but *He had cut his hair* means that he cut it himself some time before the time of speaking (past perfect tense).

When **have** is used in this way the negative and interrogative of its present and past tenses are formed with **do**:

Do you have your windows cleaned every month? ~ I don't have them cleaned; I clean them myself.
He was talking about having central heating put in. Did he have it put in in the end?

It can also be used in continuous tenses:

I can't ask you to dinner this week as I am having my house painted at the moment.
While I was having my hair done the police towed away my car.
The house is too small and he is having a room built on.

get can be used in the same way as **have** above but is more colloquial.
get is also used when we mention the person who performs the action:

She got him to dig away the snow. (She paid/persuaded him to dig etc.)

(**have** with a bare infinitive can be used in the same way, e.g. *She had him dig away the snow*, but the **get** construction is much more usual in British English.)

B   The **have** + object + past participle construction can also be used colloquially to replace a passive verb, usually one concerning some accident or misfortune:

His fruit was stolen before he had a chance to pick it
can be replaced by
He had his fruit stolen before he had a chance to pick it, and
Two of his teeth were knocked out in the fight can be replaced by
He had two of his teeth knocked out.

It will be seen that, whereas in A above the subject is the person who orders the thing to be done, here the subject is the person who suffers as a result of the action. The subject could be a thing:

The houses had their roofs ripped off by the gale.

get can also replace **have** here:

The cat got her tail singed through sitting too near the fire. (The cat's tail was singed etc.)

120 had better + bare infinitive

had here is an unreal past; the meaning is present or future:

I had/I'd better ring him at once/tomorrow. (This would be a good thing to do/the best thing to do.)

The negative is formed with **not** after **better**:

You had better not miss the last bus. (It would be unwise to miss it, or I advise/warn you not to miss it.)

had here is usually contracted after pronouns and in speech is sometimes so unstressed as to be almost inaudible.

had better is not normally used in the ordinary interrogative, but is sometimes used in the negative interrogative as an advice form:

Hadn't you better ask him first? =
Wouldn't it be a good thing to ask him first?

you had better is a very useful advice form:

You had better fly. (It would be best for you to fly, or I advise you to fly.)

In indirect speech **had better** with the first or third person remains unchanged; **had better** with the second person can remain unchanged or be reported by **advise** + object + infinitive:

He said, 'I'd better hurry' =
He said (that) he'd better hurry.
He said, 'Ann had better hurry' =
He said (that) Ann had better hurry.
He said, 'You'd better hurry' =
He said (that) I'd better hurry or
He advised me to hurry.

121 have + object + present participle

A This expression is often used with a period of future time:

I'll have you driving in three days. (As a result of my efforts, you will be driving in three days.)

It can also be used in the past or present:

He had them all dancing. (He taught/persuaded them all to dance.)
I have them all talking to each other. (I encourage/persuade them all to talk to each other.)

It can be used in the interrogative:

Will you really have her driving in three days?

but is not often used in the negative.

B *If you give all-night parties you'll have the neighbours complaining.*
(The neighbours will complain/will be complaining.)
If film-stars put their numbers in telephone books they'd have everyone ringing them up. (Everyone would ring/would be ringing them up.)

you'll have in the first example conveys the idea 'this will happen to you'. Similarly *they'd have* in the second example conveys the idea 'this would happen to them'.

If you don't put a fence round your garden you'll have people walking in and stealing your fruit. (People will walk in and steal/will be walking in and stealing it, i.e. this will happen to you.)

The construction can be used in the interrogative and negative:

When they move that bus stop, you won't have people sitting on your steps waiting for the bus any more.

This structure is chiefly used for actions which would be displeasing to the subject of **have**, as in the above example, but it can be used for an action which is not displeasing:

When he became famous, he had people stopping him in the street and asking for his autograph =

When he became famous, people stopped him in the street and asked for his autograph.

But **I won't have** + object + present participle normally means 'I won't/don't allow this':

I won't have him sitting down to dinner in his overalls. I make him change them. (I won't/don't allow him to sit down etc.)

This use is restricted to the first person.

(For **have** used for obligation, see chapter 14.)

have as an ordinary verb

122 **have** meaning 'possess' and 'suffer (from) pain/illness/disability'

A Examples:

He has a black beard.   I have had this car for ten years.
Have you got a headache? ~ Yes, I have.
The twins have mumps.
He has a weak heart.

B Form

	Affirmative	Negative	Interrogative
Present	*have (got)* or *have*	*haven't (got)* or *don't have*	*have I (got)?* etc. or *do you have?* etc.
Past	*had*	*hadn't (got)* or *didn't have*	*had you (got)?* etc. or *did you have?* etc.

Note that the negative and interrogative can be formed in two ways.

C **have** is conjugated with **do** for habitual actions:

Do you often have headaches? ~ No, I don't.

When there is not this idea of habit, the **have not (got)/have you (got)** forms are more usual in Britain, whereas other English-speaking countries (notably America) use the **do** forms here also.

An American might say:

Can you help me now? Do you have time?

where an Englishman would probably say:

> *Can you help me now? Have you got time?*

do forms can therefore be used safely throughout, but students living in Britain should practise the other forms as well.

D **got** can be added to **have/have not/have you** etc. as shown above. It makes no difference to the sense so it is entirely optional, but it is quite a common addition. **got**, however, is not added in short answers or question tags:

> *Have you got an ice-axe? ~ Yes, I have.*
> *She's got a nice voice, hasn't she?*

have (affirmative) followed by **got** is usually contracted:

> *I've got my ticket.   He's got a flat in Pimlico.*

The stress falls on **got**. The **'ve** or **'s** is often barely audible.

have (affirmative) without **got** is often not contracted. The **have** or **has** must then be audible.

123   **have** meaning 'take' (a meal), 'give' (a party) etc.

A **have** can also be used to mean:

'take' (a meal/food or drink, a bath/a lesson etc.)

'give' (a party), 'entertain' (guests)

'encounter' (difficulties/trouble)

'experience', 'enjoy', usually with an adjective, e.g. *good*.

> *We have lunch at one.*
> *They are having a party tomorrow.*
> *Did you have trouble with Customs?*
> *I hope you'll have a good holiday.*

B **have** when used as above obeys the rules for ordinary verbs:

It is never followed by **got**.

Its negative and interrogative are made with **do/did**.

It can be used in the continuous tenses.

> *We are having breakfast early tomorrow.* (near future)
> *She is having twenty people to dinner next Monday.* (near future)
> *I can't answer the telephone; I am having a bath.* (present)
> *How many English lessons do you have a week? ~ I have six.*
> *You have coffee at eleven, don't you?* (habit)
> *Ann has breakfast in bed, but Mary doesn't.* (habit)
> *Will you have some tea/coffee etc.?* (This is an invitation. We can also omit *Will you* and say *Have some tea* etc.)
> *Did you have a good time at the theatre?* (Did you enjoy yourself?)
> *Have a good time!* (Enjoy yourself!)
> *I am having a wonderful holiday.*
> *I didn't have a very good journey.*
> *Do you have earthquakes in your country? ~ Yes, but we don't have them very often.*

do

124   Form

Principal parts: *do, did, done*
Gerund/present participle: *doing*

Present tense:

Affirmative	Negative	Interrogative
I do	*I do not/don't*	*do I?*
you do	*you do not/don't*	*do you?*
he does	*he does not/doesn't*	*does he?*
she does	*she does not/doesn't*	*does she?*
it does	*it does not/doesn't*	*does it?*
we do	*we do not/don't*	*do we?*
you do	*you do not/don't*	*do you?*
they do	*they do not/don't*	*do they?*

Negative interrogative: *do I not/don't I? do you not/don't you?*
does he not/doesn't he? etc.

do as an ordinary verb has the affirmative shown above. But for
negative and interrogative we add the infinitive **do** to the above forms:
What does/did she do? (See 126.)

Past tense:
Affirmative: *did* for all persons
Negative: *did not/didn't* for all persons
Interrogative: *did he?* etc.
Negative interrogative: *did he not/didn't he?* etc.

do is followed by the bare infinitive:
   I don't know.   *Did you see it?*   *He doesn't like me.*

125   **do** used as an auxiliary

A   **do** is used to form the negative and interrogative of the present simple
and past simple tenses of ordinary verbs (see 103-5):
   He doesn't work.   He didn't work.
   Does he work?   Did he work?

B   It is possible to use **do/did** + infinitive in the affirmative also when we
wish to add special emphasis. It is chiefly used when another speaker
has expressed doubt about the action referred to:
   You didn't see him. ~ I 'did see him. (The *did* is strongly stressed
   in speech. This is more emphatic than the normal *I saw him.*)
   I know that you didn't expect me to go, but I 'did go.

C   **do** is used to avoid repetition of a previous ordinary verb:

1   In short agreements and disagreements (see 109):
    Tom talks too much. ~ Yes, he does/No, he doesn't.
    He didn't go. ~ No, he didn't/Oh yes, he did.

2   In additions (see 112):
    He likes concerts and so do we. (Note inversion.)
    He lives here but I don't.   He doesn't drive but I do.

3   In question tags (see also 110):
    He lives here, doesn't he?   He didn't see you, did he?

D   **do** is used in short answers to avoid repetition of the main verb:
    Do you smoke? ~ Yes, I do (not *Yes, I smoke*)/*No, I don't.*
    Did you see him? ~ Yes, I did/No, I didn't.   (See 108.)

E   Similarly in comparisons (see 22): *He drives faster than I do.*

F   **do** + imperative makes a request or invitation more persuasive:
    Do come with us. (more persuasive than *Come with us.*)
    Do work a little harder.   Do help me, please.

G   It can similarly be used as an approving or encouraging affirmative
    answer to someone asking for approval of, or permission to do, some
    action: *Shall I write to him? ~ Yes, do* or *Do* alone.

126   do used as an ordinary verb

do, like **have**, can be used as an ordinary verb. It then forms its
negative and interrogative in the simple present and past with **do/did**:

    I do not do   do you do?   don't you do?
    he does not do   does he do?   doesn't he do?
    I did not do   did he do?   didn't he do? etc.

It can be used in the continuous forms, or simple forms:
    What are you doing (now)? ~ I'm doing my homework.
    What's he doing tomorrow? (near future)
    What does he do in the evenings? (habit)
    Why did you do it? ~ I did it because I was angry.

How do you do? is said by both parties after an introduction:
    HOSTESS: *Mr Day, may I introduce Mr Davis? Mr Davis, Mr Day.*
Both men say *How do you do?* Originally this was an enquiry about the
other person's health. Now it is merely a formal greeting.

Some examples of other uses of **do**:
    He doesn't do what he's told. (doesn't obey orders)
    What do you do for a living? ~ I'm an artist.
    How's the new boy doing? (getting on)
    I haven't got a torch. Will a candle do? (= be suitable/adequate) ~
    A candle won't do. I'm looking for a gas leak. (A candle would be
    unsuitable.)
    Would £10 do? (= be adequate) ~ *No, it wouldn't. I need £20.*

to do with (in the infinitive only) can mean 'concern'. It is chiefly used
in the construction **it is/was something/nothing to do with** + noun/
pronoun/gerund: *It's nothing to do with you = It doesn't concern you.*

12 **may** and **can** for permission and possibility

Permission

127 **may** used for permission: forms

may for all persons in the present and future.
might in the conditional and after verbs in a past tense.
Negative: *may not/mayn't, might not/mightn't*
Interrogative: *may I? might I?* etc.
Negative interrogative: *may I not/mayn't I? might I not/mightn't I?* etc.
Other forms are supplied by *allow, be allowed*.
may is followed by the bare infinitive.

128 **can** used for permission: forms

can for all persons in the present and future.
could for past and conditional.
Negative: *cannot/can't, could not/couldn't*
Interrogative: *can I? could I?* etc.
Negative interrogative: *can I not/can't I? could I not/couldn't I?* etc.
Other forms are supplied by *allow, be allowed*.
can is followed by the bare infinitive.

129 **may** and **can** used for permission in the present or future

A First person
I/we can is the most usual form:
I can take a day off whenever I want.
I/we may meaning 'I/we have permission to . . .' is possible:
I may leave the office as soon as I have finished.
But this is not a very common construction and it would be much more usual to say:
I can leave/I'm allowed to leave . . .
I/we may/might is a little more usual in indirect speech:
'You may leave when you've finished,' he says/said =
He says we may leave/He said we might leave . . .
But in colloquial speech we would use **can/could**:
He says we can leave/He said we could leave.

B   Second person
Here **may** is chiefly used when the speaker is giving permission. *You may park here* means 'I give you permission to park'. It does not normally mean 'The police etc. allow you to park' or 'You have a right to park'.
can can be used as an informal alternative to **may** here. But it can also be used to express the idea of having permission. *You can park here* can mean 'I allow it/The police allow it/You have a right to park here'. Similarly *You can take two books home with you* can mean 'I allow it/The library allows it' and *You can't eat sandwiches in the library* can mean 'I don't allow it/The librarian doesn't allow it' or 'It isn't the proper thing to do'.
could can be used when there is an idea of condition:
    Why don't you ring him? You can/could use my phone.
could is also used in indirect speech introduced by a verb in a past tense:
    He said I could use his phone.

C   Third person
may can be used as in B above when the speaker is giving permission:
    He may take my car. (I give him permission to take it.)
    They may phone the office and reverse the charges.
    (I give them permission.)
But it is chiefly used in impersonal statements concerning authority and permission:
    In certain circumstances a police officer may (= has the right to) *ask a driver to take a breath test.*
    If convicted, an accused person may (= has the right to) *appeal.*
    SCRABBLE RULES: *No letter may be moved after it has been played.*
In|informal English **can/can't** would be used:
    He can take the car.
    They can phone the office.
    A police officer can ask a driver . . .
    An accused person can appeal.
    No letter can be moved . . .

130   **could** or **was/were allowed to** for permission in the past

could can also express general permission in the past:
    On Sundays we could (= were allowed to) *stay up late.*
When a particular action was permitted and performed we use **was/were allowed** instead of **could**:
    I had a visa so I was allowed to cross the frontier.
couldn't however can be used a little more widely than **could**:
    We couldn't bring our dog into the restaurant.
The opposite of this would be:
    We were allowed to bring etc.

For perfect and continuous tenses and passives **allowed** must be used:
Since his accident he hasn't been allowed to drive.
As a child he had been allowed to do exactly what he liked.
(For **might/could** in indirect speech, see 129 A.)

131 Requests for permission (see also 283)

A **can I?, could I?, may I?, might I?** are all possible and can be used for the present or future. **can I?** is the most informal.
could I? is the most generally useful of the four, as it can express both formal and informal requests.
may I? is a little more formal than **could I?** but can also be used for both types of requests.
might I? is more diffident than **may I?** and indicates greater uncertainty about the answer.

B The negative interrogative forms **can't I?** and **couldn't I?** are used to show that the speaker hopes for an affirmative answer:
Can't I stay up till the end of the programme?
Couldn't I pay by cheque?
may and **might** are not used in this way.

C Answers to **can I/could I** requests will normally be:
Yes, you can.   Yes, of course (you can).   No, you can't.
Affirmative answers to **may I/might I** requests are normally:
Yes, you may.   Yes, of course (you may).
For a negative answer *No, you may not* is possible but it would normally be replaced by a milder expression:
I'd rather you didn't.   I'm afraid not.

D Questions about permission are expressed by **can** or **am/is/are allowed to** in the present and by **could** or **was/were allowed to** in the past:
Can Tom use the car whenever he likes?
Is Tom allowed to use the car . . . ?
Could students choose what they wanted to study?
Were students allowed to choose . . . ?

Possibility

132 may/might for possibility

A Form
may/might for present and future.
might in the conditional and after verbs in the past tense.
Negative: *may not/mayn't, might not/mightn't*
Interrogative: see E below
Infinitive: *to be + likely*

B   **may/might** + present infinitive can express possibility in the present
     or future:
>   *He may/might tell his wife.* (Perhaps he tells/will tell his wife.)
>   *He may/might emigrate.* (Perhaps he will emigrate.)
>   *Ann may/might know Tom's address.* (Perhaps Ann knows etc.)
     Similarly with the continuous infinitive:
>   *He may/might be waiting at the station.* (Perhaps he is waiting at
>   the station.)
>   *He may/might be waiting at the station when we arrive.* (Perhaps he
>   will be waiting etc.)

C   **may** or **might** for present or future possibility

     Normally either can be used. **might** slightly increases the doubt.

     Note that in speech we can also indicate increased doubt by stressing
     may/might. *Tom 'may lend you the money* (with a strong stress on
     may) implies that this is not very likely. *Tom 'might lend you the money*
     (with a strong stress on *might*) implies 'I don't think this is at all likely/
     I think it is unlikely'.

D   **might** must be used in the conditional and when the expression is
     introduced by a verb in the past tense:
>   *If 'you invited him he might come.*
>   *I knew we might have to wait at the frontier.*
>   *He said he might hire a car.* (indirect speech)

E   **may/might** in the negative and interrogative
     The negative presents no problems:
>   *He may/might not believe your story.* (Perhaps he won't/doesn't
>   believe your story.)
     The interrogative is normally expressed by **do you think?** or a
     construction with **be + likely**:
>   *Do you think he's alone?*
>   *Do you think he believes your story?*
>   *Is it likely that the plane will be late?*
>   *Is the plane likely to be late?*
     may? for possibility very seldom introduces a sentence. It may be
     placed later on:
>   *When may we expect you?*
>   *What may be the result of the new tax?*
     But a construction with **be + likely** or **think** is more usual:
>   *When are you likely to arrive?*
>   *What do you think the result will be?*
     might? is just possible:
>   *Might they be waiting outside the station?*
     But *Could they be waiting?* or *Do you think they are waiting?* would be
     more usual (see 134).
     may/might in the affirmative, however, can form part of a question:
>   *Do you think he may/might not be able to pay?*
     (See 104 for this type of question.)

133   may/might + perfect infinitive

A   This is used in speculations about past actions:

He may/might have gone =
It is possible that he went/has gone or
Perhaps he went/has gone.

might must be used, as shown in 132 D, when the main verb is in a past tense:

He said/thought that she might have missed the plane.

might, not **may**, must be used when the uncertainty no longer exists:

He came home alone. You shouldn't have let him do that; he might have got lost. (But he didn't get lost.)

So in the sentence:

You shouldn't have drunk the wine: it may/might have been drugged

the words *it may have been drugged* would indicate that we are still uncertain whether it was drugged or not. *it might have been drugged* could have the same meaning but could also mean that we know it wasn't drugged.

might, not **may**, is also used when the matter was never put to the test, as in:

Perhaps we should have taken the other road. It might have been quicker.
It's a good thing you didn't lend him the money. You might never have got it back.

Sentences of this kind are very similar to the third type of conditional sentence:

If we had taken the other road we might have arrived earlier.

B   **may/might** can be used in conditional sentences instead of **will/would** to indicate a possible instead of a certain result:

If he sees you he will stop. (certain)
If he sees you he may stop. (possible)

Similarly:

If you poured hot water into it, it might crack and
If you had left it there someone might have stolen it.

(See 223 B.)

134   could as an alternative to may/might

A   **could be** can be used instead of **may/might be**:

I wonder where Tom is. ~ He may/might/could be in the library.
(Perhaps he is in the library.)

Similarly when **be** is part of the continuous infinitive:

I wonder why Bill isn't here? ~ He may/might/could still be waiting for a bus. (Perhaps he is still waiting for a bus.)

And when **be** is part of a passive infinitive:

Do you think the plane will be on time? ~ I don't know. It may/might/could be delayed by fog. (Perhaps it will be delayed by fog.)

In the interrogative we can use either **could** or **might**:
> *Might/Could he be waiting for us at the station?* (Do you think he is waiting . . . ?)

In the negative, though, there is a difference of meaning between **could** and **may/might**:
> *He may/might not be driving the car himself.* (Perhaps he isn't driving the car himself.)

But *He couldn't be driving the car himself* expresses a negative deduction. It means 'This is impossible. He can't drive'.

B **could** + the perfect infinitive of any verb can be used instead of **may/might** + perfect infinitive (possibility):
> *I wonder how Tom knew about Ann's engagement.* ~
> *He may/might/could have heard it from Jack.* (Perhaps he heard it from Jack.)

As in A above, in the interrogative we can use **might** or **could**:
> *Could/Might the bank have made a mistake?* (Do you think it is possible that the bank (has) made a mistake?)

But in the negative the meanings differ:
> *Ann might not have seen Tom yesterday* (perhaps she didn't see him) but
> *Ann couldn't have seen Tom yesterday.* (negative deduction: perhaps Ann and Tom were in different towns)

135 **can** used to express possibility

A General possibility

Subject + **can** can mean 'it is possible', i.e. circumstances permit (this is quite different from the kind of possibility expressed by **may**):
> *You can ski on the hills.* (There is enough snow.)
> *We can't bathe here on account of the sharks.* (It isn't safe.)
> *Can you get to the top of the mountain in one day?* (Is it possible?)

B **can** can also express occasional possibility:
> *Measles can be quite dangerous.* (Sometimes it is possible for them to be quite dangerous/Sometimes they are quite dangerous.)
> *The Straits of Dover can be very rough.* (It is possible for the Straits to be rough; this sometimes happens.)

could is used in the past:
> *He could be very unreasonable.* (Sometimes he was unreasonable; this was a possibility.)

can is used in this way in the present or past tense only, and chiefly in the affirmative.

13 **can** and **be able** for ability

136 **can** and **be able**: forms

can is used here in conjunction with **be** + the adjective **able**, which supplies the missing parts of **can** and provides an alternative form for the present and past tense. We have therefore the following forms:

Infinitive: *to be able*
Past participle: *been able*

	Affirmative	Negative	Interrogative
Future	*will/shall* *be able*	*will/shall not* *be able*	*shall/will I be able?* *will he be able?* etc.
Present	*can* or *am able*	*cannot* or *am not able*	*can I?* or *am I able?* etc.
Past	*could* or *was able*	*could not* or *was not able*	*could I?* or *was I able?* etc.

There is only one future form. In the conditional, however, we have two forms: *could* and *would be able.*

All other tenses are formed with **be able** according to the rules for ordinary verbs:
Present perfect: *have been able*
Past perfect: *had been able*
Negative interrogative: *could you not/couldn't you? were you not/weren't you able? will you not/won't you be able?* etc.
can/be/will/shall not and **have** can be contracted in the usual way:
I wasn't able, he won't be able, I've been able.
can is followed by the bare infinitive.
be able is followed by the full infinitive.

137 **can/am able, could/was able**

A **can** and **be able**

1 **shall/will be able** is the only future form:
   Our baby will be able to walk in a few weeks.

2   Either **can** or **am able** may be used in the present. **can** is the
more usual:
> *Can you/Are you able to type?*
> *I can't pay you today. Can you wait till tomorrow?* or
> *Could you wait?* (request; see B2 below)

3   For the present perfect, however, we must use the **be able** form:
> *Since his accident he hasn't been able to leave the house.*

B   **could**

1   **could** can be used with a present meaning when there is an idea of
condition:
> *Could you run the business by yourself?* (if this was necessary)
> *Could he get another job?* (if he left this one)
> *I could get you a copy.* (if you want one)

In the first two examples **could** is replaceable by **would be able**.

2   **could you?** is a very good way of introducing a request. It is an
alternative to **would you?** and a little more polite:
> *Could you show me the way/lend me £5/wait half an hour?*
> *Could you please send me an application form?*

couldn't you? is also useful:
> HOUSEHOLDER: *Could you come and mend a leak in a pipe?*
> PLUMBER: *Would sometime next month suit you?*
> HOUSEHOLDER: *Couldn't you come a little earlier?*

C   **could** and **was able** used for past ability

1   For ability only, either can be used:
> *When I was young I could/was able to climb any tree in the forest.*

2   For ability + particular action, use **was able**:
> *Although the pilot was badly hurt he was able to explain what had
> happened.* (He could and did explain.)
> *The boat capsized quite near the bank so the children were able to
> swim to safety.* (They could and did swim.)

This rule, however, is relaxed in the negative when the action did not
take place, and with verbs of the senses:
> *He read the message but he couldn't/wasn't able to understand it.*
> *I could/was able to see him through the window.*

D   **had been able** is the past perfect form:
> *He said he had lost his passport and hadn't been able to leave the
> country.*

(For **could** in reported speech, see 312.)

138 could + perfect infinitive

A This form is used for past ability when the action was not performed:

I could have lent you the money. Why didn't you ask me?
(see also 154)

or when we don't know whether it was performed or not:

The money has disappeared! Who could have taken it?
Tom could have (taken it); he was here alone yesterday.

Compare:

He was able to send a message. (He sent it.)
He could have sent a message. (He didn't send it or we don't know whether he sent it or not. See also 135.)

B **could** + perfect infinitive can also express irritation at or reproach for the non-performance of an action:

You could have told me =
I am annoyed/disappointed that you didn't tell me. You should have told me.

There would be a strong stress on the word the speaker wishes to emphasize.

(For **might** used in the same way, see 285.)

14 ought, should, must, have to, need for obligation

139 ought: forms

ought is a modal verb (see 107 B).
The same form can be used for present and future and for the past when preceded by a verb in a past tense or followed by a perfect infinitive:

I ought to write to him today/tomorrow.
I knew I ought to write to him.
She said I ought to write.
I know/knew that I ought to have written.

Negative: *ought not/oughtn't*
Interrogative: *ought I?* etc.
Negative interrogative: *ought I not/oughtn't I?* etc.
ought takes the full infinitive, and to remind students of this, it is sometimes referred to as **ought to**.
Questions or remarks with **ought** may be answered by **should** and vice versa:

You ought to put in central heating. ~ Yes, I suppose I should.

140 should: forms

should is also a modal verb.
Like **ought**, the same form can be used for present and future and for the past when preceded by a verb in a past tense. **should** could replace **ought to** in the above examples.
Negative: *should not/shouldn't*
Interrogative: *should I?* etc.
Negative interrogative: *should I not/shouldn't I?* etc.
should is followed by the bare infinitive.
should and **ought**, used for obligation, normally have the same meaning but **should** is the more usual form.
In conversation **should/ought to** can often be used alone, the infinitive being understood but not mentioned:

You should paint/ought to paint your door. ~ Yes, I know I should/
I know I ought to.

141 ought/should compared to must and have to

A Differences in use

1 **ought/should** is used to express the subject's obligation or duty:
> *You should send in accurate income tax returns*

or to indicate a correct or sensible action:
> *They shouldn't allow parking here; the street is too narrow.*
> *This word is spelt wrongly. There should be another 's'.*

Here there is neither the speaker's authority, as with **must**, or external authority, as with **have to** (see 145). It is more a matter of conscience or good sense:
> PIANIST TO PUPIL: *You must practise at least an hour a day.*
> PUPIL TO MUSICAL FRIEND: *I have to practise an hour a day!*
> MUSICAL FRIEND: *You ought to/should practise for more than an hour.*

2 Another difference beween **ought/should** and **must** and **have to** is that with **must** and **have to** we normally have the impression that the obligation is being or will be fulfilled. This is particularly the case with the first person but quite often applies to the other persons too. With **ought/should** we do not necessarily feel that the obligation is being or will be fulfilled. Quite often, especially in the first person, the reverse is the case.

If a driver says *I ought to/should go slowly here; it's a built-up area* he usually implies that he isn't going to go slowly. If he really intended to go slowly he would say, *I must go/I have to go/I will have to go slowly here.*

Similarly, if someone says *We must have a party to celebrate your engagement*, his friends are reasonably confident that there will be a party. But if he says *We should have a party . . .* it is not so certain that the party will take place. His tone or expression might indicate that it will not be possible.

B Similarities in use

1 **should** (but not **ought**) can be used in formal notices and on information sheets etc.:
> *Candidates should be prepared to answer questions on . . .*
> *Intending travellers should be in possession of the following documents . . .*
> *On hearing the alarm bell, hotel guests should leave their rooms . . .*

must could be used here without change of meaning, but **should** expresses the obligation more gently.

2 **ought** and **should** can express advice:
> *You ought to/should read this. It's very good.*

But for more emphatic advice **must** is better:
> *You must read this. It's marvellous!*

142 ought/should with the continuous infinitive

ought/should with the continuous infinitive expresses the idea that the subject is not fulfilling his obligations or that he is acting foolishly, rashly etc. or not acting sensibly, prudently etc.:

> *He ought to be studying for his exam. He shouldn't be spending all his time on the beach.*
> *We should be wearing seat belts.* (But we are not wearing them.)
> *I shouldn't be telling you this. It's supposed to be a secret.*

143 ought/should with the perfect infinitive

This construction is used to express an unfulfilled obligation or a sensible action that was neglected. In the negative it expresses a wrong or foolish action in the past.

> *You ought to have told him that the paint on that seat was wet.*
> *You|should have turned his omelette; he likes it turned.*
> *They ought to have stopped at the traffic lights.*
> *She shouldn't have opened the letter; it wasn't addressed to her.*
> *The Emergency Exit doors shouldn't have been blocked.*

144 must and have to: forms

A **must**

must is a modal verb (see 107 B). It is used in the present or future.
Negative: *must not/mustn't*
Interrogative: *must I?* etc.
Negative interrogative: *must I not/mustn't I?* etc.
The past tense is supplied by *had to*.
must takes the bare infinitive.
It can express obligation and emphatic advice:

> FATHER: *You must get up earlier in the morning.* (obligation)
> *You must take more exercise. Join a squash club.* (advice)

B **have to**

	Obligation		No obligation
	Speaker's authority	External authority	
Future	*must*	*shall/will have to*	*shan't/won't have to*
Present	*must*	*have to** *have (got) to**	*don't/doesn't have to** *haven't (got) to**
Past	*had to*	*had to*	*didn't have to* *hadn't (got) to*

*See C below.

C Difference between the starred **have to** forms

have to (without **got**) and its negative **don't/doesn't have to** are the correct forms for habitual actions but can be used for single actions also, and are common in American English.

have (got) to and **haven't (got) to** are for single actions only:

TOM: *I have to go to work every day except Sunday. But I don't have to work a full day on Saturday.*

But on Sunday he could say:

I'm glad I haven't (got) to go to work today or
I'm glad I don't have to go to work today.

In the past **didn't have to** can be used for both habitual and single actions in the past.

hadn't (got) to is used more for single actions.

didn't have to is the more generally used form.

have to in the affirmative expresses obligation.

have to in the negative expresses absence of obligation. This can also be expressed by **need not, don't need** etc. (see 149).

145 Difference between **must** and **have to** in the affirmative

A **must** expresses obligation imposed by the speaker:

MOTHER: *You must wipe your feet when you come in.*

have to expresses external obligation:

SMALL BOY: *I have to wipe my feet every time I come in.*

B Second person examples

1 Speaker's authority

MOTHER: *You must wear a dress tonight. You can't go to the opera in those dreadful jeans.*

EMPLOYER: *You must use a dictionary. I'm tired of correcting your spelling mistakes.*

DOCTOR: *You must cut down on your smoking.*

2 External authority

You have to wear uniform on duty, don't you?
You have to train very hard for these big matches, I suppose.
You'll have to get up earlier when you start work, won't you?
You'll have to cross the line by the footbridge.

C Third person examples

Here **must** is chiefly used in written orders or instructions:

RAILWAY COMPANY: *Passengers must cross the line by the footbridge.*

OFFICE MANAGER: *Staff must be at their desks by 9.00.*

REGULATION: *A trailer must have two rear lamps.*

When we are merely stating or commenting on another person's obligations we use **have to**:

In this office even the senior staff have to be at their desks by 9.00.
She has to make her children's clothes. She can't afford to buy them.
They'll have to send a diver down to examine the hull.

If we used **must** instead of **have to** above it might imply that the speaker had authority to order these actions.
But **must** may be used when the speaker approves of an obligation:
> *A driver who has knocked someone down must stop.* (The speaker thinks it is the driver's duty to stop.)

Or when the speaker feels strongly:
> *Something must be done to stop these accidents.*

D   First person examples
In the first person the difference between **must** and **have to** is less important and very often either form is possible:
> TYPIST: *I must/will have to buy a dictionary.*
> PATIENT: *I must/have to/will have to cut down on my smoking.*

But **have to** is better for habits:
> *I have to take two of these pills a day*

and **must** is better when the obligations are urgent or seem important to the speaker:
> *I must tell you about a dream I had last night.*
> *Before we do anything I must find my cheque book.*

E   Some other examples (all persons)
> *You must come and see us some time.* (This is quite a usual way of expressing a casual invitation.)
> *The children have to play in the street till their parents come home.*
> *This sort of thing must stop!* (The speaker either has authority or feels very strongly about it.)
> *You must write to your uncle and thank him for his nice present.*
> *If there are no taxis we'll have to walk.*
> *If your father was a poor man you'd have to work.*
> *We have to walk our dog twice a day.*
> NOTICE IN SHOP WINDOW: *Closing down sale! Everything must go!*

F   Affirmative obligations in the past: **had to**
Here the distinction between the speaker's authority and external authority cannot be expressed and there is only one form, **had to**:
> *I ran out of money and had to borrow from Tom.*
> *You had to pay duty on that, I suppose?*
> *There were no buses so he had to walk.*

146   need not and **must not** in the present and future

need not can be used for present and future. It has the same form for all persons. (See 148.)
need not expresses absence of obligation. The speaker gives permission for an action not to be performed or sometimes merely states that an action is not necessary:
> EMPLOYER: *You needn't make two copies. One will do.*
> *Give them this cheque. They needn't send me a receipt.*
> *You needn't change (your clothes). Just come as you are.*

must not expresses a negative obligation imposed by the speaker or very emphatic advice:

You mustn't repeat this to anyone.

NOTICE IN SHOP: *Staff must not smoke when serving customers.*

You mustn't leave your car unlocked. This place is full of thieves.

147 **need not, must not** and **must** in the present and future

DOCTOR: *You needn't go on a diet; but you must eat sensibly and you mustn't overeat.*

ZOO NOTICE: *Visitors must not feed the animals.*

RAILWAY NOTICE: *Passengers must not walk on the line.*

You mustn't drive fast. There is a speed limit here.

You needn't drive fast. We've plenty of time.

You needn't strike a match. I can see well enough.

You mustn't strike a match. This room is full of gas.

SCHOOL NOTICE: *The lifts must not be used during Fire Drill.*

You mustn't wear that dress again. You look terrible in yellow.

TEACHER: *You needn't read the whole book but you must read the first four chapters.*

You must cut down that dead tree or it will fall on your house.

DOCTOR: *You mustn't take more than two of these pills at once. Three might be fatal.*

DOCTOR (to patient's wife): *If the pain has gone he needn't take any more of these.*

148 **need**: forms

A **need** can be both an auxiliary and an ordinary verb. As an auxiliary it is a semi-modal, i.e. it has both modal and 'ordinary verb' forms. As a modal, its forms are *need* or *need not/needn't* for all persons in the present and future and in indirect speech. (See C below.)

Interrogative: *need I?* etc.

Negative interrogative: *need I not/needn't I?* etc.

need conjugated as above takes the bare infinitive.

B **need** as an auxiliary is seldom used in the affirmative except when a negative or interrogative sentence is preceded by an expression which changes the negative or interrogative verb into an affirmative:

I needn't wear a coat or *I don't suppose I need wear a coat.*

Need I tell Tom? or *Do you think I need tell Tom?*

It is however sometimes used in fairly formal English with *hardly/ scarcely* or *only*:

I need hardly say how pleased we are to welcome Mr X. (I needn't say . . .)

You need only touch one of the pictures for all the alarm bells to start ringing. (If you even touch one of the pictures all the bells . . .)

C   '**needn't**' in direct speech can be reported unchanged:
> *'You needn't pay till the 31st' he says/said =*
> *He says/said I needn't pay till the 31st.*

(See also 325 C.)

D   **need** can also be conjugated as an ordinary verb with negative forms as shown in 149 below. Corresponding **have to** forms are also shown. For interrogative forms, see 151.

need conjugated with **will/shall**, **do/does/did** etc. takes the full infinitive and is sometimes referred to as **need to**.

149   Absence of obligation: forms

	Speaker's authority	External authority
Future	*need not*	*shan't/won't need to* *shan't/won't have to*
Present	*need not*	*don't/doesn't need to* *don't/doesn't have to* *haven't/hasn't got to*
Past (see 150 B)	*didn't need to* *didn't have to* *hadn't got to*	

But see 148 C above for *needn't* in indirect speech.

shan't/won't need to = shan't/won't have to
don't/doesn't need to = don't/doesn't have to
didn't need to = didn't have to (but *didn't have to* is the more usual form)
There are no exact *need* equivalents of *haven't/hasn't got to* and *hadn't got to* as can be seen from the table.

150   Difference between **need not** and the other forms

A 1   As already stated, **need not** expresses the speaker's authority or advice:
> *You needn't write me another cheque. Just change the date and initial it.*
> *I'm in no hurry. He needn't send it by air. He can send it by sea.*
> *You needn't do it by hand. I'll lend you my machine.*
> *You needn't call me Mr Jones. We all use first names here.*
> COLLEGE LECTURER: *You needn't type your essays but you must write legibly.*

2   The other forms express external authority:

> *Tom doesn't have to wear uniform at school.*
> *We don't have to type our essays but we have to write legibly.*
> *When I'm an old age pensioner I won't have to pay any more*
> *bus fares.*
> *Ann hasn't got to go/doesn't have to go to this lecture. Attendance*
> *is optional.*
> *When I have a telephone of my own I won't have to waste time*
> *waiting outside these wretched telephone boxes.*
> *Ann doesn't have to cook for herself. She works at a hotel and gets*
> *all her meals there.*

3   Sometimes, however, **need not** can be used for external authority
also, as an alternative to **won't/don't need to** or **won't/don't have
to** forms. This is particularly common in the first person:

> *I needn't type/I won't/don't have to type this report today. Mr Jones*
> *said that there was no hurry about it.*

Note, however, that though it is possible to use **need not** for a future
habitual action:

> *I'm retiring. After Friday I need never go to the office again.*

it is not possible to use it for a present habitual action:

> *I don't have to queue for my bus. I get on at the terminus.* (**need
> not** could not be used here.)

B   Past

Here the distinction between the speaker's authority and external
authority disappears, and we have a choice of three forms: **didn't have
to, didn't need to** and **hadn't got to**. There is no difference in
meaning, but **hadn't got to** is not normally used for habitual actions.
didn't have to is the most usual form:

> *I didn't have to wait long. He was only a few minutes late.*
> *When he was at university he didn't have to/need to pay anything for*
> *his keep, for he stayed with his uncle.*

151   must, have to and need in the interrogative

	Asking the authority	External authority	
Future	*must I?* etc.	*shall I/we have to?*	*shall I/we need to?*
	need I? etc.	*will he have to?* etc.	*will he need to?* etc.
Present	*must I?* etc.	*do I/we have to?*	*do I/we need to?*
	need I? etc.	*does he have to?* etc.	*does he need to?* etc.
		have I/we (got) to?	
		has he (got) to? etc.	
Past		*did he have to?* etc.	
		did he need to? etc.	
		had he got to? etc.	

Both **need?** and **must?** imply that the person addressed is the
authority concerned. **need?** also implies that the speaker is hoping for a
negative answer: *Must I go, mother?* and *Need I go, mother?* mean the
same, but in the second question the speaker is hoping that his mother
will say *No*. The other interrogative form of **need, do I need?** etc.,
can be used similarly. Note possible answers:

> *Shall I have to go? ~ Yes, you will/No, you won't.*
> *Have I got to go? ~ Yes, you have/No, you haven't.*
> *Does he have to go? ~ Yes, he does/No, he doesn't.*
> *Need I go? ~ Yes, you must/No, you needn't.*
> *Must I go? ~ Yes, you must/No, you needn't.*

152 needn't + perfect infinitive

This structure is used to express an unnecessary action which was
nevertheless performed:

> *I needn't have written to him because he phoned me shortly
> afterwards.* (But I had written, thus wasting my time.)
> *You needn't have brought your umbrella for we are going by car.*
> (You brought your umbrella unnecessarily.)
> *He needn't have left home at 6.00; the train doesn't start till 7.30.*
> (So he will have an hour to wait.)

153 needn't have (done) compared with didn't have/need (to do)

A **needn't have done**: no obligation but action performed
(unnecessarily), i.e. time wasted:

> *You needn't have watered the flowers, for it is going to rain.* (You
> wasted your time.)
> *You needn't have written such a long essay. The teacher only asked
> for 300 words, and you have written 600.*
> *He needn't have bought such a large house. His wife would have been
> quite happy in a cottage.* (waste of money)
> *You needn't have carried all these parcels yourself. The shop would
> have delivered them if you had asked them.*

B **didn't have/need to do**: no obligation, and normally no action:

> *I didn't have to translate it for him for he understands Dutch.*
> *I didn't have to cut the grass myself. My brother did it.* (no obligation
> and no action)

Some people do use **didn't have to/didn't need to** for actions which
were performed. The **have** or **need** is then usually stressed: *You
didn't 'have to give him my name* would then mean 'It wasn't necessary
to give him my name, but you gave it to him'. But the student is
advised to use **needn't have** + past participle when an unnecessary
action was performed:

> *You needn't have given him my name.*

154 needn't, could and should + perfect infinitive

A **needn't** + perfect infinitive is often combined with **could** + perfect infinitive. The use of this combination is best shown by examples:

> *I wanted a copy of the letter, so I typed it twice.* ~ *You needn't have typed it twice. You could have used a carbon.*
> *I walked up six flights of stairs.* ~ *You needn't have walked up; you could have taken the lift.*
> *She stood in a queue to get an Underground ticket.* ~ *But she needn't have stood in a queue. She could have got a ticket from the machine.*

B **needn't have** and **should have** compared
should or **ought to** could be used instead of **need** or **could** in all the examples in A above:

> *She shouldn't have stood in a queue. She should have got tickets from the machine.*

But there is a difference in meaning:

> *She shouldn't have stood in a queue.* (It was wrong or foolish of her to stand in a queue.)
> *She needn't have stood in a queue.* (It was not necessary to do this, but she did it.)

shouldn't have (done) implies criticism.
needn't have (done) does not imply criticism.

155 to need as an ordinary verb, meaning 'require'

As shown in 149, **need** can be conjugated as an ordinary verb. It then has the normal regular forms, but no continuous tense.
to need can be used with an infinitive or with a noun/pronoun object:

> *I need to know the exact size.*
> *How much money do you need? I need £5.*

to need can also be used with the passive infinitive or the gerund in such sentences as:

> *Your hair needs to be cut/needs cutting.*
> *The windows need to be washed/need washing.*

want + gerund can be used instead of **need** here:

> *Your hair wants cutting.*

15 must, have, will and should
for deduction and assumption

156 **must** used for deduction

A Forms
Present
must + present infinitive: *He must live here,* or
must + continuous infinitive: *He must be living here.*
Past
must + perfect infinitive: *He must have lived here,* or
must + continuous perfect infinitive: *He must have been living here.*
Note the difference between the past forms of **must** used for deduction
and the past equivalent of **must** used for obligation: **had to.**
must is not used for negative deduction (see 159) and is not normally
used in the interrogative except when querying a deduction with **must:**
> *There's a lot of noise from upstairs. It must be Tom.* ~ *Why must it
> be Tom? Other people use that flat.*

B Examples
> *He has a house in London and another in Paris, so he must be rich.*
> *I've had no sleep for 48 hours.* ~ *You must be exhausted.*
> *He develops his own films. That must save him a lot of money.*
> *I keep meeting him on the bus. He must live/must be living near by.*
> *The police are stopping all cars. They must be looking for the escaped
> prisoner.*
> *What explosion? I didn't hear any.* ~ *You must have heard it! The
> whole town heard it!*
> *He must have taken sleeping pills last night. He didn't wake up till
> lunch time.*
> *I waited under the clock!* ~ *So did I, but I didn't see you! We must
> have been waiting under different clocks.*
> *It was a head-on collision, but the drivers weren't hurt.* ~ *They must
> have been wearing their seat belts.*

157 **must** (deduction) compared to **may/might**

The difference is best seen by examples:

(a) Imagine that we have three keys on a ring and we know that one of
these keys opens the cellar door. We might begin by picking one key
and saying:
> *This may/might be the key.* (Perhaps this is the key.)
But after trying two keys unsuccessfully, we will pick up the third key
and say *This must be the key.* No other choice remains.

(b) *I wonder why Tom hasn't answered my letter.* ~ *He may/might be ill.*
(Perhaps he is ill. But there are other possibilities also: he may be
away or too busy to answer.)
But imagine that Bill never has any visitors. If an ambulance stops at his
door the neighbours will say *Bill must be ill.* This is the only possible
explanation of the arrival of the ambulance.

(c) Similarly, when considering a past action:
He may have come by train. (Perhaps he came by train. But there
are other possibilities: he might have come by taxi or bus.)
But *He must have come by taxi* implies that he had no choice. There was
no other way of making this journey.

158 have/had used for deduction

This is an American usage which is sometimes heard in Britain.
have/had here is chiefly used with **to be**:
There's a tall grey bird fishing in the river. ~ *It has to be/must
be a heron.*
had + **to be** can express the speaker's feeling of certainty in the past:
There was a knock on the door. It had to be Tom. (She was sure it
was Tom.)
had + **to be** can also be an alternative to **must** + perfect infinitive:
I wonder who took the money. ~ *It had to be Tom/It must have been
Tom. He's the only one who was there.*
But, to avoid confusion, the student is advised to stick to the **must**
forms.

159 can't and couldn't used for negative deduction

A Negative deductions about a present event can be expressed by
can't/couldn't with the present infinitive of the verb **be** or with the
continuous infinitive of any verb:
CHILD: *Can I have some sweets? I'm hungry.*
MOTHER: *You can't/couldn't be hungry. You've just had dinner.*

ANN (looking through binoculars): *An aeroplane is pulling up people
from the boat!*
TOM: *It can't/couldn't be an aeroplane. It must be a helicopter.*

He says he's still reading 'The Turn of the Screw'. ~ *He
can't/couldn't still be reading it. I lent it to him ages ago and it's
quite a short book.*

B Negative deductions about a past event are expressed by
can't/couldn't + the perfect infinitive or continuous perfect infinitive
of any verb:
A man answered the phone. I suppose it was her husband. ~ *It
can't/couldn't have been her husband. He's been dead for ages.*

I took a Circle Line train to St Paul's. ~ You can't/couldn't have taken the Circle Line. It doesn't go through St Paul's. You must have been on the Central Line.

couldn't must be used when the deduction is made in the past or introduced by a verb in the past tense:

She said I couldn't have come on the Circle Line.
He said it couldn't be an aeroplane.

Otherwise either **can't** or **couldn't** can be used.

160 will and should for assumption

A **will** used for assumptions about present or past actions

will here can be used with the present infinitive (for non- deliberate actions only) or with the continuous or perfect infinitive:

Ring his home number. He'll be at home now. (I'm sure he's at home.)
He'll be expecting a call from you. (I'm sure he's expecting a call.)
He'll have finished his supper. (I'm sure he has finished his supper.)
It's no use asking Tom; he won't know. (I'm sure he doesn't.)
Will Bill be at the club now, do you think? (Do you think he is?)

B **should** used for assumptions about present or past actions

should here is used mainly with the present infinitive (for non-deliberate actions only) in the affirmative or negative. It is sometimes also possible with the continuous and perfect infinitives:

The plane should be landing now. (I expect it is landing.)
The letter should have arrived by now. (I expect it has arrived.)

Assumptions with **should** are less confident than assumptions with **will**:

Tom should know the address. (I expect Tom knows it.) But
Tom'll know the address. (I'm sure Tom knows it.)
He should have finished by now. (I expect he has finished.) But
He'll have finished by now. (I'm sure he has finished.)

should is not used for assumptions which displease the speaker:

Let's not go shopping now. The shops will be very crowded. (**should** would not be used.)

But for the opposite (agreeable) assumption, either word could be used:

Let's go shopping now. The shops will be/should be fairly empty or
The shops won't be/shouldn't be too crowded.

C **will** and **should** can also express assumptions about the future:

He should/will have plenty of time to get to the station.
They shouldn't/won't have any difficulty in finding the house.

will + present infinitive used for assumptions about the future is not restricted to non-deliberate actions. (See also 209.)

D **ought to** can be used in the same way as **should** in B and C above:

The plane ought to be/should be taking off in a minute.

But **should** is the more usual form.

16 The auxiliaries **dare** and **used**

161 dare

A In the affirmative **dare** is conjugated like an ordinary verb, i.e.
dare/dares in the present, *dared* in the past. But in the negative and
interrogative it can be conjugated either like an ordinary verb or like an
auxiliary, i.e. it is a semi-modal.

Negative:	present	*do/does not dare*	*dare not*
	past	*did not dare*	*dared not*
Interrogative:	present	*do you/does he dare?*	*dare you/he?*
	past	*did you/did he dare?*	*dared you/he?*

The ordinary verb construction is more commonly used.

B Infinitives after **dare**
Negatives and interrogative forms with **do/did** are in theory followed by
the infinitive with **to**, but in practice the **to** is often omitted:
> *He doesn't dare (to) say anything.*
> *Did he dare (to) criticize my arrangements?*

dare I/he/you? etc. and **dare not** forms take the infinitive without **to**:
> *Dare we interrupt?*   *They dared not move.*

When **dare** is preceded by *nobody, anybody* etc. the **to** is optional:
> *Nobody dared (to) speak.*

C **dare** is not much used in the affirmative except in the expression
I daresay. **I daresay** (or **I dare say**) has two idiomatic meanings:

1 'I suppose':
> *I daresay there'll be a restaurant car on the train.*

2 'I accept what you say (but it doesn't make any difference)':
> ENGLISH TOURIST: *But I drive on the left in England!*
> SWISS POLICEMAN: *I daresay you do, but we drive on the right here.*
>
> TRAVELLER: *But the watch was given to me; I didn't buy it.*
> CUSTOMS OFFICER: *I daresay you didn't, but you'll have to pay duty
> on it all the same.*

daresay is used in this way with the first person singular only.

D **how dare(d) you? how dare(d) he/they?** can express indignation:
> *How dare you open my letters?* (I am angry with you for
> opening them.)
> *How dared he complain?* (I am indignant because he complained.)

E **dare** is also an ordinary transitive verb meaning 'challenge' (but only to
deeds requiring courage). It is followed by object + full infinitive:
> MOTHER: *Why did you throw that stone through the window?*
> SON: *Another boy dared me (to throw it).*

162 used

A Form

used is the past tense of a defective verb which has no present tense.
Affirmative: *used* for all persons
Negative: *used not/usedn't* for all persons
Interrogative: *used you/he/they?* etc.
Negative interrogative: *used you not/usedn't you?* etc.
Negative and interrogative can also be formed with **did**:

  didn't use to *did you use to?* *didn't you use to?*

This is a more informal form, common in conversation.
used is followed by the full infinitive, and to remind students of this it is
often referred to as **used to** (just as **have** used for obligation is
referred to as **have to**).

B Use

used is used:

1 To express a discontinued habit or a past situation which contrasts with
the present:

  I used to smoke cigarettes; now I smoke a pipe.
  He used to drink beer; now he drinks wine.
  She usedn't to like Tom but she quite likes him now or
  She used to dislike Tom but she quite likes him now.

used is not normally stressed, but it can be stressed if the speaker
wishes to emphasize the contrast between past and present.

2 To express a past routine or pattern. Here we are not making a
contrast between past and present; we are merely describing
someone's routine during a certain period. Very often there is a
succession of actions. **used to** here is replaceable by **would** (but
would cannot replace **used to** for a discontinued habit etc. as in 1
above). **used** here is always unstressed.

  Tom and Ann were a young married couple. Every morning Tom
  used to kiss Ann and set off for work. Ann used to stand at the
  window and wave goodbye. In the evening she used to welcome him
  home and ask him to tell her about his day.

If we use **would** we have:

  Every morning Tom would kiss Ann and set off for work. Ann would
  stand at the window and wave goodbye etc.

Remember that **used** has no present form. So for present habits or
routines we must use the simple present tense.

163 used as an adjective: to be/become/get used to

used can also be an adjective meaning 'accustomed'. It is then preceded by **be, become** or **get** in any tense and followed by the preposition **to** + noun/pronoun or gerund:

I am used to noise.
I am used to working in a noisy room.
You will soon get used to the electric typewriters.
You will soon get used to typing on electric typewriters.
They soon got used to the traffic regulations.
They soon got used to driving on the left.

I am used to . . . etc. is a psychological statement. *I am used to working in a noisy room* means that I have worked in a noisy room, so the noise doesn't bother me; I don't mind it. *You'll soon get used to typing on electric typewriters* means that after you have used them for a while you will find them quite easy to use.

Very often *I'm used to it* has the meaning 'I don't mind it/It doesn't give me any trouble', as in the above examples. But it can work the other way. Imagine our canteen serves only tea with its meals. A Frenchman, newly arrived from France, might say:

I'm used to wine with my meals, so I find these lunches rather unsatisfying.

Do not confuse subject + **be/become/get** + **used to** with subject + **used to** (see 162).

In the first, **used** is an adjective and **to** is a preposition.

In the second, **used** is a verb and **to** is part of the following infinitive.

Do not confuse these forms with the regular verb **to use** /ju:z/ meaning 'employ'.

17 The present tenses

There are two present tenses in English:
The present continuous: *I am working.*
The simple present: *I work.*

The present continuous

164 Form

The present continuous tense is formed with the present tense of the
auxiliary verb **be** + the present participle:

A Affirmative

Affirmative	Negative	Interrogative
I am working	*I am not working*	*am I working?*
you are working	*you are not working*	*are you working?*
he/she/it is working	*he/she/it is not working*	*is he/she/it working?*
we are working	*we are not working*	*are we working?*
you are working	*you are not working*	*are you working?*
they are working	*they are not working*	*are they working?*

Negative interrogative: *am I not working? are you not working?*
is he not working? etc.

B Contractions: the verb **be** can be contracted as shown in 102 B, so the
present continuous of any verb can be contracted:

Affirmative	Negative	Negative interrogative
I'm working	*I'm not working*	*aren't I working?*
you're working	*you're not/you aren't working*	*aren't you working?*
he's working etc.	*he's not/he isn't working* etc.	*isn't he working?* etc.

Note the irregular contraction *aren't I?* for *am I not?*

Interrogative contractions: **am, is, are** may be contracted as shown
in 104 B:

> *Why's he working?*   *Where're you working?*

153

165 The spelling of the present participle

A   When a verb ends in a single **e**, this **e** is dropped before **ing**:
   argue, arguing   hate, hating   love, loving
except after **age, dye** and **singe**:
   ageing   dyeing   singeing
and verbs ending in **ee**:
   agree, agreeing   see, seeing

B   When a verb of one syllable has one vowel and ends in a single
consonant, this consonant is doubled before **ing**:
   hit, hitting   run, running   stop, stopping
Verbs of two or more syllables whose last syllable contains only one
vowel and ends in a single consonant double this consonant if the stress
falls on the last syllable:
   ad'mit, admitting   be'gin, beginning   pre'fer, preferring
but
   'budget, budgeting   'enter, entering
(stress not on the last syllable).
A final **l** after a single vowel is, however, always doubled:
   signal, signalling   travel, travelling
except in American English.

C   **ing** can be added to a verb ending in **y** without affecting the spelling of
the verb:
   carry, carrying   enjoy, enjoying   hurry, hurrying

166 Uses of the present continuous tense

A   For an action happening now:
   It is raining.
   I am not wearing a coat as it isn't cold.
   Why are you sitting at my desk?
   What's the baby doing? ~ He's tearing up a £5 note.

B   For an action happening about this time but not necessarily at the
moment of speaking:
   I am reading a play by Shaw. (This may mean 'at the moment of
   speaking' but may also mean 'now' in a more general sense.)
   He is teaching French and learning Greek. (He may not be doing
   either at the moment of speaking.)
When two continuous tenses having the same subject are joined by
and, the auxiliary may be dropped before the second verb, as in the
above example. This applies to all pairs of compound tenses:
   She was knitting and listening to the radio.

C   For a definite arrangement in the near future (the most usual way of expressing one's immediate plans):

I'm meeting Peter tonight. He is taking me to the theatre.
Are you doing anything tomorrow afternoon? ~ Yes, I'm playing tennis with Ann.

Note that the time of the action must always be mentioned, as otherwise there might be confusion between present and future meanings. **come** and **go**, however, can be used in this way without a time expression. (See 202 B.)

167   Other possible uses of the present continuous

A   With a point in time to indicate an action which begins before this point and probably continues after it:

At six I am bathing the baby. (I start bathing him before six.)
Similarly with a verb in the simple present:
They are flying over the desert when one of the engines fails.
The present continuous is rarely used in this way except in descriptions of daily routine and in dramatic narrative, but the past continuous is often combined with a point in time or a verb in the simple past.
(See 179 C, E.)

B   With **always**:

He is always losing his keys.
This form is used, chiefly in the affirmative:

1   For a frequently repeated action, usually when the frequency annoys the speaker or seems unreasonable to him: *Tom is always going away for weekends* (present continuous) would imply that he goes away very often, probably too often in the speaker's opinion. But it does not necessarily mean that he goes away every weekend. It is not a literal statement. Compare with **always** + simple present:

Tom always goes away at weekends =
Tom goes away every weekend. (a literal statement)
I/we + **always** + continuous tense is also possible here. The repeated action is then often accidental:
I'm always making that mistake.

2   For an action which appears to be continuous:

He's always working = He works the whole time.
This sort of action quite often annoys the speaker but doesn't necessarily do so: *He's always reading* could imply that he spends too much time reading, but could also be said in a tone of approval.
The first person could be used here too. The action then, like the other actions here in 2, is usually deliberate.

168 Verbs not normally used in the continuous tenses

Stative verbs (expressing a state) in contrast to action verbs (e.g. *run, strike, wink*) are not normally used in the continuous tenses and have only one present tense, the simple present. These verbs can be grouped as follows:

A   Verbs of the senses (involuntary actions): **feel, hear, see, smell**; also **notice** and **observe** (= notice), and **feel, look, smell, taste** used as link verbs (see 18 B, C).
For **feel, look, smell, taste**, see also 169. For **hear** and **see**, see also 170.
Verbs such as **gaze, listen, look (at), observe** (= watch), **stare** and **watch** imply deliberate use of the senses, and can, of course, be used in the continuous tenses:
Watch! ~ I am watching but I don't see anything unusual.
He is listening to a tape, but he's wearing earphones so nobody else hears it.

B   Verbs expressing feelings and emotions, e.g. **admire** (= respect), **adore, appreciate** (= value), **care for** (= like), **desire, detest, dislike, fear, hate, like, loathe, love, mind** (= care), **respect, value, want, wish**.
But the continuous can be used with **admire** meaning 'look at with admiration', **appreciate** meaning 'increase in value', **care for** meaning 'look after', **long for, mind** meaning 'look after/concern oneself with', **value** meaning 'estimate the financial worth of', **enjoy** and sometimes **like/love** meaning 'enjoy', and **hate** meaning the opposite, though it is safer to use the simple tenses with **like, love** and **hate**:
He's enjoying his holiday in the Arctic. He hates touristy places and he doesn't mind the cold.
I'm minding my own business.
How are you liking/Do you like your new job? ~
I'm hating it/I hate it. I just don't like work, you see.

C   Verbs of mental activity, e.g. **agree, appreciate** (= understand), **assume, believe, expect** (= think), **feel** (= think), **feel sure/certain, forget, know, mean, perceive, realize, recall, recognize, recollect, remember, see** (= understand), **see through** someone (= penetrate his attempt to deceive), **suppose, think** (= have an opinion), **trust** (= believe/have confidence in), **understand**.
But the continuous can be used with **appreciate** meaning 'to increase in value'. See also 171 for **think, assume, expect**.

D   Verbs of possession: **belong, owe, own, possess**:
How much do I owe you?

E   The auxiliaries, except **be** and **have** in certain uses.
(See 113 B, 115 B, 123.)

F   **appear** (= seem), **concern, consist, contain, hold** (= contain),
    keep (= continue), **matter, seem, signify, sound** (= seem/appear):
       It concerns us all.   This box contains explosives.
    But **appear** meaning 'to come before the public' can be used in the
    continuous.

169   **feel, look, smell** and **taste** used in the continuous forms

A   **feel**
    feel, when followed by an adjective indicating the subject's emotions or
    physical or mental condition, e.g. *angry/pleased, happy/sad, hot/cold,
    tense/relaxed, nervous/confident*, is normally used in the simple tenses
    but can also be used in the continuous:
       How do you feel/are you feeling? ~ I feel/am feeling better.
    feel meaning 'touch' (usually in order to learn something) can be used
    in the continuous:
       The doctor was feeling her pulse.
    Similarly, **feel for** meaning 'try to find something by touching':
       He was feeling for the keyhole in the dark.
    But **feel** is not used in the continuous when it means 'sense':
       Don't you feel the house shaking?
    when it means 'think':
       I feel you are wrong
    and when it is used as a link verb:
       The water feels cold.

B   **look**
    The continuous is not used with **look** used as a link verb, e.g. *That
    cake looks good*, or with **look on** (= consider), **look up to**
    (= respect) and **look down on** (= despise) (see chapter 38).
    But **look (at), look for/in/into/out** and **look on** (= watch) are
    deliberate actions and can be used in the continuous tenses:
       He is looking for his glasses.
       I'm looking out for a better job.

C   **smell**
    The continuous is not used with **smell** meaning 'perceive a scent/an
    odour', e.g. *I smell gas*, or with **smell** used as a link verb, but can be
    used with **smell** meaning 'sniff at':
       Why are you smelling the milk? Does it smell sour?

D   **taste**
    taste as a link verb is not used in the continuous:
       This coffee tastes bitter. (has a bitter taste)
    But **taste** meaning 'to test the flavour of' can be used in the
    continuous:
       She was tasting the pudding to see if it was sweet enough.

170 **see** and **hear** used in the continuous forms

A **see** can be used in the continuous when it means 'meet by appointment' (usually for business), 'interview':

The director is seeing the applicants this morning.
I am seeing my solicitor tomorrow. (See 202.)

Also when it means 'visit' (usually as a tourist):

Tom is seeing the town/the sights.

It can also be used in the continuous in the following combinations:

see about = make arrangements or enquiries:

We are seeing about a work permit for you. (trying to arrange this)

see to = arrange, put right, deal with:

The plumber is here. He is seeing to the leak in our tank.

see somebody **out** = escort him/her to the door.

see somebody **home** = escort him/her home.

see somebody **to** + place = escort him/her to + place:

ANN: *Is Bill seeing you home after the party?*
MARY: *No, he's just seeing me to my bus.*

see someone **off** = say goodbye to a departing traveller at the starting point of his journey (usually the station, airport etc.):

We're leaving tomorrow. Bill is seeing us off at the airport.

B **hear** can be used in the continuous when it means 'listen formally to' (complaints/evidence etc.):

The court is hearing evidence this afternoon.

hear meaning 'receive news or letters' can also be used in the continuous form but only in the present perfect and future:

I've been hearing all about your accident.
You'll be hearing about the new scheme at our next meeting.

171 **think, assume** and **expect** used in the continuous forms

A **think** can be used in the continuous when no opinion is given or asked for:

What are you thinking about? ~ *I'm thinking about the play we saw last night.* But

What do you think of it? (opinion asked for) ~ *I don't think much of it.* (opinion given)

Tom is thinking of emigrating. What do you think of the idea? ~ *I think it is a stupid idea. He should stay where he is.*

B **assume** can be used in the continuous when it means 'accept as a starting point':

I'm assuming that you have time to do a lot of research.

assume power/control of a country or organization can also be used in the continuous:

The new government is assuming power at once.

C **expect** can be used in the continuous when it means 'await':

I'm expecting a letter.   *She's expecting a baby in May.*

The simple present tense

172 Form

A   In the affirmative the simple present has the same form as the infinitive
but adds an **s** for the third person singular.

Affirmative	Negative	Interrogative	Negative interrogative
I work	*I do not work*	*do I work?*	*do I not work?*
you work	*you do not work*	*do you work?*	*do you not work?*
he/she/it works	*he/she/it does not work*	*does he/she/it work?*	*does he/she/it not work?*
we work	*we do not work*	*do we work?*	*do we not work?*
you work	*you do not work*	*do you work?*	*do you not work?*
they work	*they do not work*	*do they work?*	*do they not work?*

Irregular verbs form this tense in exactly the same way.

B   Contractions: the verb **do** is normally contracted in the negative and
negative interrogative (see 103 A): *I don't work, he doesn't work, don't
I work? doesn't he work?*

C   Spelling notes
Verbs ending in **ss, sh, ch, x** and **o** add **es**, instead of **s** alone, to form
the third person singular:

> *I kiss, he kisses*   *I box, he boxes*
> *I rush, he rushes*   *I do, he does*
> *I watch, he watches*   *I go, he goes*

When **y** follows a consonant we change the **y** into **i** and add **es**:

> *I carry, he carries*   *I copy, he copies*   *I try, he tries*

but verbs ending in **y** following a vowel obey the usual rule:

> *I obey, he obeys*   *I say, he says*

173 The simple present used to express habitual action

A   The main use of the simple present tense is to express habitual actions:

> *He smokes.*   *Dogs bark.*   *Cats drink milk.*

This tense does not tell us whether or not the action is being performed
at the moment of speaking, and if we want to make this clear we must
add a verb in the present continuous tense:

> *He's working. He always works at night.*
> *My dog barks a lot, but he isn't barking at the moment.*

B   The simple present tense is often used with adverbs or adverb phrases
such as: *always, never, occasionally, often, sometimes, usually, every
week, on Mondays, twice a year* etc.:

> *How often do you wash your hair?*
> *I go to church on Sundays.*   *It rains in winter.*

or with time clauses expressing routine or habitual actions.
whenever and **when** (= whenever) are particularly useful:

Whenever it rains the roof leaks.
When you open the door a light goes on.

174 Other uses of the simple present tense

A It is used, chiefly with the verb **say**, when we are asking about or
quoting from books, notices or very recently received letters:

What does that notice say? ~ It says, 'No parking.'
What does the book say? ~ It says, 'Cook very slowly.'
*I see you've got a letter from Ann. What does she say? ~ She says
she is coming to London next week.*
Shakespeare says, 'Neither a borrower nor a lender be.'

Other verbs of communication are also possible:

Shakespeare advises us not to borrow or lend.
A notice at the end of the road warns people not to go any further.

B It can be used in newspaper headlines:

MASS MURDERER ESCAPES   PEACE TALKS FAIL

C It can be used for dramatic narrative. This is particularly useful when
describing the action of a play, opera etc., and is often used by radio
commentators at sports events, public functions etc.:

*When the curtain rises, Juliet is writing at her desk. Suddenly the
window opens and a masked man enters.*

D It can be used for a planned future action or series of actions,
particularly when they refer to a journey. Travel agents use it
a good deal.

*We leave London at 10.00 next Tuesday and arrive in Paris at
13.00. We spend two hours in Paris and leave again at 15.00. We
arrive in Rome at 19.30, spend four hours in Rome etc.*

E It must be used instead of the present continuous with verbs which
cannot be used in the continuous form, e.g. **love, see, believe** etc.,
so that we can say *I love you* but not *I am loving you.* (See 168.)

F It is used in conditional sentences, type 1 (see 221):

If I see Ann I'll ask her.
Unless you take the brake off the car won't move.

G It is used in time clauses
(a) when there is an idea of routine:

As soon as he earns any money he spends it.
She takes the boy to school before she goes to work.

(b) when the main verb is in a future form (see 342):

It will stop raining soon. Then we'll go out. =
When it stops raining we'll go out.

18 The past and perfect tenses

The simple past tense

175 Form

A The simple past tense in regular verbs is formed by adding **ed** to
the infinitive:
Infinitive: *to work*   Simple past: *worked*

Verbs ending in **e** add **d** only:
Infinitive: *to love*   Simple past: *loved*

The same form is used for all persons:
I worked   you worked   he worked   etc.

The negative of regular and irregular verbs is formed with **did not
(didn't)** and the infinitive:
I did not/didn't work
you did not/didn't work   etc.

The interrogative of regular and irregular verbs is formed with **did** +
subject + infinitive:
did I work?   did you work?   etc.

Negative interrogative: *did you not/didn't you work?* etc.

B Spelling notes
The rules about doubling the final consonant when adding **ing** (see 165)
apply also when adding **ed**:
admit, admitted   stop, stopped   travel, travelled
Verbs ending in **y** following a consonant change the **y** into **i** before
adding **ed**:
carry, carried   try, tried
but **y** following a vowel does not change: *obey, obeyed*.

176 Irregular verbs: form

These vary considerably in their simple past form:
Infinitive: *to eat, to leave, to see, to speak*
Simple past: *ate, left, saw, spoke*
The simple past form of each irregular verb must therefore be learnt,
but once this is done there is no other difficulty, as irregular verbs (like
regular verbs) have no inflexions in the past tense.
A list of irregular verbs will be found in chapter 39.

161

177   Use for the relation of past events

A   It is used for actions completed in the past at a definite time. It is
therefore used:

1   for a past action when the time is given:
I met him yesterday.   Pasteur died in 1895.

2   or when the time is asked about:
When did you meet him?

3   or when the action clearly took place at a definite time even though this
time is not mentioned:
The train was ten minutes late.
How did you get your present job?
I bought this car in Montreal.

4   Sometimes the time becomes definite as a result of a question and
answer in the present perfect:
Where have you been? ~ I've been to the opera. ~ Did you enjoy it?
(See 184 A for further examples.)

B   The simple past tense is used for an action whose time is not given but
which (a) occupied a period of time now terminated, or (b) occurred at a
moment in a period of time now terminated. These may be expressed
diagrammatically. TS here stands for time of speaking in the present.

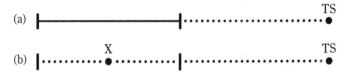

Examples of type (a):
He worked in that bank for four years. (but he does not work
there now)
She lived in Rome for a long time. (but she is not living there now)
Examples of type (b):
My grandmother once saw Queen Victoria.
Did you ever hear Maria Callas sing?
These will be clearer when compared with the present perfect
(see 182-4).

C   The simple past tense is also used for a past habit:
He always carried an umbrella.
They never drank wine.
(For **used to** indicating past habits, see 162.)

D   The simple past is used in conditional sentences, type 2 (see 222).
(For use of the unreal past after *as if, as though, it is time, if only, wish,*
would sooner/rather, see chapters 28, 29.)

The past continuous tense

178 Form

The past continuous tense is formed by the past tense of the verb **to be** + the present participle:

Affirmative	Negative	Interrogative
I was working	*I was not working*	*was I working?*
you were working	*you were not working*	*were you working?*
he/she/it was working	*he/she/it was not working*	*was he/she/it working?*
we were working	*we were not working*	*were we working?*
you were working	*you were not working*	*were you working?*
they were working	*they were not working*	*were they working?*

Negative contractions: *I wasn't working, you weren't working* etc.
Negative interrogative: *was he not/wasn't he working?* etc.

See 165 for spelling of the present participle. Remember that some verbs cannot be used in the continuous tenses (see 168).

179 Main uses of the past continuous tense

A   The past continuous is chiefly used for past actions which continued for some time but whose exact limits are not known and are not important. It might be expressed diagrammatically. '. . . . .' indicates uncertainty about times of starting or finishing:

. . . . . ———————————— . . . . .

B   Used without a time expression it can indicate gradual development:
   It was getting darker.   *The wind was rising.*

C   Used with a point in time, it expresses an action which began before that time and probably continued after it. *At eight he was having breakfast* implies that he was in the middle of breakfast at eight, i.e. that he had started it before eight. *He had breakfast at eight* would imply that he started it at eight.

D   If we replace the time expression with a verb in the simple past tense:
   When I arrived

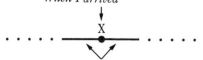

   Tom was talking on the phone
we convey the idea that the action in the past continuous started before

the action in the simple past and probably continued after it. The diagram may help to show this relationship. The action in the simple past is indicated by X. Compare this combination with a combination of two simple past tenses, which normally indicates successive actions:

When he saw me he put the receiver down.

E   We use the continuous tense in descriptions. Note the combination of description (past continuous) with narrative (simple past):

A wood fire was burning on the hearth, and a cat was sleeping in front of it. A girl was playing the piano and (was) singing softly to herself. Suddenly there was a knock on the door. The girl stopped playing. The cat woke up.

180   Other uses of the past continuous

This tense can be used as a past equivalent of the present continuous:

A   Direct speech: *He said, 'I am living in London.'*
Indirect speech: *He said he was living in London.*

B   Just as the present continuous can be used to express a definite future arrangement:

I'm leaving tonight. I've got my plane ticket.

so the past continuous can express this sort of future in the past:

He was busy packing, for he was leaving that night. (The decision to leave had been made some time previously.)

C   The past continuous with **always**:

He was always ringing me up.   *He was always working.*

(See 167 B for present continuous with **always**.)

181   Past continuous as an alternative to the simple past

The past continuous can be used as an alternative to the simple past to indicate a more casual, less deliberate action:

I was talking to Tom the other day.

The past continuous here gives the impression that the action was in no way unusual or remarkable. It also tends to remove responsibility from the subject. In the above example it is not clear who started the conversation, and it does not matter. Note the contrast with the simple past tense, *I talked to Tom*, which indicates that I took the initiative. Similarly:

From four to six Tom was washing the car.

This would indicate that this was a casual, possibly routine action. Compare with:

From four to six Tom washed the car. (implying a deliberate action by Tom)

Note that continuous tenses are used only for apparently continuous uninterrupted actions. If we divide the action up, or say how many times it happened, we must use the simple past:

I talked to Tom several times.   Tom washed both cars.

But we may, of course, use the continuous for apparently parallel actions:

Between one and two I was doing the shopping and walking the dog.

This tense is normally used in this way with a time expression such as *today, last night, in the afternoon,* which could either be regarded as points in time or as periods. Periods can also be indicated by exact times as shown above.

In questions about how a period was spent, the continuous often appears more polite than the simple past: *What were you doing before you came here?* sounds more polite than *What did you do before you came here?*

On the other hand, *What were you doing in my room?* could indicate a feeling that I think you had no right to be there, while *What did you do in my room?* could never give this impression.

The present perfect tense

182 Form and use

A   Form

The present perfect tense is formed with the present tense of **have** + the past participle: *I have worked* etc.

The past participle in regular verbs has exactly the same form as the simple past, i.e. *loved, walked* etc. (see spelling rules, chapter 37).

In irregular verbs, the past participles vary (see 364).

The negative is formed by adding **not** to the auxiliary.

The interrogative is formed by inverting the auxiliary and subject.

Affirmative	Negative	Interrogative
I have worked	*I have not worked*	*have I worked?*
you have worked	*you have not worked*	*have you worked?*
he/she/it has worked	*he/she/it has not worked*	*has he/she/it worked?*
we have worked	*we have not worked*	*have we worked?*
you have worked	*you have not worked*	*have you worked?*
they have worked	*they have not worked*	*have they worked?*

Negative interrogative: *has he not worked?* etc.

Contractions: *have/has* and *have not/has not* can be contracted thus (see 118): *I've worked, you haven't worked, hasn't he worked?* etc. Affirmative contracted forms are often almost inaudible in speech. **have?** and **has?** may also be contracted as shown in 104 B:

Where've you been?   What's he done?

B Use

This tense may be said to be a sort of mixture of present and past. It always implies a strong connexion with the present and is chiefly used in conversations, letters, newspapers and television and radio reports.

183 The present perfect used with **just** for a recently completed action

He has just gone out = *He went out a few minutes ago.*
This is a special use of this tense. **just** must be placed between the auxiliary and the main verb. This combination is used chiefly in the affirmative, though the interrogative form is possible:

Has he just gone out?
It is not normally used in the negative.

184 The present perfect used for past actions whose time is not definite

A The present perfect is used for recent actions when the time is not mentioned:

I have read the instructions but I don't understand them.
Have you had breakfast? ~ No, I haven't had it yet.
Compare with:

I read the instructions last night. (time given, so simple past)
Did you have breakfast at the hotel? (i.e. before you left the hotel: simple past)
Note possible answers to questions in the present perfect:

Have you seen my stamps? ~ Yes, I have/No, I haven't or
Yes, I saw them on your desk a minute ago.
Have you had breakfast? ~ Yes, I have or
No, I haven't had it yet or
Yes, I had it at seven o'clock or
Yes, I had it with Mary. (time implied)

B Recent actions in the present perfect often have results in the present:

Tom has had a bad car crash. (He's probably still in hospital.)
The lift has broken down. (We have to use the stairs.)
I've washed the car. (It looks lovely.)
But actions expressed by the simple past without a time expression do not normally have results in the present:

Tom had a bad crash. (but he's probably out of hospital now)
The lift broke down. (but it's probably working again now)
I washed the car. (but it may be dirty again now)
Actions expressed by the present perfect + **yet** usually have results in the present:

He hasn't come yet. (so we are still waiting for him)

C It can also be used for actions which occur further back in the past, provided the connexion with the present is still maintained, that is that the action could be repeated in the present:

I have seen wolves in that forest

implies that it is still possible to see them, and

John Smith has written a number of short stories

implies that John Smith is still alive and can write more.

If, however, the wolves have been killed off and John Smith is dead we would say:

I saw wolves in that forest once/several times or

I used to see wolves here and

John Smith wrote a number of short stories.

Note also that when we use the present perfect in this way we are not necessarily thinking of any one particular action (the action may have occurred several times) or of the exact time when the action was performed. If we are thinking of one particular action performed at a particular time we are more likely to use the simple past.

185 The present perfect used for actions occurring in an incomplete period

A This may be expressed by the following diagram:

Each X represents an action.
TS stands for 'time of speaking' in the present.

B An incomplete period may be indicated by *today* or *this morning/ afternoon/evening/week/month/year/century* etc.

Note that the present perfect can be used with *this morning* only up to about one o'clock, because after that *this morning* becomes a completed period and actions occurring in it must be put into the simple past:

(at 11 a.m.) *Tom has rung up three times this morning already.*

(at 2 p.m.) *Tom rang up three times this morning.*

Similarly, *this afternoon* will end at about five o'clock:

(at 4 p.m.) *I haven't seen Tom this afternoon.*

(at 6 p.m.) *I didn't see Tom this afternoon.*

The present perfect used with an incomplete period of time implies that the action happened or didn't happen at some undefined time during this period:

Have you seen him today? (at any time today) ~ *Yes, I have/ Yes, I've seen him today.* (at some time during the day)

But if we know that an action usually happens at a certain time or in a certain part of our incomplete period we use the simple past tense. If my alarm clock normally goes off at six, I might say at breakfast:

My alarm clock didn't go off this morning.

Imagine that the postman normally comes between nine and ten. From nine till ten we will say:

Has the postman come yet/this morning?

But after this nine to ten period we will say:

Did the postman come this morning?

We use the past tense here because we are thinking about a complete period of time even though we do not mention it.

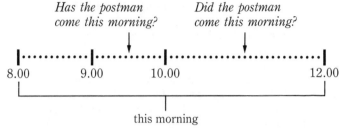

C **lately, recently** used with the present perfect also indicate an incomplete period of time.

In the sentences *Has he been here lately/recently?* and *He hasn't been here lately/recently*, **lately/recently** means 'at any time during the last week/month etc.'; and in *He has been here recently*, **recently** means 'at some undefined time during the last week/month etc.'

lately is less usual with the affirmative, except for actions covering periods of time:

There have been some changes lately/recently.

He's had a lot of bad luck lately/recently.

recently, used with a simple past tense, means 'a short time ago':

He left recently = He left a short time ago.

D The present perfect can be used similarly with *ever, never, always, occasionally, often, several times* etc. and *since* + a point in time, *since* + clause, or *since*, adverb:

1 ANN: *Have you ever fallen off a horse?*
   TOM: *Yes, I've fallen off quite often/occasionally.*
   But if Tom's riding days are over, we would have:
   ANN: *Did you ever fall off a horse?* (past tense)
   TOM: *Yes, I did occasionally/frequently.*

2 *I haven't seen him since November.*
   Has he written since he left home?
   We had a letter last week. We haven't heard since.
   I've since changed my mind = I've changed my mind since then.

3 The present perfect can be used here for habitual actions:
   They've always answered my letters.
   I've never been late for work.

   Sometimes these appear to be continual rather than repeated actions:
   Since my accident I have written with my left hand.
   I've worn glasses since my childhood.

We can then use **for** + a period of time as an alternative to **since** +
a point in time:

> *I've used my left hand for a month now.*
> *I've worn glasses for ten years.* (See 186.)

4 Note also sentences of this type:

> *This is the best wine I have ever drunk.*
> *This is the worst book I have ever read.*
> *This is the easiest job I have ever had.*

We can use this construction, without *ever*, with *the first, the second* etc.
and *the only*:

> *It/This is the first time I have seen a mounted band.*
> *It is only the second time he has been in a canoe.*
> *This is the only book he has written.*

186 The present perfect used for an action which lasts throughout an incomplete period

Time expressions include *for, since* (see 187), *all day/night/week,*
all my etc. *life, all the time, always, lately, never, recently.*

A The action usually begins in the past and continues past the time of
speaking in the present:

> *He has been in the army for two years.* (He is still in the army.)
> *I have smoked since I left school.* (I still smoke.)
> *We have waited all day.* (We are still waiting.)
> *He has lived here all his life.* (He still lives here.)
> *He has always worked for us.* (He still works for us.)

This type of action might be expressed by a diagram thus:

Compare the above sentences with:

> *He was in the army for two years.* (He is not in the army now.)
> *I smoked for six months.* (and then stopped smoking)
> *He lived here all his life.* (Presumably he is now dead.)

In each of the last three examples we are dealing with a completed
period of time:

so the simple past tense is used (see 177 B).

B Sometimes, however, the action finishes at the time of speaking:

> ANN (on meeting someone): *I haven't seen you for ages.*
> (but I see you now)
> *This room hasn't been cleaned for months.* (but we are
> cleaning it now)
> *It has been very cold lately but it's just beginning to get warmer.*

This type of action could be expressed by a diagram thus:

TS

C   Verbs of knowing, believing and understanding cannot be used in the
     present perfect except as shown in A above:
     I have known him for a long time.
     I have never believed their theories.
     So recent actions, even when the time is not mentioned, must be
     expressed by the simple past:
     Did you know that he was going to be married? (*Have you known*
     would not be possible) and
     Hello! I didn't know you were in London. How long have you been
     here?
     think and **wonder** however can be used as in 185 D:
     I have sometimes thought that I should have emigrated.
     I have often wondered why he didn't marry her.

D   Note that questions/answers such as:
     How long have you been here? ~ I've been here six months
     will normally be followed by general inquiries in the present perfect
     about actions occurring within the period mentioned, which is regarded
     as an incomplete period of time:

TS

because the action of staying, being etc., is not yet finished:
     Have you been to the zoo/the theatre/the museums/the casino?
     Have you enrolled in a school/found a job/met many people?
The answers will be in the same tense if no time is mentioned,
otherwise they will be in the simple past tense:
     Yes, I have (been to the zoo etc.) or
     Yes, I went there last week.
     No, I haven't enrolled yet or
     Yes, I enrolled on Monday/this morning.

187 The present perfect used with **for** and **since**

A   **for** is used with a period of time: *for six days, for a long time.*
     for used with the simple past tense denotes a terminated period
     of time:
     We lived there for ten years. (but we don't live there now)
     for used with the present perfect denotes a period of time extending
     into the present:
     We have lived in London for ten years. (and still live there)
     for can sometimes be omitted, especially after *be, live* and *wait*:
     We've been here an hour/two days.

for (of time) is not used before expressions beginning with *all*:
   They've worked all night.

B   **since** is used with a point or period in time and means 'from
   then to the time of speaking'. It is always used with a perfect
   tense, except as shown in D below and in 188.
   She has been here since six o'clock. (and is still here)
   We've been friends since our schooldays.

C   Note that there is a difference between **last** and **the last**. Compare:
   (a) *I have been here since last week (month, year* etc.) and
   (b) *I have been here for the last week.*
   last week, in (a), means a point in time about seven days ago.
   the last week, in (b), means the period of seven days just completed.

D   **since** + clause:
   I've worked here since I left school
   ever since (adverb) can be used alone in end position:
   He had a bad fall last year and has been off work ever since.

88   **it is** + period + **since** + past or perfect tense

We can say:
   It is three years since I (last) saw Bill or
   It is three years since I have seen Bill.
   I last saw Bill three years ago or
   I haven't seen Bill for three years.
   It is two months since Tom (last) smoked a cigarette or
   It is two months since Tom has smoked a cigarette.
   He last smoked a cigarette two months ago or
   He hasn't smoked a cigarette for two months.
We can use the **it is . . . since** construction without the adverb *last*:
   It is two years since he left the country.
This, however, is replaceable only by:
   He left the country two years ago.
We could not use a negative present perfect here as in the sentence
about Bill above. *He hasn't been (living) in this country for the last two
years* is possible but isn't an exact equivalent of *He left two years ago.*
This construction can be used in the past:
   *He invited me to go riding with him. But it was two years since I had
   ridden a horse.* (I hadn't ridden a horse for two years previous to
   the invitation so I wasn't sure that I would enjoy it.)

189   Further examples of the use of the present perfect and
   simple past

A   TOM (visiting Philip for the first time): *I didn't know you lived in a
   houseboat.*
   PHILIP: *I've always lived in a houseboat. I was born in one.*

I thought you were still on holiday. When did you get back? ~ I came back last week.
Has your term started yet? ~ Yes, it started on Monday.

B Note that a conversation about a past action often begins with a question and answer in the present perfect, but normally continues in the simple past, even when no time is given. This is because the action first mentioned has now become definite in the minds of the speakers:

Where have you been? ~ I've been to the cinema. ~
What did you see?/What was the film? ~ (I saw) 'Amadeus'. ~
Did you like it?

HUSBAND: *Where have you been?*
WIFE: *I've been at the sales.*
HUSBAND: *What have you bought?/What did you buy?*
WIFE: *I have bought/I bought you some yellow pyjamas.*
HUSBAND: *Why did you buy yellow? I hate yellow.*

C The present perfect is often used in newspapers and broadcasts to introduce an action which will then be described in the simple past tense. The time of the action is very often given in the second sentence:

Thirty thousand pounds' worth of jewellery has been stolen from Jonathan Wild and Company, the jewellers. The thieves broke into the flat above some time during Sunday night and entered the shop by cutting a hole in the ceiling.

But even if the time of the action is not given the past tense will normally be used in the second sentence:

Two prisoners have escaped from Dartmoor. They used a ladder which had been left behind by some workmen, climbed a twenty-foot wall and got away in a stolen car.

D The present perfect is often used in letters:

I am sorry I haven't written before but I've been very busy lately as Tom has been away.
We have carefully considered the report which you sent us on 26 April, and have decided to take the following action.

The present perfect continuous tense

190 Form

This tense is formed by the present perfect of the verb **to be** + the present participle:
Affirmative: *I have been working, he has been working* etc.
Negative: *I have not/haven't been working* etc.
Interrogative: *have I been working?* etc.
Negative interrogative: *have I not/haven't I been working?* etc.

191 Use

This tense is used for an action which began in the past and is still continuing:

or has only just finished:

> *I've been waiting for an hour and he still hasn't turned up.*
> *I'm so sorry I'm late. Have you been waiting long?*

Remember that a number of verbs are not normally used in the continuous form (see 168), but that some of these can be used in this form in certain cases (see 169-71). We can therefore say:

> *Tom has been seeing about a work permit for you.*
> *She has been having a tooth out.*
> *I've been thinking it over.*
> *I've been hearing all about his operation.*

In addition, the verb *want* is often used in this tense, and *wish* is also possible:

> *Thank you so much for the binoculars. I've been wanting a pair*
> *for ages.*

The present perfect continuous tense does not exist in the passive. The nearest passive equivalent of a sentence such as *They have been repairing the road* would normally be *The road has been repaired lately* (present perfect passive), which is not exactly the same thing.

192 Comparison of the present perfect simple and continuous

A   An action which began in the past and is still continuing or has only just finished can, with certain verbs, be expressed by either the present perfect simple or the present perfect continuous. Verbs which can be used in this way include *expect, hope, learn, lie, live, look, rain, sleep, sit, snow, stand, stay, study, teach, wait, want, work*:

> *How long have you learnt English?*
> *How long have you been learning English?*
> *He has slept for ten hours.*
> *He has been sleeping for ten hours.*
> *It has snowed for a long time.*
> *It has been snowing for a long time.*

This is not of course possible with verbs which are not used in the continuous forms (see 168), i.e. the present perfect continuous could not replace the simple present perfect in the following examples:

> *They've always had a big garden.*
> *How long have you known that?*
> *He's been in hospital since his accident.*

Notice also that the present perfect continuous can be used with or without a time phrase. In this way it differs from the simple present perfect, which can only express this type of action if a time phrase is added such as *for six days, since June, never*. When used without a time expression of this kind, the simple present perfect refers to a single completed action.

B A repeated action in the simple present perfect can sometimes be expressed as a continuous action by the present perfect continuous:

> *I've written six letters since breakfast.*
> *I've been writing letters since breakfast.*
> *I have knocked five times. I don't think anyone's in.*
> *I've been knocking. I don't think anybody's in.*

Note that the present perfect continuous expresses an action which is apparently uninterrupted; we do not use it when we mention the number of times a thing has been done or the number of things that have been done.

C There is, however, a difference between a single action in the simple present perfect and an action in the present perfect continuous:
(a) *I've polished the car* means that this job has been completed.
(b) *I've been polishing the car* means 'this is how I've spent the last hour'. It does not necessarily mean that the job is completed.

Note also that a single action in the present perfect continuous continues up to the time of speaking, or nearly up to this time:

> *He's been taking photos* (he's probably still carrying his camera) but
> *He has taken photos.* (This action may or may not be very recent.)

193 Some more examples of the present perfect and the present perfect continuous

> A: *I haven't seen your brother lately. Has he gone away?*
> B: *Yes, he's/he has been sent to America.*
> A: *When did he go?*
> B: *He went last month.*
> A: *Have you had any letters from him?*
> B: *I haven't, but his wife has been hearing from him regularly.*
> A: *Does she intend to go out and join him?*
> B: *They've been thinking about it but haven't quite decided yet. Unfortunately they've had a lot of expense lately and perhaps haven't got the money for her fare.*

> TOM: *What have you done with my knife?* (Where have you put it?)
> ANN: *I put it back in your drawer.*
> TOM (taking it out): *But what have you been doing with it? The blade's all twisted! Have you been using it to open tins?*

> A: *Do you see those people on that little sandy island? They've been waving handkerchiefs for the last half hour. I wonder why.*
> B: *They need help. The tide's coming in and very soon that little island will be under water. Have you been sitting here calmly and doing nothing to help them?*
> A: *I've never been here before. I didn't know about the tides.*

The past perfect tense

194 Form and use

A Form
This tense is formed with **had** and the past participle:
Affirmative: *I had/I'd worked* etc.
Negative: *I had not/hadn't worked* etc.
Interrogative: *had I worked?* etc.
Negative interrogative: *had I not/hadn't I worked?* etc.

B Use

1 The past perfect is the past equivalent of the present perfect.
Present: *Ann has just left. If you hurry you'll catch her.* (See 183.)
Past: *When I arrived Ann had just left.*
Present: *I've lost my case.* (See 184.)
Past: *He had lost his case and had to borrow Tom's pyjamas.*
Unlike the present perfect the past perfect is not restricted to actions
whose time is not mentioned. We could therefore say:
   He had left his case on the 4.40 train.

2 The present perfect can be used with *since/for/always* etc. for an action
which began in the past and is still continuing or has only just finished
(see 186). The past perfect can be used similarly for an action which
began before the time of speaking in the past, and
(a) was still continuing at that time or
(b) stopped at that time or just before it.
But note that the past perfect can also be used:
(c) for an action which stopped some time before the time of speaking.

Examples of types (a), (b) and (c) are given below:
   (a) *Bill was in uniform when I met him. He had been a soldier for
   ten years/since he was seventeen, and planned to stay in the army till
   he was thirty.*
   *Ann had lived in a cottage for sixty years/ever since she was born,
   and had no wish to move to a tower block.* (The past perfect
   continuous tense *had been living* would also be possible here.)
   (b) *The old oak tree, which had stood in the churchyard for 300
   years/since before the church was built, suddenly crashed to the
   ground.* (The past perfect continuous tense *had been standing*
   would also be possible here.)
   *Peter, who had waited for an hour/since ten o'clock, was very angry
   with his sister when she eventually turned up.* (had been waiting
   would also be possible.)
   (c) *He had served in the army for ten years; then he retired and
   married. His children were now at school.*
Here we cannot use either **since** or the past perfect continuous. Note
also that the past perfect here has no present perfect equivalent. If we
put the last verb in this sentence into the present tense the other

tenses will change to the simple past.

He served in the army for ten years; then retired and married. His children are now at school.

These structures are shown below in diagram form, with the line AB for the action in the past perfect, and TS for the time of speaking in the past:

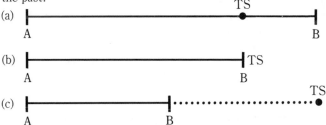

(See also 196 for the use of the past perfect in indirect speech.)

3 The past perfect is also the past equivalent of the simple past tense, and is used when the narrator or subject looks back on earlier action from a certain point in the past:

Tom was 23 when our story begins. His father had died five years before and since then Tom had lived alone. His father had advised him not to get married till he was 35, and Tom intended to follow this advice.

I had just poured myself a glass of beer when the phone rang. When I came back from answering it the glass was empty. Somebody had drunk the beer or thrown it away.

He met her in Paris in 1977. He had last seen her ten years before. Her hair had been grey then; now it was white. Or

He met her in 1967 and again ten years later. Her hair, which had been grey at their first meeting, was now white.

But if we merely give the events in the order in which they occurred no past perfect tense is necessary:

Tom's father died when Tom was eighteen. Before he died he advised Tom not to marry till he was 35, and Tom at 23 still intended to follow this advice.

He met her first in 1967 when her hair was grey. He met her again in 1977/He didn't meet her again till 1977. Her hair was now white.

There is no looking back in the above two examples so no reason for a past perfect.

Note the difference of meaning in the following examples:

She heard voices and realized that there were three people in the next room.

She saw empty glasses and cups and realized that three people had been in the room. (They were no longer there.)

He arrived at 2.30 and was told to wait in the VIP lounge.

He arrived at 2.30. He had been told to wait in the VIP lounge.

In the third example he received his instructions after his arrival. In the fourth he received them before arrival, possibly before the journey started.

195 Past and past perfect tenses in time clauses

A Clauses with **when**

When one past action follows another, *He called her a liar, She smacked his face,* we can combine them by using **when** and two simple past tenses provided that it is clear from the sense that the second action followed the first and that they did not happen simultaneously:

> *When he called her a liar she smacked his face.*

When two simple past tenses are used in this way there is usually the idea that the first action led to the second and that the second followed the first very closely:

> *When he opened the window the bird flew out.*
> *When the play ended the audience went home.*
> *When he died he was given a state funeral.*

The past perfect is used after **when** when we wish to emphasize that the first action was completed before the second one started:

> *When he had shut the window we opened the door of the cage.* (We waited for the window to be quite shut before opening the cage.)
> *When she had sung her song she sat down.* ('When she sang her song she sat down' might give the impression that she sang seated.)
> *When he had seen all the pictures he said he was ready to leave.* (When he had finished looking at them . . .)

Compare with:

> *When he saw all the pictures he expressed amazement that one man should have painted so many.* (Immediately he saw them he said this.)

The past perfect can be used similarly with **as soon as, the moment, immediately.** (For **as** as a time conjunction, see 332.)

B The past perfect can be used with **till/until** and **before** to emphasize the completion or expected completion of an action. But note that in **till/until** + past perfect + simple past combinations the simple past action may precede the past perfect action; and in **before** + past perfect + simple past combinations the simple past action will always precede the past perfect action:

> *He refused to go till he had seen all the pictures.*
> *He did not wait till we had finished our meal.*
> *Before we had finished our meal he ordered us back to work.*
> *Before we had walked ten miles he complained of sore feet.*

Past perfect tenses in both time clause and main clause are also possible:

> *It was a very expensive town. Before we had been here a week we had spent all our money.*

C **after** is normally followed by a perfect tense:

> *After the will had been read there were angry exclamations.*

D   We have already stated (see 194) that actions viewed in retrospect from a point in the past are expressed by the past perfect tense. If we have two such actions:

> *He had been to school but he had learnt nothing there, so was now illiterate*

and wish to combine them with a time conjunction, we can use **when** etc. with two past perfect tenses:

> *When he had been at school he had learnt nothing, so he was now illiterate.*

But it is more usual to put the verb in the time clause into the simple past:

> *When he was at school he had learnt nothing, . . .*

Similarly:

> *He had stayed in his father's firm till his father died. Then he had started his own business and was now a very successful man.*

E   Verbs of knowing, understanding etc. are not normally used in the past perfect tense in time clauses except when accompanied by an expression denoting a period of time:

> *When she had known me for a year she invited me to tea* but
> *When I knew the work of one department thoroughly I was moved to the next department* or *As soon as I knew* etc.

Compare with:

> *When I had learnt the work of one department I was moved.*

F   Time clauses containing past perfect tenses can be combined with a main verb in the conditional tense, but this is chiefly found in indirect speech, and some examples will be given in the next paragraph.

196   Use of the past perfect in indirect speech

A   Present perfect tenses in direct speech become past perfect tenses in indirect speech provided the introductory verb is in the past tense:

> *He said, 'I've been in England for ten years'* =
> *He said that he had been in England for ten years.*
> *He said, 'When you've worked for a year you'll get a rise'* =
> *He said that when I'd worked for a year I'd get a rise.*
> *She said, 'I'll lend you the book as soon as I have read it myself'* =
> *She said she'd lend me the book as soon as she'd read it herself.*

B   Simple past tenses in direct speech usually change similarly:

> *He said, 'I knew her well'* =
> *He said that he had known her well.*

But there are a number of cases where past tenses remain unchanged (see 309-10).

(For the past perfect after **if** (conditional), see 223; after **wish** and **if only**, see 300; after **as if, as though**, see 292.)

The past perfect continuous tense

197 Form and use

A Form
This tense is formed with **had been** + the present participle. It is therefore the same for all persons:

I had/I'd been working
they had not/hadn't been working
had you been working?
had you not/hadn't you been working?

It is not used with verbs which are not used in the continuous forms, except with **want** and sometimes **wish**:

The boy was delighted with his new knife. He had been wanting one for a long time.

Note that this tense has no passive form. The nearest passive equivalent of a sentence such as *They had been picking apples* would be *Apples had been picked*, which is not the same thing (see B3 below).

B Use
The past perfect continuous bears the same relation to the past perfect as the present perfect continuous bears to the present perfect (see 192)

1 When the action began before the time of speaking in the past, and continued up to that time, or stopped just before it, we can often use either form (see 192 A):

It was now six and he was tired because he had worked since dawn =
It was now six and he was tired because he had been working since dawn.

2 A repeated action in the past perfect can sometimes be expressed as a continuous action by the past perfect continuous (see 192 B):

He had tried five times to get her on the phone.
He had been trying to get her on the phone.

3 But there is a difference between a single action in the simple past perfect and an action in the past perfect continuous (see 192 C):

By six o'clock he had repaired the engine. (This job had been completed.)

He had been repairing the engine tells us how he had spent the previous hour/half hour etc. It does not tell us whether or not the job was completed.

Another difference is that an action in the past perfect continuous continues up to, or beyond, the time of speaking in the past. An action in the past perfect may occur shortly before the time of speaking, but there could be quite a long interval between them:

He had been painting the door. (The paint was probably still wet.)
But
He had painted the door. (Perhaps recently, perhaps some time ago.)

19 The future

198 Future forms

There are several ways of expressing the future in English. The forms are listed below and will be dealt with in the order in which they are given. Students should study them in this order, as otherwise the relationship between them will not be clear.

(a) The simple present (see 199)
(b) **will** + infinitive, used for intention (201)
(c) The present continuous (202)
(d) The **be going to** form (203-6)
(e) The 'future simple' **will/shall** + infinitive (207-10)
(f) The future continuous (211-14)
(g) The future perfect (216 A)
(h) The future perfect continuous (216 B)

For **be** + infinitive used to express future plans, see 114.
For **be about** + infinitive and **be on the point of** + gerund, see 114 C.
Note: Most of the auxiliary verbs are dealt with in chapters 11-16, but **will** + infinitive is an essential part of the future, so we have placed it here. It may seem odd that it has been separated from the future simple but logically it seems best to place it before the present continuous and the **be going to** form.

199 The simple present used for the future

This tense can be used with a time expression for a definite future arrangement:

The boys start school on Monday.   I leave tonight.
instead of the more normal present continuous tense (see 202):
The boys are starting school on Monday.   I'm leaving tonight.
The difference between them is:
(a) The simple present is more impersonal than the continuous. *I'm leaving tonight* would probably imply that I have decided to leave, but *I leave tonight* could mean that this is part of a plan not necessarily made by me.
(b) The simple present can also sound more formal than the continuous. A big store planning to open a new branch is more likely to say *Our new branch opens next week* than *Our new branch is opening next week.*

(c) The simple present is sometimes used where the continuous would sound a bit clumsy, e.g. when speaking of a series of proposed future actions, like plans for a journey; i.e. we say:

We leave at six, arrive in Dublin at ten and take the plane on . . .

instead of:

We are leaving at six, arriving in Dublin at ten and taking the plane on . . .

Note, however, that in a sentence such as *My train leaves at six* we are using the simple present for a habitual action. Here, therefore, the simple present is not replaceable by the continuous.

200 A note on the meaning of future with intention

When we say that a form expresses future with intention we mean that it expresses a future action which will be undertaken by the speaker in accordance with his wishes. **will** + infinitive and the **be going to** form can be used in this way.

When we say that a form expresses future without intention we mean that it merely states that a certain action will happen. We don't know whether it was arranged by the subject or by some other person and we don't know what the subject thinks of it. The present tense and the future continuous tense can be used in this way.

The present continuous tense in the second or third person conveys no idea of intention, though there may be a hint of intention when the first person is used.

The future simple (apart from **will** used as in 201, 205) normally conveys no idea of intention; but see **shall**, 208 B, 234.

201 will + infinitive used to express intention at the moment of decision (see also 205 E2 and E3)

(a) *The phone is ringing. ~ I'll answer it.*

(b) BILL (to waiter): *I'll have a steak, please.* (*would like* is also possible. See 210 B.)

(c) ANN: *I'd better order a taxi for tonight.*

TOM: *Don't bother. I'll drive you.*

(d) MARY (looking at a pile of letters): *I'll answer them tonight.*

(e) PAUL (who is getting fat and tired of paying parking fines): *I know what to do. I'll sell my car and buy a bike.*

(f) ALAN (on receiving a telegram saying his father is ill): *I'll go home tonight/I'll leave tonight.*

For unpremeditated actions, as above, we must use **will** (normally contracted to **'ll**). But note that if after his decision the speaker mentions the action again, he will not use **will**, but **be going to** or the present continuous. (**be going to** is always possible; the present continuous has a more restricted use. See 202.)

For example, imagine that in (b) above a friend, Tom, joins Bill before his food has arrived:

> TOM: *What are you having/going to have?*
> BILL: *I'm having/going to have a steak.*

Similarly, at a later time, in:

(c) Ann might say:
> *Tom is driving me/going to drive me to the airport tonight.*

(d) Mary, however, could only say:
> *I'm going to answer these letters tonight.* (She hasn't made an arrangement with anybody.)

(e) Paul, similarly, could say:
> *I'm going to sell the car*

though when he finds a buyer he can say:
> *I'm selling the car.*

(f) Alan, however, could say:
> *I'm going home tonight*

even though this is, as yet, only a decision. (See 202 B, D.)

(For **will** compared to **be going to**, see 205.)

202 The present continuous as a future form

Note that the time must be mentioned, or have been mentioned, as otherwise there may be confusion between present and future.

A   The present continuous can express a definite arrangement in the near future: *I'm taking an exam in October* implies that I have entered for it; and *Bob and Bill are meeting tonight* implies that Bob and Bill have arranged this. If there has merely been an expression of intention, as in 201 (d) and (e) above, we use the **be going to** form.

B   But with verbs of movement from one place to another, e.g. *arrive, come, drive, fly, go, leave, start, travel*, verbs indicating position, e.g. *stay, remain*, and the verbs *do* and *have* (food or drink), the present continuous can be used more widely. It can express a decision or plan without any definite arrangement. Alan in 201 (f) can therefore say *I'm going home tonight/I'm leaving tonight* even before he has arranged his journey.

Note also:
> *What are you doing next Saturday?* (This is the usual way of asking people about their plans.)

Possible answers:
> *I'm going to the seaside.*
> *The neighbours are coming in to watch television.*
> *I'm not doing anything. I'm staying at home. I'm going to write letters. (I'm writing . . .* would not be possible.)

C   This method of expressing the future cannot be used with verbs which are not normally used in the continuous tenses (see 168). These verbs should be put into the future simple (**will/shall**):

> *I am meeting him tonight* but *I will/shall know tonight.*
> *They are coming tomorrow* but *They will be here tomorrow.*
> *We'll think it over.*

Note, however, that **see**, when it is used for a deliberate action (**see to/about, see someone out/off/home** etc., **see** meaning 'meet by appointment'), can be used in the continuous tenses (see 170):

> *I'm seeing him tomorrow.* (I have an appointment with him.)

to be can be used in the continuous tenses when it forms part of a passive verb:

> *He is being met at the station tonight.*
> *Our new piano is being delivered this afternoon.*

D   More examples of combinations of **will** + infinitive used at the moment of decision (see 201) and the present continuous tense used as a future form:

> ANN: *I'll have to pay £150 rent at the end of this month and I don't know where to find the money.*
> TOM: *Don't worry. I'll lend you £150.*

Later, but before Tom has actually lent the money, Ann will say:

> *Tom is lending me £150.*

> TOM: *Would you like to come to the opera tonight?*
> ANN: *I'd love to. Shall I meet you there?*
> TOM: *No, I'll call for you. About seven?*
> ANN: *OK.*

Later, Ann, telling a friend about this plan, will say:

> *Tom is taking me to the opera tonight. He's calling for me at seven.*

(The be **going to** form could replace the present continuous above.)

E   In conversation, **I/we** + the present continuous negative can sometimes express decisive intention:

> *We're not letting her go alone.* (= We won't let her go . . .)
> *I'm not waiting here any longer.* (= I won't wait . . .)

203   The **be going to** form

A   Form
The present continuous tense of the verb **to go** + the full infinitive:

> *I'm going to buy a bicycle.*
> *She is not going to be there.*
> *Is he going to lecture in English?*

B   This form is used:
(a) For intention (see 204).
(b) For prediction (see 206).

204   The **be going to** form used for intention

The **be going to** form expresses the subject's intention to perform a certain future action. This intention is always premeditated and there is usually also the idea that some preparation for the action has already been made. Actions expressed by the **be going to** form are therefore usually considered very likely to be performed, though there is not the same idea of definite future arrangement that we get from the present continuous.

The following points may be noted:

1   As already shown, **be going to** can be used for the near future with a time expression as an alternative to the present continuous, i.e. we can say:

I'm/I am meeting Tom at the station at six.
I'm/I am going to meet Tom at the station at six.

But note that *I'm meeting Tom* implies an arrangement with Tom. *I'm going to meet Tom* does not: Tom may get a surprise!

2   **be going to** can be used with time clauses when we wish to emphasize the subject's intention:

He is going to be a dentist when he grows up.
What are you going to do when you get your degree?

Normally, however, the future simple (**shall/will**) is used with time clauses. (See 342.)

3   **be going to** can be used without a time expression:

I'm going to play you a Bach fugue.
He is going to lend me his bicycle.

It then usually refers to the immediate or near future.

4   As seen in (2) above, the **be going to** form can be used with the verb **to be**. It is also sometimes found with other verbs not normally used in the continuous tenses:

I am going to think about it.
I'm sure I'm going to like it.

But on the whole it is safer to use the future simple here.

5   Note that it is not very usual to put the verbs **go** and **come** into the **be going to** form. Instead we generally use the present continuous tense: i.e. instead of *I am going to go* we normally say *I am going* and instead of *I am going to come* we very often say *I am coming.*

Note that we can express intention by using **will** + infinitive. This form is compared with **be going to** in 205.

205 Comparison of the use of **be going to** and **will** + infinitive
to express intention

Very often we can use either the **be going to** form or **will** + infinitive,
but there are differences between them, as a result of which there are
occasions when only one of them is possible.

The chief difference is:

A   The **be going to** form always implies a premeditated intention, and
often an intention + plan.
will + infinitive implies intention alone, and this intention is usually,
though not necessarily, unpremeditated.
If, therefore, preparations for the action have been made, we must use
be going to:
I have bought some bricks and I'm going to build a garage.
If the intention is clearly unpremeditated, we must use **will**:
There is somebody at the hall door. ~ I'll go and open it.
(See examples in section E.)
When the intention is neither clearly premeditated nor clearly
unpremeditated, either **be going to** or **will** may be used:
I will/am going to climb that mountain one day.
I won't/am not going to tell you my age.
But **will** is the best way of expressing determination:
I ¹will help you. (with stress on *will*)
This means 'I definitely intend to help you'.

Other differences:

B   As already noted, **will** + infinitive in the affirmative is used almost
entirely for the first person. Second and third person intentions are
therefore normally expressed by **be going to**:
He is going to resign.
Are you going to leave without paying?

C   But in the negative **won't** can be used for all persons. So we can say:
He isn't going to resign or *He won't resign.*
But note that **won't** used for a negative intention normally means
'refuse':
He won't resign = He refuses to resign.
He isn't going to resign normally means 'He doesn't intend to resign'.

D   **be going to**, as already stated, usually refers to the fairly immediate
future. **will** can refer either to the immediate or to the more
remote future.

E   More examples of **be going to** and **will**

1   Examples of **be going to** used to express intention:
*What are you doing with that spade? ~ I am going to plant some
apple trees.*

She has bought some wool; she is going to knit a jumper.
Why are you taking down all the pictures? ~ *I am going to repaper the room.*
Some workmen arrived today with a roller. I think they are going to repair our road.
Why is he carrying his guitar? ~ *He is going to play it in the Underground.*

Note that it would not be possible to substitute **will** for **be going to** in any of the above examples, as in each of them there is clear evidence of premeditation.

2 Examples of **will** + infinitive (see 201):
This is a terribly heavy box. ~ *I'll help you to carry it.*
I've left my watch upstairs. ~ *I'll go and get it for you.*
Who will post this letter for me? ~ *I will.*
Will you lend me £100? ~ *No, I won't.*

3 Some comparisons of **be going to** and **will**
In answer to Tom's remark *There aren't any matches in the house* Ann might reply either *I'm going to get some today* (premeditated decision) or *I'll get some today* (unpremeditated decision). The first would imply that some time before this conversation she realized that there were no matches and decided to buy some. The second would imply that she had not previously decided to buy matches but took the decision now, immediately after Tom's remark.
Similarly, if Ann says *Where is the telephone book?* and Tom says *I'll get it for you* he is expressing a decision made immediately after Ann's question. If he said *I'm going to get it*, it would mean that he had decided to do this before Ann spoke (presumably because he had anticipated that Ann would want it, or needed it for himself).

4 Note that **will/won't** does not have any meaning of intention when it is used as indicated in 209 A-E, i.e. when it is used as part of the future simple **will/shall**. So *He won't resign* can mean *He refuses to resign* or *I don't expect that he will resign*; and in *If he hurries he'll catch up with her*, **will** doesn't express intention but merely states a fact.

206 The **be going to** form used for prediction

A The **be going to** form can express the speaker's feeling of certainty. The time is usually not mentioned, but the action is expected to happen in the near or immediate future:
Look at those clouds! It's going to rain.
Listen to the wind. We're going to have a rough crossing.
It can be used in this way after such verbs as *be sure/afraid, believe, think*:
How pale that girl is! I am sure/I believe/I think she is going to faint.

B Comparison of **be going to** (used for prediction) with **will** (used for probable future)

will is a common way of expressing what the speaker thinks, believes, hopes, assumes, fears etc. will happen (see 209 A):

It will probably be cold/I expect it will be cold.

Tomatoes will be expensive this year/I'm sure tomatoes will be expensive.

will and **be going to** are therefore rather similar and often either form can be used:

It will take a long time to photocopy all the documents =

It is going to take a long time to photocopy all the documents.

But there are two differences:

1 **be going to** implies that there are signs that something will happen, **will** implies that the speaker thinks/believes that it will happen.

2 **be going to** is normally used about the immediate/fairly immediate future; **will** doesn't imply any particular time and could refer to the remote future.

For example, *The lift is going to break down* implies that it is making strange noises or behaving in a strange way; we had better get out on the next floor. *The lift will break down* implies that this will happen some time in the future (perhaps because we always overload our lifts, perhaps because it is an XYZ Company lift and they don't last).

Similarly (of a sick man), *He is going to get better* implies that there are signs of recovery. Perhaps his temperature has gone down. *He will get better* implies confidence in his doctor or in the course of treatment, but promises eventual rather than immediate recovery.

207 The future simple

Form

There is no future tense in modern English, but for convenience we often use the term 'future simple' to describe the form **will/shall** + bare infinitive.

Affirmative	Negative	Interrogative
I will/I'll work or	*I will not/won't work* or	
I shall work	*I shall not/shan't work*	*shall I work?*
you will/you'll work	*you will not/won't work*	*will you work?*
he will/he'll work etc.	*he will not/won't work* etc.	*will he work?* etc.
we will/we'll work or	*we will not/won't work* or	
we shall work	*we shall not/shan't work*	*shall we work?*
you will/you'll work	*you will not/won't work*	*will you work?*
they will/they'll work	*they will not/won't work*	*will they work?*

For interrogative contractions, see 104.

Negative interrogative: *will he not/won't he work?* etc.

208 First person **will** and **shall**

A   Formerly **will** was kept for intention:
> *I will wait for you* = *I intend to wait for you*

and **shall** was used when there was no intention, i.e. for actions where the subject's wishes were not involved:
> *I shall be 25 next week.*
> *We shall know the result next week.* (It will be in the papers.)
> *Unless the taxi comes soon we shall miss our plane.*
> *I'm sure I shan't lose my way.*
> *I shall see Tom tomorrow.* (Perhaps we go to work on
> the same train.)

shall, used as above, is still found in formal English, but is no longer common in conversation. Instead we normally use **will**:
> *I will be 25 next week.*
> *We'll know the result tomorrow.*
> *Unless the taxi comes soon we'll miss the plane.*
> *I'm sure I won't lose my way.*

Sometimes, however, **will** might change the meaning of the sentence. If in *I shall see Tom tomorrow* we replace **shall** by **will**, we have *I will see Tom tomorrow*, which could be an expression of intention. To avoid ambiguities of this kind we use the future continuous tense:
> *I'll be seeing Tom tomorrow.* (See 211-14.)

shall, however, is still used in the interrogative:
In question tags after **let's**: *Let's go, shall we?*
In suggestions: *Shall we take a taxi?*
In requests for orders or instructions: *What shall I do with your mail?*
In speculations: *Where shall we be this time next year?* (Here, though, **will** is also possible.)

B   **shall** for determination
We have already noted (see 201, 205) that determination is normally expressed by **will**. But sometimes public speakers feel that to express determination they need a 'heavier' word, a word not normally used much, and so they say **shall**:
> (in a speech) *We shall fight and we shall win.*

We will fight and we shall win would be equally possible.
shall used in this way sometimes carries the idea of promise which we get in second person **shall**:
> *You shall have a sweet* = *I promise you a sweet.*

(See 234 A.)
In *we shall win* the speaker is promising victory.
shall can be used in this way in ordinary conversation:
> *I shall be there, I promise you.*

But **will** here is equally possible and less trouble for the student. When in doubt use **will**.

209 Uses of the future simple

A To express the speaker's opinions, assumptions, speculations about the future. These may be introduced by verbs such as *assume, be afraid, be/feel sure, believe, daresay, doubt, expect, hope, know, suppose, think, wonder* or accompanied by adverbs such as *perhaps, possibly, probably, surely*, but can be used without them:

(I'm sure) he'll come back.
(I suppose) they'll sell the house.
(Perhaps) we'll find him at the hotel.
They'll (probably) wait for us.

The future simple can be used with or without a time expression.
be going to is sometimes possible here also, but it makes the action appear more probable and (where there is no time expression) more immediate. *He'll build a house* merely means 'this is my opinion', and gives no idea when the building will start. But *He's going to build a house* implies that he has already made this decision and that he will probably start quite soon.

B The future simple is used similarly for future habitual actions which we assume will take place:

Spring will come again.
Birds will build nests.
People will make plans.
Other men will climb these stairs and sit at my desk.
(*will be coming/building/making/climbing/sitting* would also be possible.)

C The future simple is used in sentences containing clauses of condition, time and sometimes purpose:

If I drop this glass it will break. (See 221.)
When it gets warmer the snow will start to melt. (See 342.)
I'm putting this letter on top of the pile so that he'll read it first.
(See 336.)

Note that in an **if**-clause or a time clause we don't use the future simple even when the meaning is future:

He will probably be late but *If he is late . . .* and
It will get warmer soon but *When it gets warmer . . .*

D Verbs not normally used in the continuous tenses, e.g. auxiliary verbs, verbs of the senses, of emotion, thinking, possessing etc. (see 168), usually express the future by the future simple, though **be going to** is sometimes possible:

He'll be here at six.   *You'll have time for tea.*
She'll wonder where you are.   *They'll know tonight.*

E The future simple is used, chiefly in newspapers and news broadcasts, for formal announcements of future plans and for weather forecasts. In conversations such statements would normally be expressed by the present continuous or **be going to** form or, for plans only, by the present continuous:

NEWSPAPER: *The President will open the new heliport tomorrow.*
The fog will persist in all areas.
But the average reader/listener will say:
The President is going to open/is opening . . .
The fog is going to persist/continue . . .

F   **won't** can be used with all persons to express negative intention. So
He won't pay can mean either *He refuses to pay* or *I don't think
he'll pay.*
I/we will can express affirmative intention (see 201), but
he/you/they will do not normally express intention. They may appear
to do so sometimes in such sentences as *My son/brother/husband* etc.
will help you, but the intention may be the speaker's rather than the
subject's.

210 will contrasted with want/wish/would like

A   **will** must not be confused with **want/wish/would like**.
will expresses an intention + a decision to fulfil it:
I will buy it = I intend to buy it/I'm going to buy it.
want/wish/would like merely expresses a desire. They do not give
any information about intended actions. (See also 296, 299.)

B   Note, however, that **I'd like** is often a possible alternative to
I'll have/take:
CUSTOMER (in a shop): *I'd like/I'll have a pound of peas, please.*
DINER (in a restaurant): *I'd like/I'll have the soup, please.*
Both can be used for invitations:
Would you like a drink? or *Will you have a drink?*
When accepting an invitation we can use either form:
I'd like/I'll have a sherry, please.
But the two forms are not interchangeable in the negative, so if we
wish to refuse an invitation we must say:
I won't have anything, thanks or *I don't want anything, thanks.*
wouldn't like means 'would dislike', so could not be used here.

211 The future continuous tense

A   Form
This tense is made up of the future simple of **to be** + the present
participle. In the first person, **will** is more usual than **shall**, except in
the interrogative.

Affirmative	*I/we will/shall be working*
	he/she/it/you/they will be working
Negative	*I/we will/shall not be working*
	he/she/it/you/they will not be working
Interrogative	*shall/will I/we be working?*
	will he/she/it/you/they be working?

Contractions as shown in 207.
Negative interrogative: *will he not/won't he be working?* etc.

B Use

This tense has two uses:
It can be used as an ordinary continuous tense.
It can express a future without intention.

212 The future continuous used as an ordinary continuous tense

Like other continuous tenses it is normally used with a point in time, and expresses an action which starts before that time and probably continues after it. This use is best seen by examples. Imagine a class of students at this moment – 9.30 a.m. We might say:

Now they are sitting in their classroom. They are listening to a tape. This time tomorrow they will be sitting in the cinema. They will be watching a film. On Saturday there is no class. So on Saturday they will not be sitting in the classroom. They will be doing other things. Bill will be playing tennis. Ann will be shopping. George will still be having breakfast.

A continuous tense can also be used with a verb in a simple tense:

Peter has been invited to dinner with Ann and Tom. He was asked to come at eight but tells another friend that he intends to arrive at seven. The friend tries to dissuade him: 'When you arrive they'll still be cooking the meal!'

213 The future continuous used to express future without intention

Example: *I will be helping Mary tomorrow.*
This does not imply that the speaker has arranged to help Mary or that he wishes to help her. It merely states that this action will happen. The future continuous tense used in this way is somewhat similar to the present continuous, but differs from it in the following points.
The present continuous tense implies a deliberate future action. The future continuous tense usually implies an action which will occur in the normal course of events. It is therefore less definite and more casual than the present continuous:

I am seeing Tom tomorrow.
I'll be seeing Tom tomorrow.

The first implies that Tom or the speaker has deliberately arranged the meeting, but the second implies that Tom and the speaker will meet in the ordinary course of events (perhaps they work together).
This difference is not always very important, however, and very often either tense can be used. We can say:

He'll be taking his exam next week or
He is taking his exam next week.
He won't be coming to the party or
He isn't coming to the party.

The present continuous can only be used with a definite time and for the near future, while the future continuous can be used with or without a definite time and for the near or distant future. We can say:

I am meeting him tomorrow but

I'll be meeting him tomorrow/next year/some time. (or without a time expression at all)

214 The future continuous and **will** + infinitive compared

A There is approximately the same difference between **will** + infinitive and the future continuous as between **will** + infinitive and the present continuous. **will** + infinitive expresses future with intention. The future continuous expresses future without intention.
In this sentence:

*I'll **write** to Mr Pitt and tell him about Tom's new house*
the verb in bold type expresses intention. The speaker announces a deliberate future action in accordance with his own wishes. But in the sentence:

*I'll **be writing** to Mr Pitt and I'll tell him about Tom's new house*
the verb in bold type expresses no intention. It is a mere statement of fact and implies that this letter to Mr Pitt will be written either as a matter of routine or for reasons unconnected with Tom's new house. Similarly, *Tom won't cut the grass* means Tom refuses to cut it, while *Tom won't be cutting the grass* is a mere statement of fact, giving no information about Tom's feelings. Perhaps Tom is away, or ill, or will be doing some other job.

B **will** + infinitive can express invitation, request or command:

Will you have a cigarette? (See 210.)

Will you help me to lift the piano? (See 284.)

You will work in this room. (See 282.)

The future continuous can have none of the above meanings:

Will you please bring the piano in here? (request) ~ *Yes sir/OK.*
But

Will you be bringing the piano in here? (question only) ~

Yes, I think I will or *No, I think I'll put it upstairs.*

You will work in this office (command) but

You will be working here. (only a statement)

As before, the present continuous could be used here instead of the future continuous, provided that a time expression was added.

215 Examples of various future forms

A Imagine that we ask five people about their plans for the following Saturday. We say:

What are you doing/going to do on Saturday?

(a) Peter has arranged to play golf with George; so he will say:

I'm playing/going to play golf with George.

(b) Mary has decided to stay at home and make jam; so she will say:
I'm staying/going to stay at home. I'm going to make jam.

(c) Andrew's plans depend on the weather; so he may say:
If it's fine I'll work/I'm going to work in the garden.

(d) Ann hasn't made any plans, but she may say:
Perhaps I'll take/I expect I'll take/I'll probably take/I suppose I'll take my children for a walk.

(e) Bill always has to work on Saturdays; so he will say:
Oh, I'll be working as usual. (No other form would give this exact meaning.)

B   Questions about intentions

These are usually expressed by the present continuous, the **be going to** form or the future continuous. This last tense is a particularly useful interrogative form as it is considered more polite than the others. So if we are continuing to ask our five people questions we may say:

(a) *Where are you playing/are you going to play/will you be playing golf?*

(b) *What kind of jam are you going to make/will you be making?*

will you + infinitive is less usual than the other forms and is rarely found at the beginning of a sentence. (This is to avoid confusion, because **will you** + infinitive at the beginning of a sentence usually introduces a request.) It is however used in conditional sentences and when the speaker is offering something or asking the other person to make a decision:

What will you do if he is not on the plane?
Will you have a drink?
Will you have your meal now or later?

More examples of questions based on the sentences in A above:

(c) If we are questioning Andrew we will probably say:
What are you going to do/What will you be doing in the garden?
(though *What will you do?* would be possible), and
Are you going to cut/Will you be cutting the grass? (*Will you cut the grass?* would sound more like a request.)

(d) To Ann we would probably say:
If you take them, where will you go? (though *where will you be going?* is possible)

(e) To Bill we could say:
Will you be working all day?

This is the only possible form if we wish to convey the idea that Bill works on Saturday because it is the routine, not from choice.

Note that the future continuous must of course be used in questions of the type *What will you be doing this time next week?* regardless of whether the action is intentional or not (see 212).

216   The future perfect and the future perfect continuous

A   The future perfect
Form
will/shall + perfect infinitive for first persons, **will** + perfect infinitive
for the other persons.
Use
It is normally used with a time expression beginning with **by**: *by then,
by that time, by the 24th*:
> *By the end of next month he will have been here for ten years.*
It is used for an action which at a given future time will be in the past,
or will just have finished. Imagine that it is 3 December and David is
very worried about an exam that he is taking on 13 December.
Someone planning a party might say:
> *We'd better wait till 14 December. David will have had his exam by
> then, so he'll be able to enjoy himself.*
Note also:
> *I save £50 a month and I started in January. So by the end of the
> year I will/shall have saved £600.*
> BILL (looking at Tom's cellar): *You've got over 400 bottles. How long
> will that last you? Two years?*
> TOM: *Not a hope. I drink eight bottles a week. I'll have drunk all
> these by the end of this year.*

B   The future perfect continuous
Form
will/shall have been + present participle for the first persons, •
will have been + present participle for the other persons.
Use
Like the future perfect, it is normally used with a time expression
beginning with **by**:
> *By the end of this year he'll have been acting for thirty years.*
The future perfect continuous bears the same relationship to the future
perfect as the present perfect continuous bears to the present perfect,
i.e. the future perfect continuous can be used instead of the future
perfect:

1   When the action is continuous:
> *By the end of the month he will have been living/working/studying
> here for ten years.*

2   When the action is expressed as a continuous action:
> *By the end of the month he will have been training horses/climbing
> mountains for twenty years.*

But if we mention the number of horses or mountains, or divide this
action in any way, we must use the future perfect:
> *By the end of the month he will have trained 600 horses/climbed 50
> mountains.*

20 The sequence of tenses

217 Subordinate clauses

A sentence can contain a main clause and one or more subordinate clauses. A subordinate clause is a group of words containing a subject and verb and forming part of a sentence:

*We knew **that the bridge was unsafe**.*
*He gave it to me **because he trusted me**.*
*He ran faster **than we did**.*
*This is the picture **that I bought in Rome**.*

(In the examples above and in 218 the subordinate clauses are in bold type.)

For other examples see under conditional sentences, relative pronouns and clauses of purpose, comparison, time, result and concession. It is not necessary for the student to make a detailed study of clauses or even to be able to recognize the different kinds of clause, but it is necessary for him to learn to know which is the main verb of a sentence because of the important rule given below.

218 The sequence of tenses

When the main verb of a sentence is in a past tense, verbs in subordinate clauses are normally in a past tense also. See the starred sentences below.

Tense of verb in main clause		Tense of verb in subordinate clause
Present	*He thinks **that it will rain**.*	Future simple
Past	*He thought **that it would rain**.**	Conditional
Present	*He sees **that he has made a mistake**.*	Pres. perf.
Past	*He saw **that he had made a mistake**.**	Past perf.
Present	*I work so hard **that I am always tired**.*	Present
Past	*I worked so hard **that I was always tired**.**	Past
Pres. perf.	*He has done all **that is necessary**.*	Present
Past perf.	*He had done all **that was necessary**.**	Past
Present	*He says **that he is going to eat it**.*	Pres. continuous
Past	*He said **that he was going to eat it**.**	Past continuous

Note that infinitive and gerunds are not affected by the above rule:

He wants to go to Lyons.   He wanted to go to Lyons.
He likes riding.   He liked riding.

The rule about sequence of tenses applies also to indirect speech when the introductory verb is in a past tense. (See chapter 31.)

21 The conditional

The conditional tenses

219 The present conditional tense

A   This is formed with **would/should** + infinitive for the first person and
would + infinitive for the other persons.

Affirmative	*I would/I'd work* or *I should work* *you would/you'd work* etc.
Negative	*I would not/wouldn't work* or *I should not/shouldn't work* *you would not/wouldn't work* etc.
Interrogative	*would/should I work?* *would you work?* etc.
Negative interrogative	*should I not/shouldn't I work?* *would you not/wouldn't you work?* etc.

B   It is used:

(a) In conditional sentences (see 221-9).

(b) In special uses of **would** and **should** (see chapter 22).

(c) As a past equivalent of the future simple. **would/should** must be
used instead of **will/shall** when the main verb of the sentence is in the
past tense:

I hope (that) I will/shall succeed.
I hoped (that) I would/should succeed.
I know (that) he will be in time.
I knew (that) he would be in time.
He thinks (that) they will give him a visa.
He thought (that) they would give him a visa.
I expect (that) the plane will be diverted.
I expected (that) the plane would be diverted.

(For **will/shall**, **would/should** in indirect speech, see chapter 31.)

220 The perfect conditional tense

A   This is formed with **would/should** and the perfect infinitive:

Affirmative	*I would/should have worked* *you would have worked* etc.
Negative	*I would not/should not have worked* etc.
Interrogative	*would/should I have worked?* etc.
Negative interrogative	*should I not have/shouldn't I have worked?* *would you not have/wouldn't you* *have worked?* etc.

Other contractions as in 219.

B It is used:
(a) In conditional sentences (see 221-9).
(b) In special uses of **would** and **should** (see 230-7).
(c) As a past equivalent of the future perfect tense:
I hope he will have finished before we get back.
I hoped he would have finished before we got back.

Conditional sentences

Conditional sentences have two parts: the **if**-clause and the main clause. In the sentence *If it rains I shall stay at home* 'If it rains' is the **if**-clause, and 'I shall stay at home' is the main clause.
There are three kinds of conditional sentences. Each kind contains a different pair of tenses. With each type certain variations are possible but students who are studying the conditional for the first time should ignore these and concentrate on the basic forms.

221 Conditional sentences type 1: probable

A The verb in the **if**-clause is in the present tense; the verb in the main clause is in the future simple. It doesn't matter which comes first.
If he runs he'll get there in time.
The cat will scratch you if you pull her tail.
This type of sentence implies that the action in the **if**-clause is quite probable.
Note that the meaning here is present or future, but the verb in the **if**-clause is in a present, not a future tense. **if** + **will/would** is only possible with certain special meanings. (See 224.)

B Possible variations of the basic form
1 Variations of the main clause
Instead of **if** + present + future, we may have:
(a) **if** + present + **may/might** (possibility)
If the fog gets thicker the plane may/might be diverted. (Perhaps the plane will be diverted.)
(b) **if** + present + **may/can** (permission)
If your documents are in order you may/can leave at once
or **can** (permission or possibility)
If it stops snowing we can go out. (permission or possibility)
(c) **if** + present + **must, needn't, ought, should** or any expression of command, request or advice
If you want to lose weight you must/should eat less bread.
If you want to lose weight you had better eat less bread.
If you find chopsticks difficult, you needn't use them.
If you see Tom tomorrow could you ask him to ring me?

(d) **if** + present + another present tense
if + two present tenses is used to express automatic or habitual results:

> *If you heat ice it turns to water.* (*will turn* is also possible.)
> *If there is a shortage of any product prices of that product go up.*

(e) When **if** is used to mean **as/since** (see 338 A), a variety of tenses can be used in the main clause:

> *Ann hates London. ~ If she hates it why does she live there?/she ought to move out.* (*If so* could replace *If she hates it* here.)

This is not, of course, a true conditional clause.

2   Variations of the **if**-clause
Instead of **if** + present tense, we can have:
(a) **if** + present continuous, to indicate a present action or a future arrangement

> *If you are waiting for a bus* (present action) *you'd better join the queue.*
> *If you are looking for Peter* (present action) *you'll find him upstairs.*
> *If you are staying for another night* (future arrangement) *I'll ask the manager to give you a better room.*

(b) **if** + present perfect

> *If you have finished dinner I'll ask the waiter for the bill.*
> *If he has written the letter I'll post it.*
> *If they haven't seen the museum we'd better go there today.*

222   Conditional sentences type 2

A   The verb in the **if**-clause is in the past tense; the verb in the main clause is in the conditional tense:

> *If I had a map I would lend it to you.* (But I haven't a map. The meaning here is present.)
> *If someone tried to blackmail me I would tell the police.* (But I don't expect that anyone will try to blackmail me. The meaning here is future.)

There is no difference in time between the first and second types of conditional sentence. Type 2, like type 1, refers to the present or future, and the past tense in the **if**-clause is not a true past but a subjunctive, which indicates unreality (as in the first example above) or improbability (as in the second example above).

B   Type 2 is used:

1   When the supposition is contrary to known facts:

> *If I lived near my office I'd be in time for work.* (But I don't live near my office.)
> *If I were you I'd plant some trees round the house.* (But I am not you.)

2   When we don't expect the action in the **if**-clause to take place:

If a burglar came into my room at night I'd scream. (But I don't expect a burglar to come in.)

If I dyed my hair blue everyone would laugh at me. (But I don't intend to dye it.)

Some **if**-clauses can have either of the above meanings:

If he left his bicycle outside someone would steal it.

'If he left his bicycle' could imply 'but he doesn't' (present meaning, as in 1 above) or 'but he doesn't intend to' (future meaning, as in 2). But the correct meaning is usually clear from the text.

Ambiguity of this kind can be avoided by using **were/was** + infinitive instead of the past tense in type 2.

if he/she/it were can be used instead of **if he/she/it was,** and is considered the more correct form:

If he were to resign . . .   = If he resigned . . .

If I were to succeed . . .   = If I succeeded . . .

This construction with **were** is chiefly found in fairly formal sentences. **if he/she/it was** + infinitive is possible in colloquial English, but the past tense, as shown above, is much more usual.

3   Sometimes, rather confusingly, type 2 can be used as an alternative to type 1 for perfectly possible plans and suggestions:

Will Mary be in time if she gets the ten o'clock bus? ~

No, but she'd be in time if she got the nine-thirty bus or

No, but she'll be in time if she gets the nine-thirty bus.

We'll never save £200! ~ *If we each saved £10 a week we'd do it in ten weeks* or

If we each save £10 a week we'll do it in ten weeks.

A suggestion in type 2 is a little more polite than a suggestion in type 1, just as **would you** is a more polite request form than **will you.** But the student needn't trouble too much over this use of type 2.

C   Possible variations of the basic form

1   Variations of the main clause

(a) **might** or **could** may be used instead of **would:**

If you tried again you would succeed. (certain result)

If you tried again you might succeed. (possible result)

If I knew her number I could ring her up. (ability)

If he had a permit he could get a job. (ability or permission)

(b) The continuous conditional form may be used instead of the simple conditional form:

Peter is on holiday; he is touring Italy. ~ *If I were on holiday I would/might be touring Italy too.*

(c) **if** + past tense can be followed by another past tense when we wish to express automatic or habitual reactions in the past: compare **if** + two present tenses, 221 B1(d). Note that the past tenses here have a past meaning:

If anyone interrupted him he got angry. (whenever anyone interrupted him)
If there was a scarcity of anything prices of that thing went up.
(d) When **if** is used to mean 'as' or 'since', a variety of tenses is possible in the main clause. **if** + past tense here has a past meaning. The sentence is not a true conditional.

The pills made him dizzy. All the same he bought/has bought/is buying some more. ~ If they made him dizzy why did he buy/has he bought/is he buying more?
I knew she was short of money. ~ If you knew she was short of money you should have lent her some./why didn't you lend her some?

2 Variations of the **if**-clause
Instead of **if** + simple past we can have:
(a) **if** + past continuous
(We're going by air and) I hate flying. If we were going by boat I'd feel much happier.
If my car was working I would/could drive you to the station.
(b) **if** + past perfect
If he had taken my advice he would be a rich man now.
(This is a mixture of types 2 and 3. For more examples, see 223.)
(For **if** + **would**, see 224.)

223 Conditional sentences type 3

A The verb in the **if**-clause is in the past perfect tense; the verb in the main clause is in the perfect conditional. The time is past and the condition cannot be fulfilled because the action in the **if**-clause didn't happen.

If I had known that you were coming I would have met you at the airport. (But I didn't know, so I didn't come.)
If he had tried to leave the country he would have been stopped at the frontier. (But he didn't try.)

B Possible variations of the basic form

1 **could** or **might** may be used instead of **would**:
If we had found him earlier we could have saved his life. (ability)
If we had found him earlier we might have saved his life. (possibility)
If our documents had been in order we could have left at once. (ability or permission)

2 The continuous form of the perfect conditional may be used:
At the time of the accident I was sitting in the back of the car, because Tom's little boy was sitting beside him in front. If Tom's boy had not been there I would have been sitting in front.

3 We can use the past perfect continuous in the **if**-clause:
I was wearing a seat belt. If I hadn't been wearing one I'd have been seriously injured.

4   A combination of types 2 and 3 is possible:
> *The plane I intended to catch crashed and everyone was killed. If I*
> *had caught that plane I would be dead now* or
> *I would have been killed.* (type 3)
> *If I had worked harder at school I would be sitting in a comfortable*
> *office now; I wouldn't be sweeping the streets.* (But I didn't work
> hard at school and now I am sweeping the streets.)

5   **had** can be placed first and the **if** omitted:
> *If you had obeyed orders this disaster would not have happened* =
> *Had you obeyed orders this disaster would not have happened.*

224   Special uses of **will/would** and **should** in **if**-clauses

Normally these auxiliaries are not used after **if** in conditional sentences.
There are, however, certain exceptions.

A   **if you will/would** is often used in polite requests. **would** is the more
polite form.
> *If you will/would wait a moment I'll see if Mr Jones is free.*
> (Please wait.)
> *I would be very grateful if you would make the arrangements for me.*

    if you would + infinitive is often used alone when the request is one
which would normally be made in the circumstances. The speaker
assumes that the other person will comply as a matter of course.
> *If you'd fill up this form.*
> (in a hotel) *If you'd just sign the register.*
> (in a shop) *If you'd put your address on the back of the cheque.*
> (in a classroom) *If you'd open your books.*

B   **if** + **will/would** can be used with all persons to indicate willingness:
> *If he'll listen to me I'll be able to help him.* (If he is willing to
> listen . . .)
> *If Tom would tell me what he wants for his dinner I'd cook it for*
> *him.* (The speaker implies that Tom is unwilling to tell her.)

    won't used in this way can mean 'refuse':
> *If he won't listen to me I can't help him.* (If he is unwilling to
> listen/If he refuses to listen . . .)
> *If they won't accept a cheque we'll have to pay cash.* (If they refuse
> to accept . . .)

C   **will** can be used to express obstinate insistence (230 B):
> *If you ¹will play the drums all night no wonder the neighbours*
> *complain.* (If you insist on playing . . .)

D   **if** + **would like/care** can be used instead of **if** + **want/wish** and is
more polite:
> *If you would like to come I'll get a ticket for you.*
> *If you'd care to see the photographs I'll bring them round.*
> *If he'd like to leave his car here he can.*

But if we rearrange such sentences so that **would like** has no object, we can drop the **would**:

If you like I'll get a ticket for you but
If you'd like a ticket I'll get one for you.
If he likes he can leave his car here but
If he'd like to leave his car here he can or
He can leave it here if he'd like to.

E   **if + should** can be used in type 1 to indicate that the action, though possible, is not very likely. It is usually combined with an imperative and is chiefly used in written instructions:

If you should have any difficulty in getting spare parts ring this number.
If these biscuits should arrive in a damaged condition please inform the factory at once.

should can be placed first and the **if** omitted:
Should these biscuits arrive . . . (See 225 B.)

225   if + were and inversion of subject and auxiliary

A   **if + were** instead of **if + was**

1   Usually either can be used, **were** being more likely in formal English:
If she was/were offered the job she'd take it.
If Tom was/were here he'd know what to do.

2   But **were** is a little more usual than **was** in the advice form *If I were/was you I would/should . . .* :
'If I were you I would wait a bit,' he said. (See 287 C.)
were is also more usual in the infinitive construction:
If Peter were/was to apply for the post he'd get it. (See 222 B.)

3   **were**, not **was**, is used when the auxiliary is placed first:
Were I Tom I would refuse. (See B below.)
When **if** means 'since' (see 222 C) **was** cannot be replaced by **were**.
were can replace **was** after *if only* (see 228) and *wish* (see 300).

B   **if + subject + auxiliary** can be replaced in formal English by inversion of auxiliary and subject with **if** omitted:
If I were in his shoes . . . = Were I in his shoes . . .
If you should require anything . . . =
Should you require anything . . .
If he had known . . . = Had he known . . .

226   if, even if, whether, unless, but for, otherwise, provided, suppose

A   **even if = even though**
Compare:
You must go tomorrow if you are ready and
You must go tomorrow even if you aren't ready.

B   **whether . . . or** = **if . . . or**
You must go tomorrow whether you are ready or not.

C   **unless** + affirmative verb = **if** + negative
Unless you start at once you'll be late =
If you don't start at once you'll be late.
Unless you had a permit you couldn't get a job =
If you hadn't a permit you couldn't get a job.
Note the difference between:
    (a) *Don't call 'me if you need help* and
    (b) *Don't call me unless you need help.*
In (a) he won't help her even if she needs help.
In (b) he will help her if she needs help but doesn't want
non-urgent calls.
unless + **he'd/you'd like/prefer** etc. normally replaces **if he/you
wouldn't like** etc.:
*I'll ask Tom, unless you'd prefer me to ask/unless you'd rather
I asked Bill.*

D   **but for** = 'if it were not for/if it hadn't been for'
My father pays my fees. But for that I wouldn't be here.
The car broke down. But for that we would have been in time.

E   **otherwise** = 'if this doesn't happen/didn't happen/hadn't happened'
We must be back before midnight; otherwise we'll be locked out =
If we are not back by midnight we'll be locked out.
Her father pays her fees; otherwise she wouldn't be here =
If her father didn't pay her fees she wouldn't be here.
I used my calculator; otherwise I'd have taken longer =
If I hadn't used my calculator I'd have taken longer.

F   In colloquial English **or** (+ **else**) can often replace **otherwise**:
We must be early or (else) we won't get a seat.

G   **provided (that)** can replace **if** when there is a strong idea of limitation
or restriction. It is chiefly used with permission.
You can camp here provided you leave no mess.

H   **suppose/supposing . . . ?** = **what if . . . ?**
Suppose the plane is late? =
What if/What will happen if the plane is late?
Suppose no one had been there? =
What if no one had been there?
suppose can also introduce suggestions:
Suppose you ask him/Why don't you ask him?

27   **if** and **in case**

A   **in case** is followed by a present or past tense or by **should** (see 337).
It appears similar to **if** and is often confused with it. But the two are
completely different.

An **in case** clause gives a reason for the action in the main clause:

> *Some cyclists carry repair outfits in case they have a puncture* =
> *Some cyclists carry repair outfits because they may have/because it is possible they will have a puncture.*
> *I always slept by the phone in case he rang during the night* =
> *I always slept by the phone because (I knew) he might ring during the night.*

An **in case** clause can be dropped without changing the meaning of the main clause. In a conditional sentence, however, the action in the main clause depends on the action in the **if**-clause, and if the **if**-clause is dropped the meaning of the main clause changes. Compare:

> (a) BILL: *I'll come tomorrow in case Ann wants me* and
> (b) TOM: *I'll come tomorrow if Ann wants me.*

In (a) perhaps Ann will want Bill, perhaps she won't. But Bill will come anyway. His action doesn't depend on Ann's. *in case Ann wants me* could be omitted without changing the meaning of the main verb.

In (b), a conditional sentence, Tom will only come if Ann asks him. His action depends on hers. We cannot remove *if Ann wants me* without changing the meaning of the main verb.

B   An **in case** clause is normally placed after the main clause, not before it. Note, however, that **in case of** + noun = **if there is a/an** + noun:

> *In case of accident phone 999* = *If there is an accident phone 999.*

This may have led to the confusion of **if**-clauses and **in case** clauses.

228   if only

only can be placed after **if** and indicates hope, a wish or regret, according to the tense used with it.

A   **if only** + present tense/**will** expresses hope:

> *If only he comes in time* =
> *We hope he will come in time.*
> *If only he will listen to her* =
> *We hope he will be willing to listen to her.*

B   **if only** + past/past perfect expresses regret (see also **wish** + past/past perfect, 300):

> *If only he didn't smoke!* =
> *We wish he didn't smoke* or *We are sorry he smokes.*
> *If only (= I/We wish) Tom were here!*
> *If only you hadn't said, 'Liar'!* =
> *We wish you hadn't said, 'Liar'/We are sorry you said, 'Liar'.*

C   **if only** + **would** can express regret about a present action as an alternative to **if only** + past tense (it has the same meaning as **wish** + **would**):

> *If only he would drive more slowly!* =
> *We are sorry that he isn't willing to drive more slowly*

or a not very hopeful wish concerning the future:

If only (= I/We wish) the rain would stop! (We don't really expect it
to stop.)
(See also **wish**, 300-1.)
if only clauses can stand alone as above or form part of a full
conditional sentence.

229 Conditional sentences in indirect speech

A Type 1, basic form. The tenses here change in the usual way:
He said, 'If I catch the plane I'll be home by five' =
He said that if he caught the plane he would be home by five.
Type 2, basic form. No tense changes:
'If I had a permit I could get a job,' he said =
He said that if he had a permit he could get a job.
Type 3, basic form. No tense changes:
'If she had loved Tom,' he said, 'she wouldn't have left him' =
He said that if she had loved Tom she wouldn't have left him.

B Examples of **if**-clauses + commands and requests in indirect speech
(see also 320-1):

He said, 'If you have time wash the floor' or
He said, 'If you have time would you wash the floor?' =
He told/asked me to wash the floor if I had time (note change of
order) or
He said that if I had time I was to wash the floor.

'If you see Ann ask her to ring me,' he said =
He said that if I saw Ann I was to ask her to ring him.
(The infinitive construction here would be clumsy and less clear.)

PETER (on phone): *If you miss the last bus get a taxi* =
Peter says that if we miss the last bus we are to get a taxi. (The
infinitive construction would be much less usual here.)

(For **if you would** . . . requests, see 284 F.)

C **if**-clauses + expressions of advice in indirect speech:
'If you feel ill,' she said, 'why don't you go to bed?' or
' . . . you'd better go to bed' =
She advised me to go to bed if I felt ill or
She said that if I felt ill I'd better/I should go to bed.
'If I were you I'd stop taking pills,' she said =
She advised me to stop taking pills.

D **if**-clauses + questions are usually reported with the **if**-clause last:
'If the baby is a girl what will they call her?' he wondered =
He wondered what they would call the baby if it was a girl.
'If the door is locked what shall I do?' she asked =
She asked what she should/was to do if the door was locked.

22 Other uses of **will/would, shall/should**

For **will/shall** in commands, see 282.
For **will/would** in requests, see 284.
For **will/would** in invitations, see 286.
For **would/should** used with **like, prefer, wish** etc., see chapter 29.

230 Habits expressed by **will, would**

A   Habits in the present are normally expressed by the simple present tense; but **will** + infinitive can be used instead when we wish to emphasize the characteristics of the performer rather than the action performed. It is chiefly used in general statements:

> *An Englishman will usually show you the way in the street.* (It is normal for an Englishman to act in this way.)

This is not a very important use of **will**, but the past form, **would**, has a much wider use and can replace **used to** when we are describing a past routine:

> *On Sundays he used to/would get up early and go fishing. He used to/would spend the whole day by the river and in the evening used to/would come home with marvellous stories of the fish he had nearly caught.*

Note, however, that when **used to** expresses a discontinued habit, it cannot be replaced by **would**. (See 162.)

Both **will** and **would** can be contracted when used as above.

B   **will** can also express obstinate insistence, usually habitual:

> *If you 'will keep your watch half an hour slow it is hardly surprising that you are late for your appointments.*

would is used in the past:

> *We all tried to stop him smoking in bed but he 'would do it.*

will and **would** are not contracted here and are strongly stressed.

C   **would** can express a characteristic action, usually one which annoys the speaker:

> *Bill objects/objected.* ~ *He 'would!/He 'would object!* (He always objects.)

231 should/would think + that-clause or so/not

(See 347 for **so/not** used to replace clauses.)

A *Will it be expensive?* ~ *I should/would think so./I should think it would.* (= probably 'Yes') or
*I shouldn't think it would./I shouldn't/wouldn't think so./
I should/would think not.* (= probably 'No')

By this sort of answer the speaker implies that he doesn't really know but that this is his impression. *I should/would think* is therefore less confident than *I think*.

so/not is not usually possible when **should/would think** introduces a comment. A **that**-clause therefore has to be used:

He's an astrologer, looking for work. ~ *I shouldn't/wouldn't think that he'd find it easy to get work.*

B If we are commenting on a past action we use **should/would have thought**:

He actually got a job as an astrologer. ~ *I shouldn't/wouldn't have thought that it was possible to do that.*

C **should/would have expected** + an infinitive construction or a **that**-clause is also possible. The impersonal pronoun **you** can sometimes replace **I**:

She has emigrated. ~ *Has she? You'd/I'd have expected her to stay in this country.*

232 would for past intention

As has already been noted **would** is the past equivalent of **will** when **will** is used for the ordinary future:

He knows he will be late.   *He knew he would be late.*

would similarly is the past equivalent of **will** used to express intention (see 201):

I said, 'I will help him' =
I said that I would help him.
He said, 'I won't lend you a penny' =
He said that he wouldn't lend me a penny.

But notice that whereas **would** used for future or intention is restricted to subordinate clauses as in the above examples, **wouldn't** used for negative intention can stand alone:

He won't help me today. (He refuses to help.)
He wouldn't help me yesterday. (He refused to help.)

would cannot be used in this way. So to put a sentence such as *I will help him today* into the past, we have to replace **will** by another verb:

I wanted/intended/offered to help him yesterday.

233 **shall I/we?** in requests for orders or advice, offers, suggestions

Requests for orders:
How shall I cook it?   *Where shall we put this?*
When the request is for advice only we use either **shall** or **should**:
Which one shall I buy? or *Which one should I buy?*
Offers:
Shall I wait for you?   *Shall I help you to pack?*
Suggestions:
Shall we meet at the theatre?   *Let's meet at the theatre, shall we?*

(See 318 for **shall I/we?** in indirect speech.)

234 **shall** in the second and third persons

shall can express (A) the subject's intention to perform a certain action or to cause it to be performed, and (B) a command. Both these uses are old-fashioned and formal and normally avoided in modern spoken English.

A Examples of **shall** used to express the speaker's intention:
You shall have a sweet = *I'll give you a sweet* or
I'll see that you get a sweet.
He shan't come here = *I won't let him come here.*
They shall not pass = *We won't let them pass.*
In the past, i.e. in indirect speech, it is usually necessary to change the wording:
He said, 'You shall have a sweet' = *He promised me a sweet.*

B Examples of **shall** used to express a command:
Yachts shall go round the course, passing the marks in the correct order. (yacht-racing rules)
Members shall enter the names of their guests in the book provided. (club rules)
This construction is chiefly used in regulations or legal documents. In less formal English **must** or **are to** would be used instead of **shall** in the above sentences. (See also 282.)

C **shall you?** is an old-fashioned form which is occasionally still found in some novels possibly because it is shorter and neater than the future continuous tense:
Shall you go? = *Will you be going?*

235 **that . . . should** after certain verbs

Certain verbs can be followed by **that** + subject + **should** as an alternative to a gerund or infinitive construction.
that . . . should is particularly useful in the passive and sometimes is the only possible passive form.

that . . . should is more formal than a gerund or infinitive construction and usually implies less direct contact between the advisers/organizers etc. and the people who are to carry out the action.
Verbs which can be used with **that . . . should** include the following: *advise, agree, arrange, ask, beg, command, decide, demand, determine, insist, order, propose, recommend, request, stipulate, suggest, urge.* Note also: *be anxious, be determined.*

> *She advised that we should keep the gate locked.*
> *She advised that the gate should be kept locked.*
> *She advised keeping the gate locked/advised us to keep it locked.*
> (See 267.)

recommend could be used above instead of *advise* and would sound more formal.

> *They agreed/decided that the roof should be repaired.*
> *They agreed/decided to repair the roof.*

> *He arranged that I should go abroad.*
> *He arranged for me to go abroad.*
> *They arranged that the minister should be met at the airport.*
> *They arranged for the minister to be met at the airport.*

be anxious (= wish; see 27 C) takes the same construction as *arrange*:
> *He is anxious that classes should start/should be started at once.*
> *He is anxious for classes to start/to be started at once.*

> *They asked/begged/urged that relief work should be given priority.*
> *They asked/begged/urged the authorities to give relief work priority.*
> (See 243.)

> *He commanded that the army should advance.* (He was not necessarily with the army.)
> *He commanded the army to advance.* (He probably was with the army.)

> *She determined/was determined that he should study music.*
> *She determined/was determined to let him/make him study music.*
> *She insisted that he should study music/insisted on his studying music.* (See 262.)

> *He ordered that Ann should go.* (He probably told someone else to tell her.)
> *He ordered Ann to go.* (He probably told her himself.) (See 320.)
> *He ordered that the goods should be sent by air.*
> *He ordered the goods to be sent by air.*

> *He proposed/suggested that we should try homeopathic remedies.* (See 289.)
> *He proposed/suggested that homeopathic remedies should be tried.*
> *He proposed/suggested (our) trying homeopathic remedies.*

> *They stipulated that the best materials should be used.*
> *They stipulated for the best materials to be used.*

should is sometimes omitted before **be**. (See 291 C.)

236 it is/was + adjective + that . . . should

A **that . . . should** can be used after *it is/was advisable, better, desirable, essential, imperative, important, natural, necessary*; after *fair* (= just), *just, right* (these are often preceded by *only*) and after *reasonable*, as an alternative to a **for** + infinitive construction:

> *It is advisable that everyone should have a map.*
> *It is better for him to hear it from you.*
> *It is better that he should hear it from you.*
> *It is essential for him to be prepared for this.*
> *It is essential that he should be prepared for this.*
> *It is only right that she should have a share.*

should is sometimes omitted before **be**:

> *It is essential that he be prepared.*

B **that . . . should** can be used after *it is/was absurd, amazing, annoying, ludicrous, odd, ridiculous, strange, surprising* and similar adjectives as an alternative to **that** + present/past tense:

> *It is ridiculous that we should be* (= that we are) *short of water in a country where it is always raining.*

The perfect infinitive is sometimes used when referring to past events:

> *It is amazing that she should have said* (= that she said) *nothing about the murder.*

237 Other uses of should

A After *can't think why/don't know why/see no reason why* etc. when the speaker queries the reasonableness or justice of an assumption:

> *I don't know why you should think that I did it.*
> *I see no reason why you should interfere in their quarrel.*

The perfect infinitive is usual when the assumption was in the past:

> *I can't think why he should have said that it was my fault.*

B Idiomatically with **what, where, who** in dramatic expressions of surprise:

> *What should I find but an enormous spider!*

Quite often the surprise is embarrassing:

> *Who should come in but his first wife!*

C After **lest** and sometimes after **in case**:

1 In literary English **lest . . . should** is sometimes placed after expressions of fear or anxiety:

> *He was terrified lest he should slip on the icy rocks.*

should + perfect infinitive is used when the anxiety concerns a previous action:

> *She began to be worried lest he should have met with some accident.*

2 **lest** can also be used in purpose clauses to mean 'for fear that':

> *He dared not spend the money lest someone should ask where*
> *he had got it.*

As above, this is a literary form.

in case, which is more usual than **lest** here, can be followed by **should** or by an ordinary present or past tense:

> *in case someone should ask/someone asked*

(See also 227, 337.)

D **should** is sometimes used in purpose clauses as an alternative to **would/could**:

> *He wore a mask so that no one should recognize him.*

(See 336.)

E In conditional sentences instead of the present tense:

> *If the pain should return take another of these pills.*

(See 224.)

F In indirect, rather formal, commands when the recipient of the command is not necessarily addressed directly:

> *He ordered that Tom should leave the house.* (See 321 B.)

Compare with *He ordered Tom to leave* which implies that he told Tom himself.

23 The infinitive

238 Form

A   Examples of infinitive forms

Present infinitive	*to work, to do*
Present continuous infinitive	*to be working*
	to be doing
Perfect infinitive	*to have worked, to have done*
Perfect continuous infinitive	*to have been working*
	to have been doing
Present infinitive passive	*to be done*
Perfect infinitive passive	*to have been done*

B   The full infinitive consists of two words, **to** + verb, as shown above. But after certain verbs and expressions we use the form without **to**, i.e. the 'bare infinitive' (see 246):
> *You had better say nothing.* (See 120.)

C   It is not normally advisable to put any words between the **to** and the verb, but see 248, split infinitives.

D   To avoid repetition, an infinitive is sometimes represented by its **to**:
> *Do you smoke? ~ No, but I used to (smoke).* (See 247.)

239 Uses of the infinitive

A   The infinitive may be used alone, *We began to walk*, or as part of an infinitive phrase, *We began to walk down the road.*

B   The infinitive may be the subject of a sentence (see 240).

C   The infinitive may be the complement of a verb:
> *His plan is to keep the affair secret.*

D   The infinitive may be the object or part of the object of a verb.
It can follow the verb directly: *He wants to pay* (see 241, 243) or follow verb + **how, what** etc. (see 242) or follow verb + object: *He wants me to pay* (see 243, 244).

E   **be** + infinitive can express commands or instructions (see 114).

F   The infinitive can express purpose (see 334).

G   The infinitive can be used after certain adjectives:
> *angry, glad, happy, sorry* (see 26)
> *fortunate, likely, lucky* (see 27)

H   The infinitive can connect two clauses (see 249).

I   The infinitive can sometimes replace relative clauses (see 77, 250).

J   The infinitive can be used after certain nouns (see 251).

K   The infinitive can be used with **too/enough** and certain adjectives/adverbs (see 252).

L   An infinitive phrase such as *to tell the truth, to cut a long story short* can be placed at the beginning or end of a sentence (see 253).

240   The infinitive as subject

A   An infinitive or an infinitive phrase can be the subject of the verbs **appear, be, seem**. The infinitive can be placed first:
> *To compromise appears advisable.*
> *To lean out of the window is dangerous.*
> *To save money now seems impossible.*

B   But it is more usual to place the pronoun **it** first, and move the infinitive or infinitive phrase to the end of the sentence:
> *It appears advisable to compromise.*
> *It is dangerous to lean out of the window.*
> *It seemed impossible to save money.*

    it here is known as the introductory **it**. Note its use with interrogatives:
> *Would it be safe to camp here?*
> *Wouldn't it be better to go on?*

    The **it** construction is necessary here. *Would* + *to camp* and *Wouldn't* + *to go on* would not be possible.

C   Usually infinitive constructions of this type consist of **it** + **be** + adjective + infinitive. (See 26-7.)
    But sometimes a noun can be used instead of an adjective:
> *It would be a crime/a mistake/a pity to cut down any more trees.*
> *It is an offence to drop litter in the street.*

D   **cost/take** + object can also be used:
> *It would cost millions/take years to rebuild the castle.*

E   The gerund can be used instead of the infinitive when the action is being considered in a general sense, but it is always safe to use an infinitive. When we wish to refer to one particular action we must use the infinitive:
> *He said, 'Do come.' It was impossible to refuse.*

    But *It is not always easy to refuse invitations* can be replaced by *Refusing invitations is not always easy.* Here the action is considered in a general sense, and either gerund or infinitive is possible. (See also 258.)

F   An **it** + infinitive construction may be preceded by **believe/consider/discover/expect/find/think (that)** and **wonder (if)**:

He thought (that) it would be safer to go by train.

After **find** used in this way we can omit **that** + the verb **be**, i.e. we can say:

He found (that) it was easy to earn extra money or
He found it easy to earn extra money.
He will find (that) it is hard to make friends or
He will find it hard to make friends.

This is sometimes also possible with **think**:

He thought it safer to go.

After other verbs, however, the student is advised not to omit the **be**. (For similar gerund constructions, see 258.)

G   The perfect infinitive can also be used as the subject of a sentence:

To have made the same mistake twice was unforgivable.

Similarly with **it** first:

It is better to have loved and lost than never to have loved at all.

241   The infinitive as object or complement of the verb

A   The most useful verbs which can be followed directly by the infinitive are:

*agree***	*be determined***	*pretend**
aim	*endeavour*	*proceed*
*appear**	*fail*	*promise**
*arrange***	*forget**	*prove**
*ask***	*guarantee**	*refuse*
attempt	*happen**	*remember**
bother (negative)	*hesitate*	*resolve***
care (negative)	*hope*	*seem**
choose	*learn**	*swear**
*claim***	*long*	*tend*
condescend	*manage*	*threaten**
consent	*neglect*	*trouble* (negative)
*decide***	*offer*	*try* (= attempt)
decline	*plan*	*undertake**
*demand***	*prepare*	*volunteer*
*determine***	*be prepared*	*vow*

* See D, ** see F.

Auxiliary verbs

be	*dare*	*have*	*must*	*ought*	*will*
can	*do*	*may*	*need*	*shall*	*used*

(For verbs taking object + infinitive, see 244.
For verbs taking infinitive or gerund, see chapter 25.)

B   The following phrases can also be followed by an infinitive:

be about	*it* + *occur** + *to* + object
be able + *afford*	(negative or interrogative)
do one's best/	*set out*
do what one can	*take the trouble*
make an/every effort	*turn out** (= prove to be)
make up one's mind* (= decide)	

* See D.

C   Examples of A and B

She agreed to pay £50.
Two men failed to return from the expedition.
I managed to put the fire out.
They are preparing (= getting ready) *to evacuate the area.*
We are not prepared (= willing) *to wait any longer.*
The tenants refused to leave.   Prices always tend to go up.
She volunteered to help with Meals on Wheels.
He is just about to leave. (on the point of leaving; see 114 C)
We can't afford to live in the centre.
He didn't bother/trouble to answer personally.

Opposite of the above:

He took the trouble to answer personally.

D   Starred verbs or expressions can also be used with a **that**-clause
(see 346):

I promise to wait = I promise that I will wait.
He pretended to be angry = He pretended that he was angry.

it + **occur** + **to** + object + **that** is used in the affirmative, negative
and interrogative. Note the difference in meaning between this form
and **occur** + infinitive:

It occurred to me that he was trying to conceal something. (The idea
came to me.)
It didn't occur to me to ask him for proof of his identity. (I didn't
think of asking. So I didn't ask.)

appear, **happen**, **seem**, **turn out**, when used with a **that**
construction, require an introductory **it**:

It turned out that his 'country cottage' was an enormous bungalow.

Compare with the infinitive construction:

His 'country cottage' turned out to be an enormous bungalow.

E   A verb + infinitive does not necessarily have the same meaning as the
same verb used with a **that**-clause. With **learn**, **forget**, **occur** (see
D above) and **remember** the meaning will be different:

He learnt to look after himself.
He learnt (= was told) *that it would cost £100.*
He forgot to leave the car keys on the table. (He didn't leave them.)
He forgot that his brother wanted to use the car.

remember could be used similarly with the opposite meaning.
agree/decide + infinitive expresses an intention to act.

agree that . . . expresses an opinion.
decide that . . . expresses a conclusion or a decision not necessarily leading to action.

F   Verbs with two stars take an infinitive or a **that** . . . **should** construction. **that** . . . **should** is particularly useful in the passive (see 302).

> *They decided/agreed to divide the profits equally.*
> *They decided that the profits should be divided equally.*
> *I arranged to meet/for Tom to meet them.*
> *I arranged that Tom should meet them.*
> *I arranged that they should be met.*

G   The continuous infinitive is often used after **appear, happen, pretend, seem**:

> *I happened to be looking out of the window when they arrived.*
> *He seems to be following us.*

It is also possible after **agree, arrange, decide, determine, hope, manage, plan** and the auxiliary verbs (see 254).

H   The perfect infinitive is possible after **appear, hope, pretend, seem** and the auxiliary verbs (see 255).

242   Verb + **how/what/when/where/which/why** + infinitive

A   The verbs most frequently used in this way are **ask, decide, discover, find out, forget, know, learn, remember, see** (= understand/perceive), **show** + object, **think, understand, want to know, wonder**:

> *He discovered how to open the safe.*
> *I found out where to buy fruit cheaply.*
> *I didn't know when to switch the machine off.*
> *I showed her which button to press.*
> *She couldn't think what to say.*

(Note that this construction is not usual after **think** in the simple present or past, but can be used after other tenses of **think**, or after **think** as a second verb, as in the last example above.)

B   **whether** + infinitive can be used similarly after **want to know, wonder**:

> *I wonder/wondered whether to write or phone*

and after **decide, know, remember, think** when these verbs follow a negative or interrogative verb:

> *You needn't decide yet whether to study arts or science.*
> *He couldn't remember whether to turn left or right.*

C   **ask, decide, forget, learn, remember** can also be followed directly by the infinitive (see 241). But the meaning is not necessarily the same.

learn how + infinitive = 'acquire a skill':

> *She learnt how to make lace*

though if the skill is a fairly usual one, the **how** is normally dropped:
> *She learnt to drive a car.*

learn + infinitive (without **how**) can have another meaning:
> *She learnt to trust nobody* =
> *She found from experience that it was better to trust nobody.*

Note also:
> *I decided to do it* = *I said to myself, 'I'll do it.'*
> *I decided how to do it* = *I said to myself, 'I'll do it this way.'*
> *I remembered to get a ticket.* (I got a ticket.)
> *I remembered where to get a ticket.* (I remembered that the tickets could be obtained from the Festival Office.)

243 The infinitive after verb or verb + object

A   The most important verbs which can be used in either of these ways are **ask, beg, expect, would hate, help, intend, like** (= think wise or right), **would like** (= enjoy), **would love, mean, prefer, want, wish**:
> *He likes to eat well.*
> *He likes his staff to eat well.*
> *I want to ride. I want you to ride too.*

B   **ask** and **beg**
ask + infinitive has a different meaning from **ask** + object + infinitive:
> *I asked to speak to Mrs Jones* =
> *I said, 'Could I speak to Mrs Jones?'* but
> *I asked Bill to speak to her* =
> *I said, 'Bill, would you speak to her?'*

With **beg** there is a similar difference, though **beg** is not often followed directly by the infinitive:
> *I begged (to be allowed) to go* = *I said, 'Please let me go.'*
> *I begged him to go* = *I said, 'Please go.'*

ask and **beg** can be followed by **that . . . should** (see 235).

C   **expect** + infinitive and **expect** + object + infinitive can have the same meaning:
> *I expect to arrive tomorrow* =
> *I think it is likely that I will arrive tomorrow.*
> *I expect him to arrive tomorrow* =
> *I think it is likely that he will arrive tomorrow.*

But very often **expect** + object + infinitive conveys the idea of duty:
> *He expects his wife to bring him breakfast in bed at weekends.* (He thinks it is her duty to do this.)

expect can also be followed by **that** + subject + verb. Here there is no idea of duty.

D   For examples of **care, hate, like, love** and **prefer** used with infinitives or gerunds, see 294-8.
intend, mean, want can also be followed by gerunds (see 266).

244 Verb + object + infinitive

A   The most important of these are:

advise	*feel* (b)	*make* (b)	*show how*
allow	*forbid*	*oblige*	*teach/teach how*
bribe	*force*	*order*	*tell/tell how*
command	*hear* (b)	*permit*	*tempt*
compel	*implore*	*persuade*	*train*
convince	*induce*	*remind*	*urge*
enable	*instruct*	*request*	*warn*
encourage	*invite*	*see* (b)	*watch* (b)
entitle	*let* (b)		

(b) here means 'bare infinitive'. (See 246.)

advise, allow and **permit** can also be used with gerunds.
(For verbs of knowing and thinking, see 245.)

B   Examples of verb + object + infinitive:
> *These glasses will enable you to see in the dark.*
> *She encouraged me to try again.*
> *They forbade her to leave the house* or
> *She was forbidden to leave the house.* (more usual)
> *Nothing would induce me to do business with them.*
> *They persuaded us to go with them.*
> *They are training these dogs to sniff out drugs.*

C   **show/teach/tell + how**
show used with an infinitive requires **how**:
> *He showed me how to change a fuse.*

tell how + infinitive = 'instruct':
> *He told me how to replace a fuse.* (He gave me the necessary
> information or instructions.)

But **tell** + object + infinitive = 'order':
> *He told me to change the fuse = He said, 'Change the fuse.'*

teach how:
We can **teach** someone (**how**) to *swim, dance, type, ride* etc.:
> *He taught me how to light a fire without matches.*

how is possible, but when the skill is a fairly usual one the **how** is
normally dropped: *He taught me to ride.*

teach + object + infinitive (without **how**) can also mean to teach or
train someone to behave in a certain way:
> *He taught me to obey all commands without asking questions.*

D   **remind, show, teach, tell** can also be followed by **that**:
> *He reminded me that the road was dangerous.*
> *He showed me that it was quite easy.*

Note that **tell** + **that** does not have the same meaning as **tell** +
infinitive:
> *He told (= ordered) me to go.*
> *He told (= informed) me that I was late.*

E **request** can also be followed by **that** + **should**. This construction is chiefly used in the passive:

> *He requested that the matter should be kept secret.*

245 The infinitive after verbs of knowing and thinking etc.

A **assume, believe, consider, feel, know, suppose, understand** can be followed by object + **to be**:

> *I consider him to be the best candidate.*

But it is much more common to use **that** + an ordinary tense:

> *I consider that he is the best candidate.*

With **think, estimate** and **presume** the object + infinitive construction is extremely rare, a **that**-clause being normally used instead:

> *I think that he is the best player.*
> *They estimate that this vase is 2,000 years old.*

B When, however, these verbs are used in the passive they are more often followed by an infinitive than by the **that** construction:

> *He is known to be honest* = *It is known that he is honest.*
> *He is thought to be the best player* = *It is thought that he is* . . .
> *This vase is estimated to be 2,000 years old.*

C Note, however, that **suppose** when used in the passive often conveys an idea of duty:

> *You are supposed to know the laws of your own country* =
> *It is your duty to know/You are expected to know* . . .

D The continuous infinitive can also be used:

> *He is thought to be hiding in the woods.* (People think he is hiding.)
> *He is supposed to be washing the car.* (He should be washing it.)

E When the thought concerns a previous action we use the perfect infinitive:

> *They are believed to have landed in America.* (It is believed that they landed.)

suppose + perfect infinitive may or may not convey an idea of duty. *They are supposed to have discovered America* means 'It is thought that they did'. But *You are supposed to have read the instructions* would normally mean 'You should have read them'.

(For infinitive constructions after passive verbs, see also 306.)

246 The bare infinitive after verbs and expressions

A **can, do, may, must, shall, will**:

> *They could do it today.*   *I may as well start at once.*
> *He will probably object.*

B **need** and **dare**, except when they are conjugated with **do/did** or **will/would**:

You needn't say anything but *You don't/won't need to say anything.*
I dared not wake him but *I didn't/wouldn't dare (to) wake him.*
In theory the **to** is required in the last example but in practice it is often omitted. The theory is that if **dare** and **used** are treated as auxiliaries, they take the bare infinitive like most auxiliaries. If they are treated as ordinary verbs, with **do/did** etc., they take the full infinitive like ordinary verbs.

C **feel, hear, see** and **watch**:
   I heard him lock the door.   *I saw/watched him drive off.*
   But **see** and **hear** in the passive take the full infinitive:
   He was seen to enter the office.   *He was heard to say that . . .*
   But **feel, hear, see** and **watch** are more often used with present participles:
   I heard them shouting.   (See 273.)

D **let** takes the bare infinitive in both active and passive. But **let** in the passive is often replaced by another verb: *They let me know . . .* would be replaced in the passive by *I was told . . .* and *They let him see the documents* by *He was allowed to see them.*
   The infinitive/infinitive phrase after **let** is sometimes dropped to avoid repetition:
   She wants to go out to work but he won't let her (go out to work).
   let is used without an object in the expression:
   Live and let live.
   (For **let us/let's** used for imperatives and suggestions, see 281, 289.)

E **make**
   make in the active takes the bare infinitive:
   He made me move my car.
   But in the passive it takes the full infinitive:
   I was made to move my car.
   Sometimes the infinitive after **make** (active) is dropped to avoid repetition.
   Why did you tell him? ~ He made me (tell him)!
   An infinitive after **make** (passive) can be represented by its **to**:
   I was made to (tell him).

F **would rather/sooner, rather/sooner than** (see 297-8):
   Shall we go today? ~ I'd rather wait till tomorrow.
   Rather/Sooner than risk a bad crossing, he postponed his journey.

G **had better** (see 120):
   'You had better start at once,' he said.

H **help** may be followed by a full or bare infinitive:
   He helped us (to) push it.

I If two infinitives are joined by **and**, the **to** of the second infinitive is normally dropped:
   I intend to sit in the garden and write letters.
   I want you to stand beside me and hold the torch.

J   **but** and **except** take the bare infinitive when they follow **do +
anything/nothing/everything**:

> *He does nothing but complain.   My dog does everything but speak.*
> *Can't you do anything but ask silly questions?*
> *There's nothing to do but wait.*

K   The **to** is optional in sentences such as:

> *The only thing to do/we can do is (to) write to him* or
> *All we can do is (to) write to him.*

247   The infinitive represented by its **to**

An infinitive can be represented by **to** alone to avoid repetition. This is
chiefly done after such verbs as **hate, hope, intend, would
like/love, make** (passive), **mean, plan, try, want**, after the
auxiliaries **have, need, ought**, and with **used to, be able to** and the
be going to form:

> *Would you like to come with me? ~ Yes, I'd love to.*
> *Did you get a ticket? ~ No, I tried to, but there weren't any left.*
> *Why did you take a taxi? ~ I had to (take one). I was late.*
> *Do you ride? ~ Not now but I used to.*
> *He wanted to go but he wasn't able to.*
> *Have you fed the dog? ~ No, but I'm just going to.*

248   Split infinitives

It used to be considered bad style to split an infinitive (i.e. to put a
word between the **to** and the verb), but there is now a more relaxed
attitude to this.
really is often placed after the **to** in colloquial English:

> *It would take ages to really master this subject*

instead of . . . *really to master*, which sounds rather formal.
Some other degree adverbs such as *completely, entirely, (un)duly* can be
treated similarly, i.e. we can say:

> (a) *to completely cover the floor* instead of
> (b) *to cover the floor completely*
> (a) *to unduly alarm people* instead of
> (b) *to alarm people unduly.*

But it is safer to keep to the conventional order, as in (b) above.

249   The infinitive used as a connective link

A   The infinitive is used after **only** to express a disappointing sequel:

> *He hurried to the house only to find that it was empty =*
> *He hurried to the house and was disappointed when he found that it
> was empty.*
> *He survived the crash only to die in the desert =*
> *He survived the crash but died in the desert.*

B   The infinitive can also be used as a connective link without **only**, and
without any idea of misfortune:
  *He returned home to learn that his daughter had just become
  engaged.*
But this use is mainly confined to such verbs as **find, hear, learn,
see, be told** etc., as otherwise there might be confusion between an
infinitive used connectively and an infinitive of purpose.

250   The infinitive used to replace a relative clause

A   The infinitive can be used after **the first, the second** etc., **the last,
the only** and sometimes after superlatives (see 77):
  He loves parties; he is always the first to come and the last to leave.
  (the first who comes and the last who leaves)
  She was the only one to survive the crash. (the only one who
  survived)
Infinitives used in this way replace subject pronoun + verb. Compare
with infinitive used to replace object pronoun + verb, as in B below.

Note that the infinitive here has an active meaning. When a passive
sense is required a passive infinitive is used:
  He is the second man to be killed in this way. (the second man who
  was killed)
  the best play to be performed that year (the best play that was
  performed that year)
Compare this with:
  the best play to perform (the best play for you to perform/the play
  you should perform)

B 1   The infinitive can be placed after nouns/pronouns to show how they can
be used or what is to be done with them, or sometimes to express the
subject's wishes (see 77):
  I have letters to write. (that I must write)
  Does he get enough to eat?
  Have you anything to say? (that you want to say)
  AT THE CUSTOMS: *I have nothing to declare.* (that I need to declare)
  a house to let (a house that the owner wants to let)
Similarly with infinitives + prepositions:
  someone to talk to   *a case to keep my records in*
  cushions to sit on   *a glass to drink out of*
  a tool to open it with *a table to write on*

2   Use of passive infinitive
  There is plenty to do =
  (a) plenty of things we can do, i.e. amusements, or
  (b) plenty of work we must do.
In the **there** + **be** + noun/pronoun + infinitive construction, when
there is an idea of duty, as in (b) above, a passive infinitive is possible:
  There is a lot to be done.
But the active infinitive is more usual.

251 The infinitive after certain nouns

A number of nouns can be followed directly by the infinitive. Some of the most useful are:

ability	*demand*	*failure*	*request*
ambition	*desire*	*offer*	*scheme*
anxiety	*determination*	*plan*	*willingness*
attempt	*eagerness*	*promise*	*wish*
decision	*effort*	*refusal*	

His ability to get on with people is his chief asset.
He made an attempt/effort to stand up.
Failure to obey the regulations may result in disqualification.
Their offer/plan/promise to rebuild the town was not taken seriously.
She was annoyed by his unwillingness to do his share of the work.

252 The infinitive after **too, enough** and **so . . . as**

A **too** + adjective/adverb + infinitive

1 **too** + adjective + infinitive
(a) The infinitive can refer to the subject of the sentence. It then has an active meaning:
> *You are too young to understand.* (You are so young that you cannot understand.)
> *He was too drunk to drive home.* (He was so drunk that he couldn't drive home.)

(b) The infinitive can also refer to the object of a verb. It then has a passive meaning:
> *The plate was so hot that we couldn't touch it*
could be expressed:
> *The plate was too hot to touch.* (too hot to be touched)
Note that *it*, the object of *touch* in the first sentence, disappears in the infinitive construction, because the infinitive, though active in form, is passive in meaning.
Sometimes either an active or a passive infinitive may be used:
> *This parcel is too heavy to send/to be sent by post.*
But this is not always possible, so students are advised to stick to the active infinitive.
for + noun/pronoun can be placed before the infinitive in this construction:
> *The case was too heavy (for a child) to carry =*
> *The case was too heavy to be carried by a child.*

(c) The infinitive can refer similarly to the object of a preposition:
> *The grass was so wet that we couldn't sit on it.*
> *The grass was too wet (for us) to sit on.*
> *The light is so weak that we can't read by it.*
> *The light is too weak to read by.*

2 **too** + adjective + **a** + noun + infinitive
> *He was too shrewd a businessman to accept the first offer =*
> *As a businessman he was too shrewd to accept the first offer.*
> *He is too experienced a conductor to mind what the critics say =*
> *As a conductor he is too experienced to mind what the critics say.*

The infinitive here always refers to the subject of the sentence as in 1 above. A passive infinitive is also possible:
> *He was too experienced a conductor to be worried by what the critics said.*

3 **too** + adverb + infinitive
> *It is too soon (for me) to say whether the scheme will succeed or not.*
> *He spoke too quickly for me to understand. (for me is necessary here.)*
> *She works too slowly to be much use to me.*

B Adjective/adverb + **enough** + infinitive

1 Adjective + **enough** + infinitive
(a) As with the **too** construction, the infinitive can refer to the subject of the verb:
> *She is old enough to travel by herself.*
> *He was tall enough to see over the heads of the other people.*

(b) Or it can refer to the object of a verb:
> *The case is light enough for me to carry =*
> *The case is so light that I can carry it.*
> *After a few minutes the coffee was cool enough (for us) to drink.*

(c) It can refer to the object of a preposition:
> *The ice was thick enough to walk on.*
> *The light was strong enough to read by.*

2 **enough** may be used as pronoun or adjective:
> *He doesn't earn enough (money) to live on.*
> *We haven't enough time to do it properly.*
> *She had enough sense to turn off the gas.*

have + **enough** + abstract noun here is sometimes replaceable by **have** + **the** + noun:
> *She had the sense to turn off the gas.*
> *He had the courage to admit his mistake.*
> *I hadn't the patience to listen to any more.*

But **the** is optional before **time** here:
> *We haven't (the) time to do it properly.*

3 Adverb + **enough** + infinitive:
> *He didn't jump high enough to win a prize.*
> *He spoke slowly enough for everyone to understand.*

C **so** + adjective + **as** + infinitive:
> *He was so foolish as to leave his car unlocked.*

This is an alternative to the **enough** construction in B1 above, but note that *He was foolish enough to leave his car unlocked* can mean either that he did it or that he was capable of doing it, but *He was so foolish as to leave* etc. implies that he actually did so.

The **so . . . as** construction is not very often used as shown above, but it is quite common as a request form:

> *Would you be so good as to forward my letters?* =
> *Would you be good enough to forward my letters?*

There is no difference in meaning here between the two forms. It is important not to forget the **as**.
(For other adjective + infinitive constructions, see 26 - 7.)

253 Introductory or final infinitive phrases

Certain infinitive phrases can be placed at the beginning or sometimes at the end of a sentence and are then similar to sentence adverbs (see 40):

> *To be perfectly frank, you're a bad driver.*
> *To be honest, I just don't like him.*
> *To be fair (to him), he wasn't entirely to blame.*
> *To cut a long story short, we said 'No!'*
> *To tell you the truth, I've never met him* or
> *I've never met him, to tell you the truth.*

254 The continuous infinitive

A   Form
to be + present participle: *He seems to be following us.*

B   Use
The continuous infinitive can be used:

1   After the auxiliary verbs:
> *They'll be wondering where you are.*
> *He may/might be watching TV.* ~ *He can't/couldn't be watching TV.*
> *There are no programmes today because of the strike.*
> (negative deduction)
> *He must be coming by bus.* (deduction)
> *You shouldn't be reading a novel. You should be reading a textbook.*

2   After **appear, happen, pretend, seem**:
> *He appears/seems to be living in the area* =
> *It appears/seems that he is living in the area.*
> *He appeared/seemed to be living in the area* =
> *It appeared/seemed that he was living in the area.*
> *I happened to be standing next to him when he collapsed* =
> *It happened that I was standing next to him when he collapsed.*
> *He pretended to be looking for a book* =
> *He pretended that he was looking for a book.*

3   After **hope** and **promise** and, but less usually, after **agree, arrange, decide, determine/be determined, plan, undertake**:
> *I hope/hoped to be earning my living in a year's time* =
> *I hope I will/I hoped I would be earning* etc.

determine/be determined, plan could replace **hope** above with slight changes of meaning:

I promised to be waiting at the door when he came out.

agree, arrange, decide, determine/be determined, plan, undertake could be used instead of **promise** above with slight changes of meaning.

4 After **believe, consider, suppose, think** etc. in the passive:

He is believed to be living in Mexico. (See 306.)

255 The perfect infinitive

A Form

to have + past participle: *to have worked, to have spoken*

B Use with auxiliary verbs

1 With **was/were** to express an unfulfilled plan or arrangement (see 114):

The house was to have been ready today. (but it isn't)

2 With **should, would, might** and **could** to form the perfect conditional (see 223):

If I had seen her I should have invited her.

3 With **should** or **ought** to express unfulfilled obligation; or, in the negative, a wrong or foolish action (see 143):

He should have helped her. (but he didn't)
I shouldn't/oughtn't to have lied to him. (but I did)

4 With **should/would like** to express an unfulfilled wish (see 296 D):

He would like to have seen it. (but it wasn't possible) or
He would have liked to see it.

i.e. we can put either verb into the perfect infinitive without changing the meaning.

5 With **could** to express past unused ability or past possibility:

I could have made a lot of money. (but I didn't)
He could/might have phoned her. (Perhaps he (has) phoned.)
(See also 134, 138.)

6 With **might/could** to indicate that the speaker feels upset or indignant at the non-performance of an action:

He might/could have told me! =
I am annoyed that he didn't tell me. (See 285 D.)

7 With **may/might** in speculations about past actions:

He may/might have left =
It is possible that he (has) left. (See 133.)
You might/could have been killed!

8 With **can't/couldn't** to express negative deduction (see 159):

He can't/couldn't have moved the piano himself.
We knew he couldn't have paid for it, because he had no money.

9   With **must** to express affirmative deduction (see 156):
He must have come this way; here are his footprints.

10   With **needn't** to express an unnecessary past action (see also 152-3):
You needn't have hurried. Now we are too early.
You needn't have cooked it. We could have eaten it raw.

C   With certain other verbs

1   With **appear, happen, pretend, seem**
Note the difference between present and perfect infinitives here:
Present infinitive:
He seems to be a great athlete = It seems that he is . . .
He seemed to be a great athlete = It seemed that he was . . .
Perfect infinitive:
He seems to have been . . . = It seems that he was . . .
He seemed to have been . . . = It seemed that he had been . . .
i.e. the action of the perfect infinitive is an earlier action; it happens
before the time of the main verb. Other examples:
I happened to have driven that kind of car before =
It happened that I had driven that kind of car before.
He pretended to have read the book =
He pretended that he had read it.

2   With the following verbs in the passive voice: **acknowledge, believe, consider, find, know, report, say, suppose, think, understand**:
He is understood to have left the country. (See 306.)

3   The perfect infinitive is possible but less usual with **claim, expect, hope, promise**:
He expects/hopes to have finished by June =
He expects/hopes that he will have finished by June.

256   The perfect infinitive continuous

A   Form
to have been + present participle:
He seems to have been spying for both sides.

B   Use
It is used chiefly after auxiliary verbs and after **appear** and **seem**, but
it can also be used after **happen, pretend** and the passive of **believe, know, report, say, understand**:
He says he was talking to Tom. ~ He couldn't have been talking to Tom. Tom wasn't there.
I was following Peter closely. ~ You shouldn't have been following him closely; you should have left a good space between the two cars.
He appears to have been waiting a long time =
It appears that he has been waiting a long time.
He pretended to have been studying =
He pretended that he had been studying.

24 The gerund

257 Form and use

The gerund has exactly the same form as the present participle:
running, speaking, working etc.
It can be used in the following ways:
(a) as subject of a sentence: *Dancing bored him.* (see 258)
(b) as complement of a verb: *Her hobby is painting.*
(c) after prepositions: *He was accused of smuggling.* (259)
(d) after certain verbs (261, 266)
(e) in noun compounds: *a ˈdiving board* (a board for diving off). The gerund here carries the main stress. (See 16.)

258 The gerund as subject

As already seen in 240 E, either infinitive or gerund can be the subject of a sentence when an action is being considered in a general sense. We can say:

> *It is easier to read French than to speak it* or
> *Reading French is easier than speaking it.*

The gerund, like the infinitive (see 240 F), can be the subject of a clause placed after **believe, consider, discover, expect, find, think, wonder** etc.

After **find** we can omit **that** and the verb **be**, i.e. we can say:

> *He found that parking was difficult* or
> *He found parking difficult.*

But it is safer not to omit **be** after the other verbs.
Note the possible difference between gerund and infinitive here:
He found parking difficult would mean that he usually/always found it difficult. *He found it difficult to park* could refer to one particular occasion. It could also mean that he always found it difficult, but it is more usual to express this idea by a gerund.
The gerund is used in short prohibitions:

> *No smoking.   No waiting.   No fishing.*

But these cannot be followed by an object, so prohibitions involving an object are usually expressed by an imperative:

> *Do not touch these wires.   Do not feed the lions.*

Gerunds are used in the saying *Seeing is believing.*

259 Gerunds after prepositions (see also 98)

A When a verb is placed immediately after a preposition the gerund form must be used:

What can you do besides typing?
I have no objection to hearing your story again.
Touch your toes without bending your knees!
He is good at diving.   She is fond of climbing.
I'm not keen on gambling. I'm too afraid of losing.
He was fined for being drunk in charge of a car.
I'm against saying anything/I'm for saying nothing.
I'm tired of arguing.   I'm fed up waiting. (colloquial)
This is a tool for opening tins.   Do you feel like going out?
After swimming I felt cold.
She disapproves of jogging.
What about leaving it here and collecting it later?
He is thinking of emigrating.
I'm sorry for keeping you waiting.
They escaped by sliding down a rope.
We had difficulty in finding a parking place.
You should be ashamed of yourself for behaving so badly.
In spite of starting late he arrived in time.
Aren't you interested in making money?
There's no point in waiting.

B A number of verb + preposition/adverb combinations ('phrasal verbs') take the gerund. The most common of these are **be for/against, care for, give up, keep on, leave off, look forward to, put off, see about, take to.** (For **go on,** see 363.)

I don't care for standing in queues.
Eventually the dogs left off barking.
I am looking forward to meeting her.
He put off making a decision till he had more information.
He took to ringing us up in the middle of the night.

260 The word **to**

This word often causes confusion as it can be either (A) a part of an infinitive, or (B) a preposition.

A **to** placed after the auxiliary verbs **be, have, ought, used** and after **going** (in expressions such as 'the **be going to** form') is part of the infinitive of the following verb and is only added to remind students that the preceding verb takes the full infinitive, i.e. the infinitive with **to**.
to is often placed after **hate, hope, intend, would like/love, mean, plan, try, want** and some others (see 247) to avoid repetition of an infinitive already mentioned:

Did you buy cheese? ~ No, I meant to (buy some) but the shop was shut.

B   Otherwise **to** placed after a verb will probably be a preposition and will be followed by noun/pronoun or gerund. Note these expressions: **look forward to, take to, be accustomed to, be used to:**

> *I am looking forward to my holidays/to next weekend/to it.*
> *I am looking forward to seeing you.*
> *I am used to heat/hard work/bad food/noise/dust.*
> *I am used to standing in queues/to it.*

Be careful not to confuse **I used to/he used to** etc., which expresses a past habit or routine (*They used to burn coal; now they burn fuel oil only*), with **I am used to/he is used to** etc., which means 'I am/he is accustomed to/familiar with':

> *I am used to the cold.* (It doesn't worry me.)
> *He is used to working at night.* (He doesn't mind it.)   (See 162.)

A good way of finding out whether a **to** is a preposition or a part of an infinitive is to see if it is possible to put a noun/pronoun after it. For example a noun/pronoun could be placed after **I am accustomed to:**

> *I am accustomed to it/the dark.*

This **to** therefore is a preposition, and verbs used after **to** must be gerunds.

261   Verbs followed by the gerund

A   The most important of these are:

admit*	*keep* (= continue)
anticipate*	*loathe*
appreciate	*mean** (= involve)
avoid	*mind* (= object)
consider*	*miss*
defer	*pardon*
delay	*postpone*
deny*	*practise*
detest	*prevent*
dislike	*propose** (= suggest)
dread	*recollect**
enjoy	*remember** (= recollect)
escape	*resent*
excuse	*resist*
fancy* (= imagine)	*risk*
finish	*save (sb the trouble of)*
forgive	*stop* (= cease)
imagine*	*suggest**
involve	*understand**

*See B.

The gerund is also used after the expressions *can't stand* (= endure), *can't help* (= prevent/avoid), *it's no use/good* and after the adjective *worth.*

B   Other constructions with the above verbs
    Starred verbs can also take **that**-clauses (see 346).
    For **suggest** and **propose** (= suggest), see 289.
    mean/propose (= intend) take the infinitive (see 269).
    For **hate, like, love, prefer**, see 295.
    For other verbs taking gerund or infinitive, see chapter 25.
    dread + infinitive is used in 'dread to think':
        I dread to think what this will cost.

C   Examples of verb + gerund sentences:
        He admitted taking the money.   Avoid over-eating.
        Would you consider selling the property?
        He detests writing letters.
        She dreads getting old.   Do you enjoy teaching?
        He narrowly escaped being run over.
        Fancy meeting you!
        Putting in a new window will involve cutting away part of the roof.
        He kept complaining.   He didn't want to risk getting wet.
        If we buy plenty of food now it will save shopping later in the week.
        I can't understand his/him leaving his wife.
        I couldn't help laughing.   It's no good/use arguing.
        Is there anything here worth buying?

262   Verbs + possessive adjective/pronoun object + gerund

A   If the verb or verb + preposition is followed directly by the gerund, the
    gerund refers to the subject of the verb:
        Tom insisted on reading the letter. (Tom read it.)
    But if we put a possessive adjective or pronoun before the gerund,
    the gerund refers to the person denoted by the possessive
    adjective/pronoun:
        He insisted on my/me reading it. (I had to read it.)

B   Useful verbs and expressions which can take either construction are:

dislike	propose	understand
dread	recollect	approve/disapprove of
fancy	remember	insist on
involve	resent	it's no good/use
like (negative)	save	object to
mean	stop	there's no point in
mind	suggest	what's the point of

    He disliked working late.
    He disliked me/my working late.
    I object to paying twice for the same thing.
    I object to his/him making private calls on this phone.
    He resented being passed over for promotion.
    He resented my/me being promoted before him.

(For **mind**, see 263; for **suggest** and **propose**, see 289.)

C **excuse, forgive, pardon** and **prevent** are not followed directly by the gerund but take either possessive adjective/pronoun + gerund or pronoun + preposition + gerund:

Forgive my/me ringing you up so early.
Forgive me for ringing you up so early.
You can't prevent his/him spending his own money.
You can't prevent him from spending his own money.

appreciate usually requires a possessive adjective or passive gerund:

I appreciate your giving me so much of your time.
I appreciate being given this opportunity.

D Possessive adjective and pronoun object compared
In formal English the possessive adjective is used with the gerund. But in informal English we very often use the pronoun. The student therefore has a choice of forms, but is recommended to use the pronoun.
With **stop** meaning 'prevent' the pronoun is more usual than the possessive adjective:

I can't stop him writing to the papers.

E Nouns with gerunds
In very formal English the possessive case is used:

I do not remember my mother's complaining about it.

But it is much more usual to omit the **'s**:

I don't remember my mother complaining.

263 The verb **mind**

A This verb is used chiefly in the interrogative and negative:

Would you mind waiting a moment?
I don't mind walking.

B It can be followed directly by a gerund, or by a noun/pronoun or possessive adjective + gerund:

I don't mind living here. (I live here and don't object to it.)
I don't mind his/him living here. (He lives here and I don't object to this./I don't object to his/him living here.)
He didn't mind leaving home. (He left home quite happily.)
He didn't mind Ann leaving home. (Ann left home and he was quite happy about it. See 262 E for case of noun.)

C **would you mind?** is one of the most usual ways of making a request:

Would you mind not smoking? (Please don't smoke.)
Would you mind moving your car? (Please move it.)

Note the change of meaning when a possessive adjective precedes the gerund:

Would you mind my moving your car? =
Would you object if I moved your car? (This is not a request but a polite query.)

Do you mind if I move it? is a possible alternative to *Would you mind my moving it?* but *Do you mind my moving it?* may mean that the action has already started.

D **mind** can never be followed by an infinitive.

E The personal pronoun object can be used with gerunds instead of a possessive adjective (see 262 D).

264 The perfect gerund (**having worked, having spoken** etc.)

This can be used instead of the present form of the gerund (**working, speaking** etc.) when we are referring to a past action:
> *He was accused of deserting his ship* or
> *He was accused of having deserted his ship.*

The perfect gerund is fairly usual after **deny**:
> *He denied having been there.*

Otherwise the present form is much the more usual.

265 The passive gerund

Present: *being written*
Past: *having been written*
> *He was punished by being sent to bed without any supper.*
> *I remember being taken to Paris as a small child.*
> *The safe showed no signs of having been touched.*

25 Infinitive and gerund constructions

266 Verbs which may take either infinitive or gerund

advise (see 267)	*need* (267)
agree (269)	*permit* (267)
allow (267)	*prefer* (295)
begin (267)	*propose* (269)
can/could bear (267)	*recommend* (267)
cease (267)	*regret* (268)
continue (267)	*remember* (268)
forget (268)	*require* (267)
hate (295)	*start* (267)
intend (267)	*stop* (270 B)
like (295)	*try* (270 C)
love (295)	*used to* (270 D)
mean (269)	*want* (267)

Note also *be ashamed (of)/afraid (of)/sorry (for)*, 271;
care (for), 294, 295; *go on*, 270.

267 Verbs taking infinitive or gerund without change of meaning

A **begin, start, continue, ceáse**

B **can't bear**

C **intend**

D **advise, allow, permit, recommend**

E **it needs/requires/wants**

A With **begin, start, continue, cease** either infinitive or gerund may be used without any difference in meaning, but the infinitive is more usual with verbs of knowing and understanding and the verb **matter**:

I began working./I began to work.
He continued living/to live above the shop.

But:

I am beginning to understand/see/realize why he acted as he did.
It ceased to matter whether or not he sold his work.
She never ceased complaining/to complain about prices.

B   After **can/could bear** (chiefly used in the negative) either gerund or infinitive can be used: *I can't bear waiting/to wait;* but when the infinitive refers to a deliberate action the expression implies that the subject's feelings prevent(ed) him from performing the action:

I couldn't bear to tell him. (so I didn't)

C   After **intend**, an infinitive:

I intend to sell it

is more usual than a gerund:

I intend selling it.

The infinitive is necessary when we have **intend** + object. This is found only in formal English:

I intend him to take over the department.

D   With **advise, allow, permit, recommend**

If the person concerned is mentioned we use the infinitive:

He advised me to apply at once.

She recommends housewives to buy the big tins.

They don't allow us to park here.

But if this person is not mentioned, the gerund is used:

He advised applying at once.

She recommends buying the big tins.

They don't allow parking.

The gerund after **allow** and **permit** cannot have an object, so if we want an **allow/permit** + verb + object construction, we must use the infinitive and mention the person concerned:

They allowed their tenants to use the garage.

E   **it needs/requires/wants** can be followed either by the gerund or by the passive infinitive, the gerund being the more usual:

The grass wants cutting or *The grass needs to be cut.*

268   regret, remember, forget

A   **regret, remember, forget** are used with a gerund when the action expressed by the gerund is the earlier action:

I regret spending so much money =

I'm sorry I spent so much money. (*spending* is the first action, *regret* is the second.)

I remember reading about the earthquake in the papers. (*reading* is the first action, *remember* is the second.)

remember can be followed by possessive adjective/object + gerund:

I remember his/him telling me about it.

I remember my father('s) telling me about it.

forget + gerund is possible only when **forget** is in the negative. It is often used after **will never forget**:

I'll never forget waiting for bombs to fall =

I'll always remember waiting for bombs to fall.

B When **regret, remember, forget** themselves express the earlier action they are followed by an infinitive:

> *I regret to say that you have failed your exam.* (*regret* is the first action, *to say* is the second.)

regret here is normally followed by a verb such as *say, inform, tell.* It is normally used only in the present tense.

remember can be used in any tense:

> *I'll remember to ring Bill.* (*remember* is the earlier action.)

forget is used similarly:

> *I often forget to sign my cheques.*
> *I remembered to lock/I didn't forget to lock the door.* (I locked it.)

Conversely:

> *I didn't remember/I forgot to lock it.* (I didn't lock it.)

C **regret, remember, forget** can also be followed by a noun/pronoun or a **that**-clause.

remember and **forget** can also be followed by noun clauses beginning *how, why, when, where, who* etc.:

> *I can't remember when I saw him last.*
> *I've forgotten where I put it.*

269 agree/agree to, mean, propose

A **agree** and **agree to** (preposition)

agree takes the infinitive. It is the opposite of **refuse** + infinitive:

> *When I asked them to wait, Tom agreed to wait a week but Bill refused to wait another day.*

agree cannot take a noun/pronoun object. The opposite of **refuse** + object is **accept** + object:

> *He refused any reward.   She accepted the post.*

agree to (preposition) can be followed by possessive adjective + gerund:

> *He agreed to my leaving early on Friday.* (I asked if I could leave early on Friday and he said that I could. The opposite here would be *He wouldn't agree to my leaving early* etc.)

agree to can be followed by noun/pronoun object:

> *He agreed to the change of plan/to this/to that.*

B **mean** meaning 'intend' takes the infinitive:

> *I mean to get to the top by sunrise.*

mean meaning 'involve' (used only with an impersonal subject) takes the gerund:

> *He is determined to get a seat even if it means standing in a queue all night.*

C **propose** meaning 'intend' usually takes the infinitive:
   I propose to start tomorrow.
   propose meaning 'suggest' takes the gerund:
   I propose waiting till the police get here.
   (For **propose + that . . . should**, see 289.)

270 go on, stop, try, used (to)

A **go on** = 'continue' and is normally followed by a gerund. But it is used
   with an infinitive, usually of a verb like *explain, talk, tell*, when the
   speaker continues talking about the same topic but introduces a new
   aspect of it:
   *He began by showing us where the island was and went on to tell us
   about its climate.*
   Compare *He went on talking about his accident*, which implies that he
   had been talking about it before, with *He went on to talk about his
   accident*, which implies that he had been speaking perhaps about himself
   or his journey but that the accident was being introduced for the first
   time.

B **stop** (= cease) is followed by the gerund: *Stop talking.*
   It can be followed by object + gerund:
   I can't stop him talking to the press.
   A possessive adjective would be possible here but is very seldom used.
   stop (= halt) can be followed by an infinitive of purpose:
   I stopped to ask the way. (I stopped in order to ask the way.)

C **try** usually means 'attempt' and is followed by the infinitive:
   They tried to put wire netting all round the garden. (They attempted
   to do this.)
   The sentence doesn't tell us whether they succeeded or not.
   try can also mean 'make the experiment' and is then followed by the
   gerund:
   They tried putting wire netting all round the garden.
   This means that they put wire netting round the garden to see if it
   would solve their problem (presumably they were trying to keep out
   rabbits and foxes). We know that they succeeded in performing the
   main action; what we don't know is whether this action had the desired
   effect, i.e. kept the foxes out.

D Subject + **used** + infinitive expresses a past habit or routine:
   I used to swim all the year round. (At one time I swam all the year
   round.) (See 162.)
   But subject + **be/become/get** + **used** + **to** (preposition) is followed by
   noun or pronoun or gerund and means 'be/become/get accustomed
   (to)':
   I am used to heat/to living in a hot climate. (I have lived in a hot
   climate for some time so I don't mind it.) (See 163.)

271 be afraid (of), be sorry (for), be ashamed (of)

A **be afraid of** + gerund or gerund + noun/pronoun
Here the gerund usually expresses an action which the subject fears
may happen. It is normally an involuntary action:

He never swam far out. He was afraid of getting cramp.
She avoids lonely streets. She is afraid of being mugged.
She didn't tell him because she was afraid of upsetting him.

be afraid + infinitive means that the subject is/was etc. too frightened
to perform the action. This is obviously a deliberate action:

He was afraid to jump. (so he didn't jump)
She was afraid to protest. (so she kept quiet)

be afraid can also be followed by a **that**-clause. This can express a
fear:

I'm afraid (that) he'll blame me for this.

But, especially in the first person, it can express (usually fairly mild)
regret:

I'm afraid (that) we haven't any tickets left.

(For **I'm afraid so/not**, see 347.)

B **be sorry for** + gerund means 'apologize/regret'. The gerund usually
refers to a previous action but can refer to an immediately following
action:

I'm sorry for making such a noise last night.
I'm sorry for disturbing you. (now)

But *I'm sorry to disturb you* would be more usual here.

be sorry + infinitive can express regret or sadness:

I'm sorry to hear that you've been ill.   (See also 26 F.)

When the action expressed by the infinitive is involuntary, the two
actions are almost simultaneous:

I was sorry to see him looking so ill. (When I saw him . . . I was
sorry.)

When the infinitive refers to a deliberate action, **be sorry** is the earlier
of the two actions and is then very similar to **regret** (see 268 B):

I'm sorry to inform you that there has been an accident.

be sorry that . . . is also possible. Note that *I'm sorry that* usually
expresses genuine regret, but that with *I'm sorry to say that* or *I'm
afraid that* the regret may be very faint, even perfunctory.

C **be ashamed of** + gerund or **be ashamed of yourself** etc. **for** +
gerund
The gerund here refers to a previous action:

You should be ashamed of lying to him or
You should be ashamed of yourself for lying to him.

In **be ashamed** + infinitive, the infinitive usually refers to a subsequent
action:

I'm ashamed to tell you what this carpet cost.

would be ashamed + infinitive often implies that the subject's feelings
(will) prevent him from performing the action:

I'd be ashamed to ask for help. (so I won't/wouldn't ask)

26 The participles

272 The present (or active) participle

A Form
The infinitive + **ing**, e.g. *working, loving, sitting.*

B Use

1 To form the continuous tenses (see 164, 178 etc.):
   He is working.   You've been dreaming.

2 As adjectives (see 17):
   running water   floating wreckage
   dripping taps   leaking pipes
   Here there is equal stress on participle and noun. Compare with gerund
   + noun combinations (see 16).

3 After **have** + object (see 121):
   He had me swimming in a week.
   We have people standing on our steps all day.
   I won't have him cleaning his bike in the kitchen.

4 A present participle can sometimes replace a relative pronoun + verb
   (see 77):
   a map that marks/marked political boundaries =
   a map marking political boundaries
   people who wish/wished to visit the caves =
   people wishing to visit the caves
   children who need/needed medical attention =
   children needing medical attention

5 Present participles/participle phrases such as **adding/pointing out/
   reminding/warning** can introduce statements in indirect speech:
   *He told me to start early, reminding me that the roads would be
   crowded.*   (See 324 C.)

The above uses have already been dealt with. The present participle
can also be used:

6 After verbs of sensation (see 273).

7 After **catch/find/leave** + object (see 274).

8 After **go, come, spend, waste, be busy** (see 275).

9 Present participles can sometimes replace subject + verb in other main
   or subordinate clauses other than those mentioned above (see 276-7).

273 Present participle after verbs of sensation

A The basic verbs of sensation **see, hear, feel, smell**, and the verbs **listen (to), notice** and **watch** can be followed by object + present participle:

> *I see him passing my house every day.*
> *Didn't you hear the clock striking?*
> *I felt the car skidding.*
> *She smelt something burning and saw smoke rising.*
> *I watched them rehearsing the play.*

The action in the present participle may be either complete or incomplete: *I saw him changing the wheel* could mean that I watched the whole action or that I saw only part of it.

B **see, hear, feel** and sometimes **listen (to), notice** and **watch** can also be followed by object + bare infinitive:

> *We saw him leave the house.*
> *I heard him make arrangements for his journey.*

The infinitive implies that the action is complete. *I saw him change the wheel* means that I saw the whole action.

C Comparison of the two forms

The participle is the more generally useful as it can express both complete and incomplete actions. But the infinitive is useful when we want to emphasize that the action is complete. It is also neater than the participle when there is a succession of actions:

> *I saw him enter the room, unlock a drawer, take out a document, photograph it and put it back.*

D In the passive the full infinitive is used after verbs of the senses:

> *He was heard to say that the minister had been bribed.*

274 catch, find, leave + object + present participle

A **catch/find**:

> *I caught them stealing my apples.* (I found them doing this.)
> *If she catches you reading her diary, she'll be furious.*

The action expressed by the participle is always one which displeases the subject.

With **find** there is no feeling of displeasure:

> *I found him standing at the door =*
> *I saw him standing/He was standing at the door when I arrived.*

With **find** the object could be inanimate:

> *He found a tree lying across the road.*

B **leave** can be used with a participle:

> *I left him talking to Bob =*
> *He was talking to Bob when I left.*

275 go, come, spend, waste, be busy

A **go** and **come**

go and come can be followed by the participles of verbs of physical activity and the verb **shop**:

They are going riding/skiing/sailing.
Come dancing. *I'm going shopping this afternoon.*

(For **go** and **come** followed by infinitives of purpose, see 335.)

B **spend/waste** + an expression of time or money + present participle:

He spends two hours (a day) travelling.
He doesn't spend much time preparing his lessons.
We wasted a whole afternoon trying to repair the car.
He spent a lot of money modernizing the house.

C **be busy** + present participle: *She is/was busy packing.*

276 A present participle phrase replacing a main clause

The participle constructions in A and B below are chiefly used in written English.

A When two actions by the same subject occur simultaneously it is usually possible to express one of them by a present participle. The participle can be before or after the finite verb:

He rode away. He whistled as he went. = He rode away whistling.
He holds the rope with one hand and stretches out the other to the boy in the water = Holding the rope with one hand, he stretches etc.

B When one action is immediately followed by another by the same subject the first action can often be expressed by a present participle. The participle must be placed first:

He opened the drawer and took out a revolver =
Opening the drawer he took out a revolver.
She raised the trapdoor and pointed to a flight of steps =
Raising the trapdoor she pointed to a flight of steps.
We take off our shoes and creep cautiously along the passage =
Taking off our shoes we creep cautiously along the passage.

It would seem more logical here to use the perfect participle and say *Having opened, Having raised, Having taken off*, but this is not necessary except when the use of the present participle might lead to ambiguity. *Eating his dinner he rushed out of the house* would give the impression that he left the house with his plate in his hand. Here, therefore, it would be better to say *Having eaten his dinner . . .*

C When the second action forms part of the first, or is a result of it, we can express the second action by a present participle:

She went out, slamming the door.
He fired, wounding one of the bandits.
I fell, striking my head against the door and cutting it. (Here we have three actions, the last two expressed by participles.)

The participle need not necessarily have the same subject as the first verb:

> *The plane crashed, its bombs exploding as it hit the ground.*

277 A present participle phrase replacing a subordinate clause

These constructions are chiefly found in written English.
The present participle can replace **as/since/because** + subject + verb, i.e. it can help to explain the action which follows:

> *Knowing that he wouldn't be able to buy food on his journey he took large supplies with him = As he knew etc.*
>
> *Fearing that the police would recognize him he never went out in daylight = As he feared etc.*

Note that **being** at the beginning of a sentence will normally mean 'as he is/as he was':

> *Being a student he was naturally interested in museums =*
> *Because/As he was a student etc.*

It could not mean 'while he was a student'.
The subject of the participle need not be the same as the subject of the following verb:

> *The day being fine, we decided to go swimming.*

In cases like this the participle must follow its noun/pronoun. *Being fine the day, we decided . . .* is incorrect, but *Being athletic, Tom found the climb quite easy* is all right, as Tom is the subject of both the participle and the following verb.
It is possible to use two or more participles, one after the other:

> *Realizing that he hadn't enough money and not wanting to borrow from his father, he decided to pawn his watch.*
>
> *Not knowing the language and having no friends in the town, he found it hard to get work.*

278 The perfect participle (active)

A Form
having + past participle, e.g. *having done, having seen.*

B Use
The perfect participle can be used instead of the present participle in sentences of the type shown in 276 B (i.e. where one action is immediately followed by another with the same subject):

> *Tying one end of the rope to his bed, he threw the other end out of the window =*
>
> *Having tied one end of the rope to his bed, he threw the other end out of the window.*

The perfect participle emphasizes that the first action is complete before the second one starts, but is not normally necessary in combinations of this kind, except when the use of the present participle might lead to confusion. *Reading the instructions, he snatched up the fire extinguisher* might give the impression that the two actions were simultaneous. Here, therefore, the perfect participle would be better:

> *Having read the instructions, he snatched up the fire extinguisher.*

The perfect participle is, however, necessary when there is an interval of time between the two actions:

> *Having failed twice, he didn't want to try again.*

It is also used when the first action covered a period of time:

> *Having been his own boss for such a long time, he found it hard to accept orders from another.*

279 The past participle (passive) and the perfect participle (passive)

A **Form**

The past participle of regular verbs is formed by adding **ed** or **d** to the infinitive, e.g. *worked, loved.*

For the past participle of irregular verbs, see chapter 39.

B **Use**

1 As an adjective:

> *stolen money*   *a written report*   *fallen trees*
> *broken glass*   *tired drivers*   *blocked roads.*

2 To form the perfect tenses/infinitives and participles and the passive voice:

> *he has seen*   *to have loved*   *it was broken*

3 The past participle can replace a subject + passive verb just as the present participle can replace subject + active verb:

> *She enters. She is accompanied by her mother.* =
> *She enters, accompanied by her mother.*
> *He was aroused by the crash and leapt to his feet* =
> *Aroused by the crash, he leapt to his feet.*
> *The bridge had been weakened by successive storms and was no longer safe* =
> *Weakened by successive storms, the bridge was no longer safe* or
> *Having been weakened etc. (see below).*
> *As he was convinced that they were trying to poison him, he refused to eat anything* =
> *Convinced that they were trying to poison him, he refused to eat anything.*

C The perfect participle passive (**having been** + past participle) is used when it is necessary to emphasize that the action expressed by the participle happened before the action expressed by the next verb:

> *Having been warned about the bandits, he left his valuables at home. (He had been warned etc.)*
> *Having been bitten twice, the postman refused to deliver our letters unless we chained our dog up. (He had been bitten etc.)*

280 Misrelated participles

A participle is considered to belong to the noun/pronoun which precedes it:

Tom, horrified at what he had done, could at first say nothing.
Romeo, believing that Juliet was dead, decided to kill himself.
A man carrying a large parcel got out of the bus.

Note that the participle may be separated from its noun/pronoun by a main verb:

Jones and Smith came in, followed by their wives.
She rushed past the policeman, hoping he wouldn't ask what she had in her suitcase.

If there is no noun/pronoun in this position the participle is considered to belong to the subject of the following main verb:

Stunned by the blow, Peter fell heavily. (Peter had been stunned.)
Believing that he is alone, the villain expresses his thoughts aloud.

If this principle is disregarded confusion results. *Waiting for a bus a brick fell on my head* makes it appear that the brick was waiting for a bus, which is nonsense. A participle linked in this way to the wrong noun/pronoun is said to be 'misrelated'. The above sentence should be rewritten *As I was waiting for a bus a brick fell on my head.*

Other examples of misrelated participles:

When using this machine it must be remembered . . .
Correct form:
When using this machine you must remember . . .

Believing that I was the only person who knew about this beach, the sight of someone else on it annoyed me very much.
Correct form:
As I believed I was the only person etc. or
Believing that I was the only person on the beach, I was annoyed by the sight of someone else.

27 Commands, requests, invitations, advice, suggestions

281 Commands expressed by the imperative

A The second person imperative

1 This has the same form as the bare infinitive:
   Hurry!   Wait!   Stop!
   For the negative we put **do not (don't)** before the verb:
   Don't hurry!

2 The person addressed is very often not mentioned, but can be expressed by a noun placed at the end of the phrase:
   Eat your dinner, boys.   Be quiet, Tom.
   These nouns can be placed before the verb, but this is much less usual.

   The pronoun **you** is rarely used unless the speaker wishes to be rude, or wishes to make a distinction, as in:
   You go on; I'll wait.

3 **do** can be placed before the affirmative imperative:
   Do hurry.   Do be quiet.
   This **do** could be persuasive, but could also express irritation.

B The first person imperative
   Form
   let us (let's) + bare infinitive:
   Let us stand together in this emergency.
   For the negative we normally put **not** before the infinitive:
   Let us not be alarmed by rumours.
   But it is possible in colloquial English to put **don't** before **let's**:
   Don't let's be alarmed by rumours.
   By **let us (let's)** the speaker can urge his hearers to act in a certain way, or express a decision which they are expected to accept, or express a suggestion (see 289).

C The third person imperative
   Form
   let him/her/it/them + bare infinitive (see also 322):
   Let them go by train.
   This is not a very common construction in modern English. It would be more usual to say:
   They are to go/must go by train.
   The negative imperative, *let him/her/them* + negative infinitive, is not used in modern English. Instead, we would use **must not** or **is/are not to**:
   They must not/are not to go by air.

282 Other ways of expressing commands

A Subject + **shall** for third person commands (in written English)

shall can be used in very formal written regulations which will normally remain in force for some time. These are very often in the passive (see also 234):

> *The Chairman, Secretary, and Treasurer shall be elected annually.* (club regulations)
> *A record shall be kept of the number of students attending each class.* (college regulations)

B Subject + **will**, mainly for third person commands:

> *When the alarm rings passengers and crew will assemble at their boat stations.* (notice on board ship)

This is a formal, impersonal, peremptory type of command, implying that the person giving the order is quite certain that he will be obeyed. It is used chiefly in written instructions by people who have some authority, e.g. captains of ships, officers of the services, headmasters of schools, trainers of sports teams etc.:

> *The team will report to the gymnasium for weight-lifting training.*

Note that if we move the **will** and place it before the subject, we turn the command into a request.

It is possible to use **you will** for spoken commands:

> *You will not mention this meeting to anyone.*

But it is more usual and more polite to use **must**:

> *You must not mention this meeting to anyone.*

C Commands are often expressed as obligations by **must**:

> *You must not smoke in the petrol store.*
> *Passengers must cross the line by the footbridge.*
> *Dogs must be kept on leads in this area.*

D Instructions or orders can be conveyed by the **be** + infinitive construction:

> *You are to report for duty immediately.*
> *The switchboard is to be manned at all times.*

E Prohibitions may be expressed in written instructions by **may not**:

> *Candidates may not bring textbooks into the examination room.*

283 Requests with **can/could/may/might I/we**

A **can/could/may/might I/we** + **have** + noun/pronoun

can is the most informal:

> (a) *'Can I have a sweet?' said the little boy.*

can I/we, when used by adults, sounds more confident than **could I/we**.

could I/we is the most generally useful form:

> (b) *Could I have a cup of tea?   Could I have two tickets, please?*

may and **might** are more formal than **could**, but possible in both spoken and written English:

(c) *May/Might I have a copy of the letter?*

These requests are usually reported by **ask** (+ indirect object) + **for** + object:

The little boy asked (me) for a sweet.
He asked for a copy of the letter.

But (c) above could also be reported:

He asked if he might have a copy of the letter.

B **can/could/may/might I/we** + verb

For the difference between them, see A above.

These could be requests for permission (see 131), but with certain verbs, e.g. *see, speak (to), talk (to),* they can be ordinary requests:

May/Could I see Mr Jones? = I would like to see Mr Jones.

This type of request is reported by **ask to see/to speak to** etc.:

I asked to see Mr Jones.

Do not put a noun/pronoun after **ask**, as this would change the meaning (see 243 B).

In colloquial English **ask for** + name etc. would also be possible, especially when reporting a telephone conversation:

CALLER: *Could I speak to the secretary, please? =*
She asked for the secretary/to speak to the secretary.

C **could/might I/we** requests can be preceded by **do you think/ I wonder(ed)/was wondering if**. These prefixes make the requests more diffident:

I wonder/was wondering if I could have tomorrow off?
Do you think I could speak to the secretary?

Note the change from interrogative to affirmative verb (see 104).

284 Requests with **could/will/would you** etc.

For starred forms, see K below.

A **could you*** is a very useful request form:

Could you please show me the way?

possibly can be added to show that the speaker is asking for something extra:

Could you possibly lend me £500?

couldn't expresses the speaker's hopes for a more favourable answer than has just been indicated:

I can't wait. ~ Couldn't you wait five minutes?

you couldn't . . . could you? can be used to express a not very hopeful request:

You couldn't wait five minutes, could you?
You couldn't give me a hand with this, could you?

(The speaker doesn't really expect a favourable answer in either case.)

B   **will/would you* (please)**:
    Will/Would you please count your change?
    would you (please) has the same meaning as **could you**.
    will you is more authoritative and therefore less polite.
    will/would you can be placed at the end of the phrase:
    Shut the door, will you?
    But this form can only be used in very friendly relaxed situations. Used
    otherwise, it would sound very rude.
    will/would can also be used for third person requests:
    *Would Mrs Jones, passenger to Leeds, please come to the Enquiry
    Desk?*
    Will anyone who saw the accident please phone this number . . . ?
    (police announcement)

C   **you'll . . . won't you?** is a persuasive type of request used mainly
    among friends:
    You'll write to me, won't you?

D   **would you mind*** + gerund (see 263):
    Would you mind moving your car?

E   **perhaps you would** implies confidence that the other person will
    perform this service. It would not be used at the beginning of a
    conversation or letter, but would be possible later on:
    *Perhaps you would let me know when your new stock arrives =
    Please let me know when your new stock arrives.*

F   **if you would** is a useful request form. It is used in spoken English for
    routine-type requests which the speaker is quite sure will be obeyed:
    If you'd fill up this form/take a seat/wait a few minutes. (in an office)
    If you'd sign the register/follow the porter. (in a hotel)
    just can be added to show that the action required is very easy:
    If you'd just put your address on the back of the cheque. (in a shop)

G   **would you like to . . . ?** is also a possible request form:
    Would you like to take a seat? = Please take a seat.

H   **I should/would be very grateful if you would** is a formal request
    form found chiefly in letters but possible in speech:
    *I should be very grateful if you would let me know if you have any
    vacancies.*

I   **Would you be good/kind enough** *to keep me informed?*
    Would you be so kind as *to keep me informed?*

J   **I wish you would** can be a request form. It sometimes implies that
    the other person should be helping or have offered to do it (see 301):
    I wish you'd give me a hand.

K   Starred **would** and **could** forms may be introduced by phrases such as
    do you think? I wonder(ed) if, I was wondering if (see 104):
    Do you think you could lend me £500?

285 Requests with **might**

A **you might** can express a very casual request:
You might post these for me.
But it can only be used in friendly relaxed situations, otherwise it would sound rude.

B With a certain intonation and a strong stress on the important word **might** can express a reproachful request: *You might 'help me* with stress on *help* might imply 'Why aren't you helping me?/You should be helping me'.

C **might** can also be used with other persons to express this sort of irritation: *He might 'pay us!* with stress on *pay* could mean 'We are annoyed that he doesn't pay/hasn't paid us'.

D **might** + perfect infinitive can express irritation at or reproach for the non-performance of an action in the past: *You might have 'told us* with stress on *told* could mean 'You should have told us'.

286 Invitations

A **will you have/would you like** + noun:
Will you have a drink? (sometimes shortened to *Have a drink.*)
Would you like a coffee?
Note that **do you want** is not an invitation.
(For **want** and **would like**, see 296.)
In indirect speech we use **offer** + indirect object (= person addressed) + noun:
She offered me a drink/a coffee.

B **will/would/could you? would you like to?**
Will you have lunch with me tomorrow? is informal, but *Would/Could you have lunch with me?* or *Would you like to have lunch with me?* can be used in both informal and formal situations.
These invitations would be reported by **invite/ask** + direct object + **to** + noun, or **invite/ask** + direct object + infinitive:
He invited me to lunch/to have lunch with him.

C Answers to invitations
Offers of a drink/a cigarette etc. are usually answered:
Yes, please or *No, thank you.*
Invitations with **would you/could you/would you like** are usually answered:
I'd like to very much/I'd love to or
I'd like to very much but I'm afraid I can't.
wouldn't like, of course, would not be possible.
An invitation and answer might be reported:
He invited us to dinner/to a party/to spend the weekend with him and we accepted/but we refused/but we had to refuse because . . .

D   When the speaker doesn't really expect his offer/invitation to be accepted he can say:

You wouldn't like another drink, would you? (Perhaps the speaker would like another drink himself, and wants an excuse. He doesn't really expect that his friend will accept, though.)

You wouldn't like to come with me, would you? (Again he doesn't really expect an acceptance.)

287 Advice forms

A   **must, ought to** and **should** can be used for advice:

You must read this book. It's marvellous.
You should grow your own vegetables.
You ought to plant some trees.

In indirect speech **must, ought to** and **should** here can remain unchanged or be reported by **advise** + object:

He advised me to plant trees.

B   **you had better** + bare infinitive (see 120):

You'd better take off your wet shoes.
You'd better not wait any longer.

had better can be used with the third person:

He'd better stop taking those pills.

C   **if I were you I should/would**:

If I were you I'd buy a car.

This is often shortened to **I should/would** with a slight stress on the **I**:

ⁱ*I'd buy a car.*

In indirect speech *If I were you I should/would . . .* is reported by **advise** + object:

He advised me to buy a car.

D   **I advise/would advise you** + infinitive:

I (would) advise you to apply at once

or **I advise/would advise** + gerund:

I('d) advise applying at once.

E   **why don't you . . . ?** can be either advice or suggestion:

Why don't you learn to play your guitar?
Why don't you take a holiday?

When this is advice it is reported by **advise** + object:

He advised me to take a holiday.

F   **it is time you** + past tense:

It is time you bought a new coat. (See 293.)

This would be reported:

He said it was time I bought a new coat.

288 Advice with **may/might as well** + infinitive

This construction can express very unemphatic advice:

You may/might as well ask him =
It would do no harm to ask him.
She said I might as well ask him.

This form can be used with the third person:

He may as well come with me

and the speaker may use it of himself:

As there isn't anything more to do, I may as well go home early.

289 Suggestions

A First person suggestions with **let's** or **shall I/we**

let's + infinitive:

Let's paint it ourselves.

shall we is sometimes added:

Let's get the paint today, shall we?

shall I/we + infinitive:

Shall we invite Bill?

Suggestions with **let's** or **shall we** can be answered affirmatively by **yes, let's**.

let's not could be used jokingly as a negative answer:

Let's take the tent. ~ Let's not!

Or it can introduce a negative suggestion:

Let's not start too early.

don't let's could also be used here:

Don't let's start too early.

B First and second person suggestions

why don't we/you + infinitive or **why not** + infinitive/expression of time or place:

Why don't we meet and discuss it?
Why not meet and discuss it?
Where shall we meet? ~ Why not here?/Why not at the hotel?

In colloquial English **what's wrong with/what's the matter with** + noun could also be used:

What's wrong with the hotel?

what/how about + gerund/noun:

Where shall we sleep? ~ What about renting a caravan?
What about a bed and breakfast place?

suppose I/we/you + present or past tense:

Suppose you offer/offered to pay him?

C First, second or third person suggestions with **suggest** or **propose**

suggest (+ possessive adjective) + gerund, or **suggest that** + subject + present tense/**should**.
propose is used in exactly the same way but is slightly more formal than **suggest**.
In the active, **suggest** + **should** + infinitive is more formal than **suggest** + a present or past tense.

> *I suggest (your) selling it.*
> *We suggest that you should sell it.* (formal)
> *I propose that the secretary sends in/should send in a report.* (formal)
> *I propose that a report (should) be sent in.* (formal)

that . . . should is necessary in the passive.
With **should be** it is possible in formal English to omit the **should**, leaving the **be** alone, as shown above.

D Suggestions in indirect speech

Suggestions can be reported by:
suggest/suggested (+ possessive adjective) + gerund, or
suggest that + subject + present tense/**should**, or
suggested that + subject + past tense/**should**, or
suggest (any tense) + noun/pronoun:

> *Tom suggests/suggested (our) having a meeting.*
> *Ann suggests that he sells/should sell his house.*
> *Ann suggested that he sold/should sell it.*
> *Mr Jones suggested a meeting.*

(For suggestions with **let's**, see also 322.)

28 The subjunctive

290 Form

A   The present subjunctive has exactly the same form as the infinitive; therefore the present subjunctive of **to be** is **be** for all persons, and the present subjunctive of all other verbs is the same as their present tense except that **s** is not added for the third person singular:
   The queen lives here. (simple present tense)
   Long live the queen! (subjunctive)

B   The past subjunctive has exactly the same form as the simple past except that with the verb **be** the past subjunctive form is either **I/he/she/it was** or **I/he/she/it were**. In expressions of doubt or unreality **were** is more usual than **was**:
   He behaves as though he were the owner. (But he is not the owner.)
   In conversation, however, **was** is often used instead of **were** (see also 225).
   Past subjunctives are often known as 'unreal pasts'.

291 Use of the present subjunctive

A   The present subjunctive is used in certain exclamations to express a wish or hope, very often involving supernatural powers:
   (God) bless you!   God save the queen!
   Heaven help us!   Curse this fog!
   Come what may, we'll stand by you!
   Notice also the phrase **if need be**, which means 'if it is necessary':
   If need be we can always bring another car.

B   It is sometimes used in poetry, either to express a wish or in clauses of condition or concession:
   STEVENSON: *Fair the day shine as it shone in my childhood.* (May the day shine/I hope it will shine.)
   SHAKESPEARE: *If this be error, and upon me proved . . .* (if this is error)
   BYRON: *Though the heart be still as loving . . .* (though the heart is)

C   As seen in 235 certain verbs are followed by **should** + infinitive constructions. When the infinitive is **be**, the **should** is sometimes omitted:
   He suggested that a petition (should) be drawn up.
   The infinitive thus left alone becomes a subjunctive.

292 **as if/as though** + past subjunctive

The past subjunctive can be used after **as if/as though** to indicate unreality or improbability or doubt in the present (there is no difference between **as if** and **as though**):

He behaves as if he owned the place. (But he doesn't own it or probably doesn't own it or we don't know whether he owns it or not.)

He talks as though he knew where she was. (But he doesn't know or he probably doesn't know or we don't know whether he knows or not.)

He orders me about as if I were his wife. (but I am not)

The verb preceding **as if/though** can be put into a past tense without changing the tense of the subjunctive:

He talks/talked as though he knew where she was.

After **as if/as though** we use a past perfect when referring to a real or imaginary action in the past:

He talks about Rome as though he had been there himself. (But he hasn't or probably hasn't or we don't know whether he has or not.)

Again, the verb preceding **as if/though** can be put into a past tense without changing the tense of the subjunctive:

He looks/looked as though he hadn't had a decent meal for a month.

293 **it is time** + past subjunctive (unreal past)

it is time can be followed by the infinitive:

It's time to start

or by **for** + object + infinitive:

It's time for us to go

or by subject + a past subjunctive:

It's time we went.   *It's time we were leaving.*

There is a slight difference in meaning between the forms.

it is time + infinitive merely states that the correct time has arrived;

it is time + subject + past subjunctive implies that it is a little late.

high can be added to emphasize this idea:

It's high time we left.

it is time + **I/he/she/it** cannot be followed by **were**:

It's time I was going.

(For past subjunctives/unreal pasts in conditional sentences, see 222; after **would rather/sooner**, see 297; after **wish** + subject, see 300; in indirect speech, see 310.)

29 care, like, love, hate, prefer, wish

294 care and like

care is chiefly used in the negative and interrogative.

A **care for** + noun/gerund is very similar to **like** + noun/gerund. We can
say:
>   (a) *Does/Did Tom care for living in the country?* or
>   *Does/Did Tom like living in the country?*
>   (b) *You don't care for science fiction, do you?* or
>   *You don't like science fiction, do you?*

(b) above could be answered:
>   *I don't care for it* or *I don't like it much* or *Oh yes, I like it.*
>   (**care** would not be possible here.)

care in the interrogative sometimes carries a hint of doubt:
>   *Does Ann care for horror movies?* (The speaker thinks that she
>   probably doesn't, or is surprised that she apparently does.)

The feeling of doubt is more noticeable with **would you care
(for) . . . ?**

B **would care** and **would like**
would care for + noun and **would care** + infinitive are similar
to **would like** + noun/infinitive. But **would care (for)** is not normally
used in the affirmative, and offers expressed by **would you care
(for) . . . ?** are less confident than **would you like . . . ?** offers:
>   (a) TOM: *Would you care for a lift, Ann?* (Perhaps his car is
>   uncomfortable and she likes comfort.)
>   (b) TOM: *Would you care to see my photos, Ann?* (He isn't sure that
>   she'll want to see them.)

A favourable answer to (b) above would be:
>   *I'd like to see them very much.*

As in the affirmative, **would like** replaces **would care**.
Similarly in negative statements:
>   *I wouldn't care to live on the 35th floor ~ Oh, I'd rather like it.*

would care for/would like can sometimes be used with gerunds.
(See 295 B.)

C **would have cared (for)** and **would have liked**
Both here refer to actions which didn't take place:
>   ANN: *I'd have liked to go with Tom.* (I wanted to go but didn't get
>   my wish. See also 296 D. **care** could not be used here.)
>   BILL: *But he walked all the way! You wouldn't have cared for/have
>   liked that, would you?* or *Would you have cared for/have liked that?*

D   Do not confuse **care** as used above with **care for** (= look after) and
    care (about):

1   **care for** (= look after) is used chiefly in the passive:
        The old people were cared for by their families.

2   **care (about)** (= feel concerned) is used chiefly in the negative and
    interrogative.
    I don't care (about) appears similar to **I don't mind**, which can often
    be used instead:
        It will be very expensive. ~ I don't care/mind or
        I don't care about/mind the expense or
        I don't care/mind what it costs.
    But note that **I don't care (about)** = 'I am indifferent (to)' while
    I don't mind = 'I don't object (to)', i.e. 'He/It doesn't worry/upset/
    annoy me.'
    I don't mind is much more polite than **I don't care**, which often
    sounds arrogant and selfish. In the negative interrogative either can be
    used:
        Don't you care/mind what happens to him?
        Didn't you care/mind what happened?
    But in the ordinary interrogative there is more difference between the
    two:
        Do you care? = Are you concerned?/Do you feel concern?
    while *Do you mind?* usually means *Do you object?*
    (See also 263.)

295   care, like, love, hate, prefer

A   When used in the conditional, these verbs are usually followed by the
    infinitive:
        Would you care/like to come with me? (Would it please you to come
        with me?)
        I'd like to (come) very much or *I'd love to (come).*
        I'd hate to spend Christmas alone.
    Here we are thinking of a particular action in the future.

B   But **would care for, would like** can be followed by gerunds when we
    are not thinking of a particular action but are considering the subject's
    tastes generally. Note also that here **would care for/would like** are
    replaceable by **would enjoy**:
        She would like/would enjoy riding if she could ride better.
        I wonder if Tom would care for/would enjoy hang-gliding.
    hate and **prefer** can be used similarly but are less common.

C   When used in the present or past tenses, **care for, like** (= enjoy),
    love, hate and **prefer** are usually followed by the gerund:
        He doesn't/didn't care for dancing.
        They love/loved wind-surfing.
        He prefers/preferred walking to cycling.

But the infinitive is not impossible and is particularly common in American English:
They love/loved to run on the sands.

D Note however that **like** can also mean 'think wise or right', and is then always followed by the infinitive:
She likes them to play in the garden. (She thinks they are safe there.)
I like to go to the dentist twice a year. (I think this wise.)
Compare this with *I like going to the dentist*, which implies that I enjoy my visits. Similarly *I don't like to go* = 'I don't think it right to go' while *I don't like going* = 'I don't enjoy going'.

Notice also another difference between these two negative forms.
I don't like to go usually means 'I don't go' (because I don't think it right). *I don't like going* usually means 'I go, although I don't enjoy it'. Similarly *I didn't like to open the letter* means 'I didn't open it because I didn't think it right to do so' but *I didn't like opening the letter* means 'I opened it reluctantly'.

E **enjoy** and **dislike** are always followed by noun/pronoun or gerund.

296 would like and want

A Sometimes either **would like** or **want** can be used:

1 In requests and questions about requests (but **would not like** is not used here: see B1 below):
CUSTOMER: *I'd like some raspberries, please* or
I want some raspberries, please.
GREENGROCER: *I'm afraid I haven't any. Would you like some strawberries?*
CUSTOMER: *No, I don't want any strawberries, thanks.* (*wouldn't like* is not possible.)
I would like is usually more polite than **I want**.

would you like? is much more polite and helpful than **do you want?** **would you like?** can imply a willingness to satisfy the other person's wishes. **do you want?** doesn't imply this. Someone dealing with a customer or client, therefore, will normally use **would you like?**:
CALLER: *I'd like to/I want to speak to Mr X, please.*
TELEPHONIST: *Mr X is out. Would you like to speak to Mr Y?*

2 When we are not making requests, but merely talking about our wishes, we can use either **would like** or **want** in affirmative, interrogative or negative. There is no difference in meaning, though *I want* usually sounds more confident than *I would like* and *I want* is not normally used for unrealizable wishes:
I would like to live on Mars.

B would like and want are not interchangeable in the following uses:

1 In invitations we use **would you like?** not **do you want?**
> *Would you like a cup of coffee?*
> *Would you like to come to the theatre?*

do you want? used here would be a question only, not an invitation.

2 **wouldn't like** and **don't want** are different.
don't want = 'have no wish for', but **wouldn't like** = 'would dislike'.
wouldn't like cannot therefore be used in answer to invitations or offers, as it would be impolite. Instead we use **don't want** or some other form:
> *Would you like some more coffee?* ~ *No, I don't want any more, thanks* or *No, thanks.*

C In the past the two forms behave differently. In indirect speech **want** becomes **wanted**, but **would like** remains unchanged:
> *Tom said, 'I would like/want to see it'* =
> *Tom said he would like/wanted to see it.*

But if we don't use a reported speech construction we have to say *Tom wanted to see it.* (We cannot use **would like** here, as *Tom would like to see it* has a present or future meaning.)

D **would like** has two past forms: **would like** + perfect infinitive or **would have liked** + infinitive/noun/pronoun. These forms express unrealized wishes only:
> *I'd like to have gone skiing* or
> *I'd have liked a day's skiing.* (But I didn't get my wish.)

297 would rather/sooner and prefer/would prefer

There is no difference between **would rather** and **would sooner**, but **would rather** is more often heard.

A **would rather/sooner** is followed by the bare infinitive when the subject of **would rather/sooner** is the same as the subject of the following action:
> *Tom would rather read than talk.*

1 **would rather/sooner** + infinitive can be used instead of **prefer** + gerund for present actions:
> *Tom prefers reading to talking.*

Note: **would rather** + infinitive + **than** + infinitive, but **prefer** + gerund + **to** + gerund.

prefer can also be followed by a noun, but **would rather** always requires a verb:
> *He prefers wine to beer* =
> *He would rather drink wine than beer.*
> *I prefer tennis to golf* =
> *I'd rather play tennis than golf.*

Some statements with **prefer** + noun have no exact **would rather** equivalent: *He prefers dogs to cats* and *He would rather have dogs than cats* are not exactly the same.

2 **would rather** + infinitive cannot express preferences in the past, so the past equivalent of *Tom would rather read than talk* would be *Tom preferred reading to talking/liked reading better than talking.* But see 4 below.

3 **would rather** + infinitive can also be used instead of **would prefer** + infinitive:
> *I'd rather fly than go by sea/I'd prefer to fly.*

Note that with **would prefer**, only the preferred action is mentioned; see above. If, therefore, we want to mention both actions we must used **would rather**.
Similarly with nouns:
> *Would you like some gin?* ~ *I'd prefer a coffee* or
> *I'd rather have coffee than gin.*

4 Both **would rather/sooner** and **would prefer** can be followed by the perfect infinitive:
> *We went by sea but I'd rather have gone by air/I'd prefer to have gone by air.* (I wanted to go by air, but didn't get my wish.)

This is somewhat similar to **would like** + perfect infinitive, which expresses an unfulfilled wish. (See 296 D.)

B Subject + **would rather/sooner** is followed by subject + past tense (subjunctive) when the two subjects are different:
> *Shall I give you a cheque?* ~ *I'd rather you paid cash.*

Note the use of **would rather** + subject + **didn't** for a negative preference:
> *Would you like him to paint it?* ~ *No, I'd rather he didn't (paint it).*
> *Ann wants to tell Tom, but I'd rather she didn't (tell him).*

prefer, however, like **like**, can take object + infinitive:
> *I'd prefer you to pay cash.*
> *I'd prefer him not to paint it.*
> *I'd prefer her not to tell Tom.*

298 More examples of preference

A *I like hot weather better than cold* =
I prefer hot weather to cold =
I'd rather/sooner have hot weather than cold.
I like skiing better than skating =
I prefer skiing to skating =
I'd rather/sooner ski than skate.

B *I liked playing in matches better than watching them* =
I preferred playing matches to watching them.
(**would rather/sooner** could not be used here.)

C   *Would you like to start today or would you rather wait/would you*
     prefer to wait till tomorrow? ~ *I'd rather go today (than wait till*
     tomorrow). I'd rather not wait. Or
     I'd prefer to start today. I'd prefer not to wait.
     I'd rather deliver it by hand than post it.
     He says he'd rather go to prison than pay the fine.
     I'd rather pay his fine for him than let him go to prison.

rather than . . . would + infinitive is possible in formal English:
     Rather than let him go to prison I would pay his fine myself.

D   *Do you want Ann to repair it herself?* ~ *I'd prefer her to ring/I'd*
     rather she rang the electrician or
     I'd rather she didn't try to repair it herself.
     They want to camp in my garden but I'd rather they didn't. I'd
     rather they camped by the river.
     He usually has a pub lunch, but she'd prefer him to come home for a
     meal/she'd rather he came home for lunch. She'd rather he didn't
     spend money in pubs.

299 wish, want and would like

wish, want and **would like** all mean 'desire'.
wish is the most formal. For **want** and **would like**, see 296.

A   **wish** can be followed directly by an infinitive or by object + infinitive:
     Why do/did you wish to see the manager? ~ *I wish/wished to make a*
     complaint.
     The government does not wish Dr Jekyll Hyde to accept a
     professorship at a foreign university.
In less formal language we would use **want** or **would like**:
     I would like/want to speak to Ann.
     I wanted to speak to Ann.
     She doesn't/didn't want the children to stay up late. (If we used **like**
     here instead of **want**, it would mean that she doesn't/didn't
     approve of the children staying up late.)

B   **want** and **would like** can be followed directly by nouns:
     I want/would like a single room.
     He wanted a single room.
wish has a more restricted use:
We can wish someone luck/success/a happy Christmas etc.:
     He said, 'Good luck!' = *He wished me luck.*
We can also send someone 'good/best wishes':
     With all good wishes, yours, Bill (at the end of a letter)
     Best wishes for the New Year (on a New Year card)
Except in greetings of this kind, **wish** is not normally followed by a
noun object.
wish + for can be followed by a noun/pronoun, but usually implies that

the subject has little hope of obtaining his wish. It is chiefly used in exclamations:

>*How he wished for a drink!* (Presumably he had no hope of getting one.)
>*What he chiefly wished for was a chance to explain.* (It seems unlikely that he was going to get this chance.)

300 wish + subject + unreal past

A **wish (that)** + subject + a past tense (subjunctive; see 290 B) expresses regret about a present situation:

>*I wish I knew his address* = *I'm sorry I don't know his address.*
>*I wish you could drive a car* = *I'm sorry you can't drive a car.*
>*I wish he was coming with us* = *I'm sorry he isn't coming with us.*

wish can be put into the past without changing the subjunctive:

>*He wished he knew the address* =
>*He was sorry he didn't know the address.*

Unreal past tenses do not change in indirect speech:

>*'I wish I lived nearer my work,' he said* =
>*He said he wished he lived nearer his work.*

B **wish (that)** + subject + past perfect (subjunctive) expresses regret about a past situation:

>*I wish (that) I hadn't spent so much money* =
>*I'm sorry I spent so much money.*
>*I wish you had written to him* = *I'm sorry you didn't write to him.*

wished can replace **wish** without changing the subjunctive:

>*I wished I hadn't spent so much money* =
>*I was sorry I had spent so much money.*

These verbs will be reported unchanged:

>*'I wished I had taken his advice,' she said* =
>*She (said she) wished she had taken his advice.*

C **if only** can be used in exactly the same way. It has the same meaning as **wish** but is more dramatic:

>*If only we knew where to look for him!*
>*If only she had asked someone's advice!*

301 wish (that) + subject + would

A **wish** + subject + past tense can express regret for a present situation, as shown in 300 above:

>*I wish that he wrote more regularly* =
>*I'm sorry he doesn't write more regularly.*

B **wish** + subject + **would** can be used similarly, but only with actions which the subject can control, i.e. actions he could change if he wished.

wish + would here can express interest in the subject's willingness/unwillingness to perform an action in the present. This is usually a habitual action.

I wish he would write more often =
I'm sorry he isn't willing to write more often.
I wish he would wear a coat = I'm sorry he refuses to wear a coat.

The subject of **wish** cannot be the same as the subject of **would**, as this would be illogical. We cannot therefore have **I wish + I would**.

C **wish + subject + would** can also be used to express dissatisfaction with the present and a wish for change in the future:

I wish he would answer my letter. (I have been waiting for an answer for a long time.)
I wish they would change the menu. (I'm tired of eating sausages.)
I wish they would stop making bombs.

But the speaker is normally not very hopeful that the change will take place, and often, as in the third example above, has no hope at all.

As in B above, **wish + subject + would** here is restricted to actions where change is possible, and **wish** and **would** cannot have the same subject.

When there is a personal subject, the action is in the subject's control and the idea of willingness/unwillingness is still present, but **wish + subject + would** here can sometimes be used with inanimate subjects:

I wish it would stop raining.   *I wish the sun would come out.*
I wish prices would come down.   *I wish the train would come.*

wish + subject + would here is rather like **would like**, but **would like** is not restricted to actions where change is possible and does not imply dissatisfaction with the present situation. Also the **would like** construction does not imply any lack of hope:

I would like Jack to study art. (I want him to study art/I hope he will study art.)
I wish Peter would study art. (Peter has presumably refused to do this.)

D **I wish you would** is a possible request form. Here there is no feeling that the person addressed will refuse to perform the request, but there is often a feeling that this person is annoying or disappointing the speaker in some way: *I wish you would help me* often implies 'You should have offered to help me', and *I wish you would stop humming/interrupting/asking silly questions* would imply that the speaker was irritated by the noise/the interruptions/the silly questions. However, the expression **I wish you would** can be used in answer to an offer of help, and does not then imply any dissatisfaction:

Shall I help you check the accounts? ~ I wish you would. (I'd be glad of your help.)

E **if only + would** can replace **wish + would** in B and C above. It cannot be used for requests as in D.
if only is more dramatic than **wish**: *If only he would join our party!*

30 The passive voice

302 Form

A   The passive of an active tense is formed by putting the verb **to be** into the same tense as the active verb and adding the past participle of the active verb. The subject of the active verb becomes the 'agent' of the passive verb. The agent is very often not mentioned. When it is mentioned it is preceded by **by** and placed at the end of the clause:

This tree was planted by my grandfather.

B   Examples of present, past and perfect passive tenses:

Active   *We keep the butter here.*
Passive   *The butter is kept here.*
Active   *They broke the window.*
Passive   *The window was broken.*
Active   *People have seen wolves in the streets.*
Passive   *Wolves have been seen in the streets.*

C   The passive of continuous tenses requires the present continuous forms of **to be**, which are not otherwise much used:

Active   *They are repairing the bridge.*
Passive   *The bridge is being repaired.*
Active   *They were carrying the injured player off the field.*
Passive   *The injured player was being carried off the field.*

Other continuous tenses are exceedingly rarely used in the passive, so that sentences such as:

They have/had been repairing the road and
They will/would be repairing the road

are not normally put into the passive.

D   Auxiliary + infinitive combinations are made passive by using a passive infinitive:

Active   *You must/should shut these doors.*
Passive   *These doors must/should be shut.*
Active   *They should/ought to have told him.*
             (perfect infinitive active)
Passive   *He should/ought to have been told.*
             (perfect infinitive passive)

E Other infinitive combinations

Verbs of liking/loving/wanting/wishing etc. + object + infinitive form their passive with the passive infinitive:
Active   *He wants someone to take photographs.*
Passive   *He wants photographs to be taken.*

With verbs of command/request/advice/invitation + indirect object + infinitive we form the passive by using the passive form of the main verb:
Active   *He invited me to go.*
Passive   *I was invited to go.*

But with **advise/beg/order/recommend/urge** + indirect object + infinitive + object we can form the passive in two ways: by making the main verb passive, as above, or by **advise** etc. + **that . . . should** + passive infinitive:
Active   *He urged the Council to reduce the rates.*
Passive   *The Council was/were urged to reduce the rates* or
             He urged that the rates should be reduced.

agree/be anxious/arrange/be determined/determine/decide/ demand + infinitive + object are usually expressed in the passive by **that . . . should**, as above:
Active   *He decided to sell the house.*
Passive   *He decided that the house should be sold.*
(See also 235.)

F Gerund combinations

advise/insist/propose/recommend/suggest + gerund + object are usually expressed in the passive by **that . . . should**, as above:
Active   *He recommended using bullet-proof glass.*
Passive   *He recommended that bullet-proof glass should be used.*
(See 235.)

it/they + **need** + gerund can also be expressed by **it/they** + **need** + passive infinitive. Both forms are passive in meaning.

Other gerund combinations are expressed in the passive by the passive gerund:
Active   *I remember them taking me to the Zoo.*
Passive   *I remember being taken to the Zoo.*

303 Active tenses and their passive equivalents

A

Tense/Verb form	Active voice	Passive voice
Simple present	*keeps*	*is kept*
Present continuous	*is keeping*	*is being kept*
Simple past	*kept*	*was kept*
Past continuous	*was keeping*	*was being kept*
Present perfect	*has kept*	*has been kept*
Past perfect	*had kept*	*had been kept*
Future	*will keep*	*will be kept*
Conditional	*would keep*	*would be kept*
Perfect conditional	*would have kept*	*would have been kept*
Present infinitive	*to keep*	*to be kept*
Perfect infinitive	*to have kept*	*to have been kept*
Present participle/gerund	*keeping*	*being kept*
Perfect participle	*having kept*	*having been kept*

B   In colloquial speech **get** is sometimes used instead of **be**:
   The eggs got (= were) *broken.*
   You'll get (= be) *sacked if you take any more time off.*

C   Note that in theory a sentence containing a direct and an indirect object,
   such as *Someone gave her a bulldog*, could have two passive forms:
   She was given a bulldog.   *A bulldog was given to her.*
   The first of these is much the more usual, i.e. the indirect object
   usually becomes the subject of the passive verb.
   (See also 302 E, F.)

D   Questions about the identity of the subject of an active verb are usually
   expressed by an affirmative (see 55):
   What delayed you?   *Which team won?*
   Questions about the subject of a passive verb are also expressed by an
   affirmative:
   Something was done. ~ *What was done?*
   One of them was sold. ~ *Which of them was sold?*
   Interrogative verbs in active questions about the object become
   affirmative verbs in passive questions:
   Active   *What did they steal?* (interrogative)
   Passive   *What was stolen?* (affirmative)
   Conversely, affirmative verbs in active questions become interrogative verbs in
   passive questions:
   Active   *Who painted it?* (affirmative)
   Passive   *Who was it painted by?* (interrogative)
   Other types of question require interrogative verbs in both active and passive:
   Active   *When/Where/Why did he paint it?*
   Passive   *When/Where/Why was it painted?*

304 Uses of the passive

The passive is used:

A When it is not necessary to mention the doer of the action as it is obvious who he is/was/will be:

The rubbish hasn't been collected.   *The streets are swept every day.*
Your hand will be X-rayed.

B When we don't know, or don't know exactly, or have forgotten who did the action:

The minister was murdered.   *My car has been moved!*
You'll be met at the station.   *I've been told that . . .*

C When the subject of the active verb would be 'people':

He is suspected of receiving stolen goods. (People suspect him of . . .)
They are supposed to be living in New York. (People suppose that they are living . . .)

(See 245, 306 for infinitive constructions with passive verbs.)

D When the subject of the active sentence would be the indefinite pronoun **one**: *One sees this sort of advertisement everywhere* would usually be expressed:

This sort of advertisement is seen everywhere.

In colloquial speech we can use the indefinite pronoun **you** (see 68) and an active verb:

You see this sort of advertisement everywhere.

But more formal English requires **one** + active verb or the more usual passive form.

E When we are more interested in the action than the person who does it:

The house next door has been bought (by a Mr Jones).

If, however, we know Mr Jones, we would use the active:

Your father's friend, Mr Jones, has bought the house next door.

Similarly:

A new public library is being built (by our local council)

though in more informal English we could use the indefinite pronoun **they** (see 68) and an active verb:

They are building a new public library

while a member of the Council will of course say:

We are/The council is building etc.

F The passive may be used to avoid an awkward or ungrammatical sentence. This is usually done by avoiding a change of subject:

When he arrived home a detective arrested him

would be better expressed:

When he arrived home he was arrested (by a detective).
When their mother was ill neighbours looked after the children

would be better expressed:

When their mother was ill the children were looked after by neighbours.

G The passive is sometimes preferred for psychological reasons.
A speaker may use it to disclaim responsibility for disagreeable
announcements:

EMPLOYER: *Overtime rates are being reduced/will have to be reduced.*
The active will, of course, be used for agreeable announcements:

I am/We are going to increase overtime rates.
The speaker may know who performed the action but wish to avoid
giving the name. Tom, who suspects Bill of opening his letters, may say
tactfully:

This letter has been opened! instead of *You've opened this letter!*

H For the **have** + object + past participle construction, *I had the car
resprayed,* see 119.

305 Prepositions with passive verbs

A As already noted, the agent, when mentioned, is preceded by **by**:
Active   *Dufy painted this picture.*
Passive *This picture was painted by Dufy.*
Active   *What makes these holes?*
Passive *What are these holes made by?*

Note, however, that the passive form of such sentences as:

Smoke filled the room.   Paint covered the lock.
will be:

The room was filled with smoke.   The lock was covered with paint.
We are dealing here with materials used, not with the agents.

B When a verb + preposition + object combination is put into the passive,
the preposition will remain immediately after the verb:
Active   *We must write to him.*
Passive *He must be written to.*
Active   *You can play with these cubs quite safely.*
Passive *These cubs can be played with quite safely.*

Similarly with verb + preposition/adverb combinations:
Active   *They threw away the old newspapers.*
Passive *The old newspapers were thrown away.*
Active   *He looked after the children well.*
Passive *The children were well looked after.*

306 Infinitive constructions after passive verbs

A After **acknowledge, assume, believe, claim, consider, estimate,
feel, find, know, presume, report, saý, think, understand** etc.
(see also 245)

Sentences of the type *People consider/know/think* etc. *that he is . . .*
have two possible passive forms:

It is considered/known/thought etc. *that he is . . .*
He is considered/known/thought etc. *to be . . .*
Similarly:
People said that he was jealous of her =
It was said that he was or *He was said to be jealous of her.*
The infinitive construction is the neater of the two. It is chiefly used with **to be** though other infinitives can sometimes be used:
He is thought to have information which will be useful to the police.
When the thought concerns a previous action we use the perfect infinitive so that:
People believed that he was =
It was believed that he was or *He was believed to be . . .*
People know that he was =
It is known that he was or *He is known to have been . . .*
This construction can be used with the perfect infinitive of any verb.

B   After **suppose**

1   **suppose** in the passive can be followed by the present infinitive of any verb but this construction usually conveys an idea of duty and is not therefore the normal equivalent of **suppose** in thé active:
You are supposed to know how to drive =
It is your duty to know/You should know how to drive
though *He is supposed to be in Paris* could mean either 'He ought to be there' or 'People suppose he is there'.

2   **suppose** in the passive can similarly be followed by the perfect infinitive of any verb. This construction may convey an idea of duty but very often does not:
You are supposed to have finished = *You should have finished* but
He is supposed to have escaped disguised as a woman =
People suppose that he escaped etc.

C   Infinitives placed after passive verbs are normally full infinitives:
Active   *We saw them go out.*   *He made us work.*
Passive   *They were seen to go out.*   *We were made to work.*

let, however, is used without **to**:
Active   *They let us go.*
Passive   *We were let go.*

D   The continuous infinitive can be used after the passive of **believe, know, report, say, suppose, think, understand**:
He is believed/known/said/supposed/thought to be living abroad =
People believe/know/say/suppose/think that he is living abroad.
You are supposed to be working = *You should be working.*
The perfect form of the continuous infinitive is also possible:
He is believed to have been waiting for a message =
People believed that he was waiting for a message.
You are supposed to have been working =
You should have been working.

31 Indirect speech

307 Direct and indirect (or reported) speech

There are two ways of relating what a person has said: direct and indirect.

In direct speech we repeat the original speaker's exact words:

> *He said, 'I have lost my umbrella.'*

Remarks thus repeated are placed between inverted commas, and a comma or colon is placed immediately before the remark. Direct speech is found in conversations in books, in plays, and in quotations.

In indirect speech we give the exact meaning of a remark or a speech, without necessarily using the speaker's exact words:

> *He said (that) he had lost his umbrella.*

There is no comma after **say** in indirect speech. **that** can usually be omitted after **say** and **tell** + object. But it should be kept after other verbs: **complain, explain, object, point out, protest** etc. Indirect speech is normally used when conversation is reported verbally, though direct speech is sometimes employed here to give a more dramatic effect.

When we turn direct speech into indirect, some changes are usually necessary. These are most easily studied by considering statements, questions, and commands separately.

308 Statements in indirect speech: tense changes necessary

A Indirect speech can be introduced by a verb in a present tense: *He says that* . . . This is usual when we are:

(a) reporting a conversation that is still going on
(b) reading a letter and reporting what it says
(c) reading instructions and reporting them
(d) reporting a statement that someone makes very often, e.g. *Tom says that he'll never get married.*

When the introductory verb is in a present, present perfect or future tense we can report the direct speech without any change of tense:

> PAUL (phoning from the station): *I'm trying to get a taxi.*
>
> ANN (to Mary, who is standing beside her): *Paul says he is trying to get a taxi.*

B But indirect speech is usually introduced by a verb in the past tense. Verbs in the direct speech have then to be changed into a corresponding past tense. The changes are shown in the following table. (The **that** has been omitted in the last five examples.)

Direct speech	Indirect speech
Simple present *'I never eat meat,' he explained*	Simple past = *He explained that he never ate meat.*
Present continuous *'I'm waiting for Ann,' he said*	Past continuous = *He said (that) he was waiting for Ann.*
Present perfect *'I have found a flat,' he said*	Past perfect = *He said (that) he had found a flat.*
Present perfect continuous *He said, 'I've been waiting for ages'*	Past perfect continuous = *He said he had been waiting for ages.*
Simple past *'I took it home with me,' she said*	Past perfect = *She said she had taken it home with her.*
Future *He said, 'I will/shall be in Paris on Monday'*	Conditional = *He said he would be in Paris on Monday.*
Future continuous *'I will/shall be using the car myself on the 24th,' she said*	Conditional continuous = *She said she'd be using the car herself on the 24th.*
But note, Conditional *I said, 'I would/should like to see it'*	Conditional = *I said I would/should like to see it.* (No tense change. See also 227.)

C Note on **I/we shall/should**
   '**I/we shall**' normally becomes **he/she/they would** in indirect speech:
   > *'I shall be 21 tomorrow,' said Bill =*
   > *Bill said he would be 21 the following day.*

   But if the sentence is reported by the original speaker, '**I/we shall**' can become either **I/we should** or **I/we would. would** is the more common.
   Similarly '**I/we should**' usually becomes **he/she/they would** in indirect speech:
   > *'If I had the instruction manual I should/would know what to do,' said Bill =*
   > *Bill said that if he had the instructions he would know what to do.*

   But if the sentence is reported by the original speaker '**I/we should**' can either remain unchanged or be reported by **would**. See last example in B above.

309 Past tenses sometimes remain unchanged

A In theory the past tense changes to the past perfect, but in spoken English it is often left unchanged, provided this can be done without causing confusion about the relative times of the actions. For example, *He said, 'I loved her'* must become *He said he had loved her* as otherwise there would be a change of meaning. But *He said, 'Ann arrived on Monday'* could be reported *He said Ann arrived/had arrived on Monday.*

B The past continuous tense in theory changes to the past perfect continuous but in practice usually remains unchanged except when it refers to a completed action:

She said, 'We were thinking of selling the house but we have decided not to' =
She said that they had been thinking of selling the house but had decided not to.
But *He said, 'When I saw them they were playing tennis'* =
He said that when he saw them they were playing tennis.

C In written English past tenses usually do change to past perfect but there are the following exceptions:

1 Past/Past continuous tenses in time clauses do not normally change:
He said, 'When we were living/lived in Paris . . .' =
He said that when they were living in Paris . . .
The main verb of such sentences can either remain unchanged or become the past perfect:
He said, 'When we were living/lived in Paris we often saw Paul' =
He said that when they were living/lived in Paris they often saw/had often seen Paul.

2 A past tense used to describe a state of affairs which still exists when the speech is reported remains unchanged:
She said, 'I decided not to buy the house because it was on a main road' =
She said that she had decided not to buy the house because it was on a main road.

310 Unreal past tenses (subjunctives) in indirect speech

A Unreal past tenses after **wish, would rather/sooner** and **it is time** do not change:

'We wish we didn't have to take exams,' said the children =
The children said they wished they didn't have to take exams.
'Bill wants to go alone,' said Ann, 'but I'd rather he went with a group' =
Ann said that Bill wanted to go alone but that she'd rather he went with a group.
'It's time we began planning our holidays,' he said =
He said that it was time they began planning their holidays.

B **I/he/she/we/they had better** remains unchanged. **you had better** can remain unchanged or be reported by **advise** + object + infinitive (see 120):

'The children had better go to bed early,' said Tom =
Tom said that the children had better go to bed early.
'You'd better not drink the water,' she said =
She advised/warned us not to drink the water.

C Conditional sentences types 2 and 3 remain unchanged (see 229):

'If my children were older I would emigrate,' he said =
He said that if his children were older he would emigrate.

311 might, ought to, should, would, used to in indirect statements

A **might** remains unchanged except when used as a request form:

He said, 'Ann might ring today' =
He said that Ann might ring (that day).

But *'You might post these for me,' he said =*
He asked me to post them for him.

(See 285 for requests.)

B **ought to/should** for obligation or assumption remains unchanged:

'They ought to/should widen this road,' I said =
I said that they ought to/should widen the road.
I said, 'I should be back by six' (I assume I will be) *=*
I said I should be back by six.

C But **you ought to/you should**, if used to express advice rather than obligation, can be reported by **advise** + object + infinitive. **you must** can also express advice and be reported similarly.

'You ought to/should/must read the instructions,' said Ann =
Ann advised/urged/warned me to read the instructions.

D The advice form **'If I were you I should/would . . .'** is normally reported by **advise** + object + infinitive:

'If I were you I'd wait,' I said = I advised him to wait.

E The request form **'I should/would be (very) grateful if you would . . .'** is normally reported by **ask** + object + infinitive:

'I'd be very grateful if you'd keep me informed,' he said =
He asked me to keep him informed.

F **would** in statements doesn't change. But see 284 for **would** in requests etc.

G **used to** doesn't change:

'I know the place well because I used to live here,' he explained =
He explained that he knew the place well because he used to live there.

(For **could**, see 312; for **must**, see 325.)

312 **could** in indirect statements

(For **could** interrogative, see 283-4.)

A **could** for ability

1 **could** for present ability does not change:
> *'I can't/couldn't stand on my head,' he said* =
> *He said he couldn't stand on his head.*

2 **could** for future ability can remain unchanged or be reported by **would be able**:
> *He said, 'I could do it tomorrow'* =
> *He said he could do it/would be able to do it the next day.*

3 **could** in type 2 conditional sentences is reported similarly:
> *'If I had the tools I could mend it,' he said* =
> *He said that if he had the tools he could/would be able to mend it.*
would be able here implies that the supposition may be fulfilled. (Perhaps he'll be able to borrow tools.)

4 **could** in type 3 conditional sentences is reported unchanged.

5 **could** for past ability can remain unchanged or be reported by **had been able**:
> *'I could read when I was three!' she boasted* =
> *She boasted that she could/had been able to read when she was three.*

B **could** for permission

1 In type 2 conditional sentences **could** can remain unchanged or be reported by **would be allowed to**:
> *'If I paid my fine I could walk out of prison today,' he said* =
> *He said that if he paid his fine he could/would be allowed to walk etc.*

2 **could** in the past can remain unchanged or be reported by **was/were allowed to** or **had been allowed to**:
> *He said, 'When I was a boy I could stay up as long as I liked'* =
> *He said that when he was a boy he could/was allowed to stay up* or
> *He said that as a boy he was/had been allowed etc.*

313 Indirect speech: pronoun and adjective

A Pronouns and possessive adjectives usually change from first or second to third person except when the speaker is reporting his own words:
> *He said, 'I've forgotten the combination of my safe'* =
> *He said that he had forgotten the combination of his safe.*
> *I said, 'I like my new house'* =
> *I said that I liked my new house.* (speaker reporting his own words)

Sometimes a noun must be inserted to avoid ambiguity: *Tom said, 'He came in through the window'* would not normally be reported *Tom said he had come in through the window* as this might imply that Tom himself had come in this way; but if we use a noun there can be no confusion: *Tom said that the man/burglar/cat etc. had come in . . .*

Pronoun changes may affect the verb:

> *He says, 'I know her' = He says he knows her.*
> *He says, 'I shall be there' =*
> *He says that he will be there.*

B **this** and **these**

this used in time expressions usually becomes **that**:

> *He said, 'She is coming this week' =*
> *He said that she was coming that week.*

Otherwise **this** and **that** used as adjectives usually change to **the**:

> *He said, 'I bought this pearl/these pearls for my mother' =*
> *He said that he had bought the pearl/pearls for his mother.*

this, these used as pronouns can become **it, they/them**:

> *He showed me two bullets. 'I found these embedded in the panelling,'*
> *he said =*
> *He said he had found them embedded in the panelling.*
> *He said, 'We will discuss this tomorrow' =*
> *He said that they would discuss it/the matter the next day.*

this, these (adjectives or pronouns), used to indicate choice or to distinguish some things from others, can become **the one(s) near him** etc., or the statement can be reworded:

> *'I'll have this (one),' he said to me =*
> *He said he would have the one near him* or
> *He pointed to/touched/showed me the one he wanted.*

314 Expressions of time and place in indirect speech

A Adverbs and adverbial phrases of time change as follows:

Direct	Indirect
today	*that day*
yesterday	*the day before*
the day before yesterday	*two days before*
tomorrow	*the next day/the following day*
the day after tomorrow	*in two days' time*
next week/year etc.	*the following week/year* etc.
last week/year etc.	*the previous week/year* etc.
a year etc. *ago*	*a year before/the previous year*

> *'I saw her the day before yesterday,' he said =*
> *He said he'd seen her two days before.*
> *'I'll do it tomorrow,' he promised =*
> *He promised that he would do it the next day.*
> *'I'm starting the day after tomorrow, mother,' he said =*
> *He told his mother that he was starting in two days' time.*
> *She said, 'My father died a year ago' =*
> *She said that her father had died a year before/the previous year.*

B   But if the speech is made and reported on the same day these time changes are not necessary:

At breakfast this morning he said, 'I'll be very busy today' =
At breakfast this morning he said that he would be very busy today.

C   Logical adjustments are of course necessary if a speech is reported one/two days after it is made. On Monday Jack said to Tom:

I'm leaving the day after tomorrow.

If Tom reports this speech on the next day (Tuesday) he will probably say:

Jack said he was leaving tomorrow.

If he reports it on Wednesday, he will probably say:

Jack said he was leaving today.

D   **here** can become **there** but only when it is clear what place is meant:

At the station he said, 'I'll be here again tomorrow' =
He said that he'd be there again the next day.

Usually **here** has to be replaced by some phrase:

She said, 'You can sit here, Tom' =
She told Tom that he could sit beside her etc.

But *He said, 'Come here, boys'* would normally be reported:

He called the boys.

315   Infinitive and gerund constructions in indirect speech

A   **agree/refuse/offer/promise/threaten** + infinitive can sometimes be used instead of **say (that):**

ANN: *Would you wait half an hour?*
TOM: *All right* = *Tom agreed to wait* or *Tom said he would wait.*

ANN: *Would you lend me another £50?*
TOM: *No, I won't lend you any more money* =
Tom refused to lend her any more money or
Tom said that he wouldn't lend etc.

PAUL: *I'll help you if you like, Ann* =
Paul offered to help her or
Paul said that he'd help her. (See also **shall I?**, 318.)

ANN: *I'll pay you back next week. Really I will.* =
Ann promised to pay him back the following week or
Ann said that she would pay him back or
Ann assured him that she would pay him back.

KIDNAPPERS: *If you don't pay the ransom at once we'll kill your daughter* =
The kidnappers threatened to kill his daughter if he didn't pay the ransom at once or *The kidnappers said that they would kill* etc.

(For object + infinitive constructions, see 320.)

B **accuse . . . of/admit/apologize for/deny/insist on** + gerund can sometimes be used instead of **say (that)**:

> *'You took the money!'* might be reported
> *He accused me of taking the money.*
> *'I stole/didn't steal it'* might be reported
> *I admitted/denied stealing it.*
> *'I'm sorry I'm late,'* he said might be reported
> *He apologized for being late* or
> *He said | he was sorry he was late.*
> BILL: *Let me pay for myself.*
> TOM: *Certainly not! I'll pay!* might be reported
> *Tom insisted on paying.*

316 say, tell and alternative introductory verbs

A **say** and **tell** with direct speech

1 **say** can introduce a statement or follow it:

> *Tom said, 'I've just heard the news'* or
> *'I've just heard the news,' Tom said.*

Inversion of **say** and noun subject is possible when **say** follows the statement:

> *'I've just heard the news,' said Tom.*

say + to + person addressed is possible:

> *'I'm leaving at once,' Tom said to me.*

Inversion is also possible: *'I'm coming with you,' said Jim to his uncle.*

2 **tell** requires the person addressed:

> *Tell me.   He told us.   I'll tell Tom.*

except with **tell lies/stories/the truth**, when the person addressed need not be mentioned:

> *He told (me) lies.   I'll tell (you) a story.*

tell used with direct speech must be placed after the direct statement:

> *'I'm leaving at once,' Tom told me.*

Inversion is not possible with **tell**.

B **say** and **tell** with indirect speech

Indirect statements are normally introduced by **say**, or **tell** + object.

say + to + object is possible but much less usual than **tell** + object:

> *He said (that) he'd just heard the news.*
> *He told me (that) he'd just heard the news.*

Note also **tell . . . how/about**:

> *He told us how he had crossed the mountains.*
> *He told us about crossing the mountains.*
> *He told us about his journeys.*

(For **say** and **tell** with indirect commands, see 320-1.)

C   Verbs which can be used with direct or indirect speech include:

add*	*complain**	*point out*	*respond*
admit*	*deny**	*promise**	*warn*
answer*	*explain**	*protest**	
argue*	*grumble**	*remark**	
assure + object	*object**	*remind* + object	
boast*	*observe**	*reply**	

With direct speech they follow direct statements:
'It won't cost more,' Tom assured us.
Starred verbs can be inverted, provided the subject is a noun:
'But it will take longer,' Bill objected/objected Bill.
'It'll cost too much,' Jack grumbled/grumbled Jack.
They can all introduce indirect statements.
that should be placed after the verb:
Tom assured us that it wouldn't cost more. But Bill objected/pointed out that it would take longer.

D   **murmur, mutter, shout, stammer, whisper** can precede or follow direct statements or questions. With noun subjects the verb can be inverted as shown above:
'You're late,' whispered Tom/Tom whispered.
They can introduce indirect statements. **that** is usually necessary:
Tom whispered that we were late.
There are, of course, a lot of other verbs describing the voice or the tone of voice, e.g. *bark, growl, roar, scream, shriek, snarl, sneer, yell.*
But these are more common with direct than indirect speech.

317   Questions in indirect speech

Direct question: *He said, 'Where is she going?'*
Indirect question: *He asked where she was going.*

A   When we turn direct questions into indirect speech, the following changes are necessary.
Tenses, pronouns and possessive adjectives, and adverbs of time and place change as in statements.
The interrogative form of the verb changes to the affirmative form. The question mark (?) is therefore omitted in indirect questions:
He said, 'Where does she live?' = He asked where she lived.
With affirmative verb questions (see 55) this change is obviously not necessary:
'Who lives next door?' he said = He asked who lived next door.
'What happened?' she said = She asked what had happened.

B   If the introductory verb is .say, it must be changed to a verb of inquiry, e.g. **ask, inquire, wonder, want to know** etc.:
He said, 'Where is the station?' = He asked where the station was.

ask, inquire, wonder can also be used in direct speech. They are then usually placed at the end of the sentence:
'Where is the station?' he inquired.

C **ask** can be followed by the person addressed (indirect object):
He asked, 'What have you got in your bag?' =
He asked (me) what I had got in my bag.

But **inquire, wonder, want to know** cannot take an indirect object, so if we wish to report a question where the person addressed is mentioned, we must use **ask**:
He said, 'Mary, when is the next train?' =
He asked Mary when the next train was.

If we use **inquire, wonder** or **want to know** we must omit *Mary*.

D If the direct question begins with a question word (**when, where, who, how, why** etc.) the question word is repeated in the indirect question:
He said, 'Why didn't you put on the brake?' =
He asked (her) why she hadn't put on the brake.
She said, 'What do you want?' =
She asked (them) what they wanted.

E If there is no question word, **if** or **whether** must be used:
'Is anyone there?' he asked =
He asked if/whether anyone was there.

1 Normally we can use either **if** and **whether. if** is the more usual:
'Do you know Bill?' he said =
He asked if/whether I knew Bill.
'Did you see the accident?' the policeman asked =
The policeman asked if/whether I had seen the accident.

2 **whether** can emphasize that a choice has to be made:
'Do you want to go by air or sea?' the travel agent asked =
The travel agent asked whether I wanted to go by air or by sea.
Note **whether or not**:
'Do you want to insure your luggage or not?' he asked =
He asked whether or not I wanted to insure my luggage or
He asked if I wanted to insure my luggage or not.

3 **whether** + infinitive is possible after **wonder, want to know**:
'Shall/Should I wait for them or go on?' he wondered =
He wondered whether to wait for them or go on or
He wondered whether he should wait for them or go on.
inquire + **whether** + infinitive is possible but less usual.
(For **whether** + infinitive, see also 242 B.)

4 **whether** is neater if the question contains a conditional clause as otherwise there would be two **if**s:
'If you get the job will you move to York?' Bill asked =
Bill asked whether, if I got the job, I'd move to York.

18 Questions beginning **shall I/we?** in indirect speech

Questions beginning **shall I/we?** can be of four kinds.

A Speculations or requests for information about a future event:
> *'Shall I ever see them again?' he wondered.*
> *'When shall I know the result of the test?' she asked.*

These follow the ordinary rule about **shall/will**. Speculations are usually introduced by **wonder**:
> *He wondered if he would ever see them again.*
> *She asked when she would know the result of the test.*

B Requests for instructions or advice:
> *'What shall I do with it?'* = *'Tell me what to do with it.'*

These are expressed in indirect speech by **ask, inquire** etc., with **should** or the **be** + infinitive construction. Requests for advice are normally reported by **should**:
> *'Shall we post it, sir?' he said* =
> *He asked the customer if they were to post/if they should post it.*
> *'What shall I say, mother?' she said* =
> *She asked her mother what she should say.* (request for advice)

When a choice is required we normally use **whether** in indirect speech. **whether** + infinitive is sometimes possible (see also 317 E):
> *'Shall I lock the car or leave it unlocked?' he said* =
> *He asked whether he should/was to lock the car or leave it unlocked* or *He asked whether to lock the car* etc.

C Offers:
> *'Shall I bring you some tea?'* could be reported
> *He offered to bring me some tea.*

Note that *'Would you like me to bring you some tea?'* and *'I'll bring you some tea if you like'* could also be reported by **offer**.

D Suggestions:
> *'Shall we meet at the theatre?'* could be reported
> *He suggested meeting at the theatre.*

319 Questions beginning **will you/would you/could you?**

These may be ordinary questions, but may also be requests, invitations, or, very occasionally, commands (see 284, 286, 320):
> *He said, 'Will you be there tomorrow?'* (ordinary question) =
> *He asked if she would be there the next day.*
> *'Will you stand still!' he shouted* = *He shouted at me to stand still* or
> *He told/ordered me to stand still.*
> *'Would you like to live in New York?' he asked* =
> *He asked if I would like to live in New York.*
> *'Will/Would you file these letters, please?' he said* =
> *He asked/told me to file the letters.*

'Would you like a lift?' said Ann = *Ann offered me a lift.*
'Would you like to come round/Could you come round for a drink?'
he said =
He invited me (to come) round for a drink.
'Could you live on £25 a week?' he asked =
He asked if I could live on £25 a week.
'Could/Would you give me a hand?' she said =
She asked us to give her a hand.
'Could/Would you show me the photos?' she said =
She asked me to show her the photos or *She asked to see the photos.*
(For **can/could/may/might** + **I/we?**, see 283.
For requests for permission, see 131.)

320   Commands, requests, advice in indirect speech

Direct command: *He said, 'Lie down, Tom.'*
Indirect command: *He told Tom to lie down.*
Indirect commands, requests, advice are usually expressed by a verb of command/request/advice + object + infinitive (= the object + infinitive construction).

A   The following verbs can be used: **advise, ask, beg, command, encourage, entreat, forbid, implore, invite, order, recommend, remind, request, tell, urge, warn**.
(Note that **say** is not included in this list. For indirect commands/ requests reported by **say**, see 321.)
　　He said, 'Get your coat, Tom!' = *He told Tom to get his coat.*
　　'You had better hurry, Bill!' she said = *She advised Bill to hurry.*

B   Negative commands, requests etc. are usually reported by **not** + infinitive:
　　'Don't swim out too far, boys,' I said =
　　I warned/told the boys not to swim out too far.
forbid can also be used for prohibitions, but is more common in the passive than in the active.

C   Verbs in A above require object + infinitive, i.e. they must be followed directly by the person addressed without preposition (see also 89). The person addressed is often not mentioned in direct commands, requests etc.: *He said, 'Go away!'*
When reporting such commands/requests therefore we must add a noun or pronoun:
　　He told me/him/her/us/them/the children to go away.
ask differs from the other verbs in A in that it can also be followed directly by the infinitive of certain verbs, e.g. **see, speak to, talk to**:
　　He said, 'Could I see Tom, please?' =
　　He asked to see Tom.　　(See also 283.)
But this is quite different from the **ask** + object + infinitive type of request.

Both **ask** and **beg** can be followed by the passive infinitive:

'Do, please, send me to a warm climate,' he asked/begged =
He asked/begged us to send him to a warm climate or
He asked/begged to be sent to a warm climate.

D Examples of indirect commands, requests, advice
Note that direct commands are usually expressed by the imperative,
but that requests and advice can be expressed in a variety of ways
(see 283-7):

'If I were you, I'd stop taking tranquillizers,' I said =
I advised him to stop taking tranquillizers. (See 311 D.)
'Why don't you take off your coat?' he said =
He advised me to take off my coat. (See also 287.)
'Would/Could you show me your passport, please?' he said =
He asked me to show him my passport or
He asked me for/He asked to see my passport.
'You might post some letters for me,' said my boss =
My boss asked me to post some letters for him.
'If you'd just sign the register,' said the receptionist =
The receptionist asked him to sign the register.
'Do sit down,' said my hostess =
My hostess asked/invited me to sit down.
'Please, please don't take any risks,' said his wife =
His wife begged/implored him not to take any risks.
*'Forget all about this young man,' said her parents; 'don't see him
again or answer his letters'* =
*Her parents ordered her to forget all about the young man and told
her not to see him again or answer his letters* or
*She was ordered to forget all about the young man and forbidden to
see him again or answer his letters.* (passive construction)
'Don't forget to order the wine,' said Mrs Pitt =
Mrs Pitt reminded her husband to order the wine.
'Try again,' said Ann's friends encouragingly =
Ann's friends encouraged her to try again.
'Go on, apply for the job,' said Jack =
Jack urged/encouraged me to apply for the job.
*'You had better not leave your car unlocked,' said my friends;
'there's been a lot of stealing from cars'* =
*My friends warned me not to leave my car unlocked as there had been
a lot of stealing from cars.*

will you . . . sentences are normally treated as requests and
reported by **ask**:

'Will all persons not travelling please go ashore,' he said =
He asked all persons not travelling to go ashore.

But if a **will you** sentence is spoken sharply or irritably, and the
please is omitted, it might be reported by **tell** or **order**:

'Will you be quiet!/Be quiet, will you!' he said =
He told/ordered us to be quiet.

321 Other ways of expressing indirect commands

A **say/tell** + subject + **be** + infinitive:
> *He said/told me that I was to wait.*

This is a possible alternative to the **tell** + infinitive construction, so that:
> *He said, 'Don't open the door'* could be reported
> *He told me not to open the door* or
> *He said that I wasn't to open the door.*

The **be** + infinitive construction is particularly useful in the following cases:

1 When the command is introduced by a verb in the present tense:
> *He says, 'Meet me at the station'* =
> *He says that we are to meet him at the station.*

(*He tells us to meet him* would be much less likely.)

2 When the command is preceded by a clause (usually of time or condition):
> *He said, 'If she leaves the house follow her'* could be reported
> *He said that if she left the house I was to follow her.*

He told me to follow her if she left the house would be equally possible here but note that if we use the **tell** + infinitive construction we must change the order of the sentence so as to put the command first. Sometimes this would result in a rather confusing sentence. For example, the request *If you see Ann tell her to ring me* would become *He told me to tell Ann to ring him if I saw her*. Such requests can only be reported by the **be** + infinitive construction:
> *He said that if I saw Ann I was to tell her to ring him.*

B **say/tell** (+ **that**) + subject + **should**

1 **say** or **tell** with a **should** construction normally indicates advice rather than command:
> *He said, 'If your brakes are bad don't drive so fast'* =
> *He said/told me that if my brakes were bad I shouldn't drive so fast*
> or
> *He advised me not to drive so fast if my brakes were bad.* (Note change of order here, as with **tell** + infinitive above.)

2 Advice can also be expressed by **advise, recommend** and **urge** + **that . . . should**. This is particularly useful in the passive (see 302 E):
> *'I advise cancelling the meeting,' he said* =
> *He advised that the meeting should be cancelled.*

3 **command** and **order** can also be used with **should** or a passive infinitive:
> *'Evacuate the area!' ordered the superintendent* =
> *The superintendent ordered that everyone should leave the area* or
> *ordered that the area should be evacuated* or
> *ordered the area to be evacuated.*

4 Note that when an indirect command is expressed by an object + infinitive construction, as in 320, there is normally the idea that the

person who is to obey the command is addressed directly. But when the command is expressed by the **be** + infinitive construction (A above) or by a **should** construction (B3 above) the recipient of the command need not necessarily be addressed directly. The command may be conveyed to him by a third person.

322 let's, let us, let him/them in indirect speech

A let's

1 **let's** usually expresses a suggestion and is reported by **suggest** in indirect speech:
> *He said, 'Let's leave the case at the station'*
would be reported:
> *He suggested leaving the case at the station* or
> *He suggested that they/we should leave the case at the station.*
(See 289 for constructions with **suggest**.)
> *He said, 'Let's stop now and finish it later'*
would be reported:
> *He suggested stopping then and finishing it later* or
> *He suggested that they/we should stop then and finish it later.*
Similarly in the negative:
> *He said, 'Let's not say anything about it till we hear the facts' =*
> *He suggested not saying anything/saying nothing about it till they heard the facts* or
> *He suggested that they shouldn't say anything till they heard the facts.*
But **let's not** used alone in answer to an affirmative suggestion is often reported by some phrase such as *opposed the idea/was against it/objected.* So that we could report:
> *'Let's sell the house,' said Tom. 'Let's not,' said Ann* by
> *Tom suggested selling the house but Ann was against it.*
(For other suggestion forms, see 289.)

2 **let's/let us** sometimes expresses a call to action. It is then usually reported by **urge/advise** + object + infinitive (see also 320):
> *The strike leader said, 'Let's show the bosses that we are united' =*
> *The strike leader urged the workers to show the bosses that they were united.*

B let him/them

1 In theory **let him/them** expresses a command. But very often the speaker has no authority over the person who is to obey the command:
> *'It's not my business,' said the postman. 'Let the government do something about it.'*
Here, the speaker is not issuing a command but expressing an obligation. Sentences of this type are therefore normally reported by **ought/should**:
> *He said that it wasn't his business and that the government ought to/should do something about it.*

2 Sometimes, however, **let him/them** does express a command. It is
then usually reported by **say** + **be** + infinitive (see 321):
> *'Let the boys clear up this mess,' said the headmaster* =
> *The headmaster said that the boys were to clear up the mess.*
> *'Let the guards be armed,' he ordered* =
> *He ordered that the guards should be armed.*

3 Sometimes **let him/them** is more a suggestion than a command. In
such cases it is usually reported by **suggest**, or **say** + **should**
(see 289):
> *She said, 'Let them go to their consul. He'll be able to help them'* =
> *She suggested their/them going to their consul etc. or*
> *She suggested that they should go to their consul or*
> *She said that they should go to their consul.*

4 **let him/them** can also indicate the speaker's indifference:
> *'The neighbours will complain,' said Ann.*
> *'Let them (complain),' said Tom* = *Tom expressed indifference* or
> *Tom said he didn't mind (if they complained).*

C **let there be**
Here the speaker could be ordering, advising, urging or begging:
> *'Let there be no reprisals,' said the widow of the murdered man* =
> *The widow urged/begged that there should be no reprisals.*

D **let** is also an ordinary verb meaning **allow/permit**:
> *'Let him come with us, mother; I'll take care of him,' I said* =
> *I asked my mother to let him come with us and promised to take care
> of him.*

323 Exclamations and **yes** and **no**

A Exclamations usually become statements in indirect speech. The
exclamation mark disappears.

1 Exclamations beginning **What (a)** . . . or **How** . . . can be reported
(a) by **exclaim/say that**:
> *He said, 'What a dreadful idea!' or 'How dreadful!'* =
> *He exclaimed that it was a dreadful idea/was dreadful*

or (b) by **give an exclamation of** delight/disgust/horror/relief/
surprise etc.
Alternatively, if the exclamation is followed by an action we can use the
construction (c) **with an exclamation of** delight/disgust etc. +
he/she etc. + verb.

2 Other types of exclamation, such as **Good! Marvellous! Splendid!
Heavens! Oh! Ugh!** etc. can be reported as in (b) or (c) above:
> *'Good!' he exclaimed* =
> *He gave an exclamation of pleasure/satisfaction.*
> *'Ugh!' she exclaimed, and turned the programme off* =
> *With an exclamation of disgust she turned the programme off.*

3   Note also:

> *He said, 'Thank you!' = He thanked me.*
> *He said, 'Curse this fog!' = He cursed the fog.*
> *He said, 'Good luck!' = He wished me luck.*
> *He said, 'Happy Christmas!' = He wished me a happy Christmas.*
> *He said, 'Congratulations!' = He congratulated me.*
> *He said, 'Liar!' = He called me a liar.*
> *He said, 'Damn!' etc. = He swore.*
> *The notice said: WELCOME TO WALES! =*
> *The notice welcomed visitors to Wales.*

B   **yes** and **no** are expressed in indirect speech by subject + appropriate auxiliary verb:

> *He said, 'Can you swim?' and I said 'No' =*
> *He asked (me) if I could swim and I said I couldn't.*
> *He said, 'Will you have time to do it?' and I said 'Yes' =*
> *He asked if I would have time to do it and I said that I would.*

324   Indirect speech: mixed types

Direct speech may consist of statement + question, question + command, command + statement, or all three together.

A   Normally each requires its own introductory verb:

> *'I don't know the way. Do you?' he asked =*
> *He said he didn't know the way and asked her if she did/if she knew it.*
> *'Someone's coming,' he said. 'Get behind the screen' =*
> *He said that someone was coming and told me to get behind the screen.*
> *'I'm going shopping. Can I get you anything?' she said =*
> *She said she was going shopping and asked if she could get me anything.*
> *'I can hardly hear the radio,' he said. 'Could you turn it up?' =*
> *He said he could hardly hear the radio and asked her to turn it up.*

B   But sometimes, when the last clause is a statement which helps to explain the first, we can use **as** instead of a second introductory verb:

> *'You'd better wear a coat. It's very cold out,' he said =*
> *He advised me to wear a coat as it was very cold out.*
> *'You'd better not walk across the park alone. People have been mugged there,' he said =*
> *He warned her not to walk across the park alone as people had been mugged there.*

C   Sometimes the second introductory verb can be a participle:

> *'Please, please, don't drink too much! Remember that you'll have to drive home,' she said =*
> *She begged him not to drink too much, reminding him that he'd have to drive home.*

*'Let's shop on Friday. The supermarket will be very crowded on
Saturday,' she said =
She suggested shopping on Friday, pointing out that the supermarket
would be very crowded on Saturday.*

(**as** could be used in both these examples.)

325 **must** and **needn't**

A **must** used for deductions, permanent commands/prohibitions and to
express intention remains unchanged. (For **must**, expressing advice,
see 287 A.)

1 Deductions:

*She said, 'I'm always running into him; he must live near here!' =
She said that . . . he must live in the area.*

2 Permanent command:

*He said, 'This door must be kept locked' =
He said that the door must be kept locked.*

3 **must** used casually to express intention:

*He said, 'We must have a party to celebrate this' =
He said that they must have a party to celebrate it.*

B **must** used for obligation can remain unchanged. Alternatively it can be
reported by **would have to** or **had to**.

1 **I/we must** reported by **would have to**

would have to is used when the obligation depends on some future
action, or when the fulfilment of the obligation appears remote or
uncertain, i.e. when **must** is clearly replaceable by **will have to**:

*'If the floods get worse we must (will have to) leave the house,' he
said =
He said that if the floods got worse they would have to leave the
house.
'When it stops snowing we must start digging ourselves out,'
I said =
I said that when it stopped snowing we would have to start digging
ourselves out.
'We must mend the roof properly next year,' he said =
He said that they would have to mend the roof properly the following
year.
'I have just received a letter,' he said. 'I must go home' =
He said that he had just received a letter and would have to go home.*

(But **had to** would be more usual here if he went at once, i.e. **had
to** would imply that he went at once.)

2 **I/we must** reported by **had to**

had to is the usual form for obligations where times for fulfilment have
been fixed, or plans made, or when the obligation is fulfilled fairly
promptly, or at least by the time the speech is reported:

> *He said, 'I must wash my hands'* (and presumably did so) =
> *He said that he had to wash his hands.*
> *Tom said, 'I must be there by nine tomorrow'* =
> *Tom said that he had to be there by nine the next day.*

would have to would be possible here also but would imply that the obligation was self-imposed and that no outside authority was involved. **had to** could express either an outside authority (i.e. that someone had told him to be there) or a self-imposed obligation.

All difficulties about **had to/would have to** can of course be avoided by keeping **must** unchanged. In both the above examples **must** could have been used instead of **had to/would have to**.

3 **you/he/they must** is reported similarly:
> *He said, 'You must start at once'* =
> *He said that she must/had to/would have to start at once.*

But note that **would have to** removes the idea of the speaker's authority:
> *Tom said, 'If you want to stay on here you must work harder'* =
> *Tom said that if she wanted to stay on she must/would have to work harder.*

must implies that Tom himself insists on her working harder. **would have to** merely implies that this will be necessary.

4 **must I/you/he?** can change similarly but as **must** in the interrogative usually concerns the present or immediate future it usually becomes **had to**:
> *'Must you go so soon?' I said* = *I asked him if he had to go so soon.*

5 **must not**
I must not usually remains unchanged. **you/he must not** remains unchanged or is expressed as a negative command (see 320-1):
> *He said, 'You mustn't tell anyone'* =
> *He said that she mustn't tell/wasn't to tell anyone* or
> *He told her not to tell anyone.*

C **needn't**
needn't can remain unchanged and usually does. Alternatively it can change to **didn't have to/wouldn't have to** just as **must** changes to **had to/would have to**:
> *He said, 'You needn't wait'* = *He said that I needn't wait.*
> *I said, 'If you can lend me the money I needn't go to the bank* =
> *I said that if he could lend me the money I needn't/wouldn't have to go to the bank.*
> *He said, 'I needn't be in the office till ten tomorrow morning'* =
> *He said that he needn't/didn't have to be in the office till ten the next morning.*

need I/you/he? behaves exactly in the same ways as **must I/you/he?** i.e. it normally becomes **had to**:
> *'Need I finish my pudding?' asked the small boy* =
> *The small boy asked if he had to finish his pudding.*

32 Conjunctions

326 Co-ordinating conjunctions: **and, but, both . . . and, or, either . . . or, neither . . . nor, not only . . . but also**

These join pairs of nouns/adjectives/adverbs/verbs/phrases/clauses:

He plays squash and rugby.
I make the payments and keep the accounts.
He works quickly and/but accurately.
He is small but strong.   She is intelligent but lazy.
We came in first but (we) didn't win the race.
Both men and women were drafted into the army.
Ring Tom or Bill.   She doesn't smoke or drink.
He can't (either) read or write.
You can (either) walk up or take the cable car.
He can neither read nor write.
Not only men but also women were chosen.

327 **besides, however, nevertheless, otherwise, so, therefore, still, yet, though**

These adverbs/conjunctions can join clauses or sentences and are then often known as 'conjuncts'. But they can also, with the exception of **nevertheless** and **therefore** (conjuncts), be used in other ways. Their position will vary according to how they are used.

A   **besides** (preposition) means 'in addition to'. It precedes a noun/pronoun/gerund:

Besides doing the cooking I look after the garden.

besides (conjunct) means 'in addition'. It usually precedes its clause, but can follow it:

I can't go now; I'm too busy. Besides, my passport is out of date.

moreover could replace **besides** here in more formal English.

anyway or **in any case** could be used here in more informal English:

Anyway, my passport's out of date.

B   **however** (adverb of degree, see 41) precedes its adjective/adverb:

You couldn't earn much, however hard you worked.

however (conjunct) usually means 'but'. It can precede or follow its clause or come after the first word or phrase:

I'll offer it to Tom. However, he may not want it or
He may not want it however or *Tom, however, may not want it* or
If, however, he doesn't want it . . .

But when two contrasting statements are mentioned, **however** can mean 'but/nevertheless/all the same':

> *They hadn't trained hard, but/however/nevertheless/all the same they won* or *they won, however/nevertheless/all the same.*

(See also 329.)

C **otherwise** (adverb of manner) usually comes after the verb:

> *It must be used in a well-ventilated room. Used otherwise* (= in a different way) *it could be harmful.*

otherwise (conjunct) means 'if not/or else':

> *We must be early; otherwise we won't get a seat.*

or could also be used here in colloquial English:

> *We must be early or (else) we won't get a seat.*

D **so** (adverb of degree) precedes its adjective/adverb:

> *It was so hot that . . .   They ran so fast that . . .*

so (conjunct) precedes its clause:

> *Our cases were heavy, so we took a taxi.*

E **therefore** can be used instead of **so** in formal English.
It can come at the beginning of the clause or after the first word or phrase; or before the main verb:

> *There is fog at Heathrow; the plane, therefore, has been diverted/the plane has therefore been diverted/therefore the plane has been diverted.*

F **still** and **yet** can be adverbs of time (see 37):

> *The children are still up. They haven't had supper yet.*

still and **yet** (conjunct) come at the beginning of clauses.
still means 'admitting that/nevertheless'.
yet means 'in spite of that/all the same/nevertheless'.

> *You aren't rich; still, you could do something to help him.*
> *They are ugly and expensive; yet people buy them.*

G **though/although** normally introduce clauses of concession (see 340):

> *Though/Although they're expensive, people buy them.*

though (but not **although**) can also be used to link two main clauses.
though used in this way means 'but' or 'yet' and is placed sometimes at the beginning but more often at the end of its clause:

> *He says he'll pay, though I don't think he will* or
> *He says he'll pay; I don't think he will, though.*

328 Subordinating conjunctions: **if, that, though/although, unless, when** etc.

Subordinating conjunctions introduce subordinate adverb or noun clauses and are dealt with in the chapters on the different types of clause.

See chapter 21 for conditional clauses, chapter 33 for purpose clauses, chapter 34 for adverb clauses of reason, result, concession, comparison and time, and chapter 35 for noun clauses.

Some conjunctions have more than one meaning and may introduce more than one type of clause.

Pairs and groups of conjunctions which are sometimes confused with each other or with other parts of speech are dealt with below.

329 **though/although** and **in spite of** (preposition phrase), **despite** (preposition)

Two opposing or contrasting statements, such as *He had no qualifications* and *He got the job,* could be combined as follows:

A   With **but, however** or **nevertheless** as shown in 327 above:

> *He had no qualifications but he got the job.*
> *He had no qualifications; however he got the job/he got the job, however.*
> *He had no qualifications; nevertheless he got the job.*

B   With **though/although**:

> *He got the job although he had no qualifications.*
> *Although he had no qualifications he got the job.*

C   With **in spite of/despite** + noun/pronoun/gerund:

> *In spite of having no qualifications he got the job. He got the job in spite of having no qualifications.*

despite = **in spite of**. It is chiefly used in newspapers and in formal English:

> *Despite the severe weather conditions all the cars completed the course.*

D   Note that **though/although** requires subject + verb:

> *Although it was windy . . .*

and that **in spite of/despite** requires noun/pronoun or gerund:

> *In spite of the wind . . .*

Some more examples:

> *Although it smelt horrible . . . = In spite of the horrible smell . . .*
> *Although it was dangerous . . . = In spite of the danger . . .*
> *Though he was inexperienced . . . =*
> *In spite of his inexperience/his being inexperienced . . .*

330 **for** and **because**

These conjunctions have nearly the same meaning and very often either can be used. It is, however, safer to use **because**, as a clause introduced by **for** (which we will call a '**for**-clause') has a more restricted use than a clause introduced by **because**:

1   A **for**-clause cannot precede the verb which it explains:
     Because it was wet he took a taxi. (**for** is not possible.)

2   A **for**-clause cannot be preceded by **not, but** or any conjunction:
     *He stole, not because he wanted the money but because he liked
     stealing.* (**for** not possible)

3   A **for**-clause cannot be used in answer to a question:
     Why did you do it? ~ I did it because I was angry. (**for** not possible)

4   A **for**-clause cannot be a mere repetition of what has been already
    stated, but always includes some new piece of information:
     *He spoke in French. She was angry because he had spoken in
     French.* (**for** is not possible.)
    But *She was angry, for she didn't know French.* (Here **for** is correct;
     because is also possible.)

The reason for these restrictions is that a **for**-clause does not tell us
why a certain action was performed, but merely presents a piece of
additional information which helps to explain it.

Some examples of **for**-clauses:
     The days were short, for it was now December.
     He took the food eagerly, for he had eaten nothing since dawn.
     *When I saw her in the river I was frightened. For at that point the
     currents were dangerous.*

In speech a short pause is usually made before a **for**-clause and in
written English this place is usually marked by a comma, and
sometimes, as in the last example above, by a full stop.
because could be used in the above sentences also, though **for** is
better.

331   when, while, as used to express time

A   **when** is used, with simple tenses:

1   When one action occurs at the same time as another or in the span of
    another:
     When it is wet the buses are crowded.
     When we lived in town we often went to the theatre.

2   When one action follows another:
     When she pressed the button the lift stopped.

B   **as** is used:

1   When the second action occurs before the first is finished:
     As I left the house I remembered the key.
    This implies that I remembered the key before I had completed the
    action of leaving the house; I was probably still in the doorway. *While I
    was leaving* would have the same meaning here, but *When I left* would
    give the impression that the act of leaving was complete and the door
    shut behind me.

2 For parallel actions: *He sang as he worked.*

3 For parallel development:
> *As the sun rose the fog dispersed.*
> *As it grew darker it became colder* =
> *The darker it grew, the colder it became.*
> *As she came to know him better she relied on him more.*
> *As he became more competent he was given more interesting work.*

If we used **when** here we would lose all idea of simultaneous progression or development.

4 To mean **while** (= during the time that):
> *As he stood there he saw two men enter the bar.*

But there is no particular advantage in using **as** here, and **while** is safer.

332 as meaning when/while or because/since

A Restricted use of **as** (= **when/while**)

as here is chiefly used with verbs indicating action or development. It is not normally used with the type of verb listed in 168, except when there is an idea of development, as in B3 above. Nor is it normally used with verbs such as *live, stay, remain.*

B **as** used with the above verbs/types of verb normally means **because/since**:
> *As he was tired . . .* = *Because he was tired . . .*
> *As he knew her well . . .* = *Because he knew her well . . .*
> *As it contains alcohol . . .* = *Since/Because it contains alcohol . . .*
> *As he lives near here . . .* = *Since/Because he lives . . .*

C With most verbs, **as** can be used with either meaning:
> *As/While he shaved he thought about the coming interview.*
> *As/Because he shaved with a blunt razor he didn't make a very good job of it.*

If in doubt here, students should use **while** or **because**.

D **as** + noun can mean either **when/while** or **because/since**:
> *As a student he had known great poverty* =
> *When he was a student he had known great poverty.*
> *As a student he gets/got in for half price* =
> *Because he is/was a student he gets/got in . . .*
> *As a married man, he has to think of his family* =
> *Because/Since he is a married man . . .*

as meaning **when/while** here is usually followed by a perfect tense.
as meaning **because/since** can be followed by any tense.

333   as, when, while used to mean **although, but, seeing that**

A   **as** can mean **though/although** but only in the combination adjective +
as + subject + **to be/to seem/to appear**:
Tired as he was he offered to carry her =
Though he was tired he offered to carry her.
Strong as he was, he couldn't lift it.

B   **while** can mean **but** and is used to emphasize a contrast:
'At sea' means 'on a ship', while 'at the sea' means 'at the seaside'.
Some people waste food while others haven't enough.
while can also mean **although** and is then usually placed at the
beginning of a sentence:
While I sympathize with your point of view I cannot accept it.

C   **when** can mean **seeing that/although**. It is therefore very similar to
while, but is chiefly used to introduce a statement which makes
another action seem unreasonable. It is often, though not necessarily,
used with a question:
*How can you expect your children to be truthful when you yourself
tell lies?*
*It's not fair to expect her to do all the cooking when she has had no
training or experience.*

D   Do not confuse **when** and **if**
When he comes implies that we are sure he will come. *If he comes*
implies that we don't know whether he will come or not.
(For **if** in conditional sentences, see chapter 21.)

33 Purpose

334 Purpose is normally expressed by the infinitive

Purpose can be expressed by:

A The infinitive alone:
> *He went to France to learn French.*   *They stopped to ask the way.*

When there is a personal object of the main verb, the infinitive may refer to this and not to the subject:
> *He sent Tom to the shop to buy bread.* (Tom was to buy the bread.)

B **in order** or **so as** + infinitive
in order + infinitive can imply either that the subject wants to perform the action or that he wants it to happen.
so as + infinitive implies only that the subject wants the action to happen. **in order** is, therefore, the more generally useful.
in order or **so as** are used:

1 With a negative infinitive to express a negative purpose:
> *He left his gun outside in order/so as not to frighten us.*

2 With **to be** and **to have**:
> *She left work early in order/so as to be at home when he arrived.*
> *She gave up work in order/so as to have more time with the children.*

3 When the purpose is less immediate:
> *He is studying mathematics in order/so as to qualify for a better job.*
> *She learnt typing in order to help her husband with his work.*

4 Sometimes in longer sentences, to emphasize that the infinitive indicates purpose:
> *He was accused of misrepresenting the facts in order/so as to make the scheme seem feasible.*
> *He took much more trouble over the figures than he usually did in order/so as to show his new boss what a careful worker he was.*

(But **in order/so as** is not essential and is often omitted.)
When the infinitive of purpose precedes the main verb, **in order/so as** may be placed first:
> *In order/So as to show his boss what a careful worker he was, he took extra trouble over the figures.*

(But here also **in order/so as** may be omitted.)

5 When there is a personal object but we want the infinitive to refer unambiguously to the subject:
> *He sent his sons to a boarding school in order/so as to have some peace.* (He, not his sons, was going to have some peace.)

Compare with:

He sent his sons to a boarding school to learn to live in a community.
(Not he but his sons were to learn to live in a community.)
But this **in order/so as** construction is not very common. It is more
usual to say:

He sent his sons to a boarding school because he wanted to have some peace.

C   **in order** (but not **so as**), used to emphasize that the subject really had
this purpose in mind:

He bought diamonds when he was in Amsterdam! ~ *That wasn't surprising. He went to Amsterdam in order to buy diamonds.* (not
for any other purpose)

We could also, however, express this idea by stressing the first verb
and omitting **in order**: *He ¹went to Amsterdam to buy diamonds.*

D   Infinitive + noun + preposition:

I want a case to keep my records in.
I need a corkscrew to open this bottle with.

Note that here we are talking about a particular purpose.
For a general purpose we use **for** + gerund:

This is a case for keeping records in.
A corkscrew is a tool for opening bottles.

335   Infinitives of purpose after **go** and **come**

It is not usual to use an infinitive of purpose after the imperative or
infinitive of **go** and **come**. Instead of *Go to find Bill* we normally say *Go
and find Bill*; and instead of *Come to talk to Ann* we say *Come and talk
to Ann*; i.e. instead of an imperative + an infinitive of purpose we
commonly use two imperatives joined by **and**.
And instead of:

I must go to help my mother and *I'll come to check the accounts*

we normally say:

I must go and help my mother and *I'll come and check the accounts.*

i.e. instead of an infinitive + an infinitive of purpose we use two
infinitives joined by **and** (see 246 I).
But when **go** and **come** are used as gerunds or in any present or past
tense they commonly take the ordinary infinitive of purpose:

I'm thinking of going to look for mushrooms.
I went to help my mother.
I've come to check the accounts.
I didn't come to talk to Bill; I came to talk to you.

336   Clauses of purpose

Clauses are necessary when the person to whom the purpose refers is
different from the subject of the main clause, or when the original
subject is stated again:

Ships carry lifeboats so that the crew can escape if the ship sinks.
This knife has a cork handle so that it will float if it falls overboard.

A Purpose clauses are usually expressed by **so that** + **will/would** or **can/could** + infinitive.
can/could is used here to mean **will/would be able to**:

> *They make £10 notes a different size from £5 notes so that blind*
> *people can* (= will be able to) *tell the difference between them.*
> *They wrote the notices in several languages so that foreign tourists*
> *could* (= would be able to) *understand them.*

can and **will** are used when the main verb is in a present, present
perfect or future tense; **could** and **would** are used when the main verb
is in a past tense. See the examples above and also:

> *I light/am lighting/have lit/will light the fire so that the house will be*
> *warm when they return.*
> *I have given/will give him a key so that he can get into the house*
> *whenever he likes.*
> *I pinned the note to his pillow so that he would be sure to see it.*
> *There were telephone points every kilometre so that drivers whose cars*
> *had broken down would be able to/could summon help.*

If **that** is omitted from purpose clauses with **can/could**, the idea of
purpose may disappear. The sentence *He took my shoes so that I*
couldn't leave the house would normally mean 'He took my shoes to
prevent my leaving etc.' but *He took my shoes, so I couldn't leave the*
house would normally mean 'He took my shoes; therefore I wasn't able
to leave'.

B Purpose clauses can also be formed by **so that/in order that/that** +
may/might or **shall/should** + infinitive. These are merely more
formal constructions than those shown in A above. There is no
difference in meaning.
Note that **so that** can be followed by **will/can/may/shall** or their past
forms, while **in order that** or **that** are limited to **may/shall** or their
past forms.
that used alone is rarely found except in very dramatic speech or
writing, or in poetry.
The rules about sequences of tenses are the same as those shown
above. The following are very formal:

> *We carved their names on the stone so that/in order that future*
> *generations should/might know what they had done.*
> *These men risk their lives so that/in order that we may live more*
> *safely.*

may in the present tense is much more comman than **shall**, which is
rarely used. In the past tense either **might** or **should** can be used.
The student should know the above forms but should not normally need
to use them, as for all ordinary purposes **so that** + **can/could** or
will/would should be quite sufficient.

C Negative purpose clauses are made by putting the auxiliary verb
(usually **will/would** or **should**) into the negative:

> *He wrote his diary in code so that his wife wouldn't be able to read it.*
> *He changed his name so that his new friends wouldn't/shouldn't*
> *know that he had once been accused of murder.*

Criminals usually telephone from public telephone boxes so that the police won't be able to trace the call.

Negative purpose clauses can, however, usually be replaced by **to prevent** + noun/pronoun + gerund, or **to avoid** + gerund:

He dyed his beard so that we shouldn't recognize him/to prevent us recognizing him/to avoid being recognized. (passive gerund)
She always shopped in another village so that she wouldn't meet her own neighbours/to avoid meeting her own neighbours.

These infinitive phrases are preferred to negative purpose clauses.

337 in case and lest

A **in case**

1 **in case** + subject + verb can follow a statement or command:
I don't let him climb trees in case he tears his trousers.
This first action is usually a preparation for, or a precaution against, the action in the **in case** clause, which is a possible future action.

in case + present tense normally has the meaning 'because this may happen/because perhaps this will happen' or 'for fear that this may happen'.

in case + past tense normally means 'because this might happen/because perhaps this would happen' or 'for fear that this would happen'.

Both present tense and past tense here can be replaced by **should** + infinitive. **should** used here would express greater improbability, but this construction is not very usual.

2 Tenses with **in case**

Main verb

$$\left.\begin{array}{l}\text{Future} \\ \text{Present} \\ \text{Present perfect}\end{array}\right\} + \textbf{in case} + \left\{\begin{array}{l}\text{present tense or} \\ \textbf{should} + \text{infinitive}\end{array}\right.$$

$$\left.\begin{array}{l}\text{Conditional} \\ \text{Past tense} \\ \text{Past perfect}\end{array}\right\} + \textbf{in case} + \left\{\begin{array}{l}\text{past tense or} \\ \textbf{should} + \text{infinitive}\end{array}\right.$$

I'll make a cake in case someone drops in at the weekend.
I carry a spare wheel in case I have/should have a puncture.
I always keep candles in the house in case there is a power cut.
I always kept candles in the house in case there was a power cut.
(See also 227.)

B **lest** means 'for fear that' and is followed by **should**:
He doesn't/didn't dare to leave the house lest someone should recognize him.

lest is rarely found except in formal written English.

34 Clauses of reason, result, concession, comparison, time

338 Clauses of reason and result/cause

Except for the type shown in A2 and A3 below, both these clauses can be introduced by **as** or **because**. But **as** is safer for clauses of reason (see A below) and **because** is safer for clauses of result/cause (see B).

A Clauses of reason

1 Introduced by **as/because/since**:

> *We camped there as/because/since it was too dark to go on.*
> *As/Because/Since it was too dark to go on, we camped there.*

2 'in view of the fact that' can be expressed by **as/since/seeing that**, but not **because**:

> *As/Since/Seeing that you are here, you may as well give me a hand.*
> *As/Since/Seeing that Tom knows French, he'd better do the talking.*

3 Where **as/since/seeing that** refers to a statement previously made or understood, it is replaceable by **if**:

> *As/Since/Seeing that/If you don't like Bill, why did you invite him?*

Note the use of **if so**:

> *I hope Bill won't come. ~ If so (= If you hope he won't come),*
> *why did you invite him?*

For **if + so/not**, see 347.

B Clauses of result/cause (see also 339) are introduced by **because** or **as**:

> *The fuse blew because we had overloaded the circuit.*
> *He was angry because we were late.*
> *As it froze hard that night there was ice everywhere next day.*
> *As the soup was very salty we were thirsty afterwards.*

C These combinations could also be expressed by two main clauses joined by **so**:

> *It was too dark to go on, so we camped there.*
> *You are here, so you may as well give me a hand.*
> *It froze hard that night, so there was ice everywhere next day.*

therefore can also be used, but is normal only in fairly formal sentences:

> *The Finnish delegate has not yet arrived. We are therefore*
> *postponing/We have therefore decided to postpone/Therefore we are*
> *postponing the meeting.* (Notice possible positions of **therefore**.)

339 Clauses of result with **such/so . . . that**

A **such** is an adjective and is used before an adjective + noun:

> *They had such a fierce dog that no one dared to go near their house.*
> *He spoke for such a long time that people began to fall asleep.*

B **so** is an adverb and is used before adverbs and with adjectives which are not followed by their nouns:

> *The snow fell so fast that our footsteps were soon covered up.*
> *His speech went on for so long that people began to fall asleep.*
> *Their dog was so fierce that no one dared come near it.*

But **such** is never used before **much** and **many**, so **so** is used even when **much** and **many** are followed by nouns:

> *There was so much dust that we couldn't see what was happening.*
> *So many people complained that they took the programme off.*

C Note that **such** + **a** + adjective + noun is replaceable by **so** + adjective + **a** + noun, so that 'such a good man' is replaceable by 'so good a man'. This is only possible when a noun is preceded by **a/an**. It is not a very usual form but may be met in literature.

Sometimes for emphasis **so** is placed at the beginning of the sentence. It is then followed by the inverted form of the verb (see 45):

> *So terrible was the storm that whole roofs were ripped off.*

340 Clauses of concession

These are introduced by **although, though** (see 327, 329), **even though, even if, no matter, however** (see 85) and sometimes by **whatever. as** is also possible, but only in the adjective + **as** + **be** construction.

> *Although/Though/Even though/Even if you don't like him you can still be polite.*
> *No matter what you do, don't touch this switch.*
> *However rich people are, they always seem anxious to make more money.*
> *However carefully you drive, you will probably have an accident eventually.*
> *Whatever you do, don't tell him that I told you this.*
> *Patient as he was, he had no intention of waiting for three hours.*
> (though he was patient)

may + infinitive can be used in hypothetical cases:

> *However frightened you may be yourself, you must remain outwardly calm.*

may can also imply 'I accept the fact that':

> *But he's your brother! ~ He may be my brother but I don't trust him!*

But **may** used in this way is part of another main clause, not a clause of concession.

should + infinitive can be used after **even if** just as it can after **if** in conditional sentences, to express the idea that the action expressed by the infinitive is not very likely to take place:

> *Even if he should find out he won't do anything about it.*

341 Clauses of comparison

A Comparisons with adjectives and finite verbs (see also 20-2):

> *It's darker today than it was yesterday.*
> *He doesn't pay as much tax as we do/as us.*
> *He spends more than he earns.*

Note **that** + adjective, a colloquial form:

> *Will it cost £100? ~ No, it won't cost as much as (all) that. It won't be (all) that expensive.* (It won't be as expensive as that.)

that + adjective is sometimes used colloquially to mean **very**.

B Comparisons with adverbs and finite verbs (see also 31-4):

> *He didn't play as well as we expected/as well as you (did).*
> *He sings more loudly than anyone I've ever heard/than anyone else (does).*
> *You work harder than he does/than him/than I did at your age.*

C Comparisons with adjectives and infinitives or gerunds

Often either can be used, but the infinitive is more usual for a particular action, and gerunds are more usual for general statements (see also E below):

> *It's sometimes as cheap to buy a new one as (it is) (to) repair the old one.*
> *Buying a new one is sometimes as cheap as repairing the old one.*
> *He found that lying on the beach was just as boring as sitting in his office* or
> *He found lying on the beach just as boring as sitting etc.* (The infinitive would be less usual here.)
> *He thinks it (is) safer to drive himself than (to) let me drive.*
> *He thinks that driving himself is safer than letting me drive.*
> *It will soon be more difficult to get a visa than it is now.*
> *Getting a visa will soon be more difficult than it is now.*

D In comparisons of the type shown in C above, if we have an infinitive before **as/than** we will usually have an infinitive (not a gerund) after it. Similarly, if we have a gerund before **as/than** we will normally have a gerund (not an infinitive) after it. See examples above.

But if we have a finite verb + **this/that/which** before **as/than** we can have a gerund after it. An infinitive is possible but would be much less usual:

> *I'll deliver it by hand; this will be cheaper than posting it.*
> *He cleaned his shoes, which was better than doing nothing.*

E   Infinitives are used with **would rather/sooner** (see 297-8):
    Most people would rather work than starve.
    I would resign rather than accept him as a partner.

342   Time clauses

A   These are introduced by conjunctions of time such as:

after	*immediately*	*till/until*
as	*no sooner . . . than*	*when*
as soon as	*once*	*whenever*
before	*since*	*while*
hardly . . . when	*the sooner*	

They can also be introduced by **the minute, the moment.**
For examples with **when, as, while**, see 331-3.
For examples with **before**, see 195 B.

B   Remember that we do not use a future form, or a conditional tense, in a
time clause.

1   Each of the following future forms becomes a present tense when we
put it in a time clause.

Future simple:
    You'll be back soon. I'll stay till then. = *I'll stay till you get back.*

be going to:
    The parachutist is going to jump. Soon after he jumps his parachute
    will open.

The present continuous, used as a future form, and the future
continuous:
    He's arriving/He'll be arriving at six but
    When he arrives he'll tell us all about the match.
    Before he arrives I'll give the children their tea.
But the continuous tense can, of course, be used in time clauses when
it indicates a continuous action:
    Peter and John will be playing/are playing/are going to play tennis
    tonight. While they are playing (during this time) *we'll go to the*
    beach.

2   The future perfect changes to the present perfect, and the future
perfect continuous changes to the present perfect continuous:
    I'll have finished in the bathroom in a few minutes.
    The moment/As soon as I have finished I'll give you a call.

3   A conditional tense changes to a past tense:
    We knew that he would arrive/would be arriving about six.
    We knew that till he arrived nothing would be done.

But when **when** introduces a noun clause it can be followed by a future
or conditional tense:
    He said, 'When will the train get in?' =
    He asked when the train would get in.

C   Clauses with **since** (see also 187-8)
    When we have a **since** clause the verb in the main clause is usually in
    the perfect tense:
    > *They've moved house twice since they got married* or
    > *Since they got married, they've moved house twice.*
    > *He said he'd lived in a tent since his house burnt down.*
    > *It's ages since I sailed/have sailed a boat.*
    > *I haven't sailed a boat since I left college.*

D   Clauses with **after**
    In clauses **after** is often followed by perfect tenses:
    > *After/When he had rung off I remembered . . .*
    > *After/When you've finished with it, hang it up.*

E   **hardly/scarcely . . . when, no sooner . . . than** (see also 45)
    > *The performance had hardly begun when the lights went out* or
    > *Hardly had the performance begun when the lights went out.*
    scarcely could replace **hardly** here but is less usual.
    > *He had no sooner drunk the coffee than he began to feel drowsy* or
    > *No sooner had he drunk the coffee than he began to feel drowsy.*
    > *He no sooner earns any money than he spends it* or
    > *Immediately he earns any money he spends it.* (more colloquial)
    Note also **the sooner . . . the sooner**:
    > *The sooner we start, the sooner we'll be there.*

F   **once** (= when, as soon as) is chiefly used with the present and
    perfect tenses:
    > *Once you see how good it is, you'll be convinced.*
    > *Once you've tasted our coffee, you won't buy another brand.*
    > *Once they'd touched the snake, they were far less afraid.*

35 Noun clauses

Noun clauses are very often introduced by **that** and are therefore often called **that**-clauses. However, not all noun clauses are **that**-clauses.

343   Noun clauses (**that**-clauses) as subject of a sentence

A   Sentences with noun clause subjects usually begin with **it** (see 67 D):
> *It is disappointing that Tom can't come.*

'*that Tom can't come*' is the subject.

B   The usual construction is **it** + **be/seem** + adjective + noun clause (see 26-7):
> *It's splendid that you passed your exam.*
> *It's strange that there are no lights on.*

Some adjectives require or can take **that . . . should** (see 236):
> *It is essential that everybody knows/should know what to do.*

C   An alternative construction is **it** + **be/seem** + **a** + noun + noun clause.
Nouns that can be used here include **mercy, miracle, nuisance, pity, shame, relief, wonder. a good thing** is also possible.
> *It's a great pity (that) they didn't get married.*
> *It's a wonder (that) you weren't killed.*
> *It's a good thing (that) you were insured.*

344   **that**-clauses after certain adjectives/participles

The construction here is subject + **be** + adjective/past participle + noun clause:
> *I am delighted that you passed your exam.*

This construction can be used with

(a) adjectives expressing emotion: **glad, pleased, relieved, sorry** (see 26 F)

(b) adjectives/participles expressing anxiety, confidence etc.: **afraid, anxious, aware, certain, confident, conscious, convinced** (see 27). **anxious** requires **that . . . should.**
> *I'm afraid that I can't come till next week.*
> *Are you certain that this is the right road?*

345 that-clauses after certain nouns

A **that**-clause can be placed after a large number of abstract nouns. The most useful of these are: **allegation, announcement, belief, discovery, fact, fear, guarantee, hope, knowledge, news, promise, proposal, report, rumour, suggestion, suspicion. proposal** and **suggestion** require that . . . should.

> *The announcement that a new airport was to be built nearby aroused immediate opposition.*
> *The proposal/suggestion that shops should open on Sundays led to a heated discussion.*
> *A report that the area was dangerous was ignored by the residents.*

346 Noun clauses as objects of verbs

A **that**-clauses are possible after a large number of verbs. Some of the most useful are given below.

acknowledge	*find* (wh)	*recommend*
admit	*forget* (wh)	*remark*
advise	*guarantee*	*remember* (wh)
agree	*happen*	*remind*
allege	*hear* (wh)	*request*
announce	*hope*	*resolve*
appear	*imagine* (wh)	*reveal* (wh)
arrange (wh)	*imply*	*say* (wh)
ask (wh)	*indicate* (wh)	*see* (wh)
assure + object	*inform* + object	*seem*
beg	*insist*	*show* (wh)
believe (wh)	*know* (wh)	*state* (wh)
command	*learn*	*stipulate*
confess	*make out* (= state)	*suggest* (wh)
consider (wh)	*mean*	*suppose*
declare	*notice* (wh)	*suspect*
decide (wh)	*observe*	*teach*
demand	*occur to* + object	*tell* (wh)
demonstrate	*order*	*think* (wh)
determine	*perceive*	*threaten*
discover (wh)	*presume*	*turn out*
doubt	*pretend*	*understand* (wh)
estimate (wh)	*promise*	*urge*
expect	*propose*	*vow*
fear	*prove* (wh)	*warn*
feel	*realize* (wh)	*wish*
	recognize	*wonder* (wh)

and other verbs of communication, e.g. *complain, deny, explain* etc. (see 316 C).

wh: see E below.

Examples
> *They alleged/made out that they had been unjustly dismissed.*
> *He assumes that we agree with him.*
> *I can prove that she did it.*

B   Most of the above verbs can also take another construction (see chapters 23-6). Note however that a verb + **that**-clause does not necessarily have the same meaning as the same verb + infinitive/gerund/present participle: *He saw her answering the letters* means 'He watched her doing this' but *He saw that she answered the letters* could mean either 'He noticed that she did this' or 'He made sure by supervision that she did this'.

C   **appear, happen, occur, seem, turn out** require **it** as subject:
> *It appears/seems that we have come on the wrong day.*
> *It occurred to me that he might be lying.*
> *It turned out that nobody remembered the address.*

D   **that** + subject + **should** can be used after **agree, arrange, be anxious, beg, command, decide, demand, determine, be determined, order, resolve** and **urge** instead of an infinitive construction, and after **insist** and **suggest** instead of a gerund:
> *They agreed/decided that a statue should be put up.*
> *He urged that the matter should go to arbitration.*
> *He suggested that a reward should be offered.*

(See 235, 302 E.)

E   Verbs in section A marked '(wh)' can also be followed by noun clauses beginning with **wh**-words: **what, when, where, who, why,** or with **how**:
> *He asked where he was to go.*
> *They'll believe whatever you tell them.*
> *I forget who told me this.*
> *Have you heard how he is getting on?*
> *I can't think why he left his wife.*
> *I wonder when he will pay me back.*

347   so and not representing a that-clause

A   After **believe, expect, suppose, think** and after **it appears/seems**:
> *Will Tom be at the party?* ~ *I expect so/suppose so/think so* = *I think he will.*

For the negative we use:

1   A negative verb with **so**:
> *Will the scheme be a success?* ~ *I don't believe so/expect so/suppose so/think so.*
> *Are they making good progress?* ~ *It doesn't seem so.*

2   Or an affirmative verb with **not**:
> *It won't take long, will it? ~ No, I suppose not* or
> *I don't suppose so.*
> *The plane didn't land in Calcutta, did it? ~ I believe not* or
> *I don't believe so.*

B   **so** and **not** can be used similarly after **hope** and **be afraid** (= be sorry to say):
> *Is Peter coming with us? ~ I hope so.*
> *Will you have to pay duty on this? ~ I'm afraid so.*

The negative here is made with an affirmative verb + **not**:
> *Have you got a work permit? ~ I'm afraid not.*

C   **so** and **not** can be used after **say** and **tell** + object:
> *How do you know there is going to be a demonstration? ~ Jack said so/Jack told me so.*

I told you so! can mean 'I told you that this was the case/that this would happen'. This usually annoys the person addressed.

For **tell** the only negative form is negative verb + **so**:
> *Tom didn't tell me so.*

For **say** there are two negative forms, but the meaning is not the same:
> *Tom didn't say so* =
> *Tom didn't say that there would be a demonstration.*
> *Tom said not* =
> *Tom said there wouldn't be a demonstration.*

D   **if + so/not**
so/not after **if** can replace a previously mentioned/understood subject + verb:
> *Will you be staying another night? If so* (= If you are), *we can give you a better room. If not* (= If you aren't), *could you be out of your room by 12.00?*

if so/not here usually represents a clause of condition as shown above, but for **if so**, see also 338 A.

36 Numerals, dates, and weights and measures

348 Cardinal numbers (adjectives and pronouns)

1 *one*	11 *eleven*	21 *twenty-one*	31 *thirty-one* etc.
2 *two*	12 *twelve*	22 *twenty-two*	40 *forty*
3 *three*	13 *thirteen*	23 *twenty-three*	50 *fifty*
4 *four*	14 *fourteen*	24 *twenty-four*	60 *sixty*
5 *five*	15 *fifteen*	25 *twenty-five*	70 *seventy*
6 *six*	16 *sixteen*	26 *twenty-six*	80 *eighty*
7 *seven*	17 *seventeen*	27 *twenty-seven*	90 *ninety*
8 *eight*	18 *eighteen*	28 *twenty-eight*	100 *a hundred*
9 *nine*	19 *nineteen*	29 *twenty-nine*	1,000 *a thousand*
10 *ten*	20 *twenty*	30 *thirty*	1,000,000 *a million*

400 *four hundred*
140 *a/one hundred and forty*
1,006 *a/one thousand and six*
5,000 *five thousand*
260,127 *two hundred and sixty thousand, one hundred and twenty-seven*

349 Points to notice about cardinal numbers

A When writing in words, or reading, a number composed of three or more figures we place **and** before the word denoting tens or units:
713 *seven hundred and thirteen*
5,102 *five thousand, one hundred and two* but
6,100 *six thousand, one hundred* (no tens or units)
and is used similarly with hundreds of thousands:
320,410 *three hundred and twenty thousand, four hundred and ten*
and hundreds of millions:
303,000,000 *three hundred and three million*

B **a** is more usual than **one** before **hundred, thousand, million** etc.,
when these numbers stand alone or begin an expression:
100 *a hundred*   1,000 *a thousand*
100,000 *a hundred thousand*
We can also say *a hundred and one, a hundred and two* etc. up to *a hundred and ninety-nine* and *a thousand and one* etc. up to *a thousand and ninety-nine*. Otherwise we use **one**, not **a** (see above). So:
1,040 *a/one thousand and forty* but
1,140 *one thousand, one hundred and forty*

C   The words **hundred, thousand, million** and **dozen**, when
used of a definite number, are never made plural:
>   *six hundred men   ten thousand pounds   two dozen eggs*

If however, these words are used loosely, merely to convey the idea of
a large number, they must be made plural:
>   *hundreds of people   thousands of birds   dozens of times*

Note also that in this case the preposition **of** is placed after *hundreds,
thousands* etc.

of is not used with definite numbers except before **the/them/
these/those** or possessives:
>   *six of the blue ones   ten of these   four of Tom's brothers*

D   Numbers composed of four or more figures are divided into groups of
three as shown above. Decimals are indicated by '·', which is read
'point':
>   10·92 *ten point nine two*

A zero after a decimal point is usually read 'nought':
>   8·04 *eight point nought four*

But 'o' /əʊ/ and 'zero' would also be possible.

350 Ordinal numbers (adjectives and pronouns)

first	*eleventh*	*twenty-first*	*thirty-first* etc.
second	*twelfth*	*twenty-second*	*fortieth*
third	*thirteenth*	*twenty-third*	*fiftieth*
fourth	*fourteenth*	*twenty-fourth*	*sixtieth*
fifth	*fifteenth*	*twenty-fifth*	*seventieth*
sixth	*sixteenth*	*twenty-sixth*	*eightieth*
seventh	*seventeenth*	*twenty-seventh*	*ninetieth*
eighth	*eighteenth*	*twenty-eighth*	*hundredth*
ninth	*nineteenth*	*twenty-ninth*	*thousandth*
tenth	*twentieth*	*thirtieth*	*millionth*

When writing in words or reading fractions other than ½ (*a half*) and ¼
(*a quarter*), we use a combination of cardinal and ordinal numbers:
>   ⅕ *a/one fifth*   ⅟₁₀ *a/one tenth*   (*a* is more usual than *one*)
>   ⅗ *three fifths*   ⁷⁄₁₀ *seven tenths*

A whole number + a fraction can be followed directly by a plural noun:
>   2¼ *miles* = *two and a quarter miles*

½ (*half*) can be followed directly by a noun but other fractions require
of before a noun:
>   *half a second* but *a quarter of a second*

(See also 2 E.)

half + of can also be used, but the **of** is optional:
>   *Half (of) my earnings go in tax.*

351 Points to notice about ordinal numbers

A Notice the irregular spelling of *fifth, eighth, ninth* and *twelfth*.

B When ordinal numbers are expressed in figures the last two letters of
the written word must be added (except in dates):

first = 1st	*twenty-first = 21st*
second = 2nd	*forty-second = 42nd*
third = 3rd	*sixty-third = 63rd*
fourth = 4th	*eightieth = 80th*

C In compound ordinal numbers the rule about **and** is the same as for
compound cardinal numbers: *101st = the hundred and first.*
The article **the** normally precedes ordinal numbers:
   the sixtieth day   the fortieth visitor
Titles of kings etc. are written in Roman figures:
   Charles V   James III   Elizabeth II
But in spoken English we use the ordinal numbers preceded by **the**:
   Charles the Fifth   James the Third   Elizabeth the Second

352 Dates

A The days of the week   The months of the year

Sunday (Sun.)	*January (Jan.)*	*July*
Monday (Mon.)	*February (Feb.)*	*August (Aug.)*
Tuesday (Tues.)	*March (Mar.)*	*September (Sept.)*
Wednesday (Wed.)	*April (Apr.)*	*October (Oct.)*
Thursday (Thurs.)	*May*	*November (Nov.)*
Friday (Fri.)	*June*	*December (Dec.)*
Saturday (Sat.)		

Days and months are always written with capital letters.
Dates are expressed by ordinal numbers, so when speaking we say:
   March the tenth, July the fourteenth etc. or *the tenth of March* etc.
They can, however, be written in a variety of ways; e.g. *March the
tenth* could be written:

March 10	*10 March*	*10th of March*
March 10th	*10th March*	*March the 10th*

B The year
When reading or speaking we use the term **hundred** but not
thousand. The year 1987 would be read as *nineteen hundred and
eighty-seven* or *nineteen eighty-seven*.
Years before the Christian era are followed by the letters BC
(= Before Christ) and years dating from the Christian era are
occasionally preceded by the letters AD (= Anno Domini, in the year of
the Lord). The former are read in either way: *1500 BC* would be read
as *one thousand five hundred BC* or *fifteen hundred BC*.

353 Weights, length and liquid measure

A Weights

The English weights table is as follows:

16 ounces (oz.)	*=*	*1 pound (lb.)*
14 pounds	*=*	*1 stone (st.)*
8 stone	*=*	*1 hundredweight (cwt.)*
20 hundredweight	*=*	*1 ton*
1 pound	*=*	*0·454 kilogram (kg)*
2·2 pounds	*=*	*1 kilogram*
2,204·6 lbs	*=*	*1 metric tonne*

Plurals

ounce, pound and **ton** can take **s** in the plural when they are used as nouns, **stone** and **hundredweight** do not take **s**: e.g. we say *six pound of sugar* or *six pounds of sugar*, but *ten hundredweight of coal* has no alternative.

When used in compound adjectives these terms never take **s**:

a ten-ton lorry

kilo or **kilogram** usually take **s** in the plural when used as nouns:

two kilos of apples or *two kilograms of apples*

B Length

The English table of length is as follows:

12 inches (in.)	*=*	*1 foot (ft.)*
3 feet	*=*	*1 yard (yd.)*
1,760 yards	*=*	*1 mile (m.)*
1 inch	*=*	*2·54 centimetres (cm)*
1 yard	*=*	*0·914 metre (m)*
1 mile	*=*	*1·609 kilometres (km)*

Plurals

When there is more than one inch/mile/centimetre we normally use the plural form of these words:

one inch, ten inches   one mile, four miles
one centimetre, five centimetres

When there is more than one foot we can use either **foot** or **feet**. **feet** is the more usual when measuring heights. We can say:

six foot tall or *six feet tall   two foot long* or *two feet long*

When used in compound adjectives the above forms never take the plural form: *a two-mile walk, a six-inch ruler.*

C Liquid measure

2 pints (pt.)	*= 1 quart (qt.)*		*1 pint*	*= 0·568 litre (l)*
4 quarts	*= 1 gallon (gal.)*		*1 gallon*	*= 4·55 litres*

D Traditionally British measurements have been made in ounces, inches, pints etc. but there is now a gradual move towards the metric system.

37 Spelling rules

For noun plurals, see also 12.
For verb forms, see also 165, 172, 175.

354 Introduction

Vowels are: **a e i o u**
Consonants are: **b c d f g h j k l m n p q r s t v w x y z**
A suffix is a group of letters added to the end of a word:
    beauty, beautiful (*ful* is the suffix.)

355 Doubling the consonant

A Words of one syllable having one vowel and ending in a single consonant
double the consonant before a suffix beginning with a vowel:
    hit + ing = hitting   but   *keep, keeping* (two vowels)
    knit + ed = knitted   *help, helped* (two consonants)
    run + er = runner   *love, lover* (ending in a vowel)
qu here is considered as one consonant: *quit, quitting.*
When the final consonant is **w, x** or **y** it does not double:
    row + ed = rowed   *box + ing = boxing*

B Two- or three-syllable words ending in a single consonant following a
single vowel double the final consonant when the stress falls on the last
syllable. (The stressed syllable is in bold type.)
    *ac**quit** + ed = acquitted*   but   ***mur**mur + ed = murmured*
    *be**gin** + er = beginner*   ***ans**wer + er = answerer*
    *de**ter** + ed = deterred*   ***or**bit + ing = orbiting*
    *re**cur** + ing = recurring*
***fo**cus + ed*, however, can be spelt *focused* or *focussed* and ***bi**as + ed* can
be spelt *biased* or *biassed.*

C The final consonant of *handicap, kidnap, worship* is also doubled:
    handicap, handicapped   *worship, worshipped*
    kidnap, kidnapped

D Words ending in l following a single vowel or two vowels pronounced
separately usually double the **l**:
    appal, appalled   *duel, duellist*   *repel, repellent*
    cruel, cruelly   *model, modelling*   *quarrel, quarrelling*
    dial, dialled   *refuel, refuelled*   *signal, signalled*
    distil, distiller

356 Omission of a final e

A   Words ending in **e** following a consonant drop the **e** before a suffix beginning with a vowel:

> *believe + er = believer*
> *love + ing = loving*
> *move + able = movable*

But *dye* and *singe* keep their final **e** before **ing** to avoid confusion with *die* and *sing*:

> *dye, dyeing   singe, singeing*

age keeps its **e** before **ing** except in American English:

> *age, ageing*

likable can also be spelt *likeable*.

Words ending in **ce** or **ge** sometimes retain the **e**. See 357.

B   A final **e** is retained before a suffix beginning with a consonant:

> *engage, engagement   fortunate, fortunately*
> *hope, hopeful   immediate, immediately*
> *sincere, sincerely*

But the final **e** in adjectives ending in a consonant + **le** is dropped in the adverb form:

> *humble, humbly   idle, idly*

The final **e** is also dropped in the following words:

> *argue, argument   due, duly*
> *judge, judgement* or *judgment   true, truly*
> *whole, wholly* (notice the double **l** here)

C   Words ending in **ee** do not drop an **e** before a suffix:

> *agree, agreed, agreeing, agreement*
> *foresee, foreseeing, foreseeable*

357 Words ending in ce and ge

A   Words ending in **ce** or **ge** retain the **e** before a suffix beginning with **a** or **o**:

> *courage, courageous   peace, peaceably*
> *manage, manageable   replace, replaceable*
> *outrage, outrageous   trace, traceable*

This is done to avoid changes in pronunciation, because **c** and **g** are generally pronounced soft before **e** and **i**, but hard before **a** or **o**.

B   Words ending in **ce** change the **e** to **i** before **ous**:

> *grace, gracious   space, spacious*
> *malice, malicious   vice, vicious*

358 The suffix **ful**

When **full** is added to a word the second l is dropped:
> *beauty* + *full* = *beautiful* (but note adverb form *beautifully*)
> *use* + *full* = *useful* (but note adverb form *usefully*)

If the word to which the suffix is added ends in ll the second l is dropped here also: *skill* + *full* = *skilful*.
Note *full* + *fill* = *fulfil*.

359 Words ending in **y**

Words ending in **y** following a consonant change the **y** to **i** before any suffix except **ing**:
> *carry* + *ed* = *carried*   but   *carry* + *ing* = *carrying*
> *happy* + *ly* = *happily*   *hurry* + *ing* = *hurrying*
> *sunny* + *er* = *sunnier*

y following a vowel does not change:
> *obey* + *ed* = *obeyed*   *play* + *er* = *player*

For plural forms of nouns, see 12.

360 **ie** and **ei**

The normal rule is that **i** comes before **e** except after **c**:
> *believe, sieve* but *deceive, receipt*

There are however the following exceptions:

beige	*feint*	*heir*	*reign*	*their*
counterfeit	*foreign*	*inveigh*	*rein*	*veil*
deign	*forfeit*	*inveigle*	*seize*	*vein*
eiderdown	*freight*	*leisure*	*skein*	*weigh*
eight	*heifer*	*neigh*	*sleigh*	*weight*
either	*height*	*neighbour*	*sleight*	*weir*
feign	*heinous*	*neither*	*surfeit*	*weird*

361 Hyphens

A   Compound words are formed by linking two or more words to make one unit. We can write the compound:

(a) as one word: *bystander, hairdresser, teacup*
(b) as two or more words: *amusement arcade, post office*
(c) with a hyphen: *launching-pad, lay-by, tooth-brush*

It is impossible in most cases to give a firm rule on when a hyphen should be used. When a compound has become familiar through constant use, the hyphen can be omitted: *layby, toothbrush*. This, however, does not always happen and a native English writer is quite capable of writing *toothbrush, tooth brush* or *tooth-brush* at different times.

If the compound is formed of monosyllables, it is more likely to be written as one word. In cases of doubt it is better to omit hyphens or consult a modern dictionary.

B   Hyphens are necessary:
(a) when pronunciation or meaning might be unclear without them:
   co-operate   re-cover (= cover again)
(b) when words form a compound in a particular sentence:
   a do-it-yourself shop
   a go-as-you-please railway ticket
(c) in adjective phrases dealing with age, size, weight and duration of time:
   a five-year-old child   *a ten-ton vehicle*
   a six-foot wall   *a five-minute interval*
Note that the compound is not in the plural form: no **s**.
Adverb/participle compounds used as adjectives are commonly hyphenated, especially when there is a danger of misunderstanding:
   low-flying aircraft   quick-dissolving sugar

C   Hyphens are used in a temporary way to divide a word at the end of a line. The division must be made at a natural break in the word, i.e. between syllables:
   dis-couraged   look-ing   inter-val
A monosyllable should not be divided.

38 Phrasal verbs

362 Introduction

A In modern English it is very usual to place prepositions or adverbs after certain verbs so as to obtain a variety of meanings:

give away = give to someone/anyone
give up = abandon (a habit or attempt)
look after = take care of
look for = search for, seek
look out = beware

The student need not try to decide whether the combination is verb + preposition or verb + adverb, but should consider the expression as a whole.

It is also important to learn whether the combination is transitive (i.e. requires an object) or intransitive (i.e. cannot have an object):

look for is transitive: *I am looking for my passport.*
look out is intransitive: *Look out! This ice isn't safe!*

Each of the combinations given in the following pages will be marked 'tr' (= transitive) or 'intr' (= intransitive), and the examples of the use of each will help to emphasize this distinction.

Note that it is possible for a combination to have two or more different meanings, and to be transitive in one/some of these and intransitive in others. For example, **take off** can mean 'remove'. It is then a transitive expression:

He took off his hat.

take off can also mean 'rise from the ground' (used of aircraft). Here it is intransitive:

The plane took off at ten o'clock.

B Transitive expressions: the position of the object
Noun objects are usually placed at the end of these expressions:

*I am looking for **my glasses**.*

With some expressions, however, they can be placed either at the end or immediately after the verb, i.e. before the short word. We can say:

*He took off **his coat*** or *He took **his coat** off.*

Pronoun objects are sometimes placed at the end of the expression:

*I am looking for **them**.*

But they are more often placed immediately after the verb:

*He took **it** off.*

This position is usual before the following: **back, up, down, in, out, away, off** and **on** (except when used in the expression **call on** = visit).

Examples given of the use of each expression will show all possible
positions of noun or pronoun objects in the following way:

I'll give **this old coat** *away. (give away* **this old coat***/give it away)*
i.e. with this expression the noun object can come before or after the
away; the pronoun object must come before the *away*. When only one
example is given the student may assume that the pronoun object has
the same position as the noun object.

C　　When these expressions are followed by a verb object the gerund form
of the verb is used:

He kept on blowing his horn.

Where gerunds are usual this will be shown by examples.
Note that some expressions can be followed by an infinitive:

It is up to you to decide this for yourself.

Some of the younger members called on the minister to resign.

The lecturer set out to show that most illnesses were avoidable.

go on can be followed by either infinitive or gerund but there is a
considerable difference in meaning. See 270 A.

363　Verb + preposition/adverb combinations

account

account for (tr) = give a good reason for, explain satisfactorily (some
action or expenditure):

A treasurer must account for the money he spends.

*He has behaved in the most extraordinary way; I can't account for
his actions at all/I can't account for his behaving like that.*

allow

allow for (tr) = make provision in advance for, take into account
(usually some additional requirement, expenditure, delay etc.):

*It is 800 kilometres and I drive at 100 k.p.h., so I'll be there in eight
hours. ~ But you'll have to allow for delays going through towns
and for stops for refuelling.*

*Allowing for depreciation your car should be worth £2,000 this time
next year.*

answer

answer back (intr), **answer** somebody **back** = answer a reproof
impudently:

FATHER: *Why were you so late last night? You weren't in till 2 a.m.*
SON: *You should have been asleep.*
FATHER: *Don't answer me back. Answer my question.*

ask

ask after/for somebody = ask for news of:

I met Tom at the party; he asked after you. (asked how you
were/how you were getting on)

ask for

(a) = ask to speak to:
  Go to the office and ask for my secretary.
(b) = request, demand:
  The men asked for more pay and shorter hours.

ask someone **in** (object before **in**) = invite him to enter the house:
  *He didn't ask me in; he kept me standing at the door while he read
  the message.*

ask someone **out** (object before **out**) = invite someone to an
entertainment or to a meal (usually in a public place):
  *She had a lot of friends and was usually asked out in the evenings,
  so she seldom spent an evening at home.*

back

back away (intr) = step or move back slowly (because confronted by
some danger or unpleasantness):
  When he took a gun out everyone backed away nervously.

back out (intr) = withdraw (from some joint action previously agreed
on), discontinue or refuse to provide previously promised help or
support:
  He agreed to help but backed out when he found how difficult it was.

back somebody **up** = support morally or verbally:
  *The headmaster never backed up **his staff**. (backed **them** up) If a
  parent complained about a teacher he assumed that the teacher was in
  the wrong.*

be

be against (tr) = be opposed to (often used with gerund):
  *I'm for doing nothing till the police arrive./I'm against doing
  anything till the police arrive.*

be away (intr) = be away from home/this place for at least a night.

be back (intr) = have returned after a long or short absence:
  *I want to see Mrs Pitt. Is she in? ~
  No, I'm afraid she's out at the moment or
  No, I'm afraid she's away for the weekend. ~
  When will she be back? ~
  She'll be back in half an hour/next week.*

be for (tr) = be in favour of (often used with gerund).

be in (intr) = be at home/in this bulding.

be in for (tr) = be about to encounter (usually something unpleasant):
  *Did you listen to the weather forecast? I'm afraid we're in for a
  bumpy flight.
  If you think that the work is going to be easy you're in for a shock.*

be over (intr) = be finished:
  The storm is over now; we can go on.

be out (intr) = be away from home/from this building for a short
time – not overnight.

be up (intr) = be out of bed:
  *Don't expect her to answer the doorbell at eight o'clock on Sunday
  morning. She won't be up.*

be up to (tr) = be physically or intellectually strong enough (to perform a certain action). The object is usually **it,** though a gerund is possible:

After his illness the Minister continued in office though he was no longer up to the work/up to doing the work.

be up to something/some mischief/some trick/no good = be occupied or busy with some mischievous act:

Don't trust him; he is up to something/some trick.

The boys are very quiet. I wonder what they are up to.

Note that the object of **up to** here is always some very indefinite expression such as these given above. It is never used with a particular action.

it is up to someone (often followed by an infinitive) = it is his responsibility or duty:

It is up to the government to take action on violence.

I have helped you as much as I can. Now it is up to you. (You must continue by your own efforts.)

bear

bear out (tr) = confirm:

*This report bears out **my theory**. (bears **my theory** out/bears **it** out)*

bear up (intr) = support bad news bravely, hide feelings of grief:

The news of her death was a great shock to him but he bore up bravely and none of us realized how much he felt it.

blow

blow out (tr) = extinguish (a flame) by blowing:

*The wind blew out **the candle**. (blew **the candle** out/blew **it** out)*

blow up (tr or intr)

(a) = destroy by explosion, explode, be destroyed:

*They blew up **the bridges** so that the enemy couldn't follow them. (blew **the bridges** up/blew **them** up)*

Just as we got to the bridge it blew up.

(b) = fill with air, inflate, pump up:

*The children blew up **their balloons** and threw them into the air. (blew **the balloons** up/blew **them** up)*

boil

boil away (intr) = be boiled until all (the liquid) has evaporated:

I put the kettle on the gas ring and then went away and forgot about it. When I returned, the water had all boiled away and the flame had burnt a hole in the kettle.

boil over (intr) = to rise and flow over the sides of the container (used only of hot liquids):

The milk boiled over and there was a horrible smell of burning.

break

break down figures = take a total and sub-divide it under various headings so as to give additional information:

> *You say that 10,000 people use this library. Could you break that down into age-groups?* (say how many of these are under 25, over 50 etc.)

break down a door etc. = cause to collapse by using force:

> *The firemen had to break down **the door** to get into the burning house. (break **the door** down/break **it** down)*

break down (intr) = collapse, cease to function properly, owing to some fault or weakness:

(a) Used of people, it normally implies a temporary emotional collapse:
> *He broke down when telling me about his son's tragic death.* (He was overcome by his sorrow; he wept.)

(b) It can express collapse of mental resistance:
> *At first he refused to admit his guilt but when he was shown the evidence he broke down and confessed.*

(c) When used of health it implies a serious physical collapse:
> *After years of overwork his health broke down and he had to retire.*

(d) It is very often used of machines:
> *The car broke down when we were driving through the desert and it took us two days to repair it.*

(e) It can be used of negotiations:
> *The negotiations broke down* (were discontinued) *because neither side would compromise.*

break in (intr), **break into** (tr)

(a) = enter by force:
> *Thieves broke in and stole the silver.*
> *The house was broken into when the owner was on holiday.*

(b) = interrupt someone by some sudden remark:
> *I was telling them about my travels when he broke in with a story of his own.*

break in (a young horse/pony etc.) (tr) = train him for use:
> *You cannot ride or drive a horse safely before he has been broken in.*

break off (tr or intr) = detach or become detached:
> *He took a bar of chocolate and broke off **a bit**. (broke **a bit** off/broke it off)*
> *A piece of rock broke off and fell into the pool at the foot of the cliff.*

break off (tr) = terminate (used of agreements or negotiations):
> *Ann has broken off **her engagement** to Tom. (broken **her engagement** off/broken it off)*

break off (intr) = stop talking suddenly, interrupt oneself:
> *They were in the middle of an argument but broke off when someone came into the room.*

break out (intr)

(a) = begin (used of evils such as wars, epidemics, fires etc.):
> *War broke out on 4 August.*

(b) = escape by using force from a prison etc.:

They locked him up in a room but he broke out. (smashed the door and escaped)

The police are looking for two men who broke out of prison last night.

break up (tr or intr) = disintegrate, cause to disintegrate:

If that ship stays there she will break up/she will be broken up by the waves.

The old ship was towed away to be broken up and sold as scrap.

Divorce breaks up a lot of families. (breaks families up/breaks them up)

break up (intr) = terminate (used of school terms, meetings, parties etc.):

The school broke up on 30 July and all the boys went home for the holidays.

The meeting broke up in confusion.

bring

bring someone **round** (tr; object usually before **round**)

(a) = persuade someone to accept a previously opposed suggestion:

After a lot of argument I brought him round to my point of view.

(b) = restore to consciousness:

She fainted with the pain but a little brandy soon brought her round.

bring a person or thing **round** (tr; object usually before **round**) = bring him/it to my/your/his house:

I have finished that book that you lent me; I'll bring it round (to your house) tonight.

bring up (tr)

(a) = educate and train children:

She brought up her children to be truthful. (brought her children up/brought them up)

(b) = mention:

At the last committee meeting, the treasurer brought up the question of raising the annual subscription. (brought the question up/brought it up)

burn

burn down (tr or intr) = destroy, or be destroyed completely by fire (used of buildings):

The mob burnt down the embassy. (burnt the embassy down/burnt it down)

The hotel burnt down before help came.

call

1   **call** meaning 'visit' (for a short time)

call at a place:

I called at the bank and arranged to transfer some money.

call for = visit a place to collect a person or thing:

I am going to a pop concert with Tom. He is calling for me at eight so I must be ready then.

Let's leave our suitcases in the left luggage office and call for them later on when we have the car.

call in is intransitive, and has the same meaning as **look in** and the colloquial **drop in**:

Call in/Look in on your way home and tell me how the interview went.

call on a person:

He called on all the housewives in the area and asked them to sign the petition.

2 Other meanings of **call for/in/on**

call for (tr) = require, demand (the subject here is often an impersonal word or phrase such as: the situation/this sort of work/this etc.; the object is then usually some quality, e.g. courage/patience/a steady hand etc.):

The situation calls for tact.

You've got the job! This calls for a celebration.

But it can also be used with a personal subject:

The workers are calling for strike action.

The relations of the dead men are calling for an inquiry.

call in a person/**call** him **in** = send for him/ask him to come to the house to perform some service. **send for** is more authoritative than **call in** which is therefore a more polite form:

It was too late to call in an electrician. (call an electrician in/call him in)

There is some mystery about his death; the police have been called in.

call on somebody (usually + infinitive) = ask him to do something/ask him to help. This is a rather formal way of making a request and is chiefly used on formal occasions or in speeches etc. There is usually the idea that the person called upon will consider it his duty to comply with the request:

The president called upon his people to make sacrifices for the good of their country.

The chairman called on the secretary to read the minutes of the last meeting.

3 Other combinations with **call**

call off (tr) = cancel something not yet started, or abandon something already in progress:

They had to call off (= cancel) the match as the ground was too wet to play on. (call the match off/call it off)

When the fog got thicker the search was called off. (abandoned)

call out (tr) = summon someone to leave his house to deal with a situation outside. It is often used of troops when they are required to leave their barracks to deal with civil disturbances:

The police couldn't control the mob so troops were called out.

*The Fire Brigade was called out several times on the night of
5 November to put out fires started by fireworks.
Doctors don't much like being called out at night.*

call up (tr)

(a) = summon for military service:

*In countries where there is conscription **men** are called up at the age
of eighteen. (call up **men**/call **men** up/call **them** up)*

(b) = telephone:

*I called **Tom** up and told him the news. (called up **Tom**/called
him up)*

care

not to care about (tr) = to be indifferent to:

*The professor said that he was interested only in research; he didn't
really care about students.*

care for (tr)

(a) = like (seldom used in the affirmative):

He doesn't care for films about war.

(b) = look after (not much used except in the passive):

The house looked well cared for. (had been well looked after/was in
good condition)

carry

carry on (intr) = continue (usually work or duty):

I can't carry on alone any longer; I'll have to get help.

carry on with (tr) is used similarly:

The doctor told her to carry on with the treatment.

carry out (tr) = perform (duties), obey (orders, instructions), fulfil
(threats):

*You are not meant to think for yourself; you are here to carry out my
orders.*

The Water Board carried out their threat to cut off our water supply.
(They threatened to do it and they did it.)

He read the instructions but he didn't carry them out.

catch

catch up with (tr), **catch up** (tr or intr) = overtake, but not pass:

*I started last in the race but I soon caught up with **the others**.
(caught **them** up/caught up)*

*You've missed a whole term; you'll have to work hard to catch up
with the rest of **the class**. (catch **them** up/catch up)*

clean

clean out (tr) a room/cupboard/drawer etc. = clean and tidy it
thoroughly:

*I must clean out **the spare room**. (clean **the spare room**
out/clean **it** out)*

clean up (tr) a mess, e.g. anything spilt:

*Clean up **any spilt paint**. (clean **the spilt paint** up/clean **it** up)*

clean up (intr) is used similarly:
These painters always clean up when they've finished. (leave the place clean)

clear

clear away (tr) = remove articles, usually in order to make space:
*Could you clear away **these papers**? (clear **these papers** away/clear **them** away)*

clear away (intr) = disperse:
The clouds soon cleared away and it became quite warm.

clear off (intr) from an open space, **clear out** (intr) of a room, building = go away (colloquial; as a command it is definitely rude):
'You clear off,' said the farmer angrily. 'You've no right to put your caravans in my field without even asking my permission.'
Clear out! If I find you in this building again, I'll report you to the police.

clear out (tr) a room/cupboard/drawer etc. = empty it, usually to make room for something else:
*I'll clear out **this drawer** and you can put your things in it. (clear **this drawer** out/clear **it** out)*

clear up (intr) = become fine after clouds or rain:
The sky looks a bit cloudy now but I think it will clear up.

clear up (tr or intr) = make tidy and clean:
When you are cooking it's best to clear up as you go, instead of leaving everything to the end and having a terrible pile of things to deal with.
*Clear up **this mess**. (clear **this mess** up/clear **it** up)*

clear up (tr)
(a) = finish (some work which still remains to be done):
I have some letters which I must clear up before I leave tonight.
(b) = solve (a mystery):
*In a great many detective stories when the police are baffled an amateur detective comes along and clears up **the mystery**. (clears **it** up)*

close

close down (tr or intr) = shut permanently (of a shop or business):
*Trade was so bad that many small shops closed down and big shops closed some of **their branches** down. (closed down **some branches**/closed **them** down)*

close in (intr) = come nearer, approach from all sides (used of mist, darkness, enemies etc.):
As the mist was closing in we decided to stay where we were.

close up (intr) = come nearer together (of people in a line):
If you children closed up a bit there'd be room for another one on this seat.

come

come across/upon (tr) = find by chance:
> *When I was looking for my passport I came across these old photographs.*

come along/on (intr) = come with me, accompany me. 'Come on' is often said to someone who is hesitating or delaying:
> *Come on, or we'll be late.*

come away (intr) = leave (with me):
> *Come away now. It's time to go home.*

come away/off (intr) = detach itself:
> *When I picked up the teapot the handle came away in my hand.*

come in (intr), **come into** (tr) = enter:
> *Someone knocked at my door and I said, 'Come in.'*
> *Come into the garden and I'll show you my roses.*

come off (intr)

(a) = succeed, of a plan or scheme (used in negative):
> *I'm afraid that scheme of yours won't come off. It needs more capital than you have available.*

(b) = take place; happen as arranged:
> *When is the wedding coming off? ~ Next June.*

If we say *The duchess was to have opened the bazaar* we imply that this plan was made but didn't come off. (She arranged to open it but later had to cancel this arrangement.)

(c) = end its run (of a play, exhibition etc.):
> *'Lady Windermere's Fan' is coming off next week. You'd better hurry if you want to see it.*

come out (intr)

(a) = be revealed, exposed (the subject here is normally **the truth/the facts/the whole story** etc. and usually refers to facts which the people concerned were trying to keep hidden, i.e. scandals etc.):
> *They deceived everybody till they quarrelled among themselves; then one publicly denounced the others and the whole truth came out.*

(b) = be published (of books):
> *Her new novel will be coming out in time for the Christmas sales.*

(c) = disappear (of stains):
> *Tomato stains don't usually come out.*

come round (intr)

(a) = finally accept a previously opposed suggestion:
> *Her father at first refused to let her study abroad but he came round (to it) in the end.* (said she could go)

(b) = come to my (your/his etc.) house:
> *I'll come round after dinner and tell you the plan.*

come round/to (intr; stress on **to**) = recover consciousness:
> *When we found him he was unconscious but he came round/to in half an hour and explained that he had been attacked and robbed.*

come up (intr)

(a) = rise to the surface:

A diver with an aqualung doesn't have to keep coming up for air; he can stay underwater for quite a long time.

Weeds are coming up everywhere.

(b) = be mentioned:

The question of the caretaker's wages came up at the last meeting.

come up (intr), **come up to** (tr) = approach, come close enough to talk:

A policeman was standing a few yards away. He came up to me and said, 'You can't park here.'

crop

crop up (intr) = appear, arise unexpectedly or by accident (the subject is normally an abstract noun such as **difficulties/the subject** etc. or a pronoun):

At first all sorts of difficulties cropped up and delayed us. Later we learnt how to anticipate these.

cut

cut down a tree = fell it:

*If you cut down **all the trees** you will ruin the land. (cut **the trees** down/cut **them** down)*

cut down (tr) = reduce in size or amount:

We must cut down expenses or we'll be getting into debt.

'This article is too long,' said the editor. 'Could you cut it down to 2,000 words?'

cut in (intr) = slip into traffic lane ahead of another car when there isn't room to do this safely:

Accidents are often caused by drivers cutting in.

cut off (tr) = disconnect, discontinue supply (usually of gas, water, electricity etc.). The object can either be the commodity or the person who suffers:

*The Company has cut off our **electricity supply** because we haven't paid our bill. (cut **our supply** off/cut **it** off)*

They've cut off the water/our water supply temporarily because they are repairing one of the main pipes.

We were cut off in the middle of our (telephone) conversation. (This might be accidental or a deliberate action by the switchboard operator.)

cut someone **off** = form a barrier between him and safety (often used in connexion with the tide, especially in the passive):

We were cut off by the tide and had to be rescued by boat.

be cut off (intr) = be inconveniently isolated (the subject is usually a place or residents in a certain place):

You will be completely cut off if you go to live in that village because there is a bus only once a week.

cut out (tr)

(a) = cut from a piece of cloth/paper etc. a smaller piece of a desired shape:

> *When I am making a dress I mark the cloth with chalk and then cut* **it** *out. (cut out* **the dress**/cut **the dress** out)*
>
> *Young people often cut out photographs of their favourite pop stars and stick them to the walls.*

(b) = omit, leave out:

> *If you want to get thin you must cut out* **sugar**. *(cut* **it** *out)*

be cut out for (tr) = be fitted or suited for (used of people, usually in the negative):

> *His father got him a job in a bank but it soon became clear that he was not cut out for that kind of work.* (He wasn't happy and was not good at the work.)

cut up (tr) = cut into small pieces:

> *They cut down the tree and cut* **it** *up for firewood. (cut* **the tree** *up/cut up* **the tree**)*

die

die away (intr) = become gradually fainter till inaudible:

> *They waited till the sound of the guard's footsteps died away.*

die down (intr) = become gradually calmer and finally disappear (of riots, fires, excitement etc.):

> *When the excitement had died down the shopkeepers took down their shutters and reopened their shops.*

die out (intr) = become extinct (of customs, races, species of animals etc.):

> *Elephants would die out if men could shoot as many as they wished.*

do

do away with (tr) = abolish:

> *The government should do away with the regulations restricting drinking hours.*

do up (tr) = redecorate:

> *When I do* **this room** *up I'll paint the walls cream. (do up* **this room**/do **it** *up)*

do without (tr) = manage in the absence of a person or thing:

> *We had to do without petrol during the fuel crisis.*

The object is sometimes understood but not mentioned:

> *If there isn't any milk we'll have to do without (it).*

draw

draw back (intr) = retire, recoil:

> *It's too late to draw back now; the plans are all made.*

draw up (tr) = make a written plan or agreement:

> *My solicitor drew up* **the lease** *and we both signed it. (drew* **it** *up)*

draw up (intr) = stop (of vehicles):

> *The car drew up at the kerb and the driver got out.*

drop

drop in (intr) = pay a short unannounced visit:
He dropped in for a few minutes to ask if he could borrow your power drill. (**drop in** is more colloquial than 'call in'.)

drop out (intr) = withdraw, retire from a scheme or plan:
We planned to hire a coach for the excursion but now so many people have dropped out that it will not be needed.

enter

enter for (tr) = become a competitor/candidate (for a contest, examination, etc.):
Twelve thousand competitors have entered for the next London Marathon.

fade

fade away (intr) = disappear, become gradually fainter (usually of sounds):
The band moved on and the music faded away.

fall

fall back (intr) = withdraw, retreat (this is a deliberate action, quite different from **fall behind**, which is involuntary):
As the enemy advanced we fell back.

fall back on (tr) = use in the absence of something better:
We had to fall back on dried milk as fresh milk wasn't available.
He fell back on the old argument that if you educate women they won't be such good wives and mothers.

fall behind (intr) = slip into the rear through inability to keep up with the others, fail to keep up an agreed rate of payments:
At the beginning the whole party kept together but by the end of the day those who were less fit had fallen behind.
He fell behind with his rent and the landlord began to become impatient.

fall in with someone's plans = accept them and agree to co-operate:
We'd better fall in with his suggestion for the sake of peace.

fall in (intr) of troops etc. = get into line

fall out (intr) of troops etc. = leave the lines:
The troops fell in and were inspected. After the parade they fell out and went back to their barracks.

fall off (intr) = decrease (of numbers, attendance etc.):
Orders have been falling off lately; we need a new advertising campaign.
If the price of seats goes up much more theatre attendances will begin to fall off.

fall on (tr) = attack violently (the victim has normally no chance to defend himself as the attackers are too strong; it is also sometimes used of hungry men who attack their food when they get it):
The mob fell on the killers and clubbed them to death.
The starving men fell on the food. (devoured it)

fall out (intr) = quarrel:

When thieves fall out honest men get their own. (proverb; i.e. get back their property)

fall through (intr) = fail to materialize (of plans):

My plans to go to Greece fell through because the journey turned out to be much more expensive than I had expected.

feed

be fed up (intr), **be fed up with** (tr) = be completely bored (slang):

I'm fed up with this wet weather.

I'm fed up with waiting; I'm going home.

feel

feel up to (tr) = feel strong enough (to do something):

I don't feel up to tidying the kitchen now. I'll do it in the morning.

I don't feel up to it.

fill

fill in/up forms etc. = complete them:

*I had to fill in **three forms** to get my new passport. (fill **three forms** in/fill **them** in)*

find

find out (tr) = discover as a result of conscious effort:

In the end I found out what was wrong with my hi-fi.

*The dog found out **the way** to open the door. (found **it** out)*

find someone **out** = find that he has been doing something wrong (this discovery is usually a surprise because the person has been trusted):

After robbing the till for months the cashier was found out.

fix

fix up (tr) = arrange:

*The club has already fixed up **several matches** for next season. (fixed **several matches** up/fixed **them** up)*

get

get about (intr) = circulate; move or travel in a general sense:

The news got about that he had won the first prize in the state lottery and everybody began asking him for money.

He is a semi-invalid now and can't get about as well as he used to.

get away (intr) = escape, be free to leave:

Don't ask him how he is because if he starts talking about his health you'll never get away from him.

I had a lot to do in the office and didn't get away till eight.

get away with (tr) = perform some illegal or wrong act without being punished, usually without even being caught:

He began forging cheques and at first he got away with it but in the end he was caught and sent to prison.

get back (tr) = recover possession of:
> *If you lend him a book he'll lend it to someone else and you'll never get it back. (get back your book/get your book back)*

get back (intr) = reach home again:
> *We spent the whole day in the hills and didn't get back till dark.*

get off (intr) = be acquitted or receive no punishment (compare with
get away with it, which implies that the offender is not even caught):
> *He was tried for theft but got off because there wasn't sufficient evidence against him. (was acquitted)*
> *The boy had to appear before a magistrate but he got off as it was his first offence. (received no punishment)*

get on (intr), **get on with** (tr)
(a) = make progress, be successful:
> *How is he getting on at school?*
> *He is getting on very well with his English.*

(b) = live, work etc., amicably with someone:
> *He is a pleasant friendly man who gets on well with nearly everybody.*
> *How are you and Mr Pitt getting on?*

get out (intr) = escape from, leave (an enclosed space):
> *Don't worry about the snake. It's in a box. It can't get out.*
> *News of the Budget got out before it was officially announced.*
> *I'm so busy that I don't very often get out. (out of the house)*

Note that the imperative 'Get out', except when it means 'descend'
(from a vehicle), is very rude.

get out of (tr) = free oneself from an obligation or habit:
> *I said that I'd help him. Now I don't want to but I can't get out of it.*
> (free myself from my promise)
> *He says that he smokes too much but he can't get out of the habit.*
> *Some people live abroad to get out of paying heavy taxes.*

get over (tr) = recover from (illness, distress or mental weakness):
> *He is just getting over a bad heart attack.*
> *I can't get over her leaving her husband like that.* (I haven't
> recovered from the surprise; I am astonished.)
> *He used to be afraid of heights but he has got over that now.*

get it over (the object is usually **it** which normally represents
something unpleasant) = deal with it and be finished with it:
> *If you have to go to the dentist why not go at once and get it over?*
(Be careful not to confuse this with **get over it**, which is quite
different.)

get round a person = coax him into letting you do what you want:
> *Girls can usually get round their fathers.*

get round a difficulty/regulation = find some solution to it/evade it:
> *If we charge people for admission we will have to pay entertainment tax on our receipts; but we can get round this regulation by saying that we are charging not for admission but for refreshments. Money paid for refreshments is not taxed.*

get through (tr or intr) = finish a piece of work, finish successfully:
> *He got through his exam all right. (passed it)*

get through (intr) = get into telephone communication:

I am trying to call London but I can't get through; I think all the lines are engaged.

get up (tr) = organize, arrange (usually an amateur entertainment or a charitable enterprise):

*They got up **a concert** in aid of cancer research. (They got **it** up.)*

get up (intr) = rise from bed, rise to one's feet, mount:

I get up at seven o' clock every morning.

(For **get** used to mean enter/leave vehicles, see 93 D.)

give

give something **away** = give it to someone (who need not be mentioned):

*I'll give **this old coat** away. (give away **this old coat** away/give **it** away)*

give someone **away** (object before **away**) = betray him:

He said that he was not an American but his accent gave him away. (told us that he was an American)

give back (tr) = restore (a thing) to its owner:

*I must call at the library to give back **this book**. (to give **this book** back/to give **it** back)*

give in (intr) = yield, cease to resist:

At first he wouldn't let her drive the car but she was so persuasive that eventually he gave in.

give out (tr)

(a) = announce verbally:

*They gave out **the names of the winners**. (gave **the names** out/gave **them** out)*

(b) = distribute, issue:

*The teacher gave out **the books**. (gave **one/some** to each pupil)*

give out (intr) = become exhausted (of supplies etc.):

The champagne gave out long before the end of the reception.

His patience gave out and he slapped the child hard.

give up (tr or intr) = abandon an attempt, cease trying to do something:

*I tried to climb the wall but after I had failed three times I gave up. (gave up **the attempt**/gave **the attempt** up/gave **it** up)*

A really determined person never gives up/never gives up trying.

give up (tr) = abandon or discontinue a habit, sport, study, occupation:

Have you given up drinking whisky before breakfast?

*He gave up **cigarettes**. (gave **them** up)*

He tried to learn Greek but soon got tired of it and gave it up.

give oneself **up** (object before **up**) = surrender:

He gave himself up to despair.

He was cold and hungry after a week on the run so he gave himself up to the police.

go

go ahead (intr) = proceed, continue, lead the way:
While she was away he went ahead with the work and got a lot done.
You go ahead and I'll follow; I'm not quite ready.

go away (intr) = leave, leave me, leave this place:
Are you going away for your holiday? ~ No, I'm staying at home.
Please go away; I can't work unless I am alone.

go back (intr) = return, retire, retreat:
I'm never going back to that hotel. It is most uncomfortable.

go back on (tr) = withdraw or break (a promise):
He went back on his promise to tell nobody about this. (He told people about it, contrary to his promise.)

go down (intr)
(a) = be received with approval (usually of an idea):
I suggested that she should look for a job but this suggestion did not go down at all well.
(b) = become less, be reduced (of wind, sea, weight, prices etc.):
During her illness her weight went down from 50 kilos to 40.
The wind went down and the sea became quite calm.

go for (tr) = attack:
The cat went for the dog and chased him out of the hall.

go in for (tr) = be especially interested in, practise; enter for (a competition):
This restaurant goes in for vegetarian dishes. (specializes in them)
She plays a lot of golf and goes in for all the competitions.

go into (tr) = investigate thoroughly:
'We shall have to go into this very carefully,' said the detective.

go off (intr)
(a) = explode (of ammunition or fireworks), be fired (of guns, usually accidentally):
As he was cleaning his gun it went off and killed him.
(b) = be successful (of social occasions):
The party went off very well. (everyone enjoyed it)
(c) = start a journey, leave:
He went off in a great hurry.

go on (intr) = continue a journey:
Go on till you come to the crossroads.

go on (intr), **go on with** (tr), **go on** + gerund = continue any action:
Please go on playing; I like it.
Go on with the treatment. It is doing you good.

go on + infinitive:
He began by describing the route and went on to tell us what the trip would probably cost. (He continued his speech and told us etc.)

go out (intr)
(a) = leave the house:
She is always indoors; she doesn't go out enough.
(b) = join in social life, leave one's house for entertainments etc.
She is very pretty and goes out a lot.

(c) = disappear, be discontinued (of fashions):
   Crinolines went out about the middle of the last century.
(d) = be extinguished (of lights, fires etc.):
   The light went out and we were left in the dark.
go over (tr) = examine, study or repeat carefully:
   He went over the plans again and discovered two very serious mistakes.
go round (intr)
(a) = suffice (for a number of people):
   Will there be enough wine to go round?
(b) = go to his/her/your etc. house:
   I said that I'd go round and see her during the weekend. (go to her house)
go through (tr) = examine carefully (usually a number of things; **go through** is like **look through** but more thorough):
   There is a mistake somewhere; we'll have to go through the accounts and see where it is.
   The police went through their files to see if they could find any fingerprints to match those that they had found on the handle of the weapon.
go through (tr) = suffer, endure:
   No one knows what I went through while I was waiting for the verdict. (how much I suffered)
go through with (tr) = finish, bring to a conclusion (usually in the face of some opposition or difficulty):
   He went through with his plan although all his friends advised him to abandon it.
go up (intr)
(a) = rise (of prices):
   The price of strawberries went up towards the end of the season.
(b) = burst into flames (and be destroyed), explode (used of whole buildings, ships etc.):
   When the fire reached the cargo of chemicals the whole ship went up. (blew up)
   Someone dropped a cigarette end into a can of petrol and the whole garage went up in flames.
go without (tr) = do without. (But it only applies to things. 'Go without a person' has only a literal meaning; i.e. it means 'start or make a journey without him'.)

grow

grow out of (tr) = abandon, on becoming older, a childish (and often bad) habit:
   He used to tell a lot of lies as a young boy but he grew out of that later on.
grow up (intr) = become adult:
   'I'm going to be a pop star when I grow up,' said the boy.

hand

hand down (tr) = bequeath or pass on (traditions/information/possessions):
This legend has been handed down from father to son.

hand in (tr) = give by hand (to someone who need not be mentioned because the person spoken to knows already):
*I handed in **my resignation**.* (gave it to my employer)
*Someone handed **this parcel** in yesterday. (handed **it** in)*

hand out (tr) = distribute:
*He was standing at the door of the theatre handing out **leaflets**.*
*(handing **leaflets** out/handing **them** out)*

hand over (tr or intr) = surrender authority or responsibility to another:
*The outgoing Minister handed over **his department** to his successor. (handed **his department** over/handed **it** over)*

hand round (tr) = give or show to each person present:
*The hostess handed round **coffee** and **cakes**. (handed **them** round)*

hang

hang about/around (tr or intr) = loiter or wait (near):
He hung about/around the entrance all day, hoping for a chance to speak to the director.

hang back (intr) = show unwillingness to act:
Everyone approved of the scheme but when we asked for volunteers they all hung back.

hang on to (tr) = retain, keep in one's possession (colloquial):
I'd hang on to that old coat if I were you. It might be useful.

hold

hold off (intr) = keep at a distance, stay away (used of rain):
The rain fortunately held off till after the school sports day.

hold on (intr) = wait (especially on the telephone):
Yes, Mr Pitt is in. If you hold on for a moment I'll get him for you.

hold on/out (intr) = persist in spite of, endure hardship or danger:
The survivors on the rock signalled that they were short of water but could hold out for another day.
The strikers held out for six weeks before agreeing to arbitration.

hold up (tr)
(a) = stop by threats or violence (often in order to rob):
The terrorists held up the train and kept the passengers as hostages.
*Masked men held up **the cashier** and robbed the bank. (held **him** up)*

(b) = stop, delay (especially used in the passive):
The bus was held up because a tree had fallen across the road.

join

> **join up** (intr) = enlist in one of the armed services:
> *When war was declared he joined up at once.*

jump

> **jump at** (tr) = accept with enthusiasm (an offer or opportunity):
> *He was offered a place in the Himalayan expedition and jumped at the chance.*

keep

> **keep** somebody **back** (object before **back**) = restrain, hinder, prevent from advancing:
> *Frequent illnesses kept him back.* (prevented him from making normal progress)
>
> **keep down** (tr) = repress, control:
> *What is the best way to keep down **rats**? (keep **them** down)*
> *Try to remember to turn off the light when you leave the room. I am trying to keep down **expenses**. (keep **expenses** down)*
>
> **keep off** (tr or intr) = refrain from walking on, or from coming too close:
> *'Keep off the grass'.* (park notice)
>
> **keep on** = continue:
> *I wanted to explain but he kept on talking and didn't give me a chance to say anything.*
>
> **keep out** (tr) = prevent from entering:
> *My shoes are very old and don't keep out **the water**. (keep **the water** out/keep **it** out)*
>
> **keep out** (intr) = stay outside:
> *'Private. Keep out.'* (notice on door)
>
> **keep up** (tr) = maintain (an effort):
> *He began walking at four miles an hour but he couldn't keep up **that speed** and soon began to walk more slowly. (he couldn't keep **it** up)*
> *It is difficult to keep up a conversation with someone who only says 'Yes' and 'No'.*
>
> **keep up** (intr), **keep up with** (tr) = remain abreast of someone who is advancing; advance at the same pace as:
> *A runner can't keep up with a cyclist.*
> *The work that the class is doing is too difficult for me. I won't be able to keep up (with them).*
> *It is impossible to keep up with the news unless you read the newspapers.*

knock

> **knock off** (tr or intr) = stop work for the day (colloquial):
> *English workmen usually knock off at 5.30 or 6.00 p.m.*
> *We knock off work in time for tea.*

knock out (tr) = hit someone so hard that he falls unconscious:
*In the finals of the boxing championship he knocked out **his** **opponent**, who was carried out of the ring. (knocked **his opponent** out/knocked **him** out)*

lay

lay in (tr) = provide oneself with a sufficient quantity (of stores etc.) to last for some time:
She expected a shortage of dried fruit so she laid in a large supply.

lay out (tr) = plan gardens, building sites etc.:
*Le Nôtre laid out **the gardens** at Versailles. (laid **the gardens** out/laid **them** out)*

lay up (tr) = store carefully till needed again (used of ships, cars etc.):
*Before he went to Brazil for a year, he laid up **his car**, as he didn't want to sell it. (laid **it** up)*

be laid up (of a person) = be confined to bed through illness:
She was laid up for weeks with a slipped disk.

lead

lead up to (tr) = prepare the way for, introduce (figuratively):
He wanted to borrow my binoculars, but he didn't say so at once. He led up to it by talking about birdwatching.

leave

leave off (usually intr) = stop (doing something):
He was playing his trumpet but I told him to leave off because the neighbours were complaining about the noise.

leave out (tr) = omit:
We'll sing our school song leaving out the last ten verses.
*They gave each competitor a number; but they left out **No. 13** as no one wanted to have it. (left **No. 13** out/left **it** out)*

let

let down (tr) = lower:
*When she lets **her hair** down it reaches her waist. (lets down **her hair**/lets **it** down)*
You can let a coat down (lengthen it) by using the hem.

let someone **down** (object before **down**) = disappoint him by failing to act as well as expected, or failing to fulfil an agreement:
I promised him that you would do the work. Why did you let me down by doing so little?
He said he'd come to help me; but he let me down. He never turned up.

let in (tr) = allow to enter, admit:
*They let in the **ticket-holders**. (let the **ticket-holders** in/ let **them** in)*
If you mention my name to the door-keeper he will let you in.

let someone **off** (object before **off**) = refrain from punishing:

I thought that the magistrate was going to fine me but he let me off.
(Compare with **get off**.)

let out (tr)

(a) = make wider (of clothes):

*That boy is getting fatter. You'll have to let out **his clothes**. (let **his clothes** out/let **them** out)*

(b) = allow to leave, release:

*He opened the door and let out **the dog**. (let **the dog** out/let **it** out)*

live

live down a bad reputation = live in such a manner that people will forget it:

*He has never quite been able to live down **a reputation** for drinking too much which he got when he was a young man. (live **it** down)*

live in (intr) = live in one's place of work (chiefly used of domestic servants):

ADVERTISEMENT: *Cook wanted. £140 a week. Live in.*

live on (tr) = use as staple food:

It is said that for a certain period of his life Byron lived on vinegar and potatoes in order to keep thin.

live up to (tr) = maintain a certain standard – moral, economic or behavioural:

He had high ideals and tried to live up to them. (he tried to act in accordance with his ideals)

lock

lock up a house (tr or intr; usually intr) = lock all doors:

People usually lock up before they go to bed at night.

lock up a person or thing = put in a locked place, i.e. box, safe, prison:

*She locked up **the papers** in her desk. (locked **the papers** up/locked **them** up)*

look

look after (tr) = take care of:

Will you look after my parrot when I am away?

look ahead (intr) = consider the future so as to make provision for it:

It's time you looked ahead and made plans for your retirement.

look at (tr) = regard:

He looked at the clock and said, 'It is midnight.'

look back (intr), **look back on** (tr) = consider the past:

Looking back, I don't suppose we are any worse now than people were a hundred years ago.

Perhaps some day it will be pleasant to look back on these things.

look back/round (intr) = look behind (literally):
Don't look round now but the woman behind us is wearing the most extraordinary clothes.

look for (tr) = search for, seek:
I have lost my watch. Will you help me to look for it?

look forward to (tr) = expect with pleasure (often used with gerund):
I am looking forward to her arrival/to seeing her.

look in (intr) = pay a short (often unannounced) visit (= call in):
I'll look in this evening to see how she is.

look into (tr) = investigate:
There is a mystery about his death and the police are looking into it.

look on . . . as (tr) = consider:
Most people look on a television set as an essential piece of furniture.
These children seem to look on their teachers as their enemies.

look on (intr) = be a spectator only, not a participator:
Two men were fighting. The rest were looking on.

look on (tr), **look out on** (tr) (used of windows and houses) = be facing:
His house looks (out) on to the sea. (from his house you can see the sea.)

look out (intr) = be watchful, beware:
(to someone just about to cross the road) *'Look out! There's a lorry coming!'*

look out for (tr) = keep one's eyes open so as to see something (usually fairly conspicuous) if it presents itself:
I am going to the party too, so look out for me.

look over (tr) = inspect critically, read again, revise quickly (**look over** is similar to **go over** but less thorough):
Look over what you've written before handing it to the examiner.
I'm going to look over a house that I'm thinking of buying.

look through (tr) = examine a number of things, often in order to select some of them; turn over the pages of a book or newspaper, looking for information:
Look through your old clothes and see if you have anything to give away.
I'd like you to look through these photographs and try to pick out the man you saw.
He looked through the books and decided that he wouldn't like them.

look through someone = look at him without appearing to see him, as a deliberate act of rudeness:
She has to be polite to me in the office but when we meet outside she always looks through me.

look up an address/a name/word/train time/telephone number etc. = look for it in the appropriate book or paper, i.e. address book/ dictionary/timetable/directory etc.:

> *If you don't know the meaning of* **the word** *look it up. (look up* **the word**/look **the word** *up)*
>
> *I must look up the time of your train.* (look for it in the timetable)

look somebody **up** can mean 'visit'. The person visited usually lives at some distance and is not seen very often. **look up** is therefore different from **look in**, which implies that the person visited lives quite close:

> *Any time you come to London do look me up.* (come and see me)
>
> *I haven't seen Tom for ages. I must find out where he lives and look* **him** *up. (look* **Tom** *up/look up* **Tom**)

look up (intr) = improve (the subject is usually *things/business/world affairs/the weather,* i.e. nothing very definite):

> *Business has been very bad lately but things are beginning to look up now.*

look someone **up and down** = look at him contemptuously, letting your eyes wander from his head to his feet and back again:

> *The policeman looked the drunk man up and down very deliberately before replying to his question.*

look up to (tr) = respect:

> *Schoolboys usually look up to great athletes.*

look down on (tr) = despise:

> *Small boys often look down on little girls and refuse to play with them.*
>
> *She thinks her neighbours look down on her a bit because she's never been abroad.*

make

make for (tr) = travel towards:

> *The escaped prisoner was making for the coast.*

make off (intr) = run away (used of thieves etc.):

> *The boys made off when they saw the policemen.*

make out (tr)

(a) = discover the meaning of, understand, see, hear etc. clearly:

> *I can't make out* **the address**, *he has written it so badly. (make* **the address** *out/make* **it** *out)*
>
> *Can you hear what the man with the loud-hailer is saying? I can't make it out at all.*
>
> *I can't make out why he isn't here yet.*

(b) = state (probably falsely or with exaggeration):

> *He made out that he was a student looking for a job. We later learnt that this wasn't true at all.*
>
> *The English climate isn't so bad as some people like to make out.*

(c) = write a cheque:

> CUSTOMER: *Who shall I make it out to?*
>
> SHOPKEEPER: *Make it out to Jones and Company.*

make up one's mind = come to a decision:
   In the end he made up his mind to go by train.
make up a quarrel/**make it up** = end it:
   *Isn't it time you and Ann made up **your quarrel**. (made it up)*
make up a story/excuse/explanation = invent it:
   I don't believe your story at all. I think you are just making it up.
make up (tr or intr) = use cosmetics:
   *Most women make up/make up **their faces**. (make **their faces** up/make **them** up)*
   Actors have to be made up before they appear on stage.
make up (tr) = put together, compound, compose:
   *Take **this prescription** to the chemist's. They will make **it** up for you there. (make up **the presciption**/make **the prescription** up)*
   NOTICE (in tailor's window): *Customers' own materials made up.*
   The audience was made up of very young children.
make up for (tr) = compensate for (the object is very often *it*):
   You'll have to work very hard today to make up for the time you wasted yesterday/to make up for being late yesterday.
   We aren't allowed to drink when we are in training but we intend to make up for it after the race is over. (to drink more than usual then)

miss

miss out (tr) = leave out ('leave out' is more usual; see page 335).

mix

mix up (tr) = confuse:
   *He mixed up **the addresses** so that no one got the right letters. (mixed **them** up)*
be/get mixed up with = be involved (usually with some rather disreputable person or business):
   I don't want to get mixed up with any illegal organization.

move

move in (intr) = move self and possessions into new house, flat, rooms etc.
move out (intr) = leave house/flat etc., with one's possessions, vacate accommodation:
   I have found a new flat. The present tenant is moving out this weekend and I am moving in on Wednesday.
move on or **up** (intr) = advance, go higher:
   Normally in schools pupils move up every year.

order

order somebody **about** (object before **about**) = give him a lot of orders (often regardless of his convenience or feelings):
   He is a retired admiral and still has the habit of ordering people about.

pay

pay back (tr), **pay someone back** (tr or intr) = repay:
> *I must pay back the money that I borrowed. (pay the money back/pay it back)*
> *I must pay back Mr Pitt. (pay Mr Pitt back/pay him back)*
> *I must pay Mr Pitt back the money he lent me. (pay him back the money/pay it back to him)*

pay someone **back/out** = revenge oneself:
> *I'll pay you back for this. (for the harm you have done me.)*

pay up (intr) = pay money owed in full (there is often a feeling that the payer is reluctant):
> *Unless you pay up I shall tell my solicitor to write to you.*

pick

pick out (tr) = choose, select, distinguish from a group:
> *Here are six rings. Pick out the one you like best. (pick it out)*
> *In an identity parade the witness has to try to pick out the criminal from a group of about eight men. (pick the criminal out/pick him out)*
> *I know that you are in this photograph but I can't pick you out.*

pick up (tr)

(a) = raise or lift a person or thing, usually from the ground or from a table or chair:
> *He picked up the child and carried him into the house. (picked the child up)*
> *She scatters toys all over the floor and I have to pick them up.*

(b) = call for, take with one (in a vehicle):
> *I won't have time to come to your house but I could pick you up at the end of your road.*
> *The coach stops at the principal hotels to pick up tourists, but only if they arrange this in advance. (pick tourists up/pick them up)*
> *The crew of the wrecked yacht were picked up by helicopter.*

(c) = receive (by chance) wireless signals:
> *Their SOS was picked up by another ship, which informed the lifeboat headquarters.*

(d) = acquire cheaply, learn without effort:
> *Sometimes you pick up wonderful bargains in these markets.*
> *Children usually pick up foreign languages very quickly.*

point

point out (tr) = indicate, show:
> *As we drove through the city the guide pointed out the most important buildings. (pointed the buildings out/pointed them out)*

pull

pull down (tr) = demolish (used of buildings):
> *Everywhere elegant old buildings are being pulled down and*

mediocre modern erections are being put up. (pull down **houses**/*pull* **them** *down)*

pull off (tr) = succeed (the object is normally *it*):
Much to our surprise he pulled off **the deal**. (sold the goods/got the contract) *(pulled* **it** *off)*

pull through (tr or intr) = recover from illness/cause someone to recover:
We thought she was going to die but her own will-power pulled her through. (tr)
He is very ill but he'll pull through if we look after him carefully. (intr)

pull up (intr) = stop (of vehicles):
A lay-by is a space at the side of a main road, where drivers can pull up if they want a rest.

put

put aside/by (tr) = save for future use (usually money). **put aside** often implies that the money is being saved for a certain purpose:
He puts aside **£50 a month** *to pay for his summer holiday. (puts* **it** *aside)*
Don't spend all your salary. Try to put something by each month.

put away (tr) = put tidily out of sight (usually in drawers, cupboards etc.):
Put **your toys** *away, children; it's bedtime. (put away* **the toys**/*put* **them** *away)*

put something **back** = replace it where you found it/where it belongs:
When you've finished with the book put it back on the shelf.

put back a clock/watch = retard the hands: *put the clock back* is sometimes used figuratively to mean *return to the customs of the past*:
MOTHER: *Your father and I will arrange a marriage for you when the time comes.*
DAUGHTER: *You're trying to put* **the clock** *back, mother. Parents don't arrange marriages these days! (put back* **the clock**/*put* **it** *back)*

put down (tr)
(a) = the opposite of **pick up**:
He picked up **the saucepan** *and put it down at once because the handle was almost red-hot. (put* **the saucepan** *down/put* **it** *down)*
(b) = crush rebellions, movements:
Troops were used to put down **the rebellion**. *(put* **the rebellion** *down/put* **it** *down)*
(c) = write:
Put down **his phone number** *before you forget it. (put* **the number** *down/put* **it** *down)*
CUSTOMER (to shop assistant): *I'll take that one. Please put it down to me/to my account.* (enter it in my account)

put something **down to** (tr) = attribute it to:
The children wouldn't answer him, but he wasn't annoyed as he put it down to shyness.

She hasn't been well since she came to this country; I put it down to the climate.

put forward a suggestion/proposal etc. = offer it for consideration:
The older members of the committee are inclined to veto any **suggestions** *put forward by the younger ones. (put* **a suggestion** *forward/put* **it** *forward)*

put forward/on clocks and watches = advance the hands. **put forward** is the opposite of **put back**:
In March people in England put their clocks forward/on an hour. When summer time ends they put them back an hour.

put in a claim = make a claim:
He put in a claim for compensation because he had lost his luggage in the train crash.

put in for a job/a post = apply for it:
They are looking for a lecturer in geography. Why don't you put in for it?

put off an action = postpone it:
Some people put off making their wills till it is too late.
I'll put off **my visit** *to Scotland till the weather is warmer. (put* **my visit** *off/put* **it** *off)*

put a person **off**
(a) = tell him to postpone his visit to you:
I had invited some guests to dinner but I had to put them off because a power cut prevented me from cooking anything.

(b) = repel, deter him:
I wanted to see the exhibition but the queue put me off.
Many people who want to come to England are put off by the stories they hear about English weather.

put on clothes/glasses/jewellery = dress oneself etc. The opposite is **take off**:
He put on **a black coat** *so that he would be inconspicuous. (put* **a coat** *on/put* **it** *on)*
She put on her glasses and took the letter from my hand.

put on an expression = assume it:
He put on an air of indifference, which didn't deceive anybody for a moment.

put on a play = produce/perform it:
The students usually put on a play at the end of the year.

put on a light/gas or electric fire/radio = switch it on:
Put on **the light**. *(put* **the light** *on/put* **it** *on)*

put out any kind of light or fire = extinguish it:
Put out **that light**. *(put* **the light** *out/put* **it** *out)*

put someone **out** (inconvenience him):
He is very selfish. He wouldn't put himself out for anyone.

be put out = be annoyed:
She was very put out when I said that her new summer dress didn't suit her.

put up (tr)
(a) = erect (a building, monument, statue etc.):
*He put up **a shed** in the garden. (put **a shed** up/put **it** up)*
(b) = raise (prices):
*When the importation of foreign tomatoes was forbidden, home
growers put up **their prices**. (put **their prices** up/put **them** up)*
put someone **up** (object usually before **up**) = give him temporary
hospitality:
If you come to Paris I will put you up. You needn't look for an hotel.
put someone **up to** something (usually some trick) = give him the idea
of doing it/tell him how to do it:
*He couldn't have thought of that trick by himself. Someone must have
put him up to it.*
put up with (tr) = bear patiently:
We had to put up with a lot of noise when the children were at home.

ring

ring up (tr or intr) = telephone:
*I rang up **the theatre** to book seats for tonight. (rang **the theatre**
up/rang **them** up)*
If you can't come ring up and let me know.
ring off (intr) = end a telephone call by putting down the receiver:
He rang off before I could ask his name.

round

round up (tr) = drive or bring together (people or animals):
*The sheepdog rounded up the sheep (= collected them into a group)
and drove them through the gate.*
*On the day after the riots the police rounded up **all suspects**/
rounded **them** up. (arrested them)*

rub

rub out (tr) = erase pencil or ink marks with an india-rubber:
*The child wrote down the wrong word and then rubbed **it** out.
(rubbed **the word** out/rubbed out **the word**)*
rub up (tr) = revise one's knowledge of a subject:
*I am going to France; I must rub up **my French**. (rub **it** up)*

run

run after (tr) = pursue (see example below).
run away (intr) = flee, desert (one's home/school etc.), elope:
The thief ran away and the policeman ran after him.
He ran away from home and got a job in a garage.
run away with (tr) = become uncontrollable (of emotions), gallop off
out of rider's control (of horses):
Don't let your emotions run away with you.
His horse ran away with him and he had a bad fall.
run away with the idea = accept an idea too hastily:
*Don't run away with the idea that I am unsociable; I just haven't
time to go out much.*

run down (tr) = disparage, speak ill of:
He is always running down his neighbours. (running his neighbours down/running them down)

run down (intr) = become unwound/discharged (of clocks/batteries etc.):
This torch is useless; the battery has run down.

be run down (intr) = be in poor health after illness, overwork etc.:
He is still run down after his illness and unfit for work.

run into (tr) = collide with (of vehicles):
The car skidded and ran into a lamp-post. (struck the lamp-post)

run into/across someone = meet him accidentally:
I ran into my cousin in Harrods recently. (I met him.)

run out of (tr) = have none left, having consumed all the supply:
I have run out of milk. Put some lemon in your tea instead.

run over (tr) = drive over accidentally (in a vehicle):
The drunk man stepped into the road right in front of the oncoming car. The driver couldn't stop in time and ran over him.

run over (tr or intr) = overflow:
He turned on both taps full and left the bathroom. When he came back he found that the water was running over./running over the edge of the bath.

run over/through (tr) = rehearse, check or revise quickly:
We've got a few minutes before the train goes, so I'll just run through your instructions again.

run through (tr) = consume extravagantly, waste (used of supplies or money):
He inherited a fortune and ran through it in a year.

run up bills = incur them and increase them by continuing to buy things and put them down to one's account:
Her husband said that she must pay for things at once and not run up bills.

run up against difficulties/opposition = encounter them/it:
If he tries to change the rules of the club he will run up against a lot of opposition.

see

see about (tr) = make inquiries or arrangements:
I must see about getting a room ready for him.

see somebody **off** = accompany an intending traveller to his train/boat/plane etc.:
The station was crowded with boys going back to school and parents who were seeing them off.

see somebody **out** = accompany a departing guest to the door of the house:
When guests leave the host usually sees them out.
Don't bother to come to the door with me. I can see myself out.

see over a house/a building = go into every room, examine it, often with a view to buying or renting:
I'm definitely interested in the house. I'd like to see over it.

see through (tr) = discover a hidden attempt to deceive:
She pretended that she loved him but he saw through her, and realized that she was only after his money. (He wasn't taken in by her/by her pretence. See **take in**.)

see to (tr) = make arrangements, put right, repair:
If you can provide the wine I'll see to the food.
That electric fire isn't safe. You should have it seen to.
Please see to it that the door is locked.

sell

sell off (tr) = sell cheaply (what is left of a stock):
ASSISTANT: *This line is being discontinued so we are selling off the remainder of our stock; that's why they are so cheap. (selling the rest off/selling it off)*

sell out (intr) = sell all that you have of a certain type of article:
When all the seats for a certain performance have been booked, theatres put a notice saying 'Sold out' outside the booking office.

send

be sent down (intr) = be expelled from a university for misconduct:
He behaved so badly in college that he was sent down and never got his degree.

send for (tr) = summon:
One of our water pipes has burst. We must send for the plumber.
The director sent for me and asked for an explanation.

send in (tr) = send to someone (who need not be mentioned because the person spoken to knows already):
You must send in your application before Friday. (send it to the authority concerned) (send your application in/send it in)

send on (tr) = forward, send after a person:
If any letters come for you after you have gone I will send them on. (send on your letters/send your letters on)

set

set in (intr) = begin (a period, usually unpleasant):
Winter has set in early this year.

set off (tr) = start (a series of events):
That strike set off a series of strikes throughout the country. (set them off)

set off/out (intr) = start a journey:
They set out/off at six and hoped to arrive before dark.

'for' is used when the destination is mentioned:
They set out/off for Rome.

set out + infinitive (often **show/prove/explain** or some similar verb) = begin this undertaking, aim:

In this book the author sets out to prove that the inhabitants of the islands came from South America.

set up (tr) = achieve, establish (a record):

*He set up **a new record** for the 1,000 metres. (set **a new record** up/set **it** up)*

set up (intr) = start a new business:

When he married he left his father's shop and set up on his own. (opened his own shop)

settle

settle down (intr) = become accustomed to, and contented in, a new place, job etc.:

He soon settled down in his new school.

settle up (intr) = pay money owed:

Tell me what I owe you and I'll settle up.

shout

shout down (tr) = make a loud noise to prevent a speaker from being heard:

Tom tried to make a speech defending himself but the crowd wouldn't listen to his explanation and shouted him down.
The moderate speakers were shouted down.

show

show off (tr or intr) = display (skill, knowledge etc.) purely in order to win notice or applause:

Although Jules speaks English perfectly, my cousin spoke French to him all the time just to show off. (to impress us with her knowledge of French)
*He is always picking up very heavy things just to show off **his strength**. (show **it** off)*

shut

shut down (tr or intr) = close down (see page 323).

sit

sit back (intr) = relax, take no action, do no more work:

I have worked hard all my life and now I'm going to sit back and watch other people working.

sit up (intr) = stay out of bed till later than usual (usually reading, working, or waiting for someone):

I was very worried when he didn't come in and I sat up till 3 a.m. waiting for him.
She sat up all night with the sick child.

stand

stand by someone (tr) = continue to support and help him:

No matter what happens I'll stand by you, so don't be afraid.

stand for (tr) = represent:
> The symbol 'x' usually stands for the unknown quantity in mathematics.

stand for Parliament = be a candidate for Parliament, offer yourself for election:
> Mr Pitt stood for Parliament five years ago but he wasn't elected.

stand up for (tr) = defend verbally:
> His father blamed him, but his mother stood up for him and said that he had acted sensibly.
> Why don't you stand up for yourself?

stand up to (tr) = resist, defend oneself against (a person or force):
> This type of building stands up to the gales very well.
> Your boss is a bully. If you don't stand up to him he'll lead you a dog's life.

stand out (intr) = be conspicuous, be easily seen:
> She stood out from the crowd because of her height and her flaming red hair.

stay

stay up (intr) = remain out of bed till later than usual, usually for pleasure:
> Children never want to go to bed at the proper time; they always want to stay up late.

step

step up (tr) = increase rate of, increase speed of (this usually refers to industrial production):
> This new machine will step up **production**. (step it up)

take

be taken aback (intr) = be surprised and disconcerted:
> I was taken aback when I saw the bill.

take after (tr) = resemble (one's parents/grandparents etc.):
> He takes after his grandmother; she had red hair too.
> My father was forgetful and I take after him; I forget everything.

take back (tr) = withdraw (remarks, accusations etc.):
> I blamed him bitterly at first but later, when I heard the whole story, I realized that he had been right and I went to him and took back **my remarks**. (took **them** back)

take down (tr) = write, usually from dictation:
> He read out the names and his secretary took **them** down. (took down **the names**/took **the names** down)

take for (tr) = attribute wrong identity or qualities to someone:
> I took him for his brother. They are extremely alike.
> Do you take me for a fool?

take in (tr)

(a) = deceive:
> At first he took us in by his stories and we tried to help him; but later we learnt that his stories were all lies.

(b) = receive as guests/lodgers:

When our car broke down I knocked on the door of the nearest house. The owner very kindly took us in and gave us a bed for the night.

*People who live by the sea often take in **paying guests** during the summer. (take **paying guests** in/take **them** in)*

(c) = understand, receive into the mind:

I was thinking of something else while she was speaking and I didn't really take in what she was saying.

*I couldn't take in **the lecture** at all. It was too difficult for me. (couldn't take **it** in)*

(d) = make less wide (of clothes):

*I'm getting much thinner; I'll have to take in **my clothes**. (take **my clothes** in/take **them** in)*

take off (tr) = remove (when used of clothing 'take off' is the opposite of 'put on'):

*He took off **his coat** when he entered the house and put it on again when he went out. (took **his coat** off/took **it** off)*

take off (intr) = leave the ground (of aeroplanes):

There is often a spectators' balcony at airports, where people can watch the planes taking off and landing.

take on (tr)

(a) = undertake work:

*She wants someone to look after her children. I shouldn't care to take on **the job**. They are very spoilt. (take **the job** on/take **it** on)*

(b) = engage staff:

They're taking on fifty new workers at the factory.

(c) = accept as an opponent:

*I'll take **you** on at table tennis. (I'll play against you.)*

*I took on **Mr Pitt** at draughts. (took **Mr Pitt** on/took **him** on)*

take out (tr) = remove, extract:

*Petrol will take out **that stain**. (take **the stain** out/take **it** out)*

The dentist took out two of her teeth.

take somebody **out** = entertain them (usually at some public place):

Her small boy is at boarding school quite near here. I take him out every month. (and give him a meal in a restaurant)

take over (tr or intr) = assume responsibility for, or control of, in succession to somebody else:

We stop work at ten o'clock and the night shift takes over until the following morning.

Miss Smith is leaving to get married and Miss Jones will be taking over the class/Miss Jones will be taking over from Miss Smith. (see **hand over***)*

take to (tr)

(a) = begin a habit. There is usually the impression that the speaker thinks this habit bad or foolish, though this is not necessarily always the case. It is often used with the gerund:

He took to drink. (began drinking too much)
He took to borrowing money from the petty cash.

(b) = find likeable or agreeable, particularly at first meeting:
I was introduced to the new headmistress yesterday. I can't say I took to her.
He went to sea (= became a sailor) *and took to the life like a duck to water.*

(c) = seek refuge/safety in:
When they saw that the ship was sinking the crew took to the boats.
After the failure of the coup many of the rebels took to the hills and became guerillas.

take up (tr)
(a) = begin a hobby, sport or kind of study (there is no feeling of criticism here):
*He took up **golf** and became very keen on it. (took **it** up)*

(b) = occupy (a position in time or space):
He has a very small room and most of the space is taken up by a grand piano.
A lot of an MP's time is taken up with answering letters from his constituents.

talk

talk over (tr) = discuss:
*Talk it over with your wife and give me your answer tomorrow. (talk over **my suggestion**/talk **my suggestion** over)*

think

think over (tr) = consider:
*I can't decide straight away but I'll think over **your idea** and let you know what I decide. (think **your idea** over/think **it** over)*

throw

throw away/out (tr) = jettison (rubbish etc.):
*Throw away **those old shoes**. Nobody could wear them now. (throw **the shoes** away/throw **them** away)*

throw up (tr) = abandon suddenly (some work or plan):
*He suddenly got tired of the job and threw it up. (he threw up **the job**/threw **the job** up)*

tie

tie someone **up** = bind his hands and feet so that he cannot move:
*The thieves tied up **the night watchman** before opening the safe. (tied **the man** up/tied **him** up)*

try

try on (tr) = put on (an article of clothing) to see if it fits:
CUSTOMER IN DRESS SHOP: *I like this dress. Could I try it on? (try **this dress** on/try on **this dress**)*

try out (tr) = test:
> *We won't know how the plan works till we have tried it out.*
> *They are trying out* **new ways of preventing noise in hospitals.** *(trying them out)*

turn

turn away (tr) = refuse admittance to:
> *The man at the door turned away* **anybody who hadn't an invitation card.** *(turned them away)*

turn down (tr) = refuse, reject an offer, application, applicant:
> *I applied for the job but they turned* **me** *down/turned down* **my application** *because I didn't know German.*
> *He was offered £500 for the picture but he turned it down. (turned down* **the offer**/*turned* **the offer** *down)*

turn into (tr) = convert into:
> *I am going to turn my garage into a playroom for the children.*
> *She turned the silver candlestick into a reading lamp.*

turn in (intr) = go to bed (used chiefly by sailors/campers etc.):
> *The captain turned in, not realizing that the icebergs were so close.*

turn on (tr) (stress on **turn**) = attack suddenly (the attacker is normally a friend or a hitherto friendly animal):
> *The tigress turned on the trainer and struck him to the ground.*

turn on/off (tr) = switch on/off (lights, gas, fires, radios, taps etc.)

turn up/down (tr) = increase/decrease the pressure, force, volume (of gas or oil, lights, fires, or of radios):
> *Turn up the gas; it is much too low.*
> *I wish the people in the next flat would turn down* **their radio.** *You can hear every word. (turn* **the sound** *down/turn it down)*

turn out (tr)

(a) = produce:
> *The creamery turns out* **two hundred tons of butter** *a week. (turns it out)*

(b) = evict, empty:

1 turn a person out = evict him from his house/flat/room:
> *At one time, if tenants didn't pay their rent the landlord could turn them out.*

2 turn out one's pockets/handbags/drawers etc. = empty them, usually looking for something:
> *'Turn out your pockets,' said the detective.*

3 turn out a room = (usually) clean it thoroughly, first putting the furniture outside:
> *I try to turn out one room every month if I have time.*

turn out (intr)

(a) = assemble, come out into the street (usually in order to welcome somebody):
> *The whole town turned out to welcome the winning football team when they came back with the Cup.*

(b) = develop:

I've never made Yorkshire pudding before so I am not quite sure how it is going to turn out.

Marriages arranged by marriage bureaux frequently turn out well.

(c) = be revealed. Notice the two possible constructions, *it turned out that . . .* and *he turned out to be . . .*:

He told her that he was a bachelor but it turned out that he was married with six children. (She learnt this later.)

Our car broke down half way through the journey but the hiker we had picked up turned out to be an expert mechanic and was able to put things right.

Note the difference between **turn out** and **come out**. With **turn out** the fact revealed is always mentioned and there is no implication that the facts are discreditable. With **come out** we are told only that certain facts (usually discreditable) are revealed; we are not told what these facts are.

turn over (tr) = turn something so that the side previously underneath is exposed:

*He turned over **the stone**. (turned **the stone** over/turned **it** over)*

The initials 'PTO' at the bottom of a page mean 'Please turn over'.

'Turn over a new leaf.' (begin again, meaning to do better)

turn over (intr)

(a) = turn upside down, upset, capsize (used of vehicles or boats):

The car struck the wall and turned over.

The canoe turned over, throwing the boys into the water.

(b) = (of people) change position so as to lie on the other side:

It is difficult to turn over in a hammock.

When his alarm went off he just turned over and went to sleep again.

turn up (intr) = arrive, appear (usually from the point of view of someone waiting or searching):

We arranged to meet at the station but she didn't turn up.

Don't bother to look for my umbrella; it will turn up some day.

walk

walk out (intr) = march out in disgust or indignation:

Some people were so disgusted with the play that they walked out in the middle of the first act.

wait

wait on (tr) = attend, serve (at home or in a restaurant):

He expected his wife to wait on him hand and foot.

The man who was waiting on us seemed very inexperienced; he got all our orders mixed up.

wash

wash up (tr or intr) = wash the plates etc. after a meal:

*When we have dinner very late we don't wash up till the next morning. (wash up **the dishes**/wash **them** up)*

watch

watch out (intr) = look out.
watch out for (tr) = look out for (see page 357).

wear

wear away (intr) = gradually reduce; make smooth or flat; hollow out (used mostly of wood or stone. The subject is usually the weather, or people who walk on or touch the stone etc.):

> *It is almost impossible to read the inscription on the monument as most of the letters have been worn away.* (by the weather)

wear off (intr) = disappear gradually (can be used literally but is chiefly used for mental or physical feelings):

> *These glasses may seem uncomfortable at first but that feeling will soon wear off.*
> *When her first feeling of shyness had worn off she started to enjoy herself.*
> *He began to try to sit up, which showed us that the effects of the drug were wearing off.*

wear out (tr or intr)

(a) (tr) = use till no longer serviceable; (intr) become unserviceable as a result of long use (chiefly of clothes):

> *Children wear out **their shoes** very quickly. (wear **their shoes** out/wear **them** out)*
> *Cheap clothes wear out quickly.*

(b) (tr) = exhaust (used of people; very often in the passive):

> *He worked all night and wanted to go on working the next day, but we saw that he was completely worn out and persuaded him to stop.*

wind

wind up (tr or intr) = bring or come to an end (used of speeches or business proceedings):

> *The headmaster wound up **(the meeting)** by thanking the parents. (wound **the meeting** up/wound **it** up)*

wipe

wipe out (tr) = destroy completely:

> *The epidemic wiped out **whole families**. (wiped **whole families** out/wiped **them** out)*

work

work out (tr) = find, by calculation or study, the solution to some problem or a method of dealing with it; study and decide on the details of a scheme:

> *He used his calculator to work out **the cost**. (work **the cost** out)*
> *Tell me where you want to go and I'll work out a route.*
> *This is the outline of the plan. We want the committee to work out **the details**. (work **them** out)*

39 List of irregular verbs

364 Irregular verbs

The verbs in roman type are verbs which are not very common in modern English but may be found in literature. When a verb has two possible forms and one is less usual than the other, the less usual one will be printed in roman.

Compounds of irregular verbs form their past tenses and past participles in the same way as the original verb:

come	*came*	*come*
overcome	*overcame*	*overcome*
set	*set*	*set*
upset	*upset*	*upset*

Present and infinitive	Simple past	Past participle
abide	abode	abode
arise	*arose*	*arisen*
awake	*awoke*/awaked	*awoken*/awaked
be	*was*	*been*
bear	*bore*	*borne/born* *
beat	*beat*	*beaten*
become	*became*	*become*
befall	befell	befallen
beget	begot	begotten
begin	*began*	*begun*
behold	beheld	beheld
bend	*bent*	*bent*
bereave	bereaved	*bereaved/bereft* *
beseech	besought	besought
bet	*betted/bet*	*betted/bet*
bid (= *command*)	bade	bidden
bid (= *offer*)	*bid*	*bid*
bind	*bound*	*bound*
bite	*bit*	*bitten*

*These past participles are not optional but carry different meanings and should be checked by the student in a reliable dictionary.

Present and infinitive	Simple past	Past participle
bleed	*bled*	*bled*
blow	*blew*	*blown*
break	*broke*	*broken*
breed	*bred*	*bred*
bring	*brought*	*brought*
broadcast	*broadcast*	*broadcast*
build	*built*	*built*
burn	*burned/burnt*	*burned/burnt*
burst	*burst*	*burst*
buy	*bought*	*bought*
can†	*could*	*be able*
cast	*cast*	*cast*
catch	*caught*	*caught*
chide	chid	chidden
choose	*chose*	*chosen*
cleave	clove/cleft	cloven/cleft*
cling	*clung*	*clung*
clothe	*clothed/clad*	*clothed/clad*
come	*came*	*come*
cost	*cost*	*cost*
creep	*crept*	*crept*
crow	*crowed*/crew	*crowed*
cut	*cut*	*cut*
dare	*dared*/durst	*dared*/durst
deal /di:l/	*dealt* /delt/	*dealt* /delt/
dig	*dug*	*dug*
do	*did*	*done*
draw	*drew*	*drawn*
dream /dri:m/	*dreamed/dreamt* /dri:md, dremt/	*dreamed/dreamt* /dri:md, dremt/
drink	*drank*	*drunk*
drive	*drove*	*driven*
dwell	dwelled/*dwelt*	dwelled/*dwelt*
eat	*ate*	*eaten*
fall	*fell*	*fallen*
feed	*fed*	*fed*
feel	*felt*	*felt*
fight	*fought*	*fought*
find	*found*	*found*
flee	*fled*	*fled*

*See footnote on page 353.
†Present only.

Present and infinitive	Simple past	Past participle
fling	*flung*	*flung*
fly	*flew*	*flown*
forbear	*forbore*	*forborne*
forbid	*forbade* /fə'bæd/	*forbidden*
forget	*forgot*	*forgotten*
forgive	*forgave*	*forgiven*
forsake	*forsook*	*forsaken*
freeze	*froze*	*frozen*
get	*got*	*got*
gild	*gilded/gilt*	*gilded/gilt*
gird	girded/girt	girded/girt
give	*gave*	*given*
go	*went*	*gone*
grind	*ground*	*ground*
grow	*grew*	*grown*
hang	*hanged/hung*	*hanged/hung**
have	*had*	*had*
hear /hɪə(r)/	*heard* /hɜːd/	*heard* /hɜːd/
hew	*hewed*	*hewed/hewn*
hide	*hid*	*hidden*
hit	*hit*	*hit*
hold	*held*	*held*
hurt	*hurt*	*hurt*
keep	*kept*	*kept*
kneel	*knelt*	*knelt*
knit**	*knit*	*knit*
know	*knew*	*known*
lay	*laid*	*laid*
lead	*led*	*led*
lean	*leaned/leant*	*leaned/leant*
/liːn/	/liːnd, lent/	/liːnd, lent/
leap	*leaped/leapt*	*leaped/leapt*
/liːp/	/liːpt, lept/	/liːpt, lept/
learn	*learned/learnt*	*learned/learnt*
leave	*left*	*left*
lend	*lent*	*lent*
let	*let*	*let*
lie	*lay*	*lain*

*See footnote on page 353.

** = unite/draw together. *knit* (= make garments from wool) is a regular verb.

Present and infinitive	Simple past	Past participle
light	*lighted/lit*	*lighted/lit*
lose	*lost*	*lost*
make	*made*	*made*
may†	*might*	—
mean /miːn/	*meant* /ment/	*meant* /ment/
meet	*met*	*met*
mow	*mowed*	*mowed/mown*
must†	*had to*	—
ought†	—	—
pay	*paid*	*paid*
put	*put*	*put*
read /riːd/	*read* /red/	*read* /red/
rend	rent	rent
rid	*rid*	*rid*
ride	*rode*	*ridden*
ring	*rang*	*rung*
rise	*rose*	*risen* /'rɪzn/
run	*ran*	*run*
saw	*sawed*	*sawed/sawn*
say /seɪ/	*said* /sed/	*said* /sed/
see	*saw*	*seen*
seek	*sought*	*sought*
sell	*sold*	*sold*
send	*sent*	*sent*
set	*set*	*set*
sew	*sewed*	*sewed/sewn*
shake	*shook*	*shaken*
shall†	*should*	—
shear	*sheared*/shore	*sheared/shorn*
shed	*shed*	*shed*
shine /ʃaɪn/	*shone* /ʃɒn/	*shone* /ʃɒn/
shoe	*shoed*/shod	*shoed/shod*
shoot	*shot*	*shot*
show	*showed*	*showed/shown*
shrink	*shrank*	*shrunk*
shut	*shut*	*shut*
sing	*sang*	*sung*
sink	*sank*	*sunk*
sit	*sat*	*sat*
slay	slew	slain
sleep	*slept*	*slept*

†Present only.

Present and infinitive	Simple past	Past participle
slide	slid	slid
sling	slung	slung
slink	slunk	slunk
slit	slit	slit
smell	smelled/smelt	smelled/smelt
smite	smote	smitten
sow	sowed	sowed/sown
speak	spoke	spoken
speed	speeded/sped	speeded/sped
spell	spelled/spelt	spelled/spelt
spend	spent	spent
spill	spilled/spilt	spilled/spilt
spin	spun	spun
spit	spat	spat
split	split	split
spread	spread	spread
spring	sprang	sprung
stand	stood	stood
steal	stole	stolen
stick	stuck	stuck
sting	stung	stung
stink	stank/stunk	stunk
strew	strewed	strewed/strewn
stride	strode	stridden
strike	struck	struck
string	strung	strung
strive	strove	striven
swear	swore	sworn
sweep	swept	swept
swell	swelled	swelled/swollen
swim	swam	swum
swing	swung	swung
take	took	taken
teach	taught	taught
tear	tore	torn
tell	told	told
think	thought	thought
thrive	thrived/throve	thrived/thriven
throw	threw	thrown
thrust	thrust	thrust
tread	trod	trodden/trod

Present and infinitive	Simple past	Past participle
understand	*understood*	*understood*
undertake	*undertook*	*undertaken*
wake	*waked/woke*	*waked/woken*
wear	*wore*	*worn*
weave	*wove*	*woven*
weep	*wept*	*wept*
wet	*wetted/wet*	*wetted/wet*
will†	*would*	—
win	*won*	*won*
wind	*wound*	*wound*
wring	*wrung*	*wrung*
write	*wrote*	*written*

†Present only.

Index

Index

Index

Index

Index